THE INFORMED ARGUMENT

BRIEF EDITION

ROBERT K. MILLER
UNIVERSITY OF SAINT THOMAS

HARCOURT BRACE COLLEGE PUBLISHERS

FORT WORTH   PHILADELPHIA   SAN DIEGO   NEW YORK   ORLANDO   AUSTIN   SAN ANTONIO
TORONTO   MONTREAL   LONDON   SYDNEY   TOKYO

Publisher:	Earl McPeek
Acquisitions Editor:	Julie McBurney
Product Manager:	Laura Brennan
Developmental Editor:	Michell Phifer
Project Editor:	Laura Miley
Art Director:	Garry Harman
Production Manager:	Serena Barnett

Cover credit: Juan Gris. *Still Life,* 1913. Philadelphia Museum of Art: A. E. Gallatin Collection.

ISBN: 0-15-503185-6
Library of Congress Catalog Card Number: 97-077919

Copyright © 1999 by Harcourt Brace & Company

All rights reserved. No part of this publication may be reproduced or transmitted in any form or by any means, electronic or mechanical, including photocopy, recording, or any information storage and retrieval system, without permission in writing from the publisher.

Requests for permission to make copies of any part of the work should be mailed to: Permissions Department, Harcourt Brace & Company, 6277 Sea Harbor Drive, Orlando, FL 32887-6777.

Portions of this work were previously published.

Copyrights and Acknowledgments appear on pages 359–361, which constitutes a continuation of the copyright page.

Address for orders:
Harcourt Brace & Company
6277 Sea Harbor Drive
Orlando, FL 32887-6777
1-800-782-4479

Address for editorial correspondence:
Harcourt Brace & Company
301 Commerce Street, Suite 3700
Fort Worth, TX 76102

Web site address:
http://www.hbcollege.com

Printed in the United States of America

7 8 9 0 1 2 3 4 5 6   016   9 8 7 6 5 4 3 2 1

Harcourt Brace College Publishers

PREFACE

This book has been designed to help you argue on behalf of your beliefs so that other people will take them seriously. Part 1 introduces basic principles of argumentation that you will need to analyze the arguments you read and to compose arguments of your own. Part 2 introduces specific strategies for efficiently and honorably drawing upon the work of other writers so that your arguments will be well informed. The readings gathered in this book will provide you with readily available sources upon which you can draw when composing a range of writing assignments. There will be times, however, when you discover that you need additional information to clarify or support your thoughts. Part 3, "A Guide to Research," introduces essential strategies for locating what you need on those occasions.

The readings included in *The Informed Argument,* Brief Edition, are arranged in Parts 4 and 5. In Part 4, "Sources for Argument," there are five sections in each of which four different writers address issues of national concern, and then a student writes in response to reading on the issue in question. Providing you with the opportunity to examine each of these issues from multiple perspectives, the twenty-five readings gathered in Part 4 form the heart of the book. The range of ideas explored in the book is extended by Part 5, "Some Classic Arguments," eight arguments that have influenced the thinking of previous generations. In this part of the book, you will also see how argument can take the form of a satire or a letter—in addition to those patterns of arrangement emphasized in the book as a whole.

In choosing arguments for you to study, I attempted to give equal consideration to opposing viewpoints so that you could better understand different sides of the issues in question. I also included examples of different writing strategies. To fulfill these goals, I did not limit the selections to the most recent works available. You will find the date of original publication within the introductory note that comes immediately before each selection. When evaluating sources, recognize that an essay can embody a strong argument or interesting point of view many years after it was written. An old essay can include outdated information, however, so you should consider the date of each source when deciding the extent to which you can rely upon it.

If you read carefully, you will find that almost every written argument includes a point that can be questioned. This is because argument is part of an ongoing process of inquiry; a single argument is unlikely to entirely resolve a complex issue. So don't feel that an argument loses all credibility because you have discovered a flaw in it. Although you should be alert for flaws, especially in reasoning, you should consider the flaw in proportion to the argument as a whole. Some writers undermine their entire argument by contradicting themselves or by making wild charges; others are able to make a strong argument despite one or two weak points. Whatever the case, readers and writers learn from considering diverse points of view and deciding how they inform each other. Argument is not about "winning" or "losing"; it is a process devoted to finding solutions to problems. When this process is undertaken honestly, everyone stands to benefit.

The ten student essays included in this edition should help you to see how other students have satisfied assignments similar to those you may be asked to undertake. Learn what you can from them, but do not feel they represent some sort of perfection that is beyond your grasp. Each of these writers wrote several drafts, revising extensively before completing the version included in the book. And because they understand that revision is a never-ending commitment essential to good writing, these students probably will see things they would like to change now that their essays are in print. I want to thank them for giving me permission to publish their work and remind them that I hope they keep on writing. I also want to thank the many students who studied the earlier editions of this book and helped me to see how it could be improved.

For helpful advice when planning this edition, I want to thank Patrick McMahon, Tallahassee Community College; Keith Coplin, Colby Community College; Arden Jensen, Gulf Coast Community College; and Linda Warwick, Portland Community College. I also want to thank Paul Teske, who helped me locate several of the arguments I have included. At Harcourt Brace, John Meyers, acquisitions editor, realized the need for this brief version of an argumentation textbook. Michell Phifer and Laura Miley provided friendly counsel and efficiently guided the book through production; Serena Barnett, production manager, and Garry Harman, art director, provided additional support. I would also like to thank Tom Torrans the copy editor for this edition of the text. Finally, I want to thank Eleanor Garner, who once again was a model of efficiency and grace when negotiating the many permissions agreements for this book. It was my good fortune to have so much valuable assistance.

CONTENTS

PART 3
A GUIDE TO RESEARCH
89

PART 4
SOURCES FOR ARGUMENT
117

SECTION 1
SURFING THE WEB: WHO CONTROLS INFORMATION?   117

PART 5
SOME CLASSIC ARGUMENTS 295

PART 1

AN INTRODUCTION TO ARGUMENT

Argument is a means of fulfilling desire. That desire may be for something as abstract as truth or as concrete as an increase in salary. When you ask for an extension on a paper, apply for a job, propose a marriage, or recommend any change that involves someone besides yourself, you are putting yourself in a position that requires effective argumentation. You may also have occasion to argue seriously about political and ethical concerns. Someone you love may be considering an abortion, a large corporation may try to bury its chemical waste on property that adjoins your own, or you may be suddenly deprived of a benefit to which you feel entitled. By learning how to organize your beliefs and support them with information that will make other people take them seriously, you will be mastering one of the most important skills you are likely to learn in college.

Working your arguments out on paper gives you an opportunity to make changes until you are satisfied that your words do what you want them to do. This is an important benefit because constructing effective arguments requires that you think clearly without letting your feelings dominate what you say, and this can be difficult at times. But it can also be tremendously satisfying to succeed in making other people understand what you mean. You may not always convert others to your point of view, but you can earn their respect. This, in a way, is what argument is all about. When you argue for what you believe, you are asking others to believe in you. This means that you must prove to your audience that you are worth listening to. Instead of thinking in terms of "winning" or "losing" an argument, consider argumentation as an intellectual effort designed to solve problems by drawing people together.

1

Bearing this in mind, you should always be careful to treat both your audience and your opponents with respect. Few people are likely to be converted to your view if you treat them as if they are fools or dismiss their beliefs with contempt. Effective argumentation requires an ability to understand differences, for you cannot resolve a conflict you do not understand. When writing an argument, you must demonstrate that you have given consideration to beliefs that are different from your own and have recognized what makes them appealing. However strong your personal convictions may be, you must not let them keep you from learning what others believe. Becoming familiar with diverse points of view will help you to write arguments that address the concerns of people who might otherwise disagree with you. You will be able to develop your own thinking and be more persuasive than writers who seem narrow-minded or overly opinionated.

The readings that form the heart of this book were chosen to make you better informed on a number of important questions so that you can write about them more persuasively. What you read should influence what you think, but, as you read more, remember that controversial subjects are controversial because there is so much that can be said about them—much more than you may have realized at first. You do not need to become an expert on a topic before you can write a thoughtful argument about it, but you do need to be able to support whatever claims you make. If you offer opinions without support, or make a big claim based on little evidence, you are unlikely to be persuasive. Well-educated men and women recognize how little they know in proportion to how much there is to be known. Make sure the conclusions you reach are based on your best efforts toward finding knowledge and understanding.

CHOOSING A TOPIC

Almost anything *can* be argued, but not everything *should* be argued. You won't be taken seriously if you seem to argue indiscriminately. Argument should be the result of reflection, not reflex, and argumentation is a skill that should be practiced selectively.

When choosing a topic for a written argument, you should avoid questions that can be easily settled by referring to an authority, such as a dictionary or an encyclopedia. There is no point in arguing about how to spell "separate" or about what city is the capital of Australia: There is only one correct answer. Choose a topic that can inspire a variety of answers, any one of which can be "correct" to some degree. Your challenge is to define and support a position in which you believe even though other people do not yet share your belief.

Almost all thoughtful arguments involve *opinions,* but not all opinions lead to good written arguments. There is no reason to argue an opinion with which almost no one would disagree. An essay designed to "prove" that puppies are cute or that vacations can be fun is unlikely to generate much excitement. Don't belabor the obvious. Choose a topic that is likely to inspire at least some controversy, but don't feel that you suddenly need to acquire strange and eccentric opinions.

Be careful to distinguish between opinions that are a matter of taste and those that are a question of judgment. Some people like broccoli, and some people don't. You may be the world's foremost broccoli lover, but no matter how hard you try, you will not convince someone who hates green vegetables to head quickly to the produce department of the nearest supermarket. A gifted stylist, writing in the manner of Charles Lamb or E. B. White, could probably compose an amusing essay on broccoli that would be a delight to read. But it is one thing to describe personal tastes and quite another to insist that others share them. We all have firmly entrenched likes and dislikes. Persuasion in matters of taste is usually beyond the reach of what can be accomplished through the written word—unless you happen to command the resources of an unusually effective advertising agency.

Taste is a matter of personal preference. Whether we prefer green to blue or daffodils to tulips is unlikely to affect anyone but ourselves. Questions of judgment are more substantial than matters of taste because judgment cannot be divorced from logic. Our judgments are determined by our beliefs, behind which are basic principles to which we try to remain consistent. These principles ultimately lead us to decide that some judgments are correct and others are not, so judgment has greater implications than taste. Should a university require freshmen to live in dormitories? Should men and women live together before getting married? Should parents prevent their children from watching television? All these are questions of judgment.

In written argumentation, questions of judgment provide the best subjects. Because they are complex, they offer more avenues to explore. This does not mean that you must cover every aspect of a question in a single essay. Good subjects have many possibilities, and the essays that are written on them will take many different directions. If you try to explore too many directions at once, you might easily get lost—or lose your readers along the way.

When planning your written argument, you may benefit from distinguishing between a *subject* and a *topic:* A topic is part of a subject. For example, "gun control" is a subject from which many different topics can be derived. Possibilities include: state laws affecting handguns, federal laws on the possession of military weapons, the constitutional right to "keep and bear arms," and gun use in criminal activities. Each of these topics could be narrowed further. Someone interested in gun use in criminal activities might focus on the extent to which criminals benefit from easy access to guns or on whether owning a gun serves as a deterrent to crime. Because it is easier to do justice to a well-focused topic than to a broad subject, choosing a topic is one of the most important choices writers need to make.

Some writers successfully define their topics before they begin to write. Others begin to write on one topic and then discover that they are more interested in a different topic, which may or may not be related. Still other writers use specific writing techniques for generating topics. At times, you will be required to write on a topic that has been assigned to you. But whenever you have freedom to choose your own topic, remember that writing may help you to discover what you want to write about. *Freewriting*—writing nonstop for five to ten minutes without worrying about grammar, spelling, style, organization, or repetition—often leads writers to discover that they have more ideas than they had realized. Similarly, *brainstorming*—listing as many aspects about a subject or a topic as come to mind during ten minutes or so—can help to focus an essay and to identify several essential points. In short, you do not need to choose your topic before you can even begin writing, but you should choose and develop a clearly defined topic before you submit an essay for evaluation.

Whether you choose a topic before you begin to write or use writing to discover a topic, ask yourself the following questions:

- Do I know exactly what my topic is?
- Is this topic suitable for the length of the work I am planning to write?
- Do I have an opinion about this topic?
- Would anyone disagree with my opinion?
- Can I hope to persuade others to agree with my opinion?
- Can I support my opinion with evidence?

If you answer yes to all of these questions, you can proceed with confidence.

DEFINING YOUR AUDIENCE

Good writers remember their *audience*—the person or people with whom they are trying to communicate. For example, your audience might consist of a single professor (when no one else will be reading what you write), a group of students (your classmates or members of a writing group), or the citizens of your community (as in a letter to the editor of a newspaper or magazine). All of these are examples of "particular audiences," and you can make certain assumptions about these readers based on your own observations and experience with them.

Instead of writing for a particular audience, some writers prefer to write for a general or universal audience—one in which all readers will have the intelligence and goodwill to listen to a reasonable stranger. When you write for a general audience, a particular audience (such as your professor) may cooperate by reading your work as a member of the larger audience you have invoked. Whatever the size and particularity of the audience you envision, you should maintain the same sense of audience throughout your entire essay.

Defining your audience can help you to choose your topic because a particular audience is likely to find some topics more interesting than others. A clear sense of audience can also help you to shape your style. It would be a mistake, for example, to use complicated technical language when writing for a general audience, and it would be just as foolish to address an audience of experts as if they knew nothing about your topic. You need to avoid confusing people but you must also be careful not to insult their intelligence. Finally, a clear sense of audience will help you to choose the points you want to emphasize in order to be persuasive, and to anticipate the objections that might be raised by readers who disagree with you.

Whether your audience is particular or general, you should assume that intelligent and fair-minded people are usually skeptical about sweeping generalizations and unsupported claims. Unless you are the keynote speaker at a political convention, assigned to rally the members of your party by telling them exactly what they want to hear, there is no reason to expect people to agree with you. If your audience already agrees with you, what's the point of your argument? Whom are you trying to convince? Remember that the immediate purpose of an argument is almost always to reconcile differences. An audience may be entirely neutral, having no opinion at all on the subject that concerns you. But by imagining a skeptical audience, you will be able to anticipate and respond to opposing views, thus building a stronger case.

Before you draft your essay, try listing the reasons why you believe as you do. You may not have the space, in a short essay, to discuss all of the points you have listed. Moreover, you are likely to discover new ideas as you draft and revise—ideas that may prove more important than those with which you began. You can benefit, however, from preliminary planning: Rank your points in order of their importance, and consider the degree to which they would probably impress the audience for whom you are writing. Once you have done this, compose another list: reasons why people might disagree with you. Having explored the opposition's point of view, ask yourself why you have not been persuaded to abandon your own beliefs. What flaw do you see in the reasoning of your opponents? Add to your second list a short response to each of your opponents' arguments.

You are likely to discover that the opposition has at least one good argument, an argument that you cannot answer. This should not be surprising. We may like to flatter ourselves by believing that Truth is on our side. In our weaker moments, we may like to pretend that anyone who disagrees with us is either ignorant or corrupt. But serious and prolonged controversies almost always continue because the opposition has at least one valid concern. Be prepared to concede a point to your opponents when it seems appropriate to do so. You must consider and respond to their views, but your responses do not always have to take the form of rebuttals. When you have no rebuttal and recognize that your opponents' case has some merit, be honest and generous enough to say so.

By making concessions to your opposition, you demonstrate to your audience that you are trying to be fair. Far from weakening your own case, an occasional concession can help bridge the gulf between you and your opponents, making it easier for you to reach a more substantial agreement. It's hard to convince opponents that your views deserve to be taken seriously when you have belligerently insisted that they are completely wrong and you are completely right. Life is seldom so simple. Human nature being what it is, most people will listen more readily to an argument that offers some recognition of their views.

Concessions establish common ground between conflicting parties and diffuse ill feeling that can inhibit persuasion. The number of concessions in an argument will vary, depending on the complexity of the issue, the extent to which people are divided in their opinions, and the writer's ability to reconcile opponents. The length of an argument is also a factor when deciding how many concessions are appropriate. In a short essay, you can usually afford to make only one or two concessions while still advancing your own line of thought. When you are able to write at length, you can concede more.

A good sense of audience will help you decide the nature and number of the concessions you make on any one occasion. Some audiences welcome long arguments; others do not. Some need to hear concessions before they can begin to listen to new ideas; others may be confused if you seem to concede too much. When making concessions, address the most pressing concerns of your audience.

Having a good sense of audience also means illustrating your case with specific examples that your audience can readily understand. It's hard to make people care about abstractions; good writers try to make the abstract concrete. Remember that you might easily lose the attention of your audience if you fail to include specific details or if you include so many details that readers feel overwhelmed.

There is, however, a great difference between responding to the interests of your audience by discussing what it wants to know, and twisting what you say to please an audience with exactly what it wants to hear. The foremost responsibility of any writer is to tell the truth as she or he sees it. What we mean by "truth" often has many dimensions. When limited space forces us to be selective, it is wise to focus on those facets of our topic that will be the most effective with the audience we are attempting to sway. But it is one thing to focus and quite another to mislead. Never write anything for one audience that you would be compelled to deny before another. Hypocrites are seldom persuasive, and no amount of verbal agility can compensate for a loss of confidence in a writer's character.

To better understand the importance of an audience in argumentation, consider the following essay, which was originally published as an editorial in a college newspaper.

TO SKIP OR NOT TO SKIP: A STUDENT DILEMMA

This is college, right? The four-year deal offering growth, maturity, experience, and knowledge? A place to be truly independent?

2 Because sometimes I can't tell. Sometimes this place downright reeks of paternal instincts. Just ask the freshmen and sophomores, who are by class rank alone guaranteed two full years of twenty-four-hour supervision, orchestrated activities, and group showers.

But the forced dorm migration of underclassmen has been bitched about before, to no avail. University policy is, it seems, set in stone. It ranks right up there with ingrown toenails for sheer evasion and longevity.

4 But there's another university policy that has no merit as a policy and no place in a university. Mandatory Attendance Policy: wherein faculty members attempt the high school hall monitor–college instructor maneuver. It's a difficult trick to justify as professors place the attendance percentage of their choice above a student's proven abilities on graded material.

Profs rationalize out a lot of arguments to support the policy. Participation is a popular one. I had a professor whose methods for lowering grades so irritated me I used to skip on purpose. He said, "Classroom participation is a very important part of this introductory course. Obviously, if you are not present, you cannot be participating."

6 Equally obvious, though not stated by the prof, is the fact that one can be perpetually present but participate as little as one who is absent. So who's the better student—the one who makes a meaningless appearance, or the one who is busy with something else? And who gets the points docked?

The rest of his policy was characteristically vague, mentioning that absences "could" result in a lower grade. Constant ambiguity is the second big problem with formal policies. It's tough for teachers to figure out just how much to let attendance affect grade point. So they doubletalk.

8 According to the UWSP catalog, faculty are to provide "clear explanation" of attendance policy. Right. Based on the language actually used, ninety-five percent of UWSP faculty are functionally incapable of uttering a single binding statement. In an effort to offend no one while retaining all power of action, profs write things like (these are actual policies): "I trust students to make their own judgments and choices about coming, or not coming, to class." But then it continues: "Habitual and excessive absence is grounds for failure." What happened to trust? What good are the choices?

Or this: "More than three absences may negatively affect your grade." Then again, they may not. Who knows? And this one: "I consider every one of you in here to be mature adults. However, I reserve the right to alter grades based on attendance."

10 You reserve the right? By virtue of your saying so? Is that like calling the front seat?

Another argument that profs cling to goes something like, "Future employers, by God, aren't going to put up with absenteeism." Well, let's take a reality pill. I think most students can grasp the difference between cutting an occasional class, which they paid for, and cutting at work, when they're the ones on salary. See, college students are capable of bi-level thought control, nowadays. (It's all those computers.)

12 In summary, mandatory attendance should be abolished because:

1. It is irrelevant. Roughly the same number of students will either skip or attend, regardless of what a piece of paper says. If the course is worth anything.

14 2. It is ineffective. It automatically measures neither participation, ability, or gained knowledge. That's what tests are for. Grades are what you end up knowing, not how many times you sat there to figure it out.

3. It is insulting. A college student is capable of determining a personal schedule, one that may or may not always meet with faculty wishes. An institution committed to the fostering of personal growth cannot operate under rules that patron-

ize or minimize the role an adult should claim for himself.

16 4. It is arbitrary. A prof has no right and no ability to factor in an unrealistic measure of performance. A student should be penalized no more than what the natural consequence of an absence is—the missing of one day's direct delivery of material.

5. It abolishes free choice. By the addition of a factor that cannot be fought. We are not at a university to learn conformity. As adults, we reserve the right to choose as we see fit, even if we choose badly.

18 Finally, I would ask the faculty to consider this: We have for some time upheld in this nation the sacred principle of separation of church and state; i.e., You are not God.

Karen Rivedal
Editor

Karen chose a topic that would certainly interest many college students, the audience for whom she saw herself writing. Her thesis is clear: Mandatory class attendance should not be required of college students. And her writing is lively enough to hold the attention of many readers. All this is good.

Unfortunately, Karen's argument has a number of flaws. In paragraph 6, she offers what logicians call "a false dilemma." By asking, "So who's the better student—the one who makes a meaningless appearance, or the one who is busy with something else?" she has ignored at least two other possibilities. Appearance in class is likely to be meaningful to at least some students, and cutting class may be meaningless if the "something else" occupying a student's attention is a waste of time. The comparison in paragraph 10 between reserving the right to lower grades because of poor attendance and "calling the front seat" is confusing. (In conversation after the initial publication of this essay, Karen explained to me that she was making a comparison between professors who "reserve the right to alter grades" and children who call "I got the front seat" when going out in the family car. I then pointed out that this analogy could easily be used against her. The driver *must* sit in the front seat, and surely whoever is teaching a class is analogous to the driver of a car rather than to one of the passengers.) In paragraph 13, Karen claims, "Roughly the same number of students will either skip or attend, regardless of what a piece of paper says," but she offers no evidence to support this claim, which is really no more than guesswork. And because Karen herself admits that many students skip class despite mandatory attendance policies, her claim in paragraph 17 that required attendance "abolishes free choice" does not hold up.

These lapses in logic aside, the major problem with this argument is that Karen misjudged her audience. She forgot that professors, as well as students, read the school newspaper. Students cannot change the policies of their professors, but the professors themselves usually can, so she has overlooked the very audience that she most needs to reach. Moreover, not only has she failed to include professors within her audience, but she has actually insulted them. Someone who is told that she or he is "functionally incapable of uttering a single binding statement" (paragraph 8) is unlikely to feel motivated to change. Only in the very last paragraph of this essay does Karen specifically address the faculty, and this proves to be simply the occasion for a final insult. There may be professors who take themselves too seriously, but are there really that many who believe that they are divine?

It's a shame that it's so easy to poke holes in this argument, because Karen deserves credit for boldly calling attention to policies that may indeed be wrong. Recognizing that her original argument was flawed, but still believing strongly that mandatory class attendance is inappropriate for college students, Karen decided to rewrite her editorial as an essay. Here is her revision:

Absent at What Price?
Karen Rivedal

This is college, right? A place to break old ties, solve problems, and make decisions? Higher education is, I thought, the pursuit of knowledge in a way that's a step beyond the paternal hand-holding of high school. It's the act of learning performed in a more dynamic atmosphere, rich with individual freedom, discourse, and debate.

2   Because sometimes I can't tell. Some university traditions cloud the full intent of higher education. Take mandatory attendance policies, wherein faculty members attempt the high school hall monitor–college instructor maneuver. It's a difficult trick to justify as professors place the attendance percentage of their choice above a student's proven abilities on graded material.

This isn't to say that the idea of attendance itself is unsound. Clearly, personal interaction between teacher and students is preferable to textbook teaching alone. It's the mandatory attendance policy, within an academic community committed to the higher education of adults, that worries me.

4   Professors, however, offer several arguments to support the practice. Participation is a popular one. I had a professor whose methods for lowering grades so irritated me that I used to skip out of spite. He said, "Classroom participation is a very important part of

this introductory course. Obviously, if you are not present, you cannot be participating."

Equally obvious, though, is the fact that one can be perpetually present, but participate as little as one who is absent. Participation lacks an adequate definition. There's no way of knowing, on the face of it, if a silent student is necessarily a learning student. Similarly, an instructor has no way of knowing for what purpose or advantage a student may miss a class, and therefore no ability to determine its relative validity.

6   As a learning indicator, then, mandatory attendance policy is flawed. It automatically measures neither participation nor ability. That's what tests are for. A final grade should reflect what a student ends up knowing, rather than the artificial consequences of demerit points.

Some faculty recognize the shortcomings of a no-exceptions mandatory attendance policy and respond with partial policies. Constant ambiguity is characteristic of this approach and troublesome for the student who wants to know just where he or she stands. It's tough for teachers to figure out just how much to let attendance affect grade point. So they doubletalk.

8   This, for example, is taken from an actual policy: "I trust students to make their own judgments and choices about coming, or not coming, to class." It then continues: "Habitual and excessive absence is grounds for failure." What happened to trust? What good are the choices?

Or this: "More than three absences may negatively affect your grade." Then again, they may not. Who knows? And this one: "I consider every one of you in here to be mature adults. However, I reserve the right to alter grades based on attendance."

10   This seems to say, what you can prove you have learned from this class takes a back seat to how much I think you should know based on your attendance. What the teacher says goes—just like in high school.

Professors who set up attendance policies like these believe, with good reason, that they are helping students to learn by ensuring their attendance. But the securing of this end by requirement eliminates an important element of learning. Removing the freedom to make the decision is removing the need to think. An institution committed to the fostering of personal growth cannot operate under rules that patronize or minimize the role an adult should claim for himself.

12   A grading policy that relies on the student's proven abilities certainly takes the guesswork out of grade assigning for teachers. This take-no-prisoners method, however, also demands a high, some say unfairly high, level of personal student maturity. Younger students especially may need, they say, the extra structuring that a policy provides.

But forfeiting an attendance policy doesn't mean that a teacher has to resign his humanity, too. Teachers who care to can still take five minutes to warn an often absent student about the possible consequences, or let the first test score tell the story. As much as dedicated teachers want students to learn, the activity is still a personal one. Students must want to.

14 A "real-world" argument that professors often use goes something like, "Future employers aren't going to put up with absenteeism, so get used to it now." Well, let's take a reality pill. I think most students can differentiate between cutting an occasional class, which they paid for, and missing at work, when they're the ones on salary.

Students who intelligently protest an institution's policies, such as mandatory attendance requirements, are proof-in-action that college is working. These students are thinking, and learning to think and question is the underlying goal of all education. College is more than its rules, more than memorized facts. Rightly, college is knowledge, the testing of limits. To be valid, learning must include choice and the freedom to make mistakes. To rely on mandatory attendance for learning is to subvert the fullest aims of that education.

In revising her essay, Karen has retained both her thesis and her own distinctive voice. Such phrases as "the high school hall monitor–college instructor maneuver," the "take-no-prisoners method," and "let's take a reality pill" are still recognizably her own. But her argument is now more compelling. In addition to eliminating the fallacies that marred her original version, Karen included new material that strengthens her case. Paragraph 3 offers a much needed clarification, reassuring readers that an argument against a mandatory attendance policy is not the same as an argument against attending class. Paragraph 7 begins with a fairly sympathetic reference to professors, and paragraph 11 opens with a clear attempt to anticipate opposition. Paragraph 12 includes another attempt to anticipate opposition, and paragraph 13, with its reference to "dedicated teachers," is much more likely to appeal to the professors in Karen's audience than any statements in the original version did. Finally, the conclusion of this essay is now much improved. It successfully links the question of mandatory attendance policies with the purpose of higher education as defined in the opening paragraph.

Exercise 1

Choose one of the following topics, and list the concerns most likely to be raised by each of the audiences specified for that topic. Although some of these audiences could overlap—a landlord, for example, could be a member of the City Council—imagine separate groups of readers for this assignment.

1. *Topic:* Finding clean, safe, affordable housing
   Audiences: (a) landlords, (b) tenants, (c) City Council
2. *Topic:* Building a large parking garage for a college located in a residential neighborhood
   Audiences: (a) commuting students, (b) neighboring home-owners, (c) the Board of Trustees
3. *Topic:* Closing an unproductive factory
   Audiences: (a) employees, (b) stockholders, (c) owners of nearby businesses
4. *Topic:* Experimenting on animals
   Audiences: (a) people with AIDS, (b) members of the Humane Society, (c) a committee that chooses the research projects that will receive financial grants
5. *Topic:* Restricting car imports
   Audiences: (a) American automobile workers, (b) American drivers, (c) foreign car dealers

DEFINING YOUR TERMS

If you want your arguments to be convincing, they must be understood by your audience. To make sure that your ideas are understandable, you must be careful in your use of words. It is especially important to clarify any terms that are essential to your argument. Unfortunately, many writers of argument fail to define the words they use. It is not unusual, for example, to find writers advocating (or opposing) gun control without defining exactly what they mean by "gun control." Many arguments use words such as "censorship," "society," "legitimate," and "moral" so loosely that it is impossible to decide exactly what the writer means. When this happens, the entire argument can break down.

Don't feel that you need to define every word you use, but be certain to define any important word that your audience might misunderstand. Avoid defining a word by using the same term or another term that is equally complex. For example, if you are opposed to the sale of pornography, you should be prepared to define what you mean by "pornography." It would not be especially helpful to tell your audience that pornography is "printed or visual material that is obscene" because this only raises the question: What is "obscene"? In an important ruling, the U.S. Supreme Court defined "obscene" as material that "the average person, applying community standards, would find . . . as a whole, appeals to the prurient interest," but even if you happened to have this definition at hand, you should ask yourself whether "the average person" understands what "prurient" means—not to mention what the Court may have meant by "community standards." Unless you define your terms carefully, avoiding unnecessarily abstract language, you can end up writing an endless chain of definitions that require further explanation.

The easiest way to define a term is to consult a dictionary. However, some dictionaries are much better than others. For daily use, most writers usually refer to a good desk dictionary such as *The American Heritage Dictionary, The Random House Dictionary,* or *Merriam-Webster's Collegiate Dictionary,* Tenth Edition. A good general dictionary of this sort may provide you with an adequate working definition. You may also want to consider consulting the multivolume *Oxford English Dictionary,* which is available in most college libraries and is especially useful in showing how the usage of a word has changed over the years. Your audience might also appreciate the detailed information that specialized dictionaries in various subject areas can provide. Many such dictionaries are likely to be available in your college library. For example, if you are working on a paper in English literature, you might consult *A Concise Dictionary of Literary Terms* or *The Princeton Handbook of Poetic Terms.* For a paper in psychology, you might turn to *The Encyclopedic Dictionary of Psychology,* or, for a paper on a musical topic, *The New Grove's Dictionary of Music and Musicians.* There are also dictionaries for medical, legal, philosophical, and theoretical terms as well as for each of the natural sciences. When using specialized dictionaries, you will often find valuable information, but remember that the definition that appears in your paper should not be more difficult than the word or phrase you originally set out to define.

Instead of relying exclusively on dictionaries, it is often best to define a term or phrase in words of your own. You can choose from among several strategies:

- Give synonyms.
- Compare the term with other words with which it is likely to be confused, and show how your term differs.
- Define a word by showing what it is *not.*
- Provide examples.

Writers frequently use several of these strategies to create a single definition; an entire essay could be devoted to defining one term. Here is an example written by a student:

Homicide

Geoff Rulland

You sit back in your lazy-boy, cold soda in hand, grab the remote control and begin to flip through the channels in search of something interesting to watch. Something on the Channel 9 news catches your ear. You listen intently as the newscaster informs you that a man from a nearby town is being charged with homicide. A lot of people would now sit back and continue the channel scan thinking that the man was a murderer. Would that be a safe assumption?

2   When someone is charged with homicide it doesn't necessarily mean he or she is a murderer. Homicide is classified in court as being "justifiable," "excusable," or "felonious." Murder, which falls into the class of felonious homicide, is "the unlawful killing of a human being with malice aforethought," according to the American Heritage Dictionary. This means that murder is always wrong, but specifying that murder is an "unlawful killing" implies that killing a human being is not always unlawful. A justifiable homicide would be a killing committed intentionally without any evil design or under the circumstance of necessity. For example, when a police officer is trying to catch a dangerous felon, using a gun to wound and possibly kill could be justifiable. An excusable homicide would be the killing of a human being accidentally or in self-defense, such as in the case of a burglar entering your home. Killing him may be the only thing that will save you or your family. Manslaughter is another term often associated with killings that aren't murders. The name gives the impression that someone was brutally slain. Actually it is the accidental killing of one person by another, and it may have been quite mild.

Black's Law Dictionary defines homicide as "the killing of any human creature or the killing of one human being by the act, procurement, or omission of another." In other words, it's the killing of one person by another in any manner. It doesn't matter if you hit a person accidentally with your car, or if you purposely shot someone, or if you hired a professional killer. Black's then goes on to state the definition as "the act of a human being in taking away the life of another human being." The Webster's New World Dictionary shortens all of that down to "any killing of one human being by another." The key word in this definition is "any." Webster's doesn't say how the killing must be done; it just says that a person is killed.

4   Two words from the Latin language are the main composition of homicide. The first one is homo meaning man and the other is caedere, which ties it to killing, meaning to cut or kill. Homicida, meaning murderer, was the form that was made from those two words which was later changed in Latin to homicidium. After going through the Old French language, the word then made its way into English and into its present form, homicide.

Homicide is not necessarily a crime. Even though all homicides result in the loss of life, sometimes committing homicide is a person's only choice. Homicide shouldn't be immediately judged as murder or something all-out wrong. The word is "neutral" according to Black's Law Dictionary. It merely states the act of killing and pronounces no judgment on its moral or legal quality.

6   With this in mind, the next time you hear of a homicide on TV you should keep your mind open and neutral. Don't immediately

form the opinion that it was a murder, because a lot of the times you may be wrong. The word merely states that a person was killed, not necessarily murdered.

In defining *homicide,* Geoff uses three of the strategies listed on page 13: He provides examples of homicide; he compares homicide to such terms as *murder* and *manslaughter;* and, by contrasting homicide with murder, he clarifies what homicide is not. In addition to consulting two good desk dictionaries, *The American Heritage Dictionary* and *Webster's New World Dictionary,* Geoff also took the trouble to consult a legal dictionary. *Black's Law Dictionary* confirmed his sense that homicide is a much broader term than murder, and this became the central idea of his essay. In the fourth paragraph, Geoff reports the origin of the term. Any good dictionary will provide you with some information of this sort, but you must be alert for it. A brief etymology (or derivation) usually appears in italics at either the beginning or the end of dictionary definitions, and this information can often be helpful when you are trying to understand a complex term. In *Webster's New World Dictionary,* for example, the definition of *homicide* begins:

[M.E.; O Fr.; L.L. *homicidium,* manslaughter, murder < L. *homicida,* murderer < *homo,* a man + *caedere,* to cut, kill]

Note that the arrows establish the sequence of the word's history. In this case, they are pointing away from Latin (not toward it), indicating the Latin origin. (Arrows pointing to the right would indicate that the earliest term came first, with others appearing in chronological order.) A key to abbreviations used in a dictionary can be found by consulting its table of contents. When you do so, you will probably find that your dictionary contains more information than you had realized.

Before leaving this essay, note that it reveals a good sense of audience. Writing for freshmen in an English class, Geoff recognized that many of his fellow students might find definition to be dry reading. To capture their attention, he begins with an imaginary anecdote addressed, in the second person, directly to readers. Compared with the thousands of essays that have begun "According to *Webster's,* . . ." this introduction (with which the conclusion is subsequently linked) seems original and likely to encourage further reading. But you should not assume that this strategy would be appropriate for any audience or any writing occasion.

Understanding the meaning of *homicide* could be essential in an argument on capital punishment or gun control. When writing an argument, however, you will usually need to define your terms within a paragraph or two. Even if you cannot employ all the strategies that you might use in an extended definition, remember your various options and decide which will be most effective for your purpose within the space available. (For examples of essays that incorporate definition within arguments, see pages 165–170, 221–225, and 267–288.)

In addition to achieving clarity, definition helps to control an argument by eliminating misunderstandings that can cause an audience to be inappropriately hostile or to jump to a conclusion that is different from your own. By carefully defining your terms, you limit a discussion to what you want to discuss. This increases the likelihood of your gaining a fair hearing for your views.

Exercise 2

Using the strategies listed on page 13, write an essay of definition for one of the following terms:

affirmative action	learning disability
alcoholism	liberal
child abuse	middle class
civil rights	progress
eating disorder	real world
family	society
feminist	well-rounded education

PLANNING YOUR ARGUMENT

A good plan grows out of a specific assignment or challenge. Your plan should suit your topic, what you have to say about that topic, and what your audience expects of you. If you have done some preliminary planning—listing reasons why you believe as you do as well as responses to the points most likely to be made by people with differing views—you must now consider a number of questions:

- Where and how should I begin my argument?
- In what order should I arrange the points I want to make?
- How can I most efficiently respond to opposing arguments?
- How should I conclude?

The answers to these questions will vary from one essay to another.

But even if no single plan will work equally well whenever you write, you can benefit from being familiar with some basic principles—for example, classical arrangement, Rogerian argument, and ways of reasoning. For easy reference, these principles are presented here as methods of organization. You should understand, however, that organization cannot be separated from all the other work you do when planning, drafting, and revising an essay. For example, if you are planning to write an argument that follows the principles of classical arrangement, you need to generate ideas that are suitable for this plan—and modify either the plan or the content later, after you have written your first draft. Or, if you begin by generating ideas without considering how you will organize them, you must then decide what kind of organization will be best suited for your ideas and your purpose in communicating them. These steps do not happen in isolation or in a linear progression in which it is impossible to revisit an earlier part of your work. When generating ideas, you might find that a tentative outline for their arrangement is beginning to emerge. Similarly, you might need to generate new ideas after organizing those with which you began, because your plan has helped you to discover a need for more material.

As you study the following plans, you should understand that they are not mutually exclusive. In a classically arranged argument, for example, the statement of background can be done with the kind of nonjudgmental language emphasized in Rogerian argument. Similarly, the summary of opposing views in a Rogerian argument requires the kind of understanding that a writer following a classical arrangement would need to have before engaging in refutation. In both cases, writers need to be well informed and fair-minded. And both classical arrangement and Rogerian argument encourage the use of concessions. The difference between the two is best understood in terms of purpose. Although any argument is designed to be persuasive, the purpose of that persuasion varies from one occasion to another. You might write to persuade other people to accept the legitimacy of your position, even if they continue to hold very different views. You might write to invite other people to change their minds or to undertake a specific action. Or you might write to encourage conflicting parties to accept a compromise. In any case, your plan needs to suit your purpose.

Classical Arrangement

Theories of argument first developed in ancient Greece and Rome, where education emphasized the importance of persuasion. Aristotle defined rhetoric as "the study of all the available means of persuasion," and his ideas—as well as the ideas of many other classical scholars—shaped the approaches to argument that dominated Western thinking for almost two thousand years.

Because these theories developed at a time when most arguments were oral, the great works of classical rhetoric recommended strategies that could be easily understood by listeners. If speakers followed essentially the same plan, listeners were able to follow long, complex arguments because the main components were easily recognizable and the order in which they appeared signaled what was likely to happen next.

Here is the most common plan for organizing an argument along classical lines. The original name of each component in classical rhetoric appears in parentheses.

Introduction *(Exordium)*	The introduction is where you urge your audience to consider the case that you are about to present. This is the time to capture the attention of your readers and introduce your issue.
Statement of Background *(Narratio)*	In the statement of background, you narrate, or tell, the key events in the story behind your case. This is the time to provide information so that your audience will understand the nature of the facts in the case at hand.
Proposition *(Partitio)*	This component divides (or partitions) the part of the argument focused on information from the part focused on reasoning, and it outlines the major points that will follow. You must state the position you are taking, based on the information you have presented, and then indicate the lines the rest of your argument will follow.
Proof *(Confirmatio)*	Adhering carefully to your outline, you now present the heart of your argument: You make (or confirm) your case. You must discuss the reasons why you have taken your position and cite evidence to support each of those reasons.
Refutation *(Refutatio)*	In this key section, you anticipate and refute opposing views. By showing what is wrong with the reasoning of your opponents, you demonstrate that you have studied the issue thoroughly and have reached the only conclusion that is acceptable in this case.
Conclusion *(Peroratio)*	The concluding paragraph(s) should summarize your most important points. In addition, you can make a final appeal to values and feelings that are likely to leave your audience favorably disposed toward your case.

The classical rhetoricians allowed variations on this plan; for example, speakers were encouraged to begin with refutation when an audience was already strongly committed to an opposing point of view. But because the basic plan remains clear and straightforward, it can still help writers organize their thoughts. If you are looking for a way to organize an argument, experiment with classical arrangement and modify it, when necessary, to suit your needs.

The classical arrangement is especially useful when you feel strongly about an issue and must bring an audience around to agreeing with you and undertaking a proposed action. Because classical rhetoric assumes that an audience can be persuaded when presented with solid evidence and a clear explanation of what is wrong with the reasoning of opponents, this plan is most effective when you are writing for reasonable people who share many of your values.

For an example of a classical arranged essay written by a student, see "Regulation of the Internet," by B. J. Nodzon (pages 153–157).

Rogerian Argument

In recent years, many rhetoricians have been influenced by the ideas of Carl Rogers, a psychotherapist who emphasized the importance of communication as a means to resolve conflicts. Rogers believed that most people are so ready "to judge, to evaluate, to approve or disapprove" that they fail to understand what others think. He urged people to "listen with understanding," and recommended a model for communication in which listeners are required to restate what others have said before offering their own views. This restatement should be done fairly and accurately, without either praise or blame; when restatement is done properly, the original speaker should be able to confirm, "Yes, that is what I said."

Although this model may seem simple, Rogers cautioned that it takes courage to listen carefully to views that are contrary to one's own. Moreover, it is especially hard to listen carefully when feelings are strong. The greater the conflict, the greater the chance of misinterpreting what others have said. In a quarrel, for example, people can sometimes talk right over one another, which drives the opposing participants even further apart. If you're interested in what Rogers says about resolving conflicts, you can read his essay "Dealing with Breakdowns in Communication" in Part 5 of this book (pages 327–333).

Scholars are divided about the extent to which Rogers's ideas can be applied to written arguments. Rogers envisioned situations in which individuals were involved in dialogue; a written argument is ultimately a kind of monologue. His commitment to the importance of restating others' ideas (without evaluating them) rests on the assumption that language can be completely neutral—an idea that has been seriously questioned in modern linguistics. And Rogers's emphasis on *learning to listen* may be more helpful to people who are used to speaking than to those who have been silenced in the past. Feminists, for example, have argued that because public discourse has long been dominated by men, women need help in learning how to assert themselves and men need help in learning how to listen.

Nevertheless, writers of argument can benefit from viewing persuasion as a means to resolve conflict and to achieve social cooperation, instead of thinking that the point of an argument is to somehow come out on top by beating down other people's opinions. Planning a Rogerian argument means emphasizing concessions rather than refutation, and placing those concessions early in your essay. Here is one way to organize an argument along Rogerian lines.*

* This plan is adapted from the work of Richard Coe in *Form and Substance.* New York: Wiley, 1981.

Introduction	State the problem that you hope to resolve. By presenting your issue as a problem in need of a solution, you raise the possibility of positive change. This strategy can interest readers who would not be drawn to an argument that seems devoted to tearing something down.
Summary of Opposing Views	As accurately and neutrally as possible, state the views of people with whom you disagree. By doing so, you show that you are capable of listening without judging and that you have given a fair hearing to people who think differently from you—the people you most need to reach.
Statement of Understanding	Having summarized views different from your own, you now show that you understand that there are situations in which these views are valid. In other words, you are offering a kind of concession. You are not conceding that these views are always right, but you are recognizing that there are conditions under which you would share the views of your opponents.
Statement of Your Position	Having won the attention of both your opponents and those readers who do not have a position on your issue, you have secured a hearing from an audience that is in need of or is open to persuasion. Now that these readers know that you've given fair consideration to views other than your own, they should be prepared to listen fairly to your views.
Statement of Contexts	Similar to the statement of understanding, in which you have described situations where you would be inclined to share the views of your opponents, the statement of contexts describes situations in which you hope your own views would be honored. By showing that your position has merit in a specific context or contexts, you establish that you don't expect everyone to agree with you all the time. The limitations you recognize increase the likelihood that your opponents will agree with you at least in part.
Statement of Benefits	You conclude your argument by appealing to the self-interest of people who do not already share your views but are beginning to respect them because of your presentation. When you conclude by showing how such readers would benefit from accepting your position, your essay's ending is positive and hopeful.

Although divided into six parts, a Rogerian argument need not be limited to six paragraphs. Depending on the complexity of the issue, the extent to which people are divided about it, and the points you yourself want to argue, any part of a Rogerian argument can be expanded. It is not necessary to devote precisely the same amount of space to each part. For example, there is no reason why you can't devote two paragraphs to your statement of contexts even if you devoted only one to your statement of understanding. You should try to make your case as balanced as possible, however. If you seem to give only superficial consideration to the views of others and then linger at length on your own, you are defeating the purpose of a Rogerian argument.

Rogerian argument is effective in situations where people are deeply divided as the result of different values or perceptions. It is especially useful when you are trying to reconcile conflicting parties and achieve a compromise that will allow these parties to move forward even though some differences remain. Because writing a Rogerian argument makes you a kind of negotiator, this plan may not be suitable when you have strongly held opinions of your own.

For an example of Rogerian argument written by a student, see the essay on same-gender marriage by Dana Simonson (Part 4, pages 215–218).

Exercise 3

Experiment with Rogerian strategies by forming a small group that includes people who hold different views on a specific issue. Each person should speak for two or three minutes. Each new speaker should begin by restating the views of the preceding speaker, without evaluating them, and then ask, "Is that accurate?" After the first speaker, all other speakers must paraphrase the previous speaker; they can deliver their own views only when they have been told by the preceding speaker that they have accurately paraphrased what they heard. When the last speaker has spoken, the first speaker should restate that person's views. After everyone has spoken, each group member should draft a paragraph that describes what has happened in the group and evaluates how successfully the speakers have managed to restate others' views without judging them.

Using Logic

The planning of an argument is also shaped by the kind of reasoning a writer employs. The two types of logic emphasized in classical rhetoric are *inductive reasoning* and *deductive reasoning*. In addition to recognizing induction and deduction, contemporary rhetoric also employs less formal models.

Reasoning Inductively When we use *induction*, we are drawing a conclusion based on specific evidence. Our argument rests on a foundation of details that we have accumulated for its support. This is the type of reasoning that we use most frequently in daily life. In the morning, we look at the sky outside our window, check the outdoor temperature, and perhaps listen to a weather forecast before dressing to face the day. If the sun is shining, the temperature is high, and the forecast is favorable, we would be making a reasonable conclusion if we decided to dress lightly and leave our umbrellas at home. We haven't *proved* that the day will be warm and pleasant, we have only *concluded* that it will be. This is all we can usually do in an inductive argument—arrive at a conclusion that seems likely to be true. Ultimate and positive proof is usually beyond reach, and writers who recognize this and proceed accordingly will usually arrive at conclusions that are both moderate and thoughtful. Such writers recognize the possibility that an unanticipated factor can undermine even the best of arguments. A lovely morning can yield to a miserable afternoon, and we may be drenched in a downpour as we hurry home on a day that began pleasantly.

Inductive reasoning is especially important in scientific experimentation. A research scientist may have a theory that she hopes to prove. But to work toward proving this theory, hundreds, thousands, and even tens of thousands of experiments may have to be conducted to eliminate variables and gather enough data to justify a generally applicable conclusion. Well-researched scientific conclusions sometimes reach a point where they seem incontestable. For many years, Congress has required the manufacturers of cigarettes to put on every package a warning that smoking can be harmful to the smokers' health. Since then, additional research has supported the conclusion that smoking can indeed be dangerous, especially to the lungs and the heart. The statement "smoking can be harmful to your health" now seems to have entered the realm of established fact. But biologists, chemists, physicists, and physicians are usually aware that the history of science, and the history of medicine in particular, is an argumentative history full of debate. Methods and beliefs established over many generations can be overthrown by a new discovery. Within a few years, that "new discovery" can also come under challenge. So the serious researcher goes back to the lab and keeps on working—ever mindful that truth is hard to find.

Induction is also essential in law enforcement. Police officers are supposed to have evidence against someone before making an arrest. Consider, for example, the way a detective works. A good detective does not arrive at the scene of a crime already certain about what happened. If the crime seems to be part of a pattern, the detective may already have a suspicion about who is responsible. But a good investigator will want to make a careful study of every piece of evidence that can be gathered. A room may be dusted for fingerprints, a murder victim photographed as found, and if the body is lying on the floor, a chalk outline may be drawn around it for future study. Every item within the room will be cataloged. Neighbors, relatives, employers, or employees will be questioned. The best detective is usually the detective with the best eye for detail and the greatest determination to keep searching for the details that will be strong enough to bring a case to court. Similarly, a first-rate detective will also be honest enough never to overlook a fact that does not fit in with the rest of the evidence. The significance of every loose end must be examined to avoid the possibility of an unfair arrest and prosecution.

In making an inductive argument, you will reach a point at which you decide that you have offered enough evidence to support the thesis of your essay. When you are writing a college paper, you will probably decide that you have reached this point sooner than a scientist or a detective might. But whether you are writing a short essay or conducting an investigation, the process is essentially the same. When you stop citing evidence and move on to your conclusion, you have made what is known as an *inductive leap.* In an inductive essay, you must always offer interpretation or analysis of the evidence you have introduced; there will always be at least a slight gap between your evidence and your conclusion. It is over this gap that the writer must leap; the trick is to do it agilely. Good writers know that their evidence must be in proportion to their conclusion: The bolder the conclusion, the more evidence is needed to back it up. Remember the old adage about "jumping to conclusions," and realize that you'll need the momentum of a running start to make more than a moderate leap at any one time.

If you listen closely to the conversations of people around you, the chances are good that you'll hear examples of faulty inductive reasoning. When someone says, "I don't like Chinese food," and reveals, under questioning, that his only experience with Chinese food has been a frozen Chinese dinner, we cannot take the opinion seriously. A sweeping conclusion has been drawn from flimsy evidence. People who claim to know "all about" complex subjects often reveal that they actually know very little. Only a sexist claims to know all about men and women, and only a racist is foolish enough to generalize about the various racial groups that make up our society. Good writers are careful not to overgeneralize.

When you begin an inductive essay, you might cite a particular observation that strikes you as especially important. You might even begin with a short anecdote. A well-structured inductive essay would then gradually expand as the evidence accumulates, so that the conclusion is supported by numerous details. Here is an example of an inductive essay written by a student:

In Defense of Hunting
David Wagner

I killed my first buck when I was fourteen. I'd gone deer hunting with my father and two of my uncles. I was cold and wet and anxious to get home, but I knew what I had to do when I sighted the eight-point buck. Taking careful aim, I fired at his chest, killing him quickly with a single shot.

2   I don't want to romanticize this experience, turning it into a noble rite of passage. I did feel that I had proved myself

somehow. It was important for me to win my father's respect, and I welcomed the admiration I saw in his eyes. But I've been hunting regularly for many years now, and earning the approval of others no longer seems very important to me. I'd prefer to emphasize the facts about hunting, facts that must be acknowledged even by people who are opposed to hunting.

It is a fact that hunters help to keep the deer population in balance with the environment. Since so many of their natural predators have almost died out in this state, the deer population could quickly grow much larger than the land can support. Without hunting, thousands of deer would die slowly of starvation in the leafless winter woods. This may sound like a self-serving argument (like the words of a parent who beats a child and insists, "This hurts me more than it does you; I'm only doing it for your own good"). But it is a fact that cannot be denied.

4 It is also a fact that hunters provide a valuable source of revenue for the state. The registration and licensing fees we pay are used by the Department of Natural Resources to reforest barren land, preserve wetlands, and protect endangered species. Also there are many counties in this state that depend upon the money that hunters spend on food, gas, and lodging. "Tourism" is our third largest industry, and all of this money isn't being spent at luxurious lakeside resorts. Opponents of hunting should realize that hunting is the most active in some of our poorest, rural counties—and realize what hunting means to the people who live in these areas.

It is also a fact that there are hundreds of men and women for whom hunting is an economic necessity and not a sport. Properly preserved, the meat that comes from a deer can help a family survive a long winter. There probably are hunters who think of hunting as a recreation. But all the hunters I know—and I know at least twenty—dress their own deer and use every pound of the venison they salt, smoke, or freeze. There may be a lot of people who don't have to worry about spending $3.00 a pound for steak, but I'm not one of them. My family needs the meat we earn by hunting.

6 I have to admit that there are hunters who act irresponsibly by trespassing where they are not wanted and, much worse, by abandoning animals that they have wounded. But there are many different kinds of irresponsibility. Look around and you will see many irresponsible drivers, but we don't respond to them by banning driving altogether. An irresponsible minority is no reason to attack a responsible majority.

I've listened to many arguments against hunting, and it seems to me that what really bothers most of the people who are opposed to hunting is the idea that hunters <u>enjoy</u> killing. I can't speak for all hunters, but I can speak for myself and the many hunters I personally know. I myself have never found pleasure in killing a deer. I think that deer are beautiful and incredibly graceful, especially when in movement. I don't "enjoy" putting an end to a beautiful animal's life. If I find any pleasure in the act of hunting, it comes from the knowledge that I am trying to be at least partially self-sufficient. I don't expect other people to do all my dirty work for me, and give me my meat neatly butchered and conveniently wrapped in plastic. I take responsibility for what I eat.

8 Lumping all hunters together as insensitive beer-drinking thugs is an example of the mindless stereotyping that logic should teach us to avoid. The men and women who hunt are no worse than anyone else. And more often than not, the hunting we do is both honorable and important.

David has drawn on his own experience to make an articulate defense of hunting. He begins with an anecdote that helps to establish that he knows something about the subject he has chosen to write about. The first sentence in the second paragraph helps to deflect any skepticism his audience may feel at this early stage in his argument, and the last sentence in this paragraph serves as a transition into the facts that will be emphasized in the next three paragraphs. In paragraph 3, David introduces the evidence that should most impress his audience, if we assume that his audience is unhappy about the idea of killing animals. In paragraphs 4 and 5, he defends hunting on economic grounds. He offers a concession in paragraph 5 ("There probably are hunters who think of hunting as a recreation") and another concession in paragraph 6 ("I have to admit that there are hunters who act irresponsibly"). But after each of these concessions he manages to return smoothly to his own thesis. In paragraph 7, he anticipates an argument frequently made by people who oppose hunting and offers a counterargument that puts his opponents on the defensive. The concluding paragraph may be a little anticlimactic, but within the limitations of a short essay, David has made a strong argument.

Reasoning Deductively Sometimes it is best to rest an argument on a fundamental truth, value, or right rather than on specific pieces of evidence. You should try to be specific within the course of such an essay, giving examples to support your case. But in deductive reasoning, evidence is of secondary importance. Your first concern is to define a commonly accepted value or belief that will prepare the way for the argument you want to make.

The Declaration of Independence, written by Thomas Jefferson (pages 303–306), is a classic example of deductive reasoning. Although Jefferson cited numerous grievances, he rested his argument on the belief that "all men are created equal" and that they have "certain unalienable Rights," which King George III had violated. This was a revolutionary idea in the eighteenth century, and even today there are many people who question it. But if we accept the idea that "all men are created equal" and have an inherent right to "Life, Liberty, and the pursuit of Happiness," then certain conclusions follow.

The right, value, or belief from which we wish to deduce our argument is called our *premise.* Perhaps you have already had the experience, in the middle of an argument, of someone's saying to you, "What's your premise?" If you are inexperienced in argumentation, a question of this sort may embarrass you and cause your argument to break down—which is probably what your opponent had hoped. But whether it is recognized or not, a premise is almost always lurking somewhere in the back of our minds. Deduction is most effective when we think about values we have automatically assumed, and then deliberately build our arguments on them.

A good premise satisfies two requirements:

- It is general enough that your audience is likely to accept it, thus establishing a common ground between you and the audience you hope to persuade.
- It is specific enough to prepare the way for the argument that will follow.

It usually takes much careful thought to frame a good premise. Relatively few people have carefully articulated values always in mind. We often know what we want—or what our conclusion is going to be—but it takes time to articulate the fundamental beliefs that we have automatically assumed. This is really what a premise amounts to: the underlying assumption that must be agreed on before the argument can begin to move along.

Because it is difficult to formulate an effective premise, it is often useful to work backward when you are outlining a deductive argument. If you know the conclusion you expect to reach, write it down, and number it as statement 3. Now ask yourself why you believe statement 3. This should prompt a number of reasons; group them together as statement 2. Now that you can look both at your conclusion and at the immediate reasons that seem to justify it, ask yourself whether you've left anything out—something basic that you skipped over, assuming that everyone would agree with that already. When you can think back successfully to what this assumption is, knowing that it will vary from argument to argument, you have your premise, at least in rough draft form.

This process may be difficult to grasp in the abstract, so consider an outline for a sample argument. Suppose that the forests in your state are slowly dying because of the pollution known as acid rain—one of the effects of burning fossil fuel, especially coal. Coal is being burned by numerous industries not only in your own state, but in neighboring states as well. You hadn't even realized that there was a problem with acid rain until last summer, when fishing was prohibited in your favorite lake. You are very upset about this and declare, "Something ought to be done!" But as you begin to think about the problem, you recognize that you'll have to overcome at least two obstacles in deciding what that "something" should be. Only two years ago, you participated in a demonstration against nuclear power, and you'd also hate to see the United States become more dependent on foreign oil. So if you attack the process of burning coal for energy, you'll have to be prepared to recommend an acceptable alternative. The other question you must answer is: Who's responsible for a problem that seems to be springing from many places in many states? Moreover, if you decide to argue for a radical reduction in coal consumption, you'll have to be prepared to anticipate the opposition: "What's this going to do to the coal miners?" someone might well ask. "Will you destroy the livelihood of some of the hardest working men and women in America?"

You realize that you have still another problem. Your assignment is for a thousand-word deductive argument, and it's due the day after tomorrow. You feel strongly about the problem of acid rain, but you are not an energy expert and there is a limit to how much you can discuss in a short essay. Your primary concern is with the effects of acid rain, which you've witnessed with your own eyes. And although you don't know much about industrial chemistry, you do know that acid rain is caused principally by public utilities' burning coal that has a high percentage of sulfur in it. Recognizing that you lack the expertise to make a full-scale attack on coal consumption, you decide that you can at least argue on behalf of using low-sulfur coal. In doing so, you will be able to reassure your audience that you want to keep coal miners at work, you recognize the needs of industry, and you do not expect the entire country to go solar by the end of the semester.

Taking out a sheet of paper, you begin to write down your outline in reverse:

3. Public utilities should not burn coal that is high in sulfur content.
2. Burning high-sulfur coal causes acid rain, and acid rain is killing American forests, endangering wildlife, and spoiling local fishing.

Before going any further, you realize that all of your reasons for opposing acid rain cannot be taken with equal degrees of seriousness. As much as you like to fish, recreation does not seem to be in the same league with your more general concern for forests and wildlife. You know that you want to describe the condition of your favorite lake at some point in your essay, because it gave you some firsthand experience with the problem and some vivid descriptive details. But you decide that if you make too much of fishing, you risk sounding as if you care only about your own pleasure.

You now ask yourself what lies behind the "should" in your statement 3. How strong is it? Did you say "should" when you meant "must"? Thinking it over, you realize that you did mean "must," but now you must decide who or what is going to make that "must" happen. You decide that you can't trust industry to make this change on its own because you are asking it to spend money that may reduce profits. You know that, as an individual, you don't have the power to bring about the change you believe is necessary, but you also know that individuals become powerful when they band together as a group. In terms of power, the most important group is probably the government we have elected to represent us. (Be careful with a term like "government" and avoid such statements as "The government ought to do something about this." Not only is the "something" vague, but we don't know what kind of government you want to take charge.) Most of us are subject to government on at least three levels: municipal, state, and federal. You decide to argue for *federal* legislation, because acid rain is being generated in several different states—and then is carried by air currents to still others.

You should now be ready to formulate your premise. Your conclusion is going to demand federal regulation, so, at the very beginning of your argument, you need to establish the principle that supports this conclusion. You realize that the federal government cannot solve all problems; you therefore must define the nature of the government's responsibility so that it will be clear that you are appealing legitimately to the right authority. Legally, the federal government has broad powers to regulate interstate commerce, and this may be a useful fact in your argument because most of the industries burning coal ship or receive goods across state lines. More specifically, ever since the creation of Yellowstone National Park in 1872, the U.S. government has undertaken a growing responsibility for protecting the environment. Acid rain is clearly an environmental issue, so you would not be demanding anything new, in terms of governmental responsibilities, if you appealed to the type of thinking that led to the creation of a national park system in 1916 and the Environmental Protection Agency in 1970.

You know, however, that there are many people who distrust big government, and you do not want to alienate anyone by appealing to Washington too early in the essay. A premise can be a single sentence, a full paragraph, or more—depending on the length and complexity of the argument. The function of a premise is to establish a widely accepted value that even your opponents should be able to share. You would probably be wise, therefore, to open this particular argument with a fairly general statement—something like: "We all have a joint responsibility to protect the environment in which we live and preserve the balance of nature on which our lives ultimately depend." As a thesis statement, this obviously needs to be developed in the paragraph that follows. In the second paragraph, you might cite some popular examples of joint action to preserve the environment, pointing out, for example, that most people are relieved to see a forest fire brought under control or an oil slick cleaned up before it engulfs a long stretch of coastline. Once you have cited examples of this sort, you could then remind your audience of the role of state and federal government in coping with such emergencies, and emphasize that many problems are too large for states to handle. By this stage in your essay, you should be able to narrow your focus to acid rain, secure in the knowledge that you have laid the foundation for a logical argument. *If* the U.S. government has a responsibility to help protect the environment, and *if* acid rain is a serious threat to the environment of several states, then it follows logically that the federal government should act to bring this problem under control. A brief outline of your argument would look something like this:

1. The federal government has the responsibility to protect the quality of American air, water, soil, and so on—what is commonly called "the environment."
2. Acid rain, which is caused principally by burning high-sulfur coal, is slowly killing American forests, endangering wildlife, and polluting lakes, rivers, and streams.
3. Therefore, the federal government should restrict the use of high-sulfur coal.

Once again, this is only an *outline*. An essay that makes this argument—explaining the problem in detail, anticipating the opposition, and providing meaningful concessions before reaching a clear and firm conclusion—would amount to several pages.

By outlining your argument in this way, you have followed the pattern of what is called a *syllogism*, a three-part argument in which the conclusion rests on two premises, the first of which is called the *major premise* because it is the point from which the writer begins to work toward a specific conclusion. Here is a simple example of a syllogism:

MAJOR PREMISE: All people have hearts.
MINOR PREMISE: John is a person.
CONCLUSION: Therefore, John has a heart.

If the major and minor premises are both true, then the conclusion reached should be true. Note that the minor premise and the major premise share a term in common (in the example, people/person). In a written argument, the "minor premise" would usually involve a specific case that relates to the more general statement with which the essay began.

A syllogism such as the one just cited may seem very simple. And it can be simple—if you're thinking clearly. On the other hand, it's even easier to write a syllogism (or an essay) that breaks down because of faulty reasoning. Consider the following example:

MAJOR PREMISE: All women like to cook.
MINOR PREMISE: Elizabeth is a woman.
CONCLUSION: Therefore, Elizabeth likes to cook.

Technically, the form here is *valid*. The two premises have a term in common, and if we accept both the major and minor premises, then we will have to accept the conclusion. But someone who thinks along these lines may be in for a surprise, especially if he has married Elizabeth confidently expecting her to cook his favorite dishes every night just as his mother used to do. Elizabeth may *hate* to cook, preferring to go out bowling at night or read the latest issue of the *Journal of Organic Chemistry.* A syllogism may be valid in terms of its organization, but it can also be *untrue* because it rests on a premise that can be easily disputed. Always remember that your major premise should inspire widespread agreement. Someone who launches an argument with the generalization that "all women like to cook," is likely to lose many readers before making it to the second sentence. Some generalizations make sense and some do not. Don't make the mistake of confusing generally accepted truths with privately held opinions. You may argue effectively on behalf of your opinions, but you cannot expect your audience to accept an easily debatable opinion as the foundation for an argument on behalf of yet another opinion. You may have many important things to say, but nobody is going to read them if alienated by your major premise.

You should also realize that, in many arguments, a premise may be implied but not stated. You might overhear a conversation like this:

> "I hear you and Elizabeth are getting married."
> "Yes, that's true."
> "Well, now that you've got a woman to cook for you, maybe you could invite me over for dinner sometime."
> "Why do you think that Elizabeth will be doing the cooking?"
> "Because she is a woman."

The first speaker has made a number of possible assumptions. He or she may believe that all women like to cook, or perhaps that all women are required to cook whether they like it or not. If the second speaker had the patience to continue this conversation, he would probably be able to discover the first speaker's premise. A syllogism that consists of only two parts is called an *enthymeme.* The part of the syllogism that has been omitted is usually the major premise, although it is occasionally the conclusion. Enthymemes usually result when a speaker or writer decides that it is unnecessary to state a point because it is obvious. What is obvious to someone trying to convince us with an enthymeme is not necessarily obvious to those of us who are trying to understand it. Although an enthymeme might reflect sound reasoning, the unstated part of the syllogism may reveal a flaw in the argument. When you encounter an enthymeme in your reading, you will often benefit from trying to reconstruct it as a full syllogism. Ask yourself what the writer has assumed, and then ask yourself whether you agree with that assumption. One sign of a faulty deductive argument is that a questionable point has been assumed to be universally true, and you may need to discover this point before you can decide that the argument is either invalid or untrue.

Deductive reasoning, which begins with a generalization and works to a conclusion that follows from that generalization, can be thought of as the opposite of *inductive reasoning*, which begins with specific observations and ends with a conclusion that goes beyond any of the observations that led up to it. So that you can see what a deductive essay might look like, here is a short essay written by a student:

Preparation for Real Life
Kerstin LaPorte

In order for all children to reach their fullest potential as adults, it is imperative that they be prepared for careers that will help them be productive members of society. Through the school system, taxpayers are responsible for providing the educational opportunities for the development of minds, so that when these students become adults, they too will be able to take their turn for supporting the education of a future generation. But many property owners have grown increasingly angry over the continual raises in their taxes, and this hostility is being expressed toward the school system that these overtaxed people have to support.

2   Cuts in spending are made, but these cuts are not reflected in the sports department. The costs of maintaining sports programs are immense. The money that is taken out of the average annual school budget for the equipment for training players, providing uniforms, and paying coaches is more than most taxpayers realize. I too am a taxpayer whose taxes go up each year. It is my view that this money would be better spent on more up-to-date textbooks, lab equipment in the science department that is not outdated, the newest computer technology, adequate tools and machinery for the wood and metal shops, and libraries that are stocked with the necessary books and magazines to complement all academic subjects. These investments will help a much larger percentage of the school population and develop skills in accord with public needs.

It would be a terrible loss to many people who gain a great deal of satisfaction out of participating in sports activities if these activities were to be completely phased out. Therefore I advocate that sports programs for adolescents be community-sponsored. Clubs, sponsored by participating members, local merchants, and private individuals, combined with fund-raising, would provide all the sports activities that have no place in an academic field.

4   Proponents of school-sponsored sports would argue that the children of lower-income families would not be able to participate in a community club due to any costs this would incur. I firmly believe

that if a student from a poor family has a special talent, clubs would probably vie for his or her membership, helping him or her with any financial deficiencies. Once the potential for a finely tuned athlete is seen, one who can help win the game or competition for the club, funding will be available for his or her recruitment.

The importance of physical fitness is not to be understated. Students need to be physically active in order to maintain mental and physical stamina. Therefore, a scaled-down physical education department must remain within the schools. If done for at least 30 minutes 3–5 times a week, aerobic exercise such as running, walking, and Jazzercize raises the heart rate sufficiently to promote physical fitness. It is not necessary to build pools, tennis courts, football stadiums, baseball parks, and basketball courts. Neither have I ever been able to justify the purchasing of cross-country skis, archery, weight lifting, and gymnastic equipment with academic funding. The maintenance of all the sport grounds and equipment involved, plus the replacement of broken or outdated equipment, is also an added annual expense to the community.

6   Just as students who have similar interests form clubs, which meet outside of school hours, students interested in further physical fitness can organize biking, skiing, or running clubs. This would involve the use of their own equipment, occur on their own time, and fill the void left if sports training is taken out of the school curriculum.

If there were to be a major change in the approach to our sports programs, the existing buildings, equipment, and outdoor facilities in and around the schools must not be wasted. The clubs could lease those premises, and any member would be eligible to utilize the facilities during club hours. This would include student members, who could go and work out during their free hours if they wanted. In this manner, the costs would not detract from the academic necessities, and the facilities already built would not go to waste.

8   Opponents to my proposal might ask: What about funding for such extracurricular activities as band, art, drama, and choir? There too, a very basic introduction to these fields is reasonable, just as scaled-down physical education would suffice. If a child shows promise of being a gifted musician, artist, actor, or singer, he or she can go on to obtain private instruction.

What about some of the academic subjects that seem unrelated to the job market, such as history, sociology, and psychology? Successful interaction between people depends on some knowledge of human nature, and these subjects are only on an introductory basis. As far as history goes, I would be scared to death to have a generation of voters go to the polls with no knowledge of the workings of government, ours or anyone else's, and, unaware of the mistakes of the past, try to make wise decisions for the future.

10   As a future teacher, I have been reminded over and over again that it is imperative that I be a good role model for my students. Coaches of competitive sports are role models also. They promote healthy lifestyles by discouraging students from smoking and drinking. They do the best they can to make their students' experiences enjoyable by providing proper motivation and support. This need not end with the removal of the sports programs from the school. These same people can either stay in the teaching field in another capacity or work for the community clubs.

       Yes, it is true that active daily training builds a particular responsibility and perseverance that will be needed in "real life." However, this "daily training" can be accomplished within the academic field also, and will serve to engender the school spirit that pro sports people feel is necessary in the educational environment. Forensics, math competitions, essay contests, and history debates all contribute to build public speaking ability, alleviate math anxiety, and promote an increased ability for self-expression in writing, which will aid students' ability to synthesize and analyze information and formulate informed opinions.

12   Extensive sports training through the school system prepares a very small percentage of the school population for a successful future, as very few individuals are lucky enough to go on to pro careers. Let's take the money that goes for sports and use it to support an up-to-date, academic education that will prepare all children for real life.

This essay has many strengths. The topic was well chosen, not only because many people are interested in school sports, but also because Kerstin's view of sports is likely to inspire controversy—hence the need for her argument. As already noted, good writers do not belabor the obvious. Writing this essay for an audience of students (with whom she shared an earlier draft for peer review), Kerstin realized that many of her classmates believed in the importance of school sports and that their convictions on this issue could keep them from listening to what she had to say. She therefore adopted a deductive strategy in order to establish some common ground with her opponents before arguing that school systems should not fund sports. Her opening paragraph establishes the premise on which her argument is based: The function of education is to help children "reach their fullest potential as adults" and prepare them to become "productive members of society." Her minor premise appears in paragraph 12: "Extensive sports training through the school system prepares a very small percentage of the school population for a successful future. . . ." If we accept both the major and minor premises, then we should be prepared to accept the conclusion: "Let's take the money that goes for sports and use it to support an up-to-date, academic education that will prepare all children for real life."

As you can see from this example, deduction allows a writer the chance to prepare the way for a controversial argument by strategically opening with a key point that draws an audience closer, without immediately revealing what exactly is afoot. With a genuinely controversial opinion, one must face the risk of being shouted down—especially when addressing a potentially hostile audience. Like Rogerian argument (pages 19–21), deductive reasoning increases the chance of gaining a fair hearing.

A writer who uses deduction should still remember to address those concerns most likely to be raised by opponents. In "Preparation for Real Life," Kerstin begins paragraphs 4, 8, and 9 by anticipating opposition and then responding to it. She also makes a number of important concessions. In her third paragraph, she concedes, "It would be a terrible loss to many people who gain a great deal of satisfaction out of participating in sports activities if these activities were to be completely phased out." The fifth paragraph begins by recognizing, "The importance of physical fitness is not to be understated." Paragraph 11 also begins with a concession: "Yes, it is true that active daily training builds a particular responsibility and perseverance that will be needed in 'real life.' " And, in paragraph 10, Kerstin admits that coaches can be good role models. These are all concessions that should appeal to men and women who value sports. But Kerstin does not simply let these concessions sit on the page. In each case, she immediately goes on to show how the concession does not undermine her own argument. Whatever your own views on this topic may be, you should realize that concessions need not weaken an argument. On the contrary, they can strengthen an argument by making it more complex.

The moment at which writers choose to anticipate opposition will usually vary; it depends on the topic, how much the author knows about it, and how easily he or she can deal with the principal counterarguments that others might raise. But whether one is writing an inductive or deductive argument, it is usually advisable to recognize and respond to opposition fairly early in the essay. You will need at least one or two paragraphs to introduce your topic, but by the time you are about one-third of the way into your essay, you may find it useful to defuse the opposition before it grows any stronger. If you wait until the very end of your essay to acknowledge that there are points of view different from your own, your audience may have already put your essay aside, dismissing it as "one-sided" or "narrow-minded." (Classical arrangement, discussed on pages 17–19, provides an alternative strategy in which counterarguments are discussed near the end of the essay. This strategy assumes that readers are familiar with the plan being used and understand that opposing views will be considered before the writer concludes.) Also, it is usually a good idea to put the opposition's point of view at the beginning of a paragraph. By doing so, you can devote the rest of that paragraph to your response. It's not enough to recognize the opposition and include some of its arguments in your essay. You must try to show your audience what to make of the counterarguments you have acknowledged. If you study the organization of "Preparation for Real Life," you will see that Kerstin begins paragraphs 3, 4, 5, 8, and 11 with sentences that acknowledge other sides to the question of public funding for school sports. But she was able to end each of these paragraphs with her own argument still moving clearly forward.

One final note: Although it is usually best to establish your premise before your conclusion, writing an essay is not the same as writing a syllogism. In "Preparation for Real Life," the minor premise does not appear until the last paragraph. It could just as easily have appeared earlier (and actually did so in a preliminary draft). Writers benefit from flexibility and the ability to make choices, depending on what they want to say. When you read or write deductive arguments, you will find that relatively few of these arguments proceed according to a fixed formula that determines exactly what must happen in any given paragraph.

Exercise 4

Draft a list of five widely accepted values or principles. Express each as a statement that would enjoy general support. Then identify at least two specific conclusions that could be drawn from each of them if they were used as premises for deductive arguments.

Reasoning by Using the Toulmin Model Although both inductive reasoning and deductive reasoning suggest useful strategies for writers of argument, they also have their limitations. Many writers prefer not to be bound by a predetermined method of organization and regard the syllogism, in particular, as unnecessarily rigid. To make their case, some writers choose to combine inductive and deductive reasoning within a single essay—and other writers can make convincing arguments without the formal use of either induction or deduction.

In an important book first published in 1958, a British philosopher named Stephen Toulmin demonstrated that the standard forms of logic needed to be reconsidered because they did not adequately explain all logical arguments. Emphasizing that logic is concerned with probability more often than certainty, he provided a new vocabulary for the analysis of argument. In Toulmin's model, every argument consists of these elements:

CLAIM: The equivalent of the conclusion or whatever it is a writer or speaker wants to try to prove.

DATA: The information or evidence a writer or speaker offers in support of the claim.

WARRANT: A general statement that establishes a trustworthy relationship between the data and the claim.

Within any argument, the claim and the data will be explicit. The warrant may also be explicit, but it is often merely implied—especially when the arguer believes that the audience will readily agree to it.

To better understand these terms, let us consider an example adapted from one of Toulmin's:

CLAIM: Raymond is an American citizen.
DATA: Raymond was born in Puerto Rico.
WARRANT: Anyone born in Puerto Rico is an American citizen.

These three statements may remind you of the three elements in a deductive argument. If arranged as a syllogism, they might look like this:

MAJOR PREMISE: Anyone born in Puerto Rico is an American citizen.
MINOR PREMISE: Raymond was born in Puerto Rico.
CONCLUSION: Raymond is an American citizen.

The advantage of Toulmin's model becomes apparent when we realize that there is a possibility that Raymond was prematurely born to French parents who were only vacationing in Puerto Rico, and he is now serving in the French army. Or perhaps he was an American citizen but became a naturalized citizen of another country after defecting with important U.S. Navy documents. Because the formal logic of a syllogism is designed to lead to a conclusion that is *necessarily* true, Toulmin argued that it is ill-suited for working to a conclusion that is *probably* true. Believing that the importance of the syllogism was overemphasized in the study of logic, Toulmin argued that there was a need for a "working logic" that would be easier to apply in the rhetorical situations in which people most often find themselves. He designed his own model so that it can easily incorporate *qualifiers* such as "probably," "presumably," and "generally." Here is a revision of the first example:

CLAIM: Raymond is probably an American citizen.
DATA: Raymond was born in Puerto Rico.
WARRANT: Anyone born in Puerto Rico is entitled to American citizenship.

Both the claim and the warrant have now been modified. Toulmin's model does not dictate any specific pattern in which these elements must be arranged, and this is a great advantage for writers. The claim may come at the beginning of an essay, or it could just as easily come after a discussion of both the data and the warrant. Similarly, the warrant may precede the data or it may follow it—or, as already noted, the warrant may be implied rather than explicitly stated at any point in the essay.

If you write essays of your own using the Toulmin model, you may find yourself making different types of claims. In one essay, you might make a claim that can be supported entirely by facts. For example, if you wanted that follows the principles of classical arrangement, you need to generate ideas that are suitable for this plan—and modify either the plan or the content later, after you have written your first draft. Or, if you begin by generating ideas without considering how you will organize them, you must then decide what kind of organization will be best suited for your ideas and your purpose in communicating them. These steps do not happen in isolation or in a linear progression in which it is impossible to revisit an earlier part of your work. When generating ideas, you might find that a tentative outline for their arrangement is beginning to emerge. Similarly, you might need to generate new ideas after organizing those with which you began, because your plan has helped you to discover a need for more material.

As you study the following plans, you should understand that they are not mutually exclusive. In a classically arranged argument, for example, the statement of background can be done with the kind of nonjudgmental language emphasized in Rogerian argument. Similarly, the summary of opposing views in a Rogerian argument requires the kind of understanding that a writer following a classical arrangement would need to have before engaging in refutation. In both cases, writers need to be well informed and fairminded. And both classical arrangement and Rogerian argument encourage the use of concessions. The difference between the two is best understood in terms of purpose. Although any argument is designed to be persuasive, the purpose of that persuasion varies from one occasion to another. You might write to persuade other people to accept the legitimacy of your position, even if they continue to hold very different views. You might write to invite other people to change their minds or to undertake a specific action. Or you might write to encourage conflicting parties to accept a compromise. In any case, your plan needs to suit your purpose.

Classical Arrangement

Theories of argument first developed in ancient Greece and Rome, where education emphasized the importance of persuasion. Aristotle defined rhetoric as "the study of all the available means of persuasion," and his ideas—as well as the ideas of many other classical scholars—shaped the approaches to argument that dominated Western thinking for almost two thousand years.

Because these theories developed at a time when most arguments were oral, the great works of classical rhetoric recommended strategies that could be easily understood by listeners. If speakers followed essentially the same plan, listeners were able to follow long, complex arguments because the main components were easily recognizable and the order in which they appeared signaled what was likely to happen next.

Here is the most common plan for organizing an argument along classical lines. The original name of each component in classical rhetoric appears in parentheses.

Introduction *(Exordium)*	The introduction is where you urge your audience to consider the case that you are about to present. This is the time to capture the attention of your readers and introduce your issue.
Statement of Background *(Narratio)*	In the statement of background, you narrate, or tell, the key events in the story behind your case. This is the time to provide information so that your audience will understand the nature of the facts in the case at hand.
Proposition *(Partitio)*	This component divides (or partitions) the part of the argument focused on information from the part focused on reasoning, and it outlines the major points that will follow. You must state the position you are taking, based on the information you have presented, and then indicate the lines the rest of your argument will follow.
Proof *(Confirmatio)*	Adhering carefully to your outline, you now present the heart of your argument: You make (or confirm) your case. You must discuss the reasons why you have taken your position and cite evidence to support each of those reasons.
Refutation *(Refutatio)*	In this key section, you anticipate and refute opposing views. By showing what is wrong with the reasoning of your opponents, you demonstrate that you have studied the issue thoroughly and have reached the only conclusion that is acceptable in this case.
Conclusion *(Peroratio)*	The concluding paragraph(s) should summarize your most important points. In addition, you can make a final appeal to values and feelings that are likely to leave your audience favorably disposed toward your case.

The classical rhetoricians allowed variations on this plan; for example, speakers were encouraged to begin with refutation when an audience was already strongly committed to an opposing point of view. But because the basic plan remains clear and straightforward, it can still help writers organize their thoughts. If you are looking for a way to organize an argument, experiment with classical arrangement and modify it, when necessary, to suit your needs.

The classical arrangement is especially useful when you feel strongly about an issue and must bring an audience around to agreeing with you and undertaking a proposed action. Because classical rhetoric assumes that an audience can be persuaded when presented with solid evidence and a clear explanation of what is wrong with the reasoning of opponents, this plan is to argue that the stock market should be subject to greater regulation, you could define the extent of current regulation, report on the laws governing overseas markets, and cite specific abuses such as scandals involving insider trading. In another essay, however, you might make a claim that is easier to support with a mixture of facts, expert opinion, and appeals to the values of your audience. If, for example, you wanted to argue against abortion, your data might consist of facts (such as the number of abortions performed within a particular clinic in 1997), testimony on which it is possible to have a difference of opinion (such as the point at which human life begins), and an appeal to moral values that you believe your audience should share with you. In short, you will cite different types of data depending on the nature of the claim you want to argue.

The nature of the warrant will also differ from one argument to another. It may be a matter of law (such as the Jones Act of 1917, which guarantees U.S. citizenship to the citizens of Puerto Rico), an assumption that one's data have come from a reliable source (such as documents published by the Securities and Exchange Commission), or a generally accepted value (such as the sanctity of human life). But whatever your warrant, you should be prepared to back it up if called on to do so. No matter how strongly you may believe in your claim, or how compelling your data may be, your argument will not be convincing if your warrant cannot be substantiated.

The Toulmin model for argumentation does not require that you abandon everything you've learned about inductive and deductive reasoning. These different systems of logic complement one another and combine to form a varied menu from which you can choose whatever seems best for a particular occasion. Unless your instructor specifies that an assignment must incorporate a particular type of reasoning, you will often be able to choose the type of logic you wish to employ, just as you might make any number of other writing decisions. And having choices is ultimately a luxury, not a burden.

For an example of a student essay that reflects the Toulmin model for reasoning, consider the following argument on the importance of studying history:

History Is for People Who Think
Ron Tackett

Can a person consider himself a thinking, creative, responsible citizen and not care about history? Can an institution that proposes to foster such attributes do so without including history in its curriculum? Many college students would answer such a question with an immediate, "Yes!" But those who are quick to answer do so without reflecting on what history truly is and how and why it is important.

2   History is boring, complain many students. Unfortunately, a lot of people pick up a bad taste of history from the primary and secondary schools. Too many lower-level history courses (and college level, too) are just glorified Trivial Pursuit: rife with rote memorization of dates and events deemed important by the teacher and textbooks, coupled with monotone lectures that could induce comas in hyperactive children. Instead of simply making students memorize when Pearl Harbor was attacked by the Japanese, teachers should concentrate on instilling an understanding of why the Japanese felt they had no alternative but to attack the United States. History is a discipline of understanding, not memorization.

        Another common complaint is that history is unimportant. But even the most fanatic antihistory students, if they were honest, would have to admit that history is important at least within the narrow confines of their own disciplines of study. Why be an artist if you are merely going to repeat the past (and probably not as expertly, since you would have to spend your time formulating theories and rules already known and recorded in Art's history)? Why write The Great Gatsby or compose Revolution again? How could anyone hope to be a mathematician, or a scientist, without knowing the field's history? Even a genius needs a base from which to build. History helps provide that base.

4   History is also important in being a politically aware citizen. Knowing that we entered World War I on the side of the Allies in part because Woodrow Wilson was a great Anglophile, as some historians charge, is not vital to day-to-day life. But it is important to know that the economic reparations imposed on Germany after the war set the stage for the rise of Hitler and World War II and that that war ended with a Russian domination of Eastern Europe that led to the Cold War, during which political philosophies were formulated that still affect American foreign and domestic policies. This type of history enables citizens to form an intelligent worldview and possibly help our nation avoid past mistakes. Of course, this illustration is simplified, but the point is as valid as when Santayana said that without history, we are "condemned to repeat it." This does not mean that history will repeat itself exactly, but that certain patterns recur in history, and if we understand the patterns of what has gone before, perhaps we can avoid making the mistakes our ancestors made.

        A person can live a long life, get a job, and raise a family without having any historical knowledge. But citizens who possess a strong knowledge of history are better prepared to contribute intelligently to their jobs and their society. Thus, knowing which Third World nations have a history of defaulting on loans can help a bank executive save his or her institution and its customers a great deal of grief by avoiding, or seeking exceptional safeguards on, such loans. And knowing the history of U.S. involvement in Central and South America, from naval incidents with Chile in the 1890s to trying to overthrow the Sandinistas in Nicaragua in the 1980s, can help Americans understand why many people and nations are concerned about U.S. policies in the region. More importantly, Americans cannot intelligently determine what those policies should be without a knowledge of history.

6   Now, if history is important enough to be required in college, how many credits are enough and what sort of history should be taught? American, European, Eastern, Latin American, or yet another? First, a course in American history must be required. Students can little appreciate the history of others, without first knowing their own. Second, since we more and more realize that we are members of a "global community," at least one world history course should be mandated. Though there is no magic number of credits that will ensure the student's becoming a thinking, creative member of society, history can help fulfill the collegiate purpose of fashioning men and women with the potential for wisdom and the ability to critically appraise political, economic, and moral issues. Thus, history should be a required part of the college curriculum.

In arguing on behalf of history, Ron shows that he is well aware that many students would like to avoid history courses. Paragraphs 2 and 3 are devoted to anticipating and responding to opposition. Although Ron concedes that history can be boring if it is badly taught, and makes an additional concession at the beginning of paragraph 5, he still insists that all college students should be required to take at least two history courses. The *claim* of this essay is "history should be a required part of the college curriculum." The *warrant* behind this claim is a value that is likely to be widely accepted: A college education should help people to think critically and become responsible members of society. This warrant underlies the entire argument, but it can be found specifically in the last paragraph where Ron refers to "the collegiate purpose of fashioning men and women with the potential for wisdom and the ability to critically appraise political, economic, and moral issues" immediately before making his claim.

Submitting *data* to support this claim presented the writer with a challenge: It would be difficult to obtain statistics or other factual evidence to prove that the claim fulfills the warrant. A reader might agree with the warrant and still doubt whether requiring college students to study history would give them the ability to think critically about political and moral issues. Ron chose to support his claim by defining history as "a discipline of understanding, not memorization" and providing several examples of historical events that are worth understanding: the Japanese attack on Pearl Harbor, the consequences of World War I, and the nature of U.S. involvement in Central and

South America. Additional support for the claim is provided by appeals to other values, which Ron has assumed his audience to possess. Paragraph 3 includes an appeal to self-interest: Knowing the history of your own field can save you from wasting time. This same strategy is employed in paragraph 5, where Ron suggests that knowledge of history can lead to better job performance. All of the examples found within the essay are clearly related to the values that the argument has invoked, and, within the limitations of a short essay, Ron has done a good job of supporting his claim.

AVOIDING LOGICAL FALLACIES

An apparently logical argument may reveal serious flaws if we take the trouble to examine it closely. Mistakes in reasoning are called logical *fallacies*. This term comes from the Latin word for deceit, and there is some form of deception behind most of these lapses in logic. It is easy to deceive ourselves into believing that we are making a strong argument when we have actually lost our way somehow, and many fallacies are unintentional. But others are used deliberately by writers or speakers for whom "winning" an argument is more important than searching for truth. Here is a list of common fallacies that you should be careful to avoid in your own arguments and remain alert to in the arguments of others.

Appealing to Pity

Writers are often justified in appealing to the pity of their readers when the need to inspire this emotion is closely related to whatever they are arguing for, and when the entire argument does not rest on this appeal alone. For example, someone who is attempting to convince you to donate one of your kidneys for a medical transplant would probably assure you that you could live with only one kidney and that there is a serious need for the kidney you are being asked to donate. In addition to making these crucial points, the arguer might move you to pity by describing what will otherwise happen to the person who needs the transplant.

When the appeal to pity stands alone, even in charitable appeals where its use is fundamental, the result is often questionable. Imagine a large billboard advertisement for the American Red Cross. It features a close-up photograph of a distraught (but nevertheless good-looking) man, beneath which, in large letters, runs this caption: PLEASE, MY LITTLE GIRL NEEDS BLOOD. Although we may already believe in the importance of donating blood, we should question the implications of this ad. Can we donate blood and ask that it be reserved for the exclusive use of little girls? Is the life of a little girl more valuable than the life of a little boy? Are the lives of children more valuable than the lives of adults? Few people would donate blood unless they sympathized with those who need transfusions, and it may be unrealistic to expect logic in advertising. But consider how weak an argument becomes when the appeal to pity has little to do with the issue in question.

Someone who has seldom attended class and failed all his examinations but then tries to argue, "I deserve to pass this course because I've had a lot of problems at home," is making a fallacious appeal to pity. The "argument" asks the instructor to overlook relevant evidence and make a decision favorable to the arguer because the instructor has been moved to feel sorry for him. You should be skeptical of any appeal to pity that is irrelevant to the conclusion or that seems designed to distract attention from the other factors you should be considering.

Appealing to Prejudice

Writers of argument benefit from appealing to the values of their readers. Such appeals become fallacious, however, when framed in inflammatory language or when offered as a crowd-pleasing device to distract attention from whether the case at hand is reasonable and well informed. A newspaper that creates a patriotic frenzy through exaggerated reports of enemy "atrocities" is appealing to the prejudicies of its readers and is making chances for reasonable discussion less likely. Racist, sexist, classist, and homophobic language can also be used to incite a crowd—something responsible writers should take pains to avoid doing. Appeals to prejudice can also take more subtle forms. Politicians may remind you that they were born and raised in "this great state" and that they love their children and admire their spouses—all of which are factors believed to appeal to the average man and woman but which nevertheless are unlikely to affect performance in office. When candidates linger on what wonderful family life they enjoy, it may be time to ask a question about the economy.

Appealing to Tradition

Although we can learn from the past and often benefit from honoring tradition, we can seldom make decisions based on tradition alone. Appealing to tradition is fallacious when tradition becomes the only reason for justifying a position. "We cannot let women join our club because we've never let women join in the past" is the equivalent of arguing: "We shouldn't buy computers for our schools, because we didn't have computers in the past." The world changes, and new opportunities emerge. What we have done in the past is not necessarily appropriate for the future. If you believe that a traditional practice can guide us in the future, you need to show why this is the case. Do not settle for claiming: "This is the way it always has been, so this is the way it always has to be."

Arguing by Analogy

An analogy is a comparison that works on more than one level, and it is possible to use analogy effectively when reasoning inductively. You must first be sure that the things you are comparing have several characteristics in common and that these similarities are relevant to the conclusion you intend to draw. If you observe that isolation produces depression in chimpanzees, you could argue that isolation can cause a similar problem for human beings. The strength of this argument would depend on the degree to which chimps are analogous to humans, so you would need to proceed with care and demonstrate that there are important similarities between the two species. When arguing from analogy, it is important to remember that you are speculating. As is the case with any type of inductive reasoning, you can reach a conclusion that is likely to be true but not guaranteed to be true. It is always possible that you have overlooked a significant factor that will cause the analogy to break down.

Unfortunately, analogies are often misused. An argument from analogy that reaches a firm conclusion is likely to be fallacious, and it is certain to be fallacious if the analogy itself is inappropriate. If a congressional candidate asks us to vote for him because of his outstanding record as a football player, he might be able to claim that politics, like football, involves teamwork. But because a successful politician needs many skills and will probably never need to run across a field or knock someone down, it would be foolish to vote on the basis of this questionable analogy. The differences between football and politics outweigh the similarities, and it would be fallacious to pretend otherwise.

Attacking the Character of Opponents

If you make personal attacks on opponents while ignoring what they have to say, or distracting attention from it, you are using what is often called an *ad hominem* argument (Latin for "to the man"). Although an audience often considers the character of a writer or speaker in deciding whether it can trust what he or she has to say, most of us realize that good people can make bad arguments, and even a crook can sometimes tell the truth. It is always better to give a thoughtful response to an opponent's arguments than to ignore those arguments and indulge in personal attacks.

Attributing False Causes

If you assume an event is the result of something that merely occurred before it, you have committed the fallacy of false causation. Assumptions of this sort are sometimes called post hoc reasoning, from the Latin phrase *post hoc, ergo propter hoc,* which means "after this, therefore because of this." Superstitious people offer many examples of this type of fallacious thinking. They might tell you, "Everything was doing fine until the lunar eclipse last month; *that's* why the economy is in trouble." Or personal misfortune may be traced back to spilling salt, stepping on a sidewalk crack, or walking under a ladder.

This fallacy is often found in the arguments of writers who are determined to prove the existence of various conspiracies. They often seem to amass an impressive amount of "evidence"—but their evidence is frequently questionable. Or, to take a comparatively simple example, someone might be suspected of murder simply because of being seen near the victim's house a day or two before the crime occurred. This suspicion may lead to the discovery of evidence, but it could just as easily lead to the false arrest of the meter reader from the electric company. Being observed near the scene of a crime proves nothing by itself. A prosecuting attorney who would be foolish enough to base a case on such a flimsy piece of evidence would be guilty of *post hoc, ergo propter hoc* reasoning. Logic should always recognize the distinction between *causes* and what may simply be *coincidences.* Sequence is not causation; every event is preceded by an infinite number of other events, all of which cannot be held responsible for whatever happens today.

This fallacy can be found in more subtle forms in essays on abstract social problems. Writers who blame contemporary problems on such instant explanations as "the rise of television" or "the popularity of computers" are no more convincing than the parent who argues that all the difficulties of family life can be traced to the rise of rock and roll. It is impossible to understand the present without understanding the past. But don't isolate at random any one event in the past, and then try to argue that it explains everything. And be careful not to accidentally imply a cause-and-effect relationship where you did not intend to do so.

Attributing Guilt by Association

This fallacy is frequently apparent in politics, especially toward the end of a close campaign. A candidate who happens to be religious, for example, may be maneuvered by opponents into the false position of being held accountable for the actions of all the men and women who hold to that particular faith. Nothing specific has been *argued,* but a negative association has been either created or suggested through hints and innuendos.

Begging the Question

In the fallacy of begging the question, a writer begins with a premise that is acceptable only to anyone who will agree with the conclusion that is subsequently reached—a conclusion often very similar to the premise itself. Thus, the argument goes around in a circle. For instance, someone might begin an essay by claiming, "Required courses like freshman English are a waste of time," and end with the conclusion that "Freshman English should not be a required course." It might indeed be arguable that freshman English should not be required, but the author who begins with the premise that freshman English is a waste of time has assumed what the argument should be devoted to proving. Because it is much easier to *claim* that something is true than to *prove* it is true, you may be tempted to beg the question you set out to answer. This temptation should always be avoided.

Equivocating

Someone who equivocates uses vague or ambiguous language to mislead an audience. In argumentation, equivocation often takes the form of using one word in several different senses, without acknowledging the change in meaning. It is especially easy to equivocate when using abstract language. Watch out in particular for the abuse of such terms as "right," "society," "freedom," "law," "justice," and "real." When you use words like these, make sure your meaning is clear. And make doubly sure your meaning doesn't shift when you use the term again.

Ignoring the Question

When someone says, "I'm glad you asked that question!" and then promptly begins to talk about something else, she or he is guilty of ignoring the question. Politicians are famous for exploiting this technique when they don't want to be pinned down on a subject. Students (and teachers) sometimes use it too, when asked a question that they want to avoid. Ignoring the question is also likely to occur when friends or lovers have a fight. In the midst of a quarrel, we may hear remarks like, "What about you!" or "Never mind the budget! I'm sick of worrying about money! We need to talk about what's happening to our relationship!"

Jumping to Conclusions

This fallacy is so common that it has become a cliché. It means that the conclusion in question has not been supported by an adequate amount of evidence. Because one green apple is sour, it does not follow that all green apples are sour. Failing one test does not mean that you will necessarily fail the next. An instructor who seems disorganized the first day of class may eventually prove to be the best teacher you ever had. You should always try to have more than one example to support an argument. Be skeptical of arguments that seem heavy on opinion but weak on evidence.

Opposing a Straw Man

Because it is easier to demolish a man of straw than to address a live opponent fairly, arguers are sometimes tempted to pretend that they are responding to the views of their opponents when they are only setting up a type of artificial opposition which they can easily refute. The most common form of this fallacy is to exaggerate the views of others or to respond only to an extreme view that does not adequately represent the arguments of one's opponents. If you argue against abolishing Social Security, you should not think that you have defended that program from all its critics. By responding only to an extreme position, you would be doing nothing to resolve specific concerns about how Social Security is financed and administered.

Presenting a False Dilemma

A false dilemma is a fallacy in which a speaker or writer poses a choice between two alternatives while overlooking other possibilities and implying that other possibilities do not exist. If a college freshman receives low grades at the end of the first semester and then claims, "What's wrong with low grades? Is cheating any better?" he or she is pretending that there is no other possibility—for example, that of earning higher grades by studying harder, a possibility that is recognized by most students and teachers.

Reasoning that Does Not Follow

Although almost any faulty argument is likely to have gaps in reasoning, this fallacy—sometimes called the *non sequitur* (Latin for "it does not follow")—describes a conclusion that does not follow logically from the explanation given for it.

Gaps of this sort can often be found within specific sentences. The most common type of non sequitur is a complex sentence in which the subordinate clause does not clearly relate to the main clause, especially where causation is involved. An example of this type of non sequitur would be: "Because the wind was blowing so fiercely, I passed the quiz in calculus." This is a non sequitur because passing calculus should not be dependent on the weather. A cause-and-effect relationship has been claimed but not explained. It may be that the wind forced you to stay indoors, which led you to spend more time studying than you usually do, and this in turn led you to pass your quiz. But someone reading the sentence as written could not be expected to know this. A non sequitur may also take the form of a compound sentence: "Mr. Blandshaw is young, and so he should be a good teacher." Mr. Blandshaw may indeed be a good teacher, but not just because he is young. On the contrary, young Mr. Blandshaw may be inexperienced, anxious, and humorless. He may also give unrealistically large assignments because he lacks a clear sense of how much work most students can handle.

Non sequiturs sometimes form the basis for an entire argument: "William Henderson will make a good governor because he is a friend of working people. He is a friend of working people because he has created hundreds of jobs through his contracting business." Before allowing this argument to go any further, you should realize that you've been asked to swallow two non sequiturs. Being a good governor involves more than being "a friend of working people." And there is no reason to assume that Henderson is "a friend of working people" just because he is an employer. He may have acquired his wealth by taking advantage of the men and women who work for him.

Sliding Down a Slippery Slope

According to this fallacy, one step will inevitably lead to an undesirable second step. An example would be claiming that legalized abortion will lead to euthanasia or that censoring pornography will lead to the end of freedom of the press. Although it is important to consider the probable effects of any step that is being debated, it is fallacious to claim that people will necessarily tumble downhill as the result of any one step. There is always the possibility that we'll be able to keep our feet firmly on the ground even though we've moved them from where they used to be.

Exercise 5

Read a series of editorials and letters in a newspaper of your own choice. Look for examples of logical fallacies. Bring your favorite example to class and explain what is wrong in the reasoning.

UNDERSTANDING OTHER FORMS OF PERSUASION

Of the various forms of persuasive writing, logical argument is the most honorable. Although logic can be abused, its object is truth rather than manipulation. Whether we are writing a logical argument or simply trying to understand one, we have to be actively involved with ideas. That means we have to *think*. We may be influenced by what we know of the writer's credibility and by whether she or he has touched our hearts within the argument as a whole. But behind any logical argument is the assumption that reasonable people should agree with its outcome—not so much because it is gracefully written (although it may be that), but because it has brought us closer to knowing truth.

There are other types of writing that rely on an indirect appeal to the mind, exploiting what is known about the psychological makeup of an audience or its most probable fears and desires. Successful advertising is *persuasive* in that it encourages us to buy one product or another, but it is not necessarily logical. Few people have the money, time, or inclination to sample every product available for consumption. When we buy a particular mouthwash, toothpaste, soap, or soft drink—and even when we make purchases as large as a car—we may simply choose the cheapest product available. But bargain hunting aside, we are frequently led to purchase brands that advertising has taught us to associate with health, wealth, and happiness. A prominent greeting card company insists that we send their cards if we really and truly care about someone. A soft drink company assures us that we will be young and have fun if we drink its best-known brand. One popular cigarette is associated with the masculinity of mounted cowboys, and another implies a dubious link with the women's movement. Almost no one really believes this sort of thing when forced to stop and think about it. But we often act without thinking, and this is one of the reasons why advertising has been able to grow into a billion-dollar industry. Through the clever use of language and visual images, advertisers can lead people into a variety of illogical and possibly ruinous acts.

This, then, is the principal distinction between argument and other types of persuasion: Argument seeks to clarify thought; persuasion often seeks to obscure it. Argument relies on evidence or widely accepted truths and does not necessarily dictate any particular course of action. Persuasion, on the other hand, can work altogether independent of the facts as we know them (such as how much money we can afford to spend before the end of the month), and it is almost always designed to inspire action—whether it is buying a new kind of deodorant or voting for the candidate with the nicest teeth. Persuasion can thus be a form of domination. It can be used to make people agree with the will of the persuader, regardless of whether the per- suader is "right" or simply selling his or her services by the hour.

Argument may include an appeal to our emotions; persuasion is likely to emphasize such appeals. A persuasive writer or speaker knows how to evoke feelings ranging from love, loyalty, and patriotism to anger, envy, and xenophobia. An audience may be deeply moved even when nothing sub- stantial has been said. With a quickened pulse or tearful eyes, we may find ourselves convinced that we've read or heard something wonderfully pro found. A few days later, we may realize that we've been inhaling the intoxi- cating fumes of a heavily scented gasbag, rather than digesting genuine "food for thought."

Analyzing Advertisements

Although persuasion is by no means limited to advertising, advertisements represent a form of persuasion that we regularly encounter in our daily lives. Recognizing that people are often bored by ads because there are so many of them, advertisers must be doubly persuasive: Before they can persuade us to buy a particular product or engage a specific service, advertisers must begin by persuading us to pay attention to the ad. Because advertisements cannot be taken for granted, advertising agencies have attracted some highly tal- ented people, and a successful advertising campaign usually involves much planning. Different advertisements employ different strategies, and if you think about the ads you encounter, you will find that they often include more than one message. Consider the examples on pages 48 through 51.

At first glance, the advertisement for Evian® Natural Spring Water (Figure 1) seems directed exclusively at pregnant women. The use of the second person, as in "If you plan to breast feed, experts say you should drink up to *30% more water* every day," seems to exclude anyone who is *not* plan- ning to breast feed: a large market sector that includes women who are un- able to have children, as well as many other women, and all men.

But although the written text seems to target only a small percentage of potential buyers of imported spring water, the ad as a whole is designed to persuade a much larger group. By associating their product with mother- hood, the advertisers have made an appeal to feeling. According to an old adage, mothers are as American as apple pie, so by associating a European

FIGURE 1

product with motherhood, the advertisers are appealing to a widely held American value. Respect for mothers is not uniquely American, however. Mother figures are revered in many different cultures, so the ad has the potential to reach a very large market. Although it is directly addressed to pregnant women, it is subconsciously directed at anyone who values motherhood. The opening line, "Mommy, can I have a drink of water?" invites readers to assume the role of children. If we are turning to our mothers for a drink of water, and good mothers are drinking Evian Natural Spring Water, then readers can hope that they will get Evian water from their mothers. If our "mommies" are no longer around to quench our thirst, then we will have to do the next best thing: head to the store for a bottle of the water good enough for mothers to give their children. To put this ad's message simply: "Mothers are good. Evian water is good for mothers. If you are a good mother, you should buy some. If you are a good child, you should also buy some."

On closer examination, we can see that the persuasive appeal of this ad involves a number of other elements. Consider the positive connotations of such italicized words as *eating, maintain, lubricate, process, cleanse,* and *life.* The woman is wearing a white dress, emphasizing the purity that apparently comes with drinking the product in question. She is thoroughly at ease, reclining, a book in hand. What could be more peaceful? The image suggests the comfort that comes with wealth. After all, for every pregnant woman who can lounge in the French Alps, there are many hundreds who are working for a living. Thus, in addition to being the drink of mothers, Evian water becomes the drink of wealth and privilege. If you cannot afford a new BMW but want the illusion that you too live in a world like this, you can at least start buying what is being marketed as the right water for those who are healthy, wealthy, and cool.

Like the ad for Evian water, the ad for Saturn automobiles (Figure 2) also involves linking the product with a positive image. In this case, the association is with physicians. But rather than settling for a relatively simple message such as "Product X is the preferred brand of nine out of ten doctors," the Saturn ad conveys a message that is more complex. The doctors in question are all young and unconventional—so unconventional that they have apparently driven some distance from a hospital for an outdoor lunch without even removing their stethoscopes. Their youth and attire emphasize that these doctors are different from the stereotypical image of physicians as highly paid professionals who take themselves seriously. As such, these four doctors—perfectly balanced in terms of gender, and representing four different cultures—are perfect clients for "A Different Kind *of* Company. A Different Kind *of* Car."

Although both their clothing and the accompanying text emphasize that Jim, Ed, Janet, and Beth are all doctors, they are also presented as good-natured and unthreatening. Three are eating simple lunches from brown paper bags, and the fourth has a plaid lunch box reminiscent of elementary school. Moreover, it is surely no accident that two of the doctors are eating

Drs. Junkins, Kwiatkowski, Cuervo, and Huang haven't been doctors long enough to know they're supposed to drive one of those overpriced luxury imports.

When Ed, Janet, Beth, and Jim emerged, successfully, from medical school, they felt the gratification of having achieved a lifelong goal, while also confronting a hard reality common to most young doctors—a ton of student loan debt. (You could buy five Saturns with what a new M.D. typically owes.)

In Ed's case, that hard reality also included his 10-year-old car—nobody could tell him how much time it had left. Since a pediatric resident's life is ruled by a beeper (and because you can't tell a sick kid that the tow truck was late), Ed bit the bullet and went looking for a new car.

Say ahh! Our bunch is that at least 9 out of 10 doctors would really love how easy Saturns are to take care of. (But don't quote us on that. Ask your doctor.)

While he was making the rounds of the car dealerships in town, Ed discovered Saturn. Where, along with the simple, painless way one shops at our showrooms, he liked the rather healthy range of standard features offered and (especially) the fact that the price of a Saturn did not put him into a state of shock.

Since then, mostly on his referral, many of Ed's colleagues have been filling the hospital parking lot with new Saturns. (Apparently, the people who pay most attention to a doctor's advice are other doctors.)

The Saturn SL2

A Different Kind *of* Company. A Different Kind *of* Car.

The Doctors are pictured with a 1993 Saturn SL2. M.S.R.P. for the 1994 Saturn SL2 is $10,830, including retailer prep and optional passenger-side mirror. Tax, license, transportation, and other options are extra. If you'd like to know more about Saturn, and our new sedans, coupes, and wagons, please call us any time at 1-800-522-5000. © 1993 Saturn Corporation.

FIGURE 2

FIGURE 2 *(Continued)*

fruit and the background is dominated by a large tree. These images combine to suggest that Saturn is a car for intelligent, nice, young professionals who value diversity, health, and fresh air.

The written text (in which we are quickly put on a first-name basis with strangers) reinforces the message that these unknown people—whose expertise has nothing whatsoever to do with cars—are typical of the good people who know what it's like to be in debt, drive an old car, and need reliable transportation. The informal, almost gossipy text emphasizes Ed's search for a car rather than specific features of the car on display. We read briefly about a "rather healthy range of standard features," but the details of the car are presumably less important than relating to the attractive people who are pictured as representative owners. Note that the car itself is obscured by the doctors in the photograph, and product information about the car is relegated to small print at the bottom of the left-hand page. Once again, a product is being sold because of the associations advertisers establish with it—not because of its specific qualities.

Exercise 6

Two other advertisements are reproduced on pages 54–55. Choose one— or an ad that you have discovered on your own—and write an essay of approximately five hundred words explaining how the ad attempts to be persuasive.

Recognizing Flaws in Persuasion

Just as some advertisements are more appealing than others, so are some ads more questionable than others. Many ads are relatively straightforward, but others may approach dishonesty. When analyzing persuasion, wherever you encounter it and in whatever form, you should be alert not only for the various types of fallacious reasoning discussed earlier, but also for the following flaws.

Bogus Claims   A claim can be considered bogus, or false, whenever persuaders promise more than they can prove or deliver. If a Chicago restaurant offers "fresh country peas" in the middle of January, you might want to ask where these peas were freshly picked. And if a large commercial bakery advertises "homemade pies," try asking whose home they were made in. You'll probably get some strange looks, because many people don't pay close attention to language. But good writers become good writers in part because they have eyes that see and ears that hear.

If a toothpaste promises to give your mouth "sex appeal," you'd still better be careful about whom you try to kiss. A claim of this sort is fairly crude, and therefore easily recognizable. But bogus claims can take many forms, some more subtle than others. A television advertisement for a new laxative may star a woman in a white coat, with a stethoscope around her neck. The advertisement implies—without necessarily saying so—that the product in question is endorsed by physicians. Ads of this sort are also likely to speak vaguely of "recent studies," or better yet, "recent *clinical* studies," which are declared to have proved a product's value. The product may indeed have value; on the other hand, it may be indistinguishable from its competition except in price and packaging. You might like it when you try it. But well-educated people should always be a little skeptical about promises from strangers.

When writing an essay, it is easy to fall into the habit of making bogus claims when reaching for generalizations to support your point of view. Imitating the style of the advertisements with which they are familiar, careless writers sometimes refer to those ever-popular "recent studies" that conveniently seem to support whatever is being argued. Such phrases as "Recent studies have shown" enable writers to avoid identifying who did the research. A recent study may provide the evidence to prove a point, but a good writer should be prepared to cite it, especially when the claim is surprising. It is one thing to write "Recent studies have shown that nutrition plays an important role in maintaining good health"—a generalization that enjoys wide acceptance. It would be something else altogether to toss off a claim like "Recent studies have shown that Americans have the most nutritious diet in the world." A specific claim requires specific support—not just a vague reference to an unidentified study. We cannot evaluate a recent study if we do not know how it was undertaken and where the results were published.

Writers who like to refer to "recent studies" are also fond of alluding to unspecified statistics, as in "Statistics have shown . . ." or "According to statistics . . . ." Statistics can be of great value, but they can also be misleading. Ask yourself whether a statistic raises any unanswered questions, and note whether the source has been revealed. Similarly, turn a critical eye on claims like "It is a well-known fact that . . ." or "Everybody knows that . . . ." If the fact *is* well known, why is the writer boring us with what we already know? If the fact is *not* well known, as is usually the case when lines of this sort are thrown about, then the writer had better explain how he or she knows it.

In short, if you want to avoid bogus claims, never claim anything that would leave you speechless if you were called on to explain or defend what you have written.

Loaded Terms   Good writers have good diction; they know a lot of words and, just as important, they know how to use them accurately. They know that most words have positive or negative *connotations*—associations with the word that go beyond its standard definition or *denotation*. "Placid," "tranquil," or "serene" might all be used to describe someone who is "calm," but each word creates a slightly different impression. Experienced writers are likely to pause before choosing the adjective that best suits their subject.

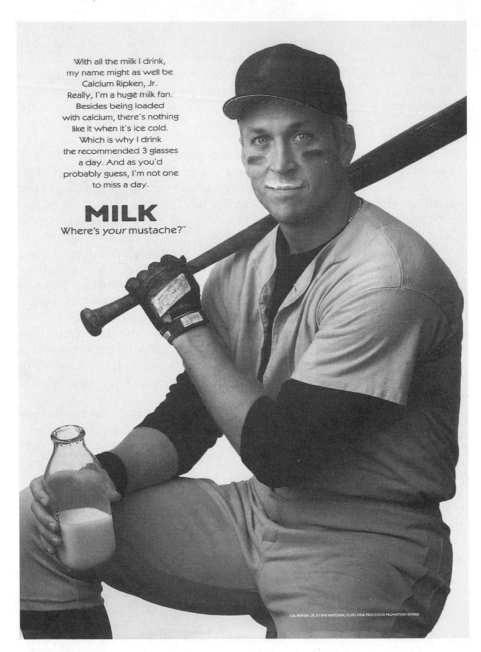

With all the milk I drink, my name might as well be Calcium Ripken, Jr. Really, I'm a huge milk fan. Besides being loaded with calcium, there's nothing like it when it's ice cold. Which is why I drink the recommended 3 glasses a day. And as you'd probably guess, I'm not one to miss a day.

MILK
Where's *your* mustache?™

CAL RIPKEN, JR. ©1998 NATIONAL FLUID MILK PROCESSOR PROMOTION BOARD

FIGURE 3

To Trena Brown, whose family has a history of breast cancer, our

search for a cure has a special urgency.

Drug companies are currently testing 73 medicines for

cancer in women, including 52 for breast cancer.

Progress like this from pharmaceutical company research provides

the best hope for conquering diseases like cancer, and dramatically reducing health costs.

Call or write to learn more about our research on new medicines for cancer and other diseases.

America's Pharmaceutical Research Companies

Pharmaceutical Manufacturers Association, 1100 15th St., NW, Box N, Wash., DC 20005. 1-800-538-2692.

FIGURE 4

A term becomes *loaded* when it is asked to carry more emotional weight than its context can legitimately support. A loaded term is a word or phrase that goes beyond connotation into the unconvincing world of the heavy handed and narrow minded. To put it simply, it is *slanted* or *biased*.

Loaded terms may appeal to the zealous, but they mislead the unwary and offend the critically minded. For example, when an aspiring journalist denounces the Clinton "regime" in the school newspaper, he is taking what many men and women would consider a cheap shot—regardless of their own politics. "Regime" is a loaded term because it is most frequently used to describe military dictatorships. Even someone who is politically opposed to Bill Clinton should be clearheaded enough to speak of the Clinton *Administration,* which is the term best suited for a political discussion of the U.S. Presidency.

Like "regime," many words have such strong connotations that they can become loaded terms very easily. In the United States, for example, terms such as "socialist," "feminist," "family," and "natural" all inspire responses that can affect how an audience responds to the context in which these words appear. Moreover, an unloaded term can become loaded within a specific context. To manipulate reader response, a writer may introduce unnecessary adjectives. A political correspondent might write "Margaret Ong, the wealthy candidate from Park Ridge, spoke today at Jefferson High School." The candidate's income has nothing to do with the news event being reported, so "wealthy" is a loaded term. It's an extra word that serves only one function: to divide the candidate from the newspaper's audience, very few of whom are wealthy. It would not be surprising if some readers began to turn against this candidate, regardless of her platform, simply because they had been led to associate her with a background that is alien to their own.

Do not make the mistake of assuming that loaded terms occur only in political discourse. They can be found almost anywhere, if you take the trouble to read critically and intelligently. You may even find some in your textbooks.

Misrepresentation Misrepresentation can take many forms. Someone may come right out and lie to you, telling you something you know—or subsequently discover—to be untrue. In the course of writing a paper, someone may invent statistics or alter research data that point to an unwelcome conclusion. And then there is *plagiarism*—taking someone else's words or ideas without acknowledgment and passing them off as your own. (For a discussion of plagiarism, see pages 68–70.)

There are always going to be people who find it easy to lie, and there isn't much we can do about this except to keep our eyes open, read well, and choose our friends with care. But we ourselves can be careful to act honorably and to follow the guidelines for working with sources that appear in Part 2 of this book. There is, however, a common misrepresentation that must be understood as part of our introduction to the principles of argument and persuasion: Dishonest writers will often misrepresent by twisting what their opponents have said.

The most common way in which writers misrepresent opposing arguments is through oversimplification. The ability to summarize what others have said or written is a skill that cannot be taken for granted, and we will turn to it shortly. There is always the possibility that someone may misrepresent an opponent accidentally—having failed to understand what has been said or having confused it in reporting it. But it is also possible to misreport others *deliberately*. A complex argument can be reduced to ridicule in a slogan, or an important element of such an argument could be entirely overlooked, creating a false impression.

Have the courage to ask for evidence whenever someone makes a questionable claim. When you find it necessary to quote someone, make sure you do so not only correctly but also *fairly*. The concept of "quoting out of context" is so familiar that the phrase has become a cliché. But clichés sometimes embody fundamental truths, and here is one of them: Quotations should be more than accurate; they should also reflect the overall nature of the quoted source. When you select a passage that truly represents the thesis of another's work, you can use it in good conscience—as long as you remember to put it in quotation marks and reveal to your readers where you got it. If you fasten onto a minor detail and quote a line that could be misunderstood if lifted away from the sentences that originally surrounded it, then you are guilty of misrepresentation.

Bogus claims, loaded terms, and misrepresentation are almost always to be found in that extreme form of persuasion known as *propaganda*. Strictly defined, propaganda means only the systematic use of words and images to propagate (or spread) ideas, but the abuse of propaganda within the past century has made the word widely associated with dishonesty. (For an extended definition of this term, see "The Purpose of Propaganda," by Adolf Hitler, pages 320–327.) Because the techniques of persuasion are easy to abuse, you should use them with great care. If you are trying to move an audience to action, you may find it useful to appeal to the heart as well as to the head, but you should try to avoid appealing to the heart alone. When appealing to the mind, it is always more honorable to address an audience as intelligent and thoughtful adults than to subtly exploit their subconscious hopes and fears.

An essay or speech that works primarily by inspiring an emotional response is most likely to succeed only when an audience can be called on for immediate action. If a senator can inspire colleagues moments before a critically important vote, or an evangelist can move a congregation to generosity just as the collection plate is about to be passed, then the results of such persuasion may be significant. But opportunities of this sort are rare for most writers. Almost everything we write can be put aside and reconsidered at another time. Irrespective of the ethical importance of arguing what is true and not just what is convenient, there is also a very practical reason for trying to argue logically: The arguments that carry the greatest weight are usually the arguments that are capable of holding up under analysis. They make *more* sense as we think about them, not less. Whereas persuasion relies on impulse, argument depends on conviction. Our impulses may determine what we do this afternoon, but our convictions shape the rest of our lives. If you make a genuinely logical argument, you may make some people angry with you, but you will not be accused of dishonesty. When you abandon logic for other persuasive techniques, make sure that you are simply making a change in writing strategy. Never write anything that you don't believe. This does not mean that there's anything wrong with writing fiction or satire. But it does mean that good writers shouldn't tell lies.

PART 2

WORKING WITH SOURCES

READING CRITICALLY

Although reading can be a pleasure, and many people find it relaxing to read material that provides a temporary escape from daily concerns, serious reading requires an active response on your part. When reading in college, or in whatever profession you are preparing for, you need to think about what you read. To make sure that you have mastered the content of what you have read, you must be able to identify key points—such as an author's thesis—and any points that you find difficult to understand. But beyond working to understand the material before you, you should also be prepared to *evaluate* it. As students, you will sometimes be confronted with more information than you can digest with ease. You will also find that different writers will tell you different things. When this happens, inexperienced readers sometimes become confused or discouraged. Being able to recognize what material deserves the closest reading, and what sources are the most reliable, is essential to coping successfully with the many academic demands made on your time. By reading critically, and reading often, you can acquire skills that will help you in almost any college course.

As you read the material collected in this book, you will find that some articles are easier to read than others. It would be a mistake to assume that the easiest material is necessarily the most reliable. On the other hand, it would also be wrong to assume that long, difficult articles are reliable simply because they are long and difficult. Whether you are preparing to write an argument of your own or simply trying to become better informed on an issue that has more than one side, you can benefit from practicing specific strategies for critical reading.

Previewing

Even before you begin to read, there are a few steps that you can take to help you benefit from the reading you are about to undertake. A quick preview, or survey, of a written text should give you an idea of how long it will take to read, what the reading will probably reveal, and how useful the reading is likely to be. When you glance through a newspaper, identifying stories that you want to read and others that you merely want to skim over, you are practicing a simple type of preview—one that is often guided primarily by your level of interest in various issues. But when previewing reading material in college, it is usually wise to ask yourself some questions that go beyond whether you happen to find a topic appealing.

How Long Is This Work?   By checking the length of a work before you begin to read, you can estimate how much reading time the material will demand, based on the speed and ease with which you normally read. The length may also be a clue in determining how useful a text may be. Although quantity is no sure guide to quality, a long work may contain more information than a short work. When reading an article in an anthology or in a magazine, you can quickly flip ahead to see where it ends. And when doing research (discussed in Part 3 of this book), you can usually learn the length of a work before you even hold it in your hand. This information is included in periodical indexes, book catalogs, and many Web sites. (See the illustrations on pages 96, 99, and 106.)

What Can I Learn from the Title?   Although some titles may be too general to communicate what you can expect when you read the works in question, a title often reveals an author's focus. An article called "Drugs and the Modern Athlete" will differ in focus from one called "Drug Testing and Corporate Responsibility." Moreover, a title can often indicate the author's point of view. Examples within this book include "In Defense of Hunting," "It's Time to Privatize," and "The Purpose of Propaganda."

Do I Know Anything about the Author?   Recognizing the names of established authorities in your field becomes easier as you do more reading, but many written sources offer information that can help you estimate an author's credibility when that author is unfamiliar to you. A magazine article may identify the author at the beginning or the end of the piece, or on a separate page (often called "Notes on Contributors" and listed in the table of contents). A biographical sketch of the author can usually be found on a book jacket, and a list of his or her other published works may appear at either the front or the back of the book. Anthologies often include introductory headnotes describing the various writers whose work has been selected. In *The Informed Argument,* Brief Edition, most headnotes indicate the authors' credentials for writing on the topic at hand. An author may have already published other works on the same subject. On the other hand, some authors choose to write about topics that are not directly related to their field of expertise. Suppose, for example, that you are about to read an argument on nuclear energy. By noting whether the article was written by a utility executive or an environmental activist, you can prepare yourself for the sort of argument you are most likely to encounter. If the article is written by a famous authority on child care, you might ask yourself whether that author will be a credible authority on nuclear power plants. Remember, however, that experts can make mistakes, and that important arguments can be written by someone new to the field. The best way to appraise any author's credibility is to read that person's work, noting how much evidence is provided to support the claims and how fairly the author seems to treat other people.

What Do I Know about the Publisher? An important work can be published by an obscure publisher, and a small magazine may be the first to publish an author destined to win a Pulitzer prize. The reputation of a publisher is not an automatic guide to the reliability of a source, but there are a few factors that can help you determine whether a source is likely to be worthwhile. University presses tend to expect a high degree of scholarship, and academic journals usually publish articles only after they have been examined by two or three other experts in that field. When you read an article in a popular magazine, the nature of that magazine may suggest what it is likely to publish. For example, an article on hunting in *Field & Stream* is almost certain to be very different from one on hunting in *Vegetarian Times*. If you read widely in periodicals, you will eventually find that some magazines and newspapers consistently reflect political positions that might be characterized as either "liberal" or "conservative." When you make a discovery of this sort, you can often make a pretty good guess about what kind of stand will be taken on issues discussed in one of these periodicals. This guess can prepare you to note any bias within the articles. Once again, remember that you are only making a preliminary estimate when previewing. The best way to judge a work is to read it carefully.

Is There Anything Else I Can Discover by Skimming through the Material? A quick examination of the text can identify a number of other features that can help you orient yourself to what you are about to read. Consider the length of the average paragraph; long paragraphs may indicate a densely written text that you will need to read slowly. Are there any special features, such as tables, figures, or illustrations that will give you visual aids? Are there any subtitles? If so, they may provide you with a rough outline of the work in question and indicate points where you may be able to take a break if necessary. Quickly reading the first sentence in every paragraph may also give you a sense of the work's outline. In some cases, a writer may actually provide you with a summary. Articles from scholarly journals are often preceded by an *abstract* (or summary) that can help you understand the article and estimate the extent to which it is likely to be of use to you.

Articles without abstracts may include a brief summary within the text itself; check the first few and last few paragraphs, the two locations where writers most often summarize their views. Finally, be sure to note whether the work includes a reference list. Scanning a bibliography—noting both how current the research seems and how extensive it is—can help you appraise a writer's scholarship and alert you to other sources that you may want to read on your own.

Annotating

Marking a text with notes, or *annotating* it, can be a great help when you are trying to understand your reading. Annotation can also help you to discover points that you might want to question when you evaluate this work. One of the advantages of owning a book—or having your own photocopy of an excerpt from a book or magazine—is that you can mark it as heavily as you wish without violating the rights of others. When you are annotating a text that is important to you, you will usually benefit from reading that text more than once and adding new annotations with each reading.

Equipped with a yellow felt-tipped pen, some students like to "highlight" the passages that seem most important to them. If this technique has worked well for you, there is no reason why you should feel compelled to abandon it. But it has two disadvantages. One is that highlighting cannot be erased. Some students find themselves with yellow-coated pages because they were initially unable to distinguish between main points and supporting details—and were later unable to remove unnecessary highlighting when they came to understand the text better. A second problem is that highlighting pens usually make broad marks ill-suited for writing. If you read with a pen like this in hand, you will need to reach for another pen or pencil whenever you want to add comments in the margin.

When reading, especially when reading a text for the first time, you might benefit from an alternative to highlighting. Try using a pen or pencil and simply marking in the margin a small check (✓) when a line seems important, an exclamation point (*!*) when you find surprising information or an unusually bold claim, and a question mark (*?*) when you have trouble understanding a particular passage or find yourself disagreeing with what it says. This simple form of annotation can be done very easily, and if you use a pencil, you will be able to erase any marks that you later find distracting.

When you are able to spend more time with a text, and want to be sure that you understand not only its content but also its strengths and weaknesses, then additional annotations are in order. Use the margins to define new words and identify unfamiliar allusions. Write comments that will remind you of what is discussed in various paragraphs. Jot down questions that you may subsequently raise in class or explore in a paper. By making cross references (like *cf.* ¶ *3* beside a later paragraph), you can remind yourself of how various components of the work fit together and also identify apparent contradictions within the work. Finally, whenever you are moved

1776 | When in the Course of human events, it becomes nec- *such as Americans* essary for one people to dissolve the political bands which have connected them with another, and to as- *such as English* sume among the powers of the earth, the separate and equal station to which the Laws of Nature and of Na- *Is "Nature's God" different from "God"?* ture's God entitle them, a decent respect to the opin- ions of mankind requires that they should declare the causes which impel them to the separation.

Why should nations have "equal station" when some are more powerful than others?

We hold these truths to be self-evident, that all *Why "self-evident"?* men are created equal, that they are endowed by their *Couldn't he prove them?* Creator with certain unalienable Rights, that among these are Life, Liberty and the pursuit of Happiness. *Permanent, "not to be separated"* That to secure these rights, Governments are insti- tuted among Men, deriving their just powers from the consent of the governed. That whenever any Form of Government becomes destructive of these ends it is *So the Civil War was ok?* the Right of the People to alter or to abolish it, and to institute new Government, laying its foundation on such principles and organizing its powers in such form, as to them shall seem most likely to effect their Safety and Happiness. Prudence, indeed, will dictate that Governments long established should not be changed for light and transient causes; and accordingly all experience has shewn, that mankind are more dis- posed to suffer, while evils are sufferable, than to right themselves by abolishing the forms to which they are accustomed. But when a long train of abuses and usurpations, pursuing invariably the same Object evinces a design to reduce them under absolute *What's the difference between a "right" and a "duty"?* Despotism, it is their right, it is their duty, to throw off such Government, and to provide new Guards for their future security. Such has been the patient suffer- ance of these Colonies; and such is now the necessity which constrains them to alter their former Systems of Government. The history of the present King of Great *George III (ruled from 1760 to 1820)* Britain is a history of repeated injuries and usurpa- tions, all having in direct object the establishment of an absolute Tyranny over these States. To prove this, *impartial* let Facts be submitted to a candid world.

Does this include women ???

If the rights to life & liberty are "unalienable" how come we have capital punishment and prisons?

wrongful seizure

Why is the capitalization so weird?

FIGURE 1

to a strong response—whether you are agreeing or disagreeing with what you have read—write that thought down before you lose it. An annotation of this sort can be useful when you are reviewing material before an exam, and it may very well be the seed from which a paper will later grow.

To give you an example of annotation, on page 63 is an annotated excerpt from The Declaration of Independence. (The full text, unannotated, appears in Part 5, pages 303–306.) As you examine it, remember that readers annotate a text in different ways. Some annotations are more thorough and reflective than others, but there are no "correct" responses against which your own annotations must be measured. You may notice different aspects of a text each time you reread it, so your annotations are likely to accumulate in layers. Annotations have been reproduced on page 63 in both printing and script, to suggest how they accumulated during more than one reading.

Summarizing

Summarizing a work is one of the best ways to demonstrate that you have understood it. On many occasions, you will be required to summarize what others have said or written—or even what you yourself have said or written. This skill is especially important in argumentation. You will have to be able to summarize the main arguments of your opponents if you want to write a convincing argument of your own. And researched papers will become ridiculously long, obscure, and unwieldy if you lack the ability to summarize your reading.

There is no clear rule to determine what passages are more significant than others. Every piece of writing must be judged on its own merits, and this means that you must consider every paragraph individually. The first sentence of a paragraph may be important if it introduces a new idea. Unfortunately for writers of summaries (but fortunately for readers, who would be easily bored if every paragraph followed the same mechanical pattern), the first sentence may simply be a transitional sentence, linking the new paragraph with whatever has preceded it. The *topic sentence* (also called the *thesis sentence*) is the single most important sentence in most paragraphs—the exceptions are very short paragraphs that serve only as transitions. (Transitional paragraphs do not advance a new idea; they simply link together longer paragraphs devoted to ideas that are related, but not closely enough so that the paragraphs can flow smoothly together.) It is important to remember that the topic sentence can occur anywhere in a paragraph.

As you read the material you want to summarize, limit yourself to marking no more than one or two sentences per paragraph. You should identify the topic sentence, and you may want to mark a line that contains an important supporting detail. At this point, you may choose to copy all the material you have noted onto a separate sheet of paper. But do not think that this means you have completed a summary. What you have are the notes for a summary: a collection of short quotations that are unlikely to flow smoothly together. A good summary should always be easy to read. After you take your notes, you must shape them into a clear, concise piece of writing.

As a writer of summary, be prepared to *paraphrase*—to restate in your own words something you've read or heard. There are many different reasons for paraphrasing, and you've probably been practicing this skill since you were a child. We frequently paraphrase the words of others to soften unpleasant truths. Sometimes we may even be tempted to restate a relatively mild statement more harshly, to make trouble for someone we don't like. But in writing summary, we should paraphrase only to make complex ideas more easily understandable. A paraphrase can be as long as the original material; under some circumstances, it may even be longer. So don't confuse paraphrase with summary. Paraphrasing is simply one of the skills that we call on when we must write a coherent summary.

Reading over the quotations you have compiled, look for lines that seem longer than they have to be and ideas that seem unnecessarily complicated. Lines of this sort are likely subjects for paraphrase. As you restate these ideas more simply, you may also be able to include details that appeared elsewhere in the paragraph and seem too important to leave out. You should not have to restate everything that someone else has written, although there's nothing necessarily wrong in doing so. A summary can include direct quotation, so long as the quotations are relatively short and have a clarity that you yourself cannot surpass.

The next step is to reread your paraphrasing and any quotations that you have included. Look for gaps between sentences, where the writing seems awkward or choppy. Eliminate all repetition, and subordinate any ideas that do not need to stand alone as separate sentences. Rearrange any sentences that would flow better in a different sequence, and add transitional phrases wherever they can help smooth the way from one idea to the next. After you have made certain that your sentences follow in a clear and easily readable sequence and have corrected any errors in grammar, spelling, or syntax, you should have an adequate summary of the material you set out to cover. You would be wise to read over what you have written at least one more time, making sure that the content accurately reflects the nature of whatever is being summarized. Be absolutely sure that any direct quotations are placed within quotation marks.

Writing summary requires good editorial judgment. A writer of summary has to be able to distinguish what is essential from what is not. If the material being summarized has a particular bias, then a good summary should indicate that the bias is part of the work in question. *But writers should not interject their own opinions into a summary of someone else's work*. The tone of a summary should be neutral. You may choose to summarize someone's work so that you can criticize it later, but do not confuse summary with criticism. When summarizing, you are taking the role of helping other writers to speak for themselves. Don't let your own ideas get in the way.

Good summaries vary in length, depending on the length and complexity of the original material and on how much time or space is available for summarizing it. It's unusual, however, to need more than 500 words to summarize most material, and you may be required to summarize an entire book in less than half that length. When summary is being used as a preliminary to some other type of work—such as argument or analysis—it is especially important to be concise. For example, if you are summarizing an argument before offering a counterargument of your own, you may be limited to a single paragraph. The general rule to follow is: Try to do justice to whatever you are summarizing in as few words as possible, and make sure that you have a legitimate reason for writing any summary that goes on for more than a page or two.

Experienced writers know that summary is a skill worth practicing. If you find summary difficult, remind yourself that it combines two skills of fundamental and inescapable importance: reading and writing. Well-educated men and women must be proficient in both. Summarizing tests not only your ability to write simply and clearly, but also your ability to comprehend what you read. The selections in Parts 4 and 5 of this book will provide you with many opportunities for summarizing.

Synthesizing

Synthesis is closely related to summary, and it demands many of the same skills. The principal difference is that while summary involves identifying the major points of a single work or passage, synthesis requires identifying related material in two or more works and tying them smoothly together. Synthesis is often an extension of summary because writers may need to summarize various sources before they can relate these sources to one another. Synthesis does not necessarily require you to cover *all* the major points of the individual sources. You may go through an entire article or book and identify only one point that relates to another work you have read. And the relationships involved in your synthesis may be of various kinds. For example, two different authors may have made the same claim, or one might provide specific information that supports a generalization made by the other. On the other hand, one author might provide information that makes another author's generalization seem inadequate or even wrong.

When reading material that you may need to synthesize, ask yourself: "How does this material relate to whatever else I have already read on this topic?" If you are unable to answer this question, consider a few more specific questions: Does the second of two works offer support for the first or does it reflect an entirely different thesis? If the two sources share a similar position, do they arrive at a similar conclusion by entirely different means or do they overlap at any points? Would it be easier to compare the two works or to contrast them? This process of identifying similarities and differences is essentially what synthesis is all about.

When you have determined the points that link your various sources to one another, you are ready to write a synthesis. To see how a synthesis can be organized, let us consider an example. Suppose you have read four articles on the subject of AIDS, written, respectively, by a scientist, a clergyman, a gay activist, and a government official. You were struck by how differently these four writers responded to the AIDS epidemic. Although they all agreed that AIDS is a serious problem, each writer advanced a different proposal for fighting the disease. Your synthesis would probably begin with an introductory paragraph that includes a clear thesis statement, for example: "Although there is widespread agreement that AIDS is a serious problem, there is no consensus about how this problem can be solved." Each of the next four paragraphs could then be devoted to a brief summary of one of the different points of view. A final paragraph might emphasize the relationship that exists among the several sources, either by reviewing the major points of disagreement among them or by emphasizing one or two points about which everyone agreed. Your outline for this type of synthesis would be:

PARAGRAPH ONE:	Introduction
PARAGRAPH TWO:	Summary of first writer (scientist)
PARAGRAPH THREE:	Summary of second writer (clergyman)
PARAGRAPH FOUR:	Summary of third writer (gay activist)
PARAGRAPH FIVE:	Summary of fourth writer (government official)
PARAGRAPH SIX:	Conclusion

Any good outline allows for some flexibility. Depending on the material and what you want to say, your synthesis might have fewer than or more than six paragraphs. For example, if two of your sources were especially long and complex, there is no reason why you couldn't devote two paragraphs to each of them, even though you were able to summarize your other two sources within single paragraphs.

An alternative method for organizing a synthesis involves linking two or more writers within paragraphs that focus on specific issues or points. This type of organization is especially useful when you have detected a number of similarities that you want to emphasize. Suppose that you have read six essays about abortion. Three writers favored legalized abortion, for much the same reasons; three writers opposing abortion offered arguments that they shared in common. Your assignment is to identify the arguments most used by people who favor legalized abortion and those most used by people who oppose it. Your outline for synthesizing this material might be organized like this:

PARAGRAPH ONE:	Introduction
PARAGRAPH TWO:	One argument in favor of abortion that was made by different writers
PARAGRAPH THREE:	A second argument in favor of abortion that was made by different writers
PARAGRAPH FOUR:	One argument against abortion that was made by different writers

PARAGRAPH FIVE: A second argument against abortion that was made by different writers

PARAGRAPH SIX: Conclusion

Suppose, during the course of your reading, you identified several other arguments both for and against legalized abortion. You have decided not to include them within your synthesis, however, because each point came up only within a single work, and your assignment was to identify the most used arguments on this subject. If you feel uneasy about ignoring these additional points, you can easily remind your audience, in either your introduction or your conclusion, that other arguments exist and you are focusing only on those most frequently put forward.

For an example of a synthesis written by a student, see the essay by Jessica Cozzens, in Part 4, at the end of the section on sexual harassment (pages 192–195).

AVOIDING PLAGIARISM

To plagiarize (from *plagiarius*, the Latin word for "kidnapper") is to steal—to be guilty of what the Modern Language Association calls "intellectual theft." Plagiarism is also a form of cheating, an activity that sometimes prompts the cliché that "Cheaters are only cheating themselves." There is some truth to this idea; someone who plagiarizes a paper is losing out on an opportunity for learning, in addition to running a serious risk. The risks are considerable. In the workplace, intellectual theft (of an essay, a song, or a proposal) can lead to lawsuits and heavy financial penalties. In a college or university, students who commit intellectual theft face penalties ranging from a failing grade on a paper to expulsion from the school. They are not the only ones who are hurt, however. In addition to hurting themselves, plagiarists injure the people they steal from; the professors who take the time to read and respond to the work of writers who are not their own students; classmates, whose grades may suffer from comparison if a clever plagiarism goes undetected; and the social fabric of the academic community, which becomes torn when values such as honesty and mutual respect are no longer cherished.

The grossest form of plagiarism involves submitting someone else's paper as your own. Services that sell papers advertise on many college campuses, and obliging friends or roommates can sometimes be persuaded to hand over one of their own papers for resubmission. In cyberspace, the World Wide Web provides ample opportunities for downloading a paper written by someone else. Many schools have home pages that include model student essays, and if you look long enough you may well find something that seems likely to fulfill an assignment you don't want to write. The electronically sophisticated can also piece a paper together by lifting paragraphs from a number of sources on the Internet and typing in commands that will paste these blocks together. No one engages in such overt plagiarism accidentally. There is usually an explanation for this kind of cheating, but an explanation is not an excuse. If ever tempted to submit someone else's work as your own, be guided by this simple rule: *Don't do it.*

On the other hand, it is also possible to plagiarize without meaning to do so. Learning how to work with sources takes instruction, time, and practice. Some students come to college inadequately prepared; their high school teachers may not have noticed when the students' papers were more or less copied out of encyclopedias or other sources. If this happens often enough, the ill-prepared student might be genuinely confused about what it means to be an honest writer. Research on plagiarism also shows that different cultures have different understandings of who "owns" ideas. Students who come to American colleges from cultures in which language and ideas are considered common property might think they are doing only what is expected of them when they patch together the unattributed words of other people.

Whatever the reason, students sometimes plagiarize by drawing too heavily on their sources. They may forget to put quotation marks around lines that they have taken word for word from another source, or they may think they don't need to quote if they have changed a few words. Such students need to learn that it is important to give credit to the *ideas* of others, as well as to their *words*. If you take most of the information another writer has provided and repeat it in essentially the same pattern, you are only a half-step away from copying the material, even if you have changed the exact wording.

Here is an example:

Original Source

Hawthorne's political ordeal, the death of his mother—and whatever guilt he may have harbored on either score—afforded him an understanding of the secret psychological springs of guilt. *The Scarlet Letter* is the book of a changed man. Its deeper insights have nothing to do with orthodox morality or religion—or the universal or allegorical applications of a moral. The greatness of the book is related to its sometimes fitful characterizations of human nature and the author's almost uncanny intuitions: his realization of the bond between psychological malaise and physical illness, the nearly perfect, if sinister, outlining of the psychological techniques Chillingsworth deployed against his victim.

Plagiarism

Nathaniel Hawthorne understood the psychological sources of guilt. His experience in politics and the death of his mother brought him deep insights that don't have anything to do with formal religion or morality. The greatness of *The Scarlet Letter* comes from its characters and the author's brilliant intuitions: Hawthorne's perception of the link between psychological and physical illness and his almost perfect description of the way Roger Chillingsworth persecuted his victim.

This student has simplified the original material, changing some of its wording. But he is clearly guilty of plagiarism. Pretending to offer his own analysis of *The Scarlet Letter,* he owes all of his ideas to another writer who is unacknowledged. Even the organization of the passage has been followed. This "paraphrase" would still be considered a plagiarism even if it ended with a reference to the original source (p. 307 of *Nathaniel Hawthorne in His Times,* by James R. Mellow). A reference or footnote would not reveal the full extent to which this student is indebted to his source.

Here is an acceptable version:

Paraphrase

As James R. Mellow has argued in *Nathaniel Hawthorne in His Times, The Scarlet Letter* reveals a profound understanding of guilt. It is a great novel because of its insight into human nature—not because of some moral about adultery. The most interesting character is probably Roger Chillingsworth because of the way he was able to make Rev. Dimmesdale suffer (307).

This student has not only made a greater effort to paraphrase the original material, but he has also introduced it with a reference to the original writer. The introductory reference to Mellow, coupled with the subsequent page reference, "brackets" the passage—showing us that Mellow deserves the credit for the ideas in between the two references. Additional bibliographical information about this source is provided by the list of works cited at the end of the paper. Turning to the student's bibliography, we find:

Mellow, James. *Nathaniel Hawthorne in His Times.* Boston: Houghton, 1980.

One final caution: It is possible to subconsciously remember a piece of someone else's phrasing and inadvertently repeat it. You would be guilty of plagiarism if the words in question embody a critically important idea or reflect a distinctive style or turn of phrase. When you revise your draft, look for such unintended quotations; if you use them, show who deserves the credit for them, and *remember to put quoted material within quotation marks.*

DOCUMENTING YOUR SOURCES

"Documenting your sources" means revealing the source of any information you report. You must provide documentation for:

- Any direct quotation.
- Any idea that has come from someone else's work.
- Any fact or statistic that is not widely known.

The traditional way to document a source is to footnote it. Strictly speaking, a "footnote" appears at the foot of the page, and an "endnote" appears at the end of the paper. But "footnote" has become a generic term covering both forms. Most writers prefer to keep their notes on a separate page because doing so is easier than providing space for them at the bottom of each page. The precise form of such notes varies, depending on the style manual being followed. Here is how a documentary footnote would look according to the style guidelines of the Modern Language Association (MLA):

A. *Bibliographic Form*

> Katz, Jonathan. The Invention of Heterosexuality. New York:
> Plume, 1996.

B. *Note Form*

> [1] Jonathan Katz, The Invention of Heterosexuality (New York: Plume,
> 1996) 37.

The indentation is reversed, the author's name is not inverted, and the publishing data are included within parentheses. Also, the author is separated from the title by a comma rather than a period. A subsequent reference to the same work would follow a shortened form:

> [5] Katz 183.

If more than one work by this same author is cited, then a shortened form of the title would also be included:

> [7] Katz, Heterosexuality 175.

Documentary footnotes require what most authorities now regard as unnecessary repetition, because the author's full name and the publishing data are already included in the bibliography. Many readers object to being obliged to turn frequently to another page if they want to check the notes. Some writers still use notes for documentation purposes. But most important style guides now urge writers to provide their documentation parenthetically within the work itself, reserving numbered notes for additional explanation or discussion that is important but cannot be included within the actual text without a loss of focus. Notes used for providing additional information are called *content notes;* for an example, see pages 206–207.

The form of your documentation will vary, depending on the subject of your paper and the requirements of your instructor. Students in the humanities are usually asked to follow the form of the Modern Language Association (MLA) or the recommendations in *The Chicago Manual of Style*. Students in the social sciences are often expected to follow the format of the American Psychological Association (APA). Students in the natural sciences are usually required to use either a parenthetical system resembling that of the APA or a system that involves numbering their sources. Make sure that you understand the requirements of your instructor, and remember that you can consult a specific manual in your field if you run into problems. Here is a list of manuals that can be found in many college libraries:

American Chemical Society. *The ACS Style Guide: A Manual for Authors and Editors*. Washington: Amer. Chemical Soc., 1986.

American Institute of Physics. *AIP Style Manual*. 4th ed. New York: Amer. Inst. of Physics, 1990.

American Mathematical Society. *A Manual for Authors of Mathematical Papers*. Rev. ed. Providence: Amer. Mathematical Soc., 1990.

American Psychological Association. *Publication Manual of the American Psychological Association*. 4th ed. Washington: Amer. Psychological Assn., 1994.

The Chicago Manual of Style. 14th ed. Chicago: U of Chicago, 1993.

Council of Biology Editors. *Scientific Style and Format: The CBE Style Manual for Authors, Editors, and Publishers*. 6th ed. New York: Cambridge UP, 1994.

Gibaldi, Joseph. *MLA Style Manual and Guide to Scholarly Publishing*. 12th ed. New York: Modern Language Assn., 1998.

Harvard Law Review Assn. *The Bluebook: A Uniform System of Citation*. 15th ed. Cambridge: Harvard Law Review Assn., 1991.

A detailed discussion of all of these styles is beyond the range of this chapter, but the following pages provide model entries for the most frequently used styles.

Parenthetical Documentation: The MLA Author/Work Style

Since 1984, the Modern Language Association has recommended that parenthetical documentation take the place of endnote or footnote citations. In MLA form, the author's name is followed by a page reference. It is not necessary to repeat within the parentheses information that is already provided within the text. If you are used to using footnotes for documentation, this format may seem a little strange at first, but it has the great merit of being easy to use and easy to understand. (Remember that additional information on these sources will be provided in a separate bibliography.)

A. A Work by a Single Author

> Henry James often identified wickedness with sexual duplicity (Kazin 227).

or

> Alfred Kazin has argued that Henry James identified wickedness with sexual duplicity (227).

There is no punctuation between the author's name and the page reference when both are cited parenthetically. Note also that the abbreviation "p." or "pp." is not used before the page reference.

B. A Work with More Than One Author

> Cleanth Brooks and Robert Penn Warren have argued that "indirection is an essential part of the method of poetry" (573).

or

> Although this sonnet may seem obscure, its meaning becomes clearer when we realize "indirection is an essential part of the method of poetry" (Brooks and Warren 573).

Note that when a sentence ends with a quotation, the parenthetical reference comes before the final punctuation mark. Note also that the ampersand (&) is not used in MLA style. When referring to a work by more than three authors, you should follow the guidelines for bibliographic entries and list only the first author's name followed by "et al." (Latin for *et alii*, "and others").

> These works "derive from a profound disillusionment with modern life" (Baym et al. 910).

C. A Work with a Corporate Author

When a corporate author has a long name, you should include it within the text rather than within parentheses. For example:

> The Council on Environmental Quality has reported that there is growing evidence of ground water contamination throughout the United States (81).

rather than

> There is growing evidence of ground water contamination throughout the United States (Council on Environmental Quality 81).

Although both of these forms are technically correct, the first is preferred because it is easier to read. Long parenthetical references intrude unnecessarily, interrupting the flow of ideas.

D. A Work with More Than One Volume

When you wish to cite a specific part of a multivolume work, include the volume number before the page reference:

> As Jacques Barzun has argued, "The only hope of true culture is to make classifications broad and criticism particular" (2: 340).

Note that the volume number is given an arabic numeral, and a space separates the colon and the page reference. The abbreviation "vol." is not used unless you wish to cite the entire volume: (Barzun, vol. 2).

E. More Than One Work by the Same Author

If you cite more than one work by the same author, you need to make your references distinct. You can do so by putting a comma after the author's name and then adding a shortened form of the title: (Hardy, *Mayor* 179). But your paper will be easier to read if you include either the author or the title directly in the text:

> Twain's late work reflects a low opinion of human nature. But when Satan complains that all men are cowards (<u>Stranger</u> 184), he is only echoing Col. Sherburn's speech in <u>Huckleberry Finn</u> (123-24).

F. A Quotation within a Cited Work

If you want to use a quotation that you have discovered in another book, your reference must show that you acquired this material secondhand and that you have not consulted the original source. Use the abbreviation "qtd. in" (for "quoted in") to make the distinction between the author of the passage being quoted and the author of the work in which you found this passage:

> In 1835, Thomas Macaulay declared the British to be "the acknowledged leaders of the human race" (qtd. in Davis 231).

G. A Quotation of Poetry

Identify line numbers when you quote poetry, but do not use the abbreviations "l." or "ll." These abbreviations can easily be confused with numbers. Write "line" or "lines" in your first citation of poetry; subsequent citations should include only the line numbers. Quotations of three lines or less should be included directly into the text of your paper. Separate the lines with a slash (/), leaving space both before and after the slash:

> Yeats returned to this theme in "The Second Coming": "The best lack all conviction, while the worst / Are full of passionate intensity" (7-8).

Each line of longer quotations should begin on a new line, indented one inch (or ten spaces) from the margin.

Parenthetical Documentation:
The APA Author/Year Style

The American Psychological Association (APA) requires that in-text documentation identify the author of the work being referred to and the year in which the work was published. This information should be provided parenthetically; it is not necessary to repeat any information that has already been provided directly in the sentence.

A. One Work by a Single Author

> It has been argued that fathers can play an important role in the treatment of eating disorders (Byrne, 1987).

or

> Byrne (1987) argued that fathers can play an important role in the treatment of eating disorders.

or

> In 1987, Katherine Byrne argued that fathers can play an important role in the treatment of eating disorders.

If the reference is to a specific chapter or page, that information should also be included. For example:

> (Byrne, 1987, p. 93)
> (Byrne, 1987, chap. 6)

Note that the abbreviations for page and chapter emphasize the distinction between the year of publication and the part of the work being referred to.

B. A Work with Two or More Authors

If a work has two authors, you should mention the names of both authors every time a reference is made to their work:

> A recent study of industry (Cole & Walker, 1997) argued that. . . .

or

> More recently, Cole and Walker (1997) have argued that. . . .

Note that the ampersand (&) is used only within parentheses.

Scientific papers often have multiple authors because of the amount of research involved. In the first reference to a work with three to five authors, you should identify each of the authors:

> Hodges, McKnew, Cytryn, Stern, and Kline (1982) have shown. . . .

Subsequent references to the same work should use an abbreviated form:

> This method was also used in an earlier study (Hodges et al., 1982).

If a work has six authors (or more), this abbreviated form should be used even for the first reference. If confusion is possible because you must refer to more than one work by the first author, list as many coauthors as necessary to distinguish between the two works.

C. A Work with a Corporate Author

When a work has a corporate author, your first reference should include the full name of the corporation, committee, agency, or institution involved. For example:

> (United States Fish and Wildlife Service [USFWS], 1997)

Subsequent references to the same source can be abbreviated:

> (USFWS, 1997)

D. A Reference to More Than One Work

When the same citation refers to two or more sources, the works should be listed alphabetically according to the first author's name and separated with semicolons:

> (Pepler & Rubin, 1982; Schlesinger, 1996; Young, 1994)

If you are referring to more than one work by the same author(s), list the works in the order in which they were published.

> The validity of this type of testing is now well established (Collins, 1988, 1994).

If you refer to more than one work by the same author published in the same year, distinguish individual works by identifying them as "a," "b," "c," etc.:

> These findings have been questioned by Scheiber (1997a, 1997b).

Organizing a Bibliography

Documenting your sources parenthetically or with notes allows you to reveal exactly which parts of your paper are supported by or owed to the works you have consulted. A bibliography, which is a list of the sources consulted, is also essential so that readers can evaluate your research and possibly draw on your sources for work of their own.

Works Cited in MLA Style

In an MLA-style bibliography, the works cited are arranged in alphabetical order determined by the author's last name. MLA style requires that the author's first name be given. Every important word in the titles of books, articles, and journals is capitalized. The titles of books, journals, and newspapers are all underlined (italicized). The titles of articles, stories, and poems appear within quotation marks. Second and subsequent lines are indented one-half inch (or leave five spaces blank). Here are some examples:

A. A Book with One Author

Mukherjee, Bharati. The Holder of the World. New York: Knopf, 1993.

Although it is important to give the author's full name, the book's full title, and the place of publication, you should use a shortened form of the publisher's name (Alfred A. Knopf, in this case).

B. A Book with Two or Three Authors

Gilbert, Sandra M., and Susan Gubar. The Madwoman in the Attic: The Woman Writer and the Nineteenth-Century Literary Imagination. New Haven: Yale UP, 1979.

Note that the subtitle is included, set off from the main title by a colon. The second author's name is not inverted, and abbreviations are used for "University Press" to provide a shortened form of the publisher's name. For books with three authors, put commas after the names of the first two authors; separate the second two authors with a comma followed by "and."

C. An Edited Book

Baldick, Chris, ed. Oxford Book of Gothic Tales. New York: Oxford UP, 1992.

D. A Book with More Than Three Authors or Editors

Black, Laurel, et al., eds. New Directions in Portfolio Assessment: Practice, Critical Theory, and Large-Scale Scoring. Portsmouth: Boynton, 1994.

Give the name of the first author or editor only, and add the abbreviation "et al."

E. Edition after the First

Champion, Larry S. The Essential Shakespeare: An Annotated Bibliography of Major Modern Studies. 2nd ed. New York: Hall, 1993.

F. A Work in an Anthology

O'Brien, Patricia. "Michael Foucault's History of Culture." The New Cultural History. Ed. Lynn Hunt. Berkeley: U of California P, 1989. 25-46.

Note that a period comes after the title of the selection but before the second quotation marks. A period is also used to separate the date of publication from the pages between which the selection can be found. No abbreviation is used before the page reference.

G. A Translated Book

> Eco, Umberto. <u>The Aesthetics of Thomas Aquinas</u>. Trans. Hugh Bredin. Cambridge: Harvard UP, 1988.

H. A Work in More Than One Volume

> Leckie, Robert. <u>The Wars of America</u>. 2 vols. New York: Harper, 1992.

I. An Introduction, Preface, Foreword, or Afterword

> Dove, Rita. Foreword. <u>Jonah's Gourd Vine</u>. By Zora Neale Hurston. New York: Harper, 1990. vii-xv.

J. An Article in an Encyclopedia

> Hunt, Roberta M. "Child Welfare." <u>The Encyclopedia Americana</u>. 1993 ed.

For citing material from well-known encyclopedias, give the author's name first, then the article title. If material is arranged alphabetically within the source, which is usually the case, there is no need to include volume and page numbers. You should give the full title of the encyclopedia, the edition if it is stated, and the year of publication (e.g., 11th ed. 1996). When no edition number is stated, identify the edition by the year of publication (e.g., 1996 ed.). If the author of the article is identified only by initials, look elsewhere within the encyclopedia for a list identifying the names these initials stand for. If the article is unsigned, give the title first. (Note: This same form can be used for other reference books, such as dictionaries and the various editions of *Who's Who*.) For an example of how to cite an electronic encyclopedia, see T.

K. A Government Publication

> United States. Federal Bureau of Investigation. <u>Handbook of Forensic Science</u>. Washington: GPO, 1994.

For many government publications, the author is unknown. When this is the case, the agency that issued the publication should be listed as the author. State the name of the government (e.g., "United States," "Florida," "United Nations") followed by a period. Then give the name of the agency that issued the work, using abbreviations only if you can do so clearly (e.g., "Bureau of the Census," "National Institute on Drug Abuse," "Dept. of Labor") followed by a period. The underlined title of the work comes next, followed by another period. Then give the place of publication, publisher, and date. Most federal publications are printed in Washington by the Government Printing Office (GPO), but you should be alert for exceptions. (Note: Treat pamphlets just as you would a book.)

L. A Journal Article with One Author

> Swann, Karen. "The Sublime and the Vulgar." <u>College English</u> 52 (1990): 7-20.

The volume number comes after the journal title without any intervening punctuation. The year of publication is included within parentheses after the volume number. A colon separates the year of publication and the page reference. Leave one space after the volume number and one space after the colon.

M. A Journal Article Paginated Anew in Each Issue

> Williams, Jeffrey. "The Life of the Mind and the Academic Situation." <u>College Literature</u> 23.3 (1996): 128-146.

In this case, the issue number is included immediately after the volume number, and the two are separated by a period without any intervening space.

N. An Article from a Magazine Published Monthly

> Renfrew, Colin. "World Linguistic Diversity." <u>Scientific American</u> Jan. 1994: 116-123.

Instead of citing the volume number, give the month and year of the issue. Abbreviate the month when it has more than four letters. (May, June, and July are spelled out.) For an example of how to cite an article from a magazine published monthly which was obtained through a computer database, see R.

O. An Article from a Magazine Issued Weekly

> Wilkinson, Alec. "The Confession." <u>New Yorker</u> 4 Oct. 1993: 162-171.

The form is the same as for an article in a magazine that is issued monthly, but you add the day immediately before the month. Note that a hyphen between page numbers indicates consecutive pages. When an article is printed on nonconsecutive pages—beginning on page 34, for example, and continuing on page 78—give only the first page number and a plus sign: 34+.

P. An Article from a Daily Newspaper

> Reich, Howard. "Limited Ambition." <u>Chicago Tribune</u> 9 Feb. 1997, final ed., sec. 7: 13.

If more than one edition is available on the date in question, specify the edition immediately after the date. If the city of publication is not part of the newspaper's name, identify the city in brackets after the newspaper title. Because newspapers often consist of separate sections, you should cite the section number if each section has separate pagination. If a newspaper consists of only one section, or if the pagination is continuous from one section to the next, then you do not need to include the section number. If separately paginated sections are identified by letters, omit the section reference (sec.) but include the letter of the section with the page number (e.g., 7B or D19). If the article is unsigned, begin the citation with the title of the article; alphabetize the article under its title, passing over small words like "a" and "the." For an example of how to cite a newspaper article accessed through a computer service, see V.

Q. An Editorial

> Wicker, Tom. "The Key to Unity." Editorial. <u>New York Times</u> 30 Jan. 1991, natl.
> ed.: A15.

Editorials are identified as such between the title of the article and the title of the newspaper or magazine.

R. Printed Material Accessed from a Periodically Published Database

> Holtzman, Henry. "Team Management: Its Time Has Come . . . Again." <u>Managing Office Technology</u> Feb. 1994: 8. <u>ABI/Inform</u>. CD-ROM. UMI Proquest. Oct. 1994.

Include the same information you would provide for a magazine or journal article: author (if known), article title, journal title, date of print publication, and page reference. Then cite the database you used, the medium through which you accessed it (e.g., a CD-ROM, a diskette) and the vendor that made this medium available. Conclude with the date of electronic publication.

S. Nonprinted Material Accessed from a Periodically Published Database

> African Development Bank. "1995 AFDB Indicative Learning Program." 19
> Sept. 1995. <u>National Trade Data Bank</u>. CD-ROM. U.S. Commercial Service. Mar. 1996.

Give the author's name (a corporate author in this case), the title of the material in quotation marks, the date it was prepared (if given), the title of the database, publication medium, vendor, and the date it was published electronically. Underline the title of the database.

T. A Non-Periodical Publication on CD-ROM

> Hogan, Robert. "Abbey Theater." <u>The Academic American Encyclopedia (1995
> Grolier Multimedia Encyclopedia)</u>. CD-ROM. Danbury: Grolier, 1995.

If no author is identified, begin with the work's title; if no author or title is available, begin with the title of the product consulted.

U. A Publication on Diskette

> Gradecki, Joe. <u>The Virtual Reality Construction Kit</u>. Diskette. New York: Wiley, 1994.

Follow the same pattern you would for a book, but add a medium description after the work's title.

V. A Printed Publication Accessed through a Computer Service

> Rothstein, Richard. "Labor Market, Not Schools, Will Aid Latino Education Woes." <u>Los Angeles Times</u> 21 July 1996, home ed.: M2. <u>Times Mirror</u>. On-line. Nexis. 10 Oct. 1996.

Follow the same pattern you would for the print equivalent (in this case, a newspaper article), then add the underlined title of the database, the publication medium, the name of the computer service, and the date you accessed it.

W. Material from an Electronic Journal or Newsletter Obtained through a Computer Network

> Brent, Doug and Joe Amato. "The Brent–Amato Exchange." <u>EJournal</u>. 1.2-1 (Oct. 1991): n. pag. Online. Internet. 31 Oct. 1994. Available FTP: http://rachel.albany.edu/~ejournal/v/n2-1.html.

Add the electronic address for your source at the end of the entry if required to do so by your instructor or if you think this information would be useful for readers.

X. An Electronic Text Obtained through a Computer Network

> Shakespeare, William. <u>A MidSummer Night's Dream</u>. <u>Annotated Hypertext Edition</u>. Ed. J.B. Siedlecki. Online. Internet. 31 Oct. 1996. Available FTP: http://quarles.unbc.edu/midsummer/info.html.

If the text has been edited, include the editor's name immediately after the title of the text.

Y. An Interview

> Nelson, Veronica. Personal interview. 16 Aug. 1997.

If you interview someone, alphabetize the interview under the name of the person interviewed.

References in APA Style

In APA style, the reference list is arranged alphabetically, the order being determined by the author's last name. The date of publication is emphasized by placing it within parentheses immediately after the author's name.

Authors submitting articles for publication are expected to indent the first line of each reference five spaces (leave five spaces blank). Additional lines are placed flush with the left margin in this case. However, the APA *Publication Manual* (4th ed.) distinguishes between papers submitted for publication and papers submitted for a college course. When papers are submitted for a college course, APA recommends a hanging indent style (similar to MLA indention), which is what is shown in the following illustrations. Ask your instructor which format is preferred at your school.

A. Book with One Author

> Sullivan, A. (1995). <u>Virtually normal</u>. New York: Knopf.

Note that the author's first name is indicated only by an initial. Capital letters are used only for the first word of the title and the first word of the subtitle if there is one. (But when a proper name appears within a title, it retains the capitalization it would normally receive, for example: *A history of ideas in Brazil.*) The name of the publisher, Alfred A. Knopf, is given in shortened form. A period comes after the parentheses surrounding the date of publication, and also after the title and the publisher.

B. Book with Two or More Authors

> Youcha, C., & Seixas, J. (1989). <u>Drugs, alcohol, and your children: How to keep your family substance-free</u>. New York: Crown.

An ampersand is used to separate the names of two authors. When there are three or more authors, separate their names with commas and put an ampersand immediately before the last author's name.

C. Edited Book

> Preston, J. (Ed.). (1992). <u>A member of the family: Gay men write about their families</u>. New York: Dutton.

The abbreviation for editor is "Ed."; it should be included within parentheses between the name of the editor and the date of publication. The abbreviation for editors is "Eds." Give the names of all editors, no matter how many there are.

D. Article or Chapter in an Edited Book

> Howard, A. (1992). Work and family crossroads spanning careers. In S. Zedeck (Ed.), <u>Work, families, and organizations</u> (pp. 70-137). San Francisco: Jossey.

Do not invert the editor's name when it is not in the author's position. Do not put the title of the article or chapter in quotation marks. Use a comma to separate the editor from the title of the edited book. The pages between which the material can be found appear within parentheses immediately after the book title. Use "p." for page and "pp." for pages.

E. Translated Book

> Calasso, R. (1993). <u>The marriage of Cadmus and Harmony</u> (T. Parks, Trans.). New York: Random. (Original work published 1988)

Within parentheses immediately after the book title, give the translator's name followed by a comma and the abbreviation "Trans." If the original work was published earlier, include this information at the end.

F. Revised Edition of a Book

> Hopkins, B. R. (1993). <u>A legal guide to starting and managing a nonprofit organization</u> (2nd ed.). New York: Wiley.

The edition is identified immediately after the title. Note that edition is abbreviated "ed." and should not be confused with "Ed." for editor.

G. Book with a Corporate Author

> American Red Cross. (1993). <u>Standard first aid</u>. St. Louis: Mosby.

H. Multivolume Work

> Jones, E. (1953-57). <u>The life and work of Sigmund Freud</u> (Vol. 2). New York: Basic.

The volume number is included within parentheses immediately after the title. When a multivolume book is published over a number of years, list the years between which it was published.

I. Journal Article with One Author

> Butler, A. C. (1996). The effect of welfare benefit levels on poverty among single-parent families. <u>Social Problems, 43,</u> 94-115.

Do not use quotation marks around the article title. Capitalize all important words in the journal title and underline. Put a comma after the journal title and then give the volume and page numbers. Abbreviations are not used for "volume" and "page." To distinguish between the numbers, underline the volume number and put a comma between it and the page numbers.

J. Journal Article with More Than One Author

> Nugent, J. K., Lester, B. M., Greene, S. M., Wieczorek-Deering, D., & O'Mahoney, P. (1996). The effects of maternal alcohol consumption and cigarette smoking during pregnancy on acoustic cry analysis. <u>Child Development, 67,</u> 1806-1815.

K. Journal Article Paginated Anew in Each Issue

> Major, B. (1993). Gender, entitlement, and the distribution of family labor. Journal of Social Issues, 49(3), 141-159.

When each issue of a journal begins with page 1, you need to include the issue number in parentheses immediately after the underlined volume number.

L. Article from a Magazine Issued Monthly

> Baker, K. (1997, February). Searching the window of nature's soul. Smithsonian, pp. 94-104.

Within parentheses immediately after the author, include the month of issue after the year of publication. Use "p." or "pp." in front of the page number(s). Do not include the volume number. Follow the same form for an article in a weekly magazine issued on a specific day, but add the day after the month:

> Hazen, R. M. (1991, February 25). Why my kids hate science. Newsweek, p. 7.

M. Article from a Newspaper

> Bishop, J. E. (1996, November 13). Heart disease may actually be rising. Wall Street Journal, p. B6.

Place the exact date of issue within parentheses immediately after the author. After the newspaper title, specify the page number(s).

N. Government Document

> National Institute of Alcohol Abuse and Alcoholism. (1980). Facts about alcohol and alcoholism (DHHS Publication No. ADM 80-31). Washington, DC: U.S. Government Printing Office.

List the agency that produced the document as the author if no author is identified. Within parentheses immediately after the document title, give the publication number (assigned to the document by the government); it can usually be found on or near the title page and should not be confused with the call number that a library may have assigned to the document.

O. Anonymous Work

> A breath of fresh air. (1991, April 29). Time, p. 49.

Alphabetize the work under the first important word in the title, and follow the form for the type of publication in question (in this case, a magazine published weekly). Use a short version of the title, in quotation marks, for the parenthetical citation in the text: ("Breath," 1991).

P. An Online Journal Article

> Fletcher, G. J. (1996, November). Assessing error in social judgment: Commenting on Koehler on base rate [9 paragraphs]. Psychology [online], 5 (10). Available E-mail: psyc212@csc.canterbury.ac.nz or http://cogsci.ecs .soten.ac.uk/cgi-bin/newpsy?5.10

Include the publication medium within brackets immediately after the journal title. A bracketed description of the article's length is optional. Because a period at the end of the citation could be mistaken as part of the electronic address, the APA recommends omitting the final period.

Q. An Online Abstract

> Dickenson, A. H. (1996, November 12). Plasticity: Implications for opioid and other pharmacological interventions in specific pain states. BBS Special Issue: Controversies in Neuroscience v: Persistent Pain: Neuronal Mechanics and Clinical Implications. [On-line]. Available FTP: http://www.cogsci .soton.ac.uk/bbs/archive/bbs.neur5.dickenson.html

In article titles, capitalize only the first letter of the first word in the title (and subtitle when there is one) and any word that would be capitalized when not part of a title. In journal titles, however, capitalize all key words.

R. An Abstract on CD-ROM

> Gowan, M. E., & Zimmerman, R. A. (1996). Impact of ethnicity, gender, and previous experience on juror judgments in sexual harassment cases. [CD-ROM]. Journal of Applied Social Psychology, 26, Abstract from: SilverPlatter File: PsychLIT Item: 83-29094

Include the item number at the end of the entry.

Numbered Systems

In a numbered system, the bibliography may be arranged in alphabetical order (determined by the authors' last names) or in the order in which the works are cited within the paper itself. Once this sequence is established, the items are assigned numbers in consecutive order beginning with 1, and these numbers are used as citations within the paper. There are many variations on the particular form of the bibliographical entries; authors of scientific papers should adopt the style recommended by the journal for which they are writing. But here are examples of two frequently used forms:

A. Biology

1. Avila, V L. Biology: A Human Endeavor. Chula Vista; Bookmark, 1992. 899 p.
2. Batistatou, A, Green, L. 1993. Internucleosomal DNA cleavage and neurona; cell survival death. The Journal of Cell Biology. 22: 523-532.

Note that neither book nor journal titles are underlined. Quotation marks are not used for article titles. The names of multiple authors are separated with a comma rather than an ampersand. The year of publication appears in different positions, depending upon the nature of the work.

B. Chemistry

> (1) Rea, W. J. <u>Chemical Sensitivity</u>; Lewis: New York, 1992.
> (2) Cargill, R. W. <u>Chem. Soc. Rev.</u> **1993**, 22, pp. 135-141.

Note that book publishers' names appear before the city of publication. Journal titles are abbreviated, and article titles are not included. Boldface the year of publication for journal articles. Lines after the first are not indented.

Although the precise form of the bibliography will vary from discipline to discipline, certain features remain constant when a numbered system is used:

- Whenever the same source is cited, the same number is cited.
- Numbers appear on the same line as the text, and they are usually either underlined or italicized to distinguish them from other numbers in the text.

With these two points in mind, you should not confuse a numbered system of references with the use of numbered footnotes. When footnotes are used, numbers appear in consecutive order and each number is used only once. When a numbered system of references is used, the same number appears whenever the source assigned that number is cited within the text, and the numbers will not necessarily be consecutive.

C. A Numbered Reference

> There are approximately 125,000 children at risk of developing Huntington's disease (4).

or

> There are approximately 125,000 children at risk of developing Huntington's disease.[4]

or

> There are approximately 125,000 children at risk of developing Huntington's disease (<u>4</u>, p. 22).

For an example of a numbered system in use, consult an issue of *Science,* a journal that can be found in most libraries, or see the paper by Amy Karlen in Part 4 (pages 290–293).

A CHECKLIST FOR DOCUMENTATION

Whether you document your sources by using footnotes or one of the recommended systems for parenthetical references, you should honor the following principles:

1. Remember to document any direct quotation, any idea that has come from someone else's work, and any fact or statistic that is not widely known.
2. Be sure to enclose all quotations in quotation marks.
3. Make sure that paraphrases are in your own words but still accurately reflect the content of the original material.
4. Remember that every source cited in a reference should have a corresponding entry in the bibliography.
5. Be consistent. Don't shift from the author/year system to the author/work system in the middle of your paper.
6. Try to vary the introductions you use for quotations and paraphrases, and make sure that the material in question has been incorporated smoothly into your text. Read your draft aloud to be better able to judge its readability.
7. When you mention authorities by name, try to identify who they are so that your audience can evaluate the source. (For example, "According to Ira Glasser, Executive Director of the American Civil Liberties Union, recent congressional legislation violates. . . .") Do not insult the intelligence of your audience by identifying well-known figures.
8. If in doubt about whether to document a source, you would probably be wise to go ahead and document it. But be careful not to overdocument your paper. A paper that is composed of one reference after another usually lacks synthesis and interpretation.

PART 3

A GUIDE TO RESEARCH

Writing effective arguments requires being able to locate and draw on information that will help you develop and support your ideas. When a topic involves an issue with which you have personal experience, you might need only to search your own mind for the information you need to write persuasively. But writers often discover that they must look beyond themselves to gather the necessary information—they must engage in *research*.

If you associate research with long papers due at the end of a semester, you may be losing sight of the many other occasions when you search for information. Any time you seek to gather information before making a decision, you are practicing a kind of research. If, for example, you are trying to decide whether to buy a particular car, you might interview people who already own the same model, read magazine articles about the car, and take a showroom vehicle out for a test drive to experience its performance. In other words, you interview people with expertise on your topic, you conduct a periodical search, and you undertake trial testing. Academic research requires all of these activities—and more—although the degree to which you need to pursue a specific research activity is likely to vary as you move from one project to another. Academic research also requires that you honor specific conventions by using sources responsibly and documenting where your information comes from. (See pages 68–87.) Nevertheless, the prospect of doing research shouldn't be frightening. Most people do research to some extent throughout their lives—and not just for long, formal papers. The key to successful research is simple: Be prepared to look in different places until you find what you need.

Scholars traditionally distinguish between primary and secondary research. *Primary research* requires firsthand experimentation or analysis. This is the sort of research done in scientific laboratories and in archives that house original manuscripts. If you interview someone, design and distribute a survey, conduct experiments, or analyze data that have not been previously published, you are also conducting primary research. Some of the "Suggestions for Writing" that appear later in this book invite you to undertake this kind of work.

You will also have many occasions for practicing *secondary research,* which means investigating what other people have already published on a given subject. College students are usually expected to be proficient at secondary research. To do this activity efficiently, you must know how to develop a search strategy. Different projects will require different strategies. The strategy outlined in this part of the book illustrates how to search for material on a public issue similar to those included in *The Informed Argument,* Brief Edition. As your research needs change from one assignment to another, you will probably use different indexes and online services. But the illustrations from the following search will provide you with sufficient information to proceed efficiently when you decide to move beyond the articles gathered in Parts 4–5 of this book.

GETTING STARTED

One of the first goals of any researcher is to decide where to focus. The more specific your search, the greater your chance for efficiently locating the material you need and then writing a well-supported paper. When you know what you are looking for, you can gauge what you need to read and what you can probably afford to pass over—a great advantage when confronted by the staggering amount of information that a good college library, or the Internet, makes available to researchers.

Do not think that you must have a clear focus before you begin your search, however. An excellent topic might emerge if you scan how information on your subject area has been classified by professional catalogers. Periodical indexes (pages 91–97) usually divide large subjects into specific components, online databases allow you to combine different terms, and search engines for navigating the Internet will alert you to diverse topics within your subject area. By using key words and checking different sources, you can discover what topics have generated the most recent interest. You can judge, at this point, which topics would be the easiest to research and which would be the most manageable. If you are overwhelmed by the number of citations in your research area, you probably need to narrow your topic. On the other hand, if you have difficulty finding material, you may need to broaden your search.

Another way to get started is to discuss your subject with other people. Talking over the possibilities with your instructor may help you to discover a topic that suits both your own interests and the requirements for the paper in question. Conversation with students and friends may be fruitful as well. A class discussion devoted to one of the arguments in this book may leave you intrigued by a topic that you had not previously considered. Electronic discussion groups, which can be accessed through the Internet, provide a further opportunity for exploring issues with other people. Talking, like writing, is a way of learning. When you have the chance, don't hesitate to bounce ideas around with people you trust. (For additional information on choosing a topic, see pages 2–4 and the writing assignments that appear at the end of each section in Part 4.)

AVOIDING SELECTIVE RESEARCH

Although you may have a tentative thesis in mind when you begin your search, do not formulate your final thesis until your research is complete. Your search strategy should be designed to answer a question that you have posed to yourself, such as: "What can be done to reduce drug-related crime?" This is very different from starting your research with your thesis predetermined. A student who is convinced that the way to reduce drug-related crime is to legalize drugs may be tempted to take notes only from sources that advocate this position—rejecting as irrelevant any source that discusses problems with this approach. Research, in this case, is not leading to greater knowledge or understanding. On the contrary, it is being used to reinforce personal beliefs that may border on prejudice.

We have seen that "anticipating the opposition" (pages 5–6, 16–21) is important even in short arguments. It is no less important in a researched paper. Almost any topic worth investigating will yield facts and ideas that could support different conclusions. The readings assembled in this book demonstrate that it is possible to take significantly different positions on sexual harassment, immigration law, and same-gender marriage—among other issues. As you may have already observed, some of the most opinionated people are also the most ignorant. Well-educated people, because they have been exposed to different points of view during their education, are usually aware that most problems are complex. Good students remember this when they are doing research. They allow their reading to influence their thought; they do not let their thoughts restrict their reading. Your own research may ultimately support a belief that you already hold, but it could just as easily lead you to realize that you were misinformed. When taking notes, remember the question that you have posed for yourself. Do not waste time recording information that is not relevant to that particular question. But you should not overlook material that directly concerns your question just because you don't agree with what the material says. If you have a good reason to reject the conclusion of someone else's work, your paper will be stronger if you recognize that this disagreement exists and then demonstrate why you favor one position over another—or show how different positions can be reconciled.

SEARCHING FOR MAGAZINE AND JOURNAL ARTICLES

Magazines, bulletins, and scholarly journals are all called *periodicals* because they are published on a regular schedule—once a week or once a month, in the case of a magazine, or four times a year, in the case of a scholarly journal. Although researchers can seldom afford to rely exclusively on periodicals for information, the indexes and abstracting services that enable them to locate relevant periodical articles are essential in most searches. Periodicals often include the most current information about a research area, and they can alert you to other important sources through book reviews as well as through the citations that support individual articles.

The best known of these indexes is the *Readers' Guide to Periodical Literature,* which is now available online through OLLC *FirstSearch* (a service which provides access to over 40 electronic indexes, all searches using the same commands), in addition to being published in the green volumes that have been familiar to library users for several decades. The *Readers' Guide* covers over 250 magazines; material is indexed by subject and by author. Because it indexes popular mass-circulation periodicals, it will lead you to articles that are relatively short and accessible. *InfoTrac,* another computerized index for periodicals in general circulation, offers a similar advantage.

Most college libraries have a variety of other indexes that will point you toward more substantial material, and you should be prepared to move beyond the *Readers' Guide* in any serious search. Almost every academic field has its own index available in regularly printed volumes, and most electronic versions of these indexes are now including *abstracts* (short summaries of the articles indexed). Among the specialized indexes most often used are the following:

Applied Science and Technology Index	*Index to Legal Periodicals*
Art Index	*Index Medicus* (for medicine)
Biological and Agricultural Index	*Music Index*
Business Periodicals Index	*Philosopher's Index*
Education Index	*Science Citation Index*
Humanities Index	*Social Sciences Index*

Anyone doing research in literature should also be familiar with the *MLA International Bibliography* (for books and articles written about English, American, and foreign-language literature) and the *Essay and General Literature Index* (for essays and articles that have appeared in books rather than in journals).

If you have difficulty finding material, or if you are in difficulty because you have found too much, you can broaden or narrow an online search by using *Boolean operators*—words that instruct a database to narrow a search or to broaden it. Suppose that you are researching the relationship between drug use and violent crime. Searching for *drugs* alone would gather an unwieldy amount of material, including articles on new prescriptions for arthritis and other information that is irrelevant to your topic. If you enter *drugs and crime* as your subject, you will be alerted only to articles that mention both drugs and crime. This is still a big subject, so if you are conducting a search along these lines, you could enter additional search terms, such as *gender,* which would narrow the search to articles discussing the role of gender in drug use and crime. Adding *women,* or *youth,* on the other hand, would identify articles mentioning both drugs and crime and either women or youth. By playing with terms this way, and discovering how much material is available on any given combination, you can find a specific topic for a researched paper within a larger subject area.

The advantage of consulting the *Readers' Guide* online is readily apparent from the accompanying illustrations. After instructing the computer to search for the subject (su) *drugs and crime,* the person conducting this online search in 1996 discovered 674 articles, compared to one article on the subject in the printed volume for May 1996. (See Figures 1 and 2.) To discover additional articles through printed volumes would require consulting other volumes and following up on a range of cross-references (see Figure 3). A computer can do that task within seconds.

A disadvantage of using the *Readers' Guide* is also readily apparent: Few college professors are likely to be impressed by the credibility of research drawn from *People, Time,* or *U.S. News & World Report.* If you have access to the *Readers' Guide* through *FirstSearch,* you should also have access to *Periodical Abstracts,* which covers approximately 1,500 journals, giving you access to the kind of material you would locate through the *Readers' Guide* as well as much more scholarly work.

```
+ * * * * * * * * * * * * * List of Records * * * * * * * * * * * * * * * +
DATABASE. ReadGuideAbs                        LIMITED TO:
SEARCH: su:drugs and crime FOUND 674 Records
____NO.___SOURCE_____TITLE_____YEAR

      1    People Wkly       Death on the border.                       1996
      2    Time              What Dole must say.                        1996
      3    U S News World R  Popgun politics.                           1996
      4    N Y Times (Late   Drugs, guns and just don't do it.          1996
      5    N Y Times (Late   Drugs, guns and vigilante justice in So    1996
      6    Public Interest   Legalization madness.                      1996
      7    N Y Times (Late   Dole campaign says it has hardly begun     1996
      8    N Y Times (Late   Campaigning on portents of doom and boo    1996

HINTS: More records type . . . F.    View a record . . type record number.
       Decrease number of records . . . . type L (to limit) or A (to 'and').
       Do a new search . . . . . . . . . . . . . . . type S or SEARCH.

ACTIONS: Help  Search  And  Limit  Print  Email  Database  Forward

RECORD NUMBER (or Action):
```

FIGURE 1
Citations from *Readers' Guide Abstracts,* an online service covering the years 1983–1996 in this case

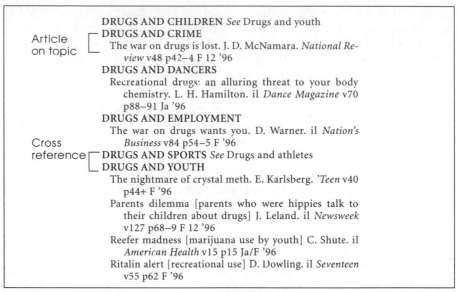

FIGURE 2
Excerpt from a bound volume of *Readers' Guide*

DRUG ABUSE
   See also
   Alcoholics and alcoholism
   Children of drug addicts
   Cocaine
   Crack (Cocaine)
   Drugs and athletes
   Drugs and blacks
   Drugs and celebrities
   Drugs and crime
   Drugs and dancers
   Drugs and employment
   Drugs and youth
   Marijuana
   Methamphetamine
   Needle exchange programs
   PCP
   United States. Office of National Drug Control Policy

FIGURE 3
Cross-reference from a bound volume of *Readers' Guide*

Although there is some overlapping from one index to another, each index covers different periodicals. The records you find in one will usually vary from the records you find in another. This is worth remembering, for two reasons:

1. You should not get easily discouraged when searching for periodical literature. If you cannot locate any material in the past few

years of one index, try another index that sounds as if it might include records on your subject.

2. Many subjects of general interest will be found in more than one index. If you consult more than one index, you are increasing the likelihood of being exposed to different points of view.

Of the various specialized indexes that can lead you exclusively to material in professional journals, the *Social Sciences Index* is especially useful for locating information on drug use and crime, for it indexes literature in sociology, psychology, and political science. Like the *Readers' Guide,* it can be consulted in bound volumes or online, with the online service providing abstracts as well as citations. Figure 4 reproduces the content of a screen providing instructions for using *Social Science Abstracts* on OLLC *FirstSearch.* Figure 5 shows the first eight citations located when searching for articles on the relationship between drug use and crime. Figure 6 shows a sample abstract from this search. Note that a scholarly publication like the *Journal of Criminal Law and Criminology* would not be indexed by the *Readers' Guide* and that a journal like this is likely to provide more credible data than an issue of *People.* Note also that the journal article identified in Figure 6 is twenty-six pages long, a length unlikely to be possible in a general-circulation magazine.

Figure 7 shows an early screen for OLLC *FirstSearch,* the online service used to discover the material from the *Social Science Abstracts* cited on page 96. Access to the *Social Science Abstracts* was obtained by entering number 13 from this screen. Access to the *Readers' Guide* was obtained by entering number 7. If you continued to research through this online service, you would find additional material on drugs and crime by selecting "News &

```
* * * * * * * * * * * * * * * * * Search * * * * * * * * * * * * * * * * * *

DATABASE: SocSciAbs

  SEARCH         DESCRIPTION                               EXAMPLES

  Subject        Type the label SU: and a word(s).         su:fashion
                 (Subjects, abstracts and titles)          su:decision making

  Author         Type the label AU: and the author         au:huether
                 name or any part of the name.             au:milton yinger

  Title          Type the label TI: and the title          ti:psychology
                 or any word(s) in the title.              ti:academic freedom


HINTS:   Other ways to search . . . . . . . type H <database name> LABELS.
         Include plural (s and es) or possessive . . . type + at end of word.
         Return to List of Records screen . . . . . . . just press Enter.

ACTIONS: Help  Limit  Database  Wordlist  Reset

SEARCH WORD(S) (or Action): su:drugs and crime
```

FIGURE 4
Instructions for using *Social Science Abstracts*

```
+ * * * * * * * * * * * * List of Records * * * * * * * * * * * * * * * +
DATABASE: SocSciAbs                    LIMITED TO:
SEARCH: su:drugs and crime FOUND 200 Records
____ NO.___SOURCE_____TITLE_____YEAR

    1      Br J Criminol    In search of the high life: drugs, crim  1996
    2      Far East Econ Re Dying for attention: lacking parents' c  1996
    3      Br J Criminol    Young adult offenders, alcohol and crim  1996
    4      Economist        Innocence lost.                          1996
    5      J Crim Justice   Recidivism among boot camp graduates: a  1996
    6      J Res Crime Deli Gender, power, and alternative living a  1996
    7      Acta Sociol      Drugs, crime, and other deviant adaptat  1995
    8      Crime Delinq     Drug policy and community context: the   1996


HINTS: More records type . . . F.    View a record . . type record number.
       Decrease number of records . . . . type L (to limit) or A (to 'and').
       Do a new search . . . . . . . . . . . . . . type S or SEARCH.

ACTIONS: Help  Search  And  Limit  Print  Email  Database  Forward

RECORD NUMBER (or Action):
```

FIGURE 5

The first of two hundred records discovered when searching *Social Science Abstracts*

```
* * * * * * * * * * * * * * Full Record Display * * * * * * * * * * * * * *
DATABASE: SocSciAbs                         LIMITED TO:
SEARCH: su:drugs and crime

 Record 15 of 200___ YOUR LIBRARY (MNT) MAY OWN THIS ITEM____( PAGE 1 OF 3)

       AUTHOR: Blumstein, Alfred.
        TITLE: Youth violence, guns, and the illicit-drug industry.
       SOURCE: The Journal of Criminal Law & Criminology v. 86 (Fall '95)
               p. 10-36
     ABSTRACTS: Part of a special issue on firearms and violence in the U.S.
               The writer investigates several empirical aspects of
               changing crime patterns in recent years and identifies the
               nature of these changing patterns. Three major changes
               between 1985 and 1992 are that homicide rates by youths aged
               18 and under, the number of homicides committed by juveniles
               with guns, and the drug arrest rates of nonwhite juveniles
               have all more than doubled. The growth in youth homicide is
               attributed to the recruitment of youths into illicit drug
               markets. The illegal nature of these markets means that
               young people are likely to carry arms for self-protection.
               This initiates an escalating process: the more arms in the
               community, the greater the incentive for people to arm
               themselves.
  STANDARD NO: 0091-4169
         DATE: 1995

HINTS:    Another page . type F or B.    Another record . type record number.
          See which libraries may own this item . . . . . . . . . type LIB.
          Return to Record List . . . . . . . . . . . . . just press Enter.

ACTIONS: Help  Search  Print  Email  Order  LIBraries  Forward  Back

RECORD NUMBER (or Action):
```

FIGURE 6

Sample abstract from *Social Science Abstracts*

```
* * * * * * * * * * * * Topic Area Selection * * * * * * * * * * * * * *

    NO. TOPIC AREA                        NO. TOPIC AREA

    1      Arts & Humanities              8      General Science
    2      Business & Economics           9      Life Sciences
    3      Conferences & Proceedings      10     Medicine & Health
    4      Consumer Affairs & People      11     News & Current Events
    5      Education                      12     Public Affairs & Law
    6      Engineering & Technology       13     Social Sciences
    7      General & Reference            14     All Databases

HINTS:    Select a topic area . . . . . . . . . . . type topic area number.
          Get help . . . . . . . . . . . . . . . . . . . . . . . . type H.
          Get News . . . . . . . . . . . . . . . . . . . . . . type H NEWS.
          See hours of operation . . . . . . . . . . . . . . type H HOURS.

ACTIONS: Help  Database  Reset

AREA NUMBER (or Action):
```

FIGURE 7
An introductory screen for *FirstSearch*

Current Events" or "Public Affairs & Law." You might also discover material through "Business & Economics" (both crime and drug abuse affect the economy) and "Conferences & Proceedings" (law enforcement officers, attorneys, and scholars are likely to give presentations on drugs and crime).

SEARCHING FOR NEWSPAPER ARTICLES

You can access many newspaper articles by using the "News & Current Events" option provided by *FirstSearch* (see Figure 7). As shown in Figure 1, the *Readers' Guide* will also lead you to some newspaper articles. For a serious electronic search of newspaper articles on a research topic involving a public policy issue, use Lexis-Nexis, a powerful database that searches for news articles and legal documents worldwide—often locating material only a day or two after its publication—and may provide wire service dispatches that have not yet made their way into the papers. Figure 8 shows one of the first screens that comes up in a search using Lexis-Nexis. You can narrow or expand your search by limiting yourself to the last two years or going back further, focusing on a particular region, or choosing to search a particular kind of text such as newsletters or newspapers. By entering MAJPAP (for major papers), and then "drugs crime and youth," the person conducting this search discovered thirty-three stories. ("Drugs and crime" alone yielded over 1,000 stories, which required narrowing the search further by focusing on "youth" in addition to "drugs and crime.") You can choose whether to view citations only, citations with summaries, and—when you find something that seems especially promising—full text, which you might then be able to print out, depending on the nature of the service your library provides. Figure 9 shows the first five citations identified during this 1996

```
MAJPAP

Please ENTER, separated by commas, the NAMES of the files you want to
search. You may select as many files as you want, including files that do
not appear below, but you must enter them all at one time. To see a
description of a file, ENTER its page (PG) number.
              FILES - PAGE 1 of 89 (NEXT PAGE for additional files)

NAME    PG DESCRIP            NAME   PG DESCRIP         NAME    PG DESCRIP

                   T H E   N E W S   L I B R A R Y
--Full-Text Group Files--  --Full-Text By Type--    --Full Text by Region--
CURNWS  1 Last 2 years      MAGS    3 Magazines          --Papers & Wires--
ARCNWS  1 Beyond 2 years    MAJPAP  3 Major Papers  NON-US 1 English Non-US
ALLNWS  1 All News Files    NWLTRS  3 Newsletters   US     1 US News
                            PAPERS  3 Newspapers        --US Sources--
                            SCRIPT  3 Transcripts   MWEST  3 Midwest
--Group File Exclusions--   WIRES   3 Wires         NEAST  3 Northeast
ALLABS  4 All Abstracts     -----Hot Files-----     SEAST  3 Southeast
NONENG  1 Non-English News  HOTTOP  2 Hot Topics*   WEST   3 West
TXTNWS  1 Textline News*    OJCIV   2 OJ Civil*        ------Assists------
TODAY   1 Today's News*                             GUIDE  2 Descriptions*
                                                    LNTHS  2 L-N Index Ths*

Files marked * may not be combined.
```

FIGURE 8

An introductory screen for Lexis-Nexis. Reprinted with the permission of
LEXIS-NEXIS, a division of Reed Elsevier Inc. LEXIS and NEXIS are registered
trademarks of Reed Elsevier Properties Inc.

```
                        LEVEL 1 - 33 STORIES

1.   Los Angeles Times, November 3, 1996, Sunday, Ventura County Edition,
Page 1 1477 words, CITIES SEEK TO STEM TIDE OF TEEN CRIME, DRUG ABUSE;
GOVERNMENT: LOCAL EFFORTS TO DEVELOP YOUTH MASTER PLANS ARE AIMED AT
REDUCING THE GROWING VIOLENCE AMONG CHILDREN OF BABY BOOMERS., MACK REED,
TIMES STAFF WRITER

2.   The Jerusalem Post, October 3, 1996, Thursday, NEWS; Pg. 3, 534
words, Drug crimes on rise among youth, Itim

3.   The Tampa Tribune, July 3, 1996, Wednesday, FLORIDA EDITION, Pg. 2,
194 words, Camp focuses on drugs and youth crime, A Tribune staff report,
FORT MEADE

4.   The Baltimore Sun, April 10, 1996, Wednesday, HOWARD EDITION, Pg. 3B,
741 words, 'Posse' created as detour on youths' road of life; Church
outreach program hopes to steer children away from drugs, crime, Alisa
Samuels, SUN STAFF

5.   Los Angeles Times, February 7, 1996, Wednesday, Home Edition, Part A;
Page 8; National Desk, 858 words, PARENTS AT CENTER OF TALE OF HORRIFIC
CHILD ABUSE; CRIME: THEY ARE IN CHICAGO JAIL, ACCUSED OF MOLESTATION,
INJECTING CHILDREN WITH DRUGS AND FEEDING THEM RATS. CHARGES BASED ON
YOUTHS' ACCOUNTS., By JUDY PASTERNAK, TIMES STAFF WRITER, CHICAGO
```

FIGURE 9

Citations from Lexis-Nexis. Reprinted with the permission of LEXIS-NEXIS, a
division of Reed Elsevier Inc. LEXIS and NEXIS are registered trademarks of
Reed Elsevier Properties Inc.

```
                     LEVEL 1 - 1 OF 33 STORIES

                  Copyright 1996 Times Mirror Company
                          Los Angeles Times

               November 3, 1996, Sunday, Ventura County Edition

SECTION: Metro; Part B; Page 1; No Desk

LENGTH: 1477 words

HEADLINE: CITIES SEEK TO STEM TIDE OF TEEN CRIME, DRUG ABUSE;
GOVERNMENT: LOCAL EFFORTS TO DEVELOP YOUTH MASTER PLANS ARE AIMED AT
REDUCING THE GROWING VIOLENCE AMONG CHILDREN OF BABY BOOMERS.

BYLINE: MACK REED, TIMES STAFF WRITER

  BODY:

    Born during a brainstorm two years ago, a method for combating the rise
of violence and drug use among teens is growing ever more popular with
governments in Ventura County: the youth master plan.

    Such plans are meant to knit together schools, police, businesses,
social service agencies and families in a safety net so tight that only
```

FIGURE 10
The beginning of a full text article found online

search; Figure 10 reproduces the beginning of the full text of one of the citations retrieved online. (Note: Not all libraries have access to Lexis-Nexis, while some which do charge for this service.)

Your college or community library may also provide you with the equipment to search online for articles in a local paper. If you are unable to search for newspapers online, look for printed volumes of the *New York Times Index,* which has been published annually since 1913 and is updated frequently throughout the current year.

USING ABSTRACTING SERVICES

Although many electronic indexing services such as *Readers' Guide Abstracts* and *Social Science Abstracts* are now offering summaries of current articles along with the citations a search identifies, they do not consistently provide abstracts for all of the material they index. There are other services that specialize in abstracts. Important abstracting services in printed volumes include:

Abstracts in Anthropology	*Historical Abstracts*
Academic Abstracts	*Physics Abstracts*
Biological Abstracts	*Psychological Abstracts*
Chemical Abstracts	*Sociological Abstracts*

These abstracts are organized in different ways, and you may need to consult one volume for the index and another volume for the matching abstracts. When using bound volumes, consult the instructions that can be found within them. Nowadays, however, there is no reason to consult printed volumes of abstracts unless you do not have access to electronic databases. Almost all college libraries provide access to at least a few electronic databases. Hundreds of databases are published, however, with new ones becoming available almost daily. Ask your reference librarian if there are electronic resources in your library that are appropriate to your research.

Although it does not cover precisely the same sources as *Psychological Abstracts,* the *PsycLIT* database provides much easier access to comparable scholarship in the field. Figure 11 shows an abstract located by searching *PsycLIT* for material on "drugs and crime." Other databases provide a similar service for research in other disciplines.

Abstracts offer a great advantage over bibliographical citations, because it can be hard to tell from a title whether an article will be useful. The summary provided by an abstracting service can help you to decide whether you want to read the entire article. A good rule to follow with abstracts is that if you can't understand the summary, you probably won't understand the article. Another point to remember is that many abstracting services are international in their coverage. Just because an article summary is written in English does not mean that this is the language of the article itself; be alert for notations such as *(Chin), (Germ),* or *(Span),* which indicate when an article is published in another language. Finally, remember that good researchers never pretend to have read an entire article when they have read only an abstract of it. Use abstracts as a tool for locating material to read, not as a substitute for a full-length reading.

USING THE INTERNET

First developed by the U.S. military, the Internet is an electronic "network of networks" linking millions of computers through telecommunication lines. This network allows the quick exchange of information between connected computers on a worldwide scale. The kind of information that can be found on the Internet is very diverse, but includes library catalogs, government documents and data, and material published by commercial organizations, special interest groups, and even individuals who wish to make contact with others who share their concerns.

Currently, the most common way to search the vast amount of information on the Internet is to use the World Wide Web, a graphical interface that makes it possible to navigate the Internet by "pointing and clicking." If you are new to the Internet, check to see whether your library or academic computing office provides introductory workshops. Your college or community bookstore may also carry one of several guides to using the Internet that have been published in recent years.

```
SilverPlatter 3.11        PsycLIT Journal Articles 1/90-12/96
No.    Records    Request
1:     12413      DRUGS
2:      1918      CRIME
3:       112      DRUGS and CRIME
4:     12413      DRUGS
5:      1918      CRIME
6:        30      (DRUGS and CRIME) in TI
                                                    1 of 1
                                        Marked in Search: #6
TI  DOCUMENT TITLE: Sweeping out drugs and crime: Residents' views of the
Chicago Housing Authority's Public Housing Drug Elimination Program.
AU  AUTHOR(S): Popkin,-Susan-J.; Olson,-Lynn-M.; Lurigio,-Arthur-J.;
Gwiasda,-Victoria-E.; et-al
IN  INSTITUTIONAL AFFILIATION OF FIRST AUTHOR: Abt Assoc, Bethesda, MD, US
JN  JOURNAL NAME: Crime-and-Delinquency; 1995 Jan Vol 41(1) 73-99
IS  ISSN: 00111287
LA  LANGUAGE: English
PY  PUBLICATION YEAR: 1995
AB  ABSTRACT: Surveyed residents' perceptions of the effects of the
Chicago Housing Authority's Public Housing Drug Elimination Program
(PHDEP) on drugs and crime in 2 housing developments chosen for their
preexisting differences in crime rates and population stability. 262
residents (aged 16 yrs or older) were surveyed, and 39 residents were
interviewed. Overall, respondents in the better organized development
reported more favorable perceptions of PHDEP's impact. (PsycLIT Database
Copyright 1995 American Psychological Assn, all rights reserved)
KP  KEY PHRASE: Chicago Housing Authority Public Housing Drug Elimination
Program; drugs & crime; 16 yr old & older residents of housing
developments
DE  DESCRIPTORS: CRIME-PREVENTION; HOUSING-; DRUGS-; ADOLESCENCE-;
ADULTHOOD-
CC  CLASSIFICATION CODE(S): 4270; 42
PO  POPULATION: Human
AG  COMPOSITE AGE GROUP: Adolescent; Adult
UD  UPDATE CODE: 9507
AN  PSYC ABS. VOL. AND ABS. NO.: 82-27532
JC  JOURNAL CODE: 1194
```

FIGURE 11

A sample abstract obtained through *PsycLIT* after narrowing a search to articles that mention both drugs and crime in their titles

Because the Internet provides access to apparently unlimited information, some users have discovered that the same technology that makes searching so efficient, in one sense, can make it time-consuming in another. You may find yourself scrolling through an endless series of documents and losing sight of your main objective while pursuing an elusive loose end.

You must also be aware of a key difference between material published on the Internet and material published in print. Writers who publish in print receive professional editorial support. Editors decide what material is worth printing and then assist writers when preparing work for publication. The Internet operates without editors, however. Anyone with a little knowledge of computers can publish whatever comes to mind. In a sense, the Internet is wonderfully democratic, and many people have enjoyed activities such as creating a Web site for their cat and connecting with other cat fanciers. On the other hand, the Internet also carries hate speech, crank editorials, and hard-core pornography. (See pages 117–157 for information on recent attempts to regulate the Internet.) When searching the Internet, you must carefully evaluate the material you locate—and recognize that this material can range from first-rate scholarship to utter trash.

Still, the Internet is a wonderful resource for anyone prepared to navigate it. The challenge is how to find your way through the huge amount of material floating around you in cyberspace. Computer experts have developed systems called *search engines* that work as indexing services for the World Wide Web. Those most commonly used today are *Yahoo!, Alta Vista, Infoseek,* and *Lycos.* Once you learn how to use one of these systems, you can easily learn how to adapt to the others. No search engine provides a complete, error-free index to electronic documents, so serious research often demands using more than one system—just as you would use more than one periodical index when looking for information.

Search engines require you to identify your research topic by typing key words into an entry box, as you would when conducting a periodical search or searching a library catalog by subject area. After you have entered your search terms, you will be given a list of Web sites that match your request. Each of these sites can, in turn, lead you to others—the kind of help you also experience when you consult the bibliography of a book or periodical article. The principal difference in searching on the Internet is the speed with which you can move from one site to another. Do not expect instant access to anything you want to view, however. Long documents, and documents from heavily visited sites, can sometimes take several minutes to download.

Like other electronic resources, search engines provide help screens with instructions on the best ways to search. These instructions change as the technology changes, and it is wise to review them whenever you are in doubt about how to proceed. Figure 12 shows the introductory screen for *Yahoo!,* one of the most widely used search engines in the 1990s. Figure 13 shows a Web page located when using *Yahoo!* to search for information on the relationship between drug use and crime.

Remember that the Internet is constantly changing. In 1996, it was estimated that a new Web page was appearing every 15 seconds. New search systems are being developed almost monthly. Because the Internet accesses so much information, some researchers make the mistake of thinking anything they need to find must be available electronically. When you retrieve documents from the Internet, do so with caution. Because you are visiting a world without editors, the documents you retrieve may include errors. And because not every scholar chooses to make completed work available electronically, you can miss important material if you try to do all your research on the Internet.

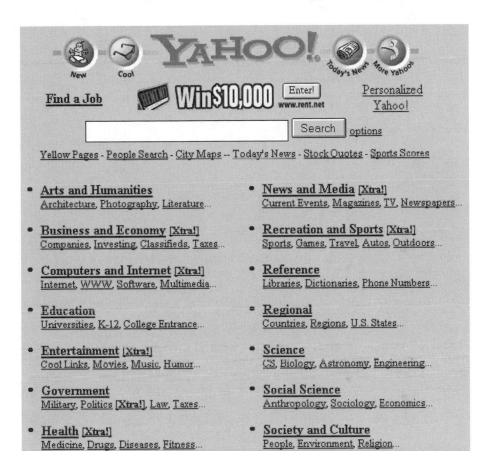

FIGURE 12
An introductory screen for searching the World Wide Web (Text and art-
work copyright 1996 by YAHOO!, INC. All rights reserved. YAHOO! and the
YAHOO! logo are trademarks of YAHOO!, INC.)

LOOKING FOR BOOKS

Now that computers make it possible to consult indexes outside of libraries,
print out the full text of periodical articles, and spend hours at a time exploring the World Wide Web, it can be tempting to avoid looking for *books*
on a subject. Books remain essential to scholarship, however. Although the
books you locate in your library may vary in quality, books often represent
the final and most prestigious result of someone else's research. It is common, for example, for a scholar to publish several journal articles in the process of writing a book. Much of the best information you can find appears
somewhere in a book, and you should never assume that your research subject is so new, or so specialized, that your library will not have books on it. A
topic that seems new to you may not necessarily be new to others.

New drug plan targets youth, crime

President to outline policy goals

April 29, 1996
Web posted at: 10:45 a.m. EDT

President Clinton arrived Monday in Coral Gables, Florida, where, in a speech at a high school, he is expected to outline a new five-part national drug control strategy.

Sources say the speech, aimed at restoring the Clinton administration's leadership in the war on drugs, will emphasize boosting drug education and reducing illegal drug use among young people. The growing use of methamphetamines is to get special attention.

Clinton left for Miami Monday morning

Other goals will include cutting drug-related crime; increasing funds for treatment of drug abusers and other steps to cut the health and welfare costs of drugs; tightening up on the flow of drugs on land, at sea and in the air; and cutting off the source of drugs, both internally and internationally.

"Our challenge right now is young people and crime," retired Gen. Barry McCaffrey, White House drug policy chief, said Sunday on NBC's "Meet the Press." "Those are the two places where it seems to me we've got to get moving."

McCaffrey, who assumed his post several weeks ago amid charges that the administration's drug policy was a failure, said that while the number of Americans using illegal drugs dropped from 22 million people 15 years ago to 11 million today, and that cocaine use is down 30 percent in the past three years, there has been a sharp rise this decade in young people smoking marijuana.

McCaffrey said the administration will continue to support drug courts, which give first-time abusers a right to stay in school or jobs and get treatment rather than serve a prison sentence. Drug courts, he said, cost $1,000 per person rather than the $15,000 it costs to keep a drug abuser locked up for a year.

McCaffrey

FIGURE 13
A CNN web page discovered through YAHOO! (Text and artwork copyright 1996 by YAHOO!, INC. All rights reserved. YAHOO! and the YAHOO! logo are trademarks of YAHOO!, INC.)

Unlike many other resources, books can accompany you wherever you go. They don't need to be plugged in, and they can be read as easily in bed as at a desk. But no matter how informative or enjoyable books may be, they still take time to read. With this in mind, some researchers look for books at the beginning of their search. Others turn to books after they have investigated the periodical literature to focus their interests and identify the most influential works in their field. Whenever you choose to look for books on your topic, be sure that you do so well before your paper is due. A book full of important information will be of little help if you haven't left yourself time to read it.

Using the Main Catalog

Although some libraries still use catalogs consisting of alphabetically arranged cards in multiple drawers, most college libraries now provide computer access to their collection of books. If you have a computer with a modem, you might be able to search your library's collection from the convenience of your own home or office. By using a computer terminal in the library, however, you can easily get help if you run into difficulties. In an age when many people feel overwhelmed by the mass of information that is available on most subjects, professional librarians can often come to the rescue.

Computerized catalogs enable users to search for books by author, title, or subject. Most of these catalogs also permit a search for material via a call number or a "key word"—a word likely to appear somewhere in the title or description. In addition to providing all of the information about a book that could be obtained from a card catalog, computerized catalogs are usually designed to report whether the book is currently available. Computerized catalogs help make research efficient by providing instant access to information that might otherwise be recorded in the different drawers of a card catalog. If you have access to a computerized catalog but are unfamiliar with how to use it, you should be able to find user information posted near the computers. The program will provide instructions on the screen once you begin.

If you are limited to a card catalog, do not be discouraged. Until fairly recently, card catalogs were the standard means through which scholars did their research. But you should be prepared to look in more than one place. Card catalogs usually include two or three cards for every book the library owns. This allows you to locate books in a variety of ways, depending on how much you know. You may be looking for books by a particular author, so find your library's *author cards*. You may know the title of a book but not who wrote it, so find your library's *title cards*. These two kinds of card are often filed in the same set of drawers and called an *author/title catalog*. In addition, you may be able to look for books on your subject through a separate *subject catalog*. When you are unable to find material under the heading you have consulted, you should explore alternative headings. Books on the Civil War, for example, might be listed under "War Between the States." You might find a cross-reference directing you to the appropriate heading, or you may need to draw on your own ingenuity. If you are sure that the library must have books on your subject and you are simply unable to find the correct subject heading, ask a librarian for help.

Figures 14 and 15 show how a catalog card compares to an entry on a computer screen. The two entries are very similar despite some minor differences in format. As you do research, you should expect to find variations on these examples. Author cards, title cards, and subject cards will each have slightly different headings so that they can be filed in different places. And the precise format of a computerized entry depends on the program employed by the library you are using.

There is no foolproof method for determining the quality or usefulness of a book from a catalog entry. The best way to judge a book is always to read it. But a catalog listing can reveal some useful clues if you know how

```
03 DEC 96   UNIVERSITY OF ST. THOMAS-O'SHAUGHNESSY-FREY LIBRARY    12:57 pm
                          Public Access Catalog
 Call Number   ST. THOMAS                              Status: checked In
               HV5825 .C88 1993
       AUTHOR   Currie, Elliott.
        TITLE   Reckoning : drugs, the cities, and the American future / Elliott
                Currie.
      EDITION   1st ed.
    PUBLISHER   New York : Hill and Wang, 1993.
      DESCRIPT   vi, 405 p. ; 24 cm.
        NOTES   Includes bibliographical references and index.

                                              ----More on Next Screen----
  Press <Enter> to see next screen :
 SO=Start Over, B=Back, RW=Related Works, R=Request, C=Copy status
 SB=Save Bib, <Enter>=Next Screen, SBLIST=Saved Bib List
 ALT-F10  HELP | VT-100 | FDX | 9600 N81 | LOG CLOSED | PRT OFF | CR | CR
```

FIGURE 14
An entry from a computer catalog

to find them. Consider, for example, the date of publication. There is no reason to assume that new books are always better than old books, but unless you are researching a historical or literary topic, you should be careful not to rely heavily on material that may be out of date. Consider also the length of the book. A book with 300 pages is likely to provide more information than a book half that size. A book with a bibliography may help you to find more material. Finally, you might also consider the reputation of the publisher. Any conclusion that you draw at this point should be tentative. But some books are better than others, and it is your responsibility as a

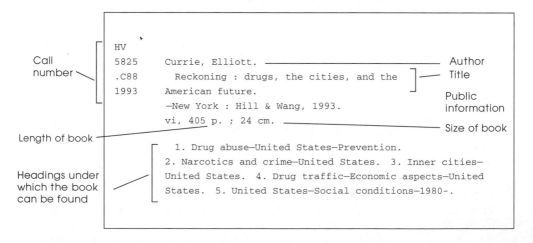

FIGURE 15
An author card from a card catalog

researcher to evaluate the material that you use. (For additional information on evaluating sources, see pages 59–62.) If you are fortunate enough to find several books on your subject, select the books that seem the best.

Understanding Classification Systems

Most American libraries use one of two systems for classifying the books in their collections: the Dewey Decimal system or the Library of Congress system. If you understand these systems, you can save valuable time in the library by knowing where to look for material when you are already working in the stacks.

The Dewey Decimal system classifies books numerically:

000–099	General Works
100–199	Philosophy
200–299	Religion
300–399	Social Sciences
400–499	Language
500–599	Natural Sciences
600–699	Technology
700–799	Fine Arts
800–899	Literature
900–999	History and Geography

These major divisions are subdivided into units of ten to identify specializations within each general field. For example, within the 800–899 category for literature, American literature is found between 810 and 819, English literature between 820 and 829, German literature between 830 and 839—and so forth. Specific numbers narrow these areas further: 811 represents American poetry, for example, and 812 is for American drama. Additional numbers after a decimal point enable catalogers to classify books more precisely: 812.54 would indicate an American play written since 1945. To distinguish individual books from others that are similar, an additional number is usually placed beneath the Dewey number.

Most libraries that use the Dewey Decimal system combine it with one of three systems for providing what is called an "author mark." These systems (referred to as Cutter two-figure, Cutter three-figure, and Cutter-Sanborn) all work according to the same principle. Librarians consult a reference table that provides a numerical representation for the first four to six letters of every conceivable last name. The first letter of the author's last name is placed immediately before this number, and the first letter of the first significant word in the title is placed after the number. Here is a complete call number for *Cat on a Hot Tin Roof,* by the American playwright Tennessee Williams:

812.54
W675c

Although the Dewey Decimal system remains the most widely used system for the classification of books in American libraries, many university libraries prefer to use the Library of Congress system, which uses selected letters of the alphabet to distinguish twenty-one major categories as opposed to the Dewey Decimal system's ten:

A	General Works
B	Philosophy, Psychology, and Religion
C	General History
D	Foreign History
E-F	American History (North and South)
G	Geography and Anthropology
H	Social Sciences
J	Political Science
K	Law
L	Education
M	Music
N	Fine Arts
P	Language and Literature
Q	Science
R	Medicine
S	Agriculture
T	Technology
U	Military Science
V	Naval Science
Z	Bibliography and Library Science

USING OTHER LIBRARY RESOURCES

Because of the great amount of material being published, most libraries are now using devices that allow for material to be stored in less space than would be required by its original form. When looking for books or articles, you may need to use some type of *microform:* printed material that has been reduced in size through microphotography. Libraries that use microform provide users with special devices that magnify the material in question—whether it is available on microfilm or microfiche—a flat sheet of microfilm.

Even when space is not an issue, most libraries can afford to purchase only a fraction of the material that is published each year. Although a good college library should give you all the sources you need for most papers, you may occasionally find it necessary to look beyond the library where you normally do your research. If you live in or near a city, several other libraries may be available. If this is not the case, remember that most libraries also provide an interlibrary loan service, which will allow you to request a book or journal article that your own library does not possess. When a library offers interlibrary loan, you will be asked to provide bibliographical information about the material you are requesting. Librarians will then do the work of locating and securing a copy of the book or article for you. You should ask for material only if you are reasonably certain that it would be useful for you, and that an equivalent resource is not already available in your own library. You should also recognize that obtaining a source through interlibrary loan can take two weeks or longer, so it will be of no use if you defer your research until a few days before your paper is due.

CONDUCTING INTERVIEWS AND SURVEYS

For some topics, you may want to conduct original research through interviews or surveys.

Although *interviews* are usually inappropriate for papers in the natural sciences, they can be useful in most other fields. If you are writing a paper on drug use and crime, for example, you might interview someone working in law enforcement, such as a police officer or a public defender. You might also interview teenagers who have used drugs, or residents in a neighborhood plagued by drug-related crime. Remember that you can learn useful information from many different kinds of people. Interviews do not have to be limited to celebrities or nationally recognized authorities. If you have the opportunity to interview a respected authority on your subject, you should take advantage of it. But many citizens in your own community have their own stories to tell.

Remember also that interviews need to be planned ahead, and you should prepare a list of questions before you go. As a general rule, it is better to compose questions that will take several sentences to answer rather than questions that might be answered with a single word. But don't feel compelled to adhere rigidly to the questions you prepare in advance. A good interviewer knows how to ask a follow-up question that is inspired by a provocative response to an earlier question. Do not get so caught up in the interview, however, that you forget to take careful notes. (If you want to use a tape recorder, courtesy demands that you ask permission to do so when you arrange for the interview.) Because you will need to include the interview in your bibliography, record the date of the interview and the full name and credentials or position of the person you interviewed.

When you ask the same questions of a number of different people, you are conducting a *survey*. When a survey is long, complex, and administered to a large sample group, researchers seeking to analyze the data they have gathered will benefit from having a working knowledge of statistics. But, for many undergraduate research projects, a relatively simple survey can produce interesting and useful data. The first step is to compose a list of relevant questions. Then decide whether you want to administer the survey orally or distribute it in a written form. Each question should be designed to elicit a clear answer that is directly related to the purpose of the survey. You must then decide how many people you will need to interview to have a credible sample of the population that concerns you; for example, if you want to survey college freshmen at your school, you should find out how many freshmen are registered and how many freshmen responses would be necessary for your audience to be persuaded that your results are representative. One advantage of an oral survey is that you are immediately aware of your response rate; with a written survey, weeks can pass before you discover that an insufficient number of people responded to your request for information. On the other hand, written surveys give you clear records to work from. A good rule to follow when conducting a written survey is to distribute at least twice as many copies as you really need to have returned to you.

Another factor to consider is whether it would be useful to analyze your results in terms of such differences as gender, race, age, income, or religion. If so, you must design a questionnaire that will provide you with this information. Be aware, however, that many potential respondents may have legitimate concerns about protecting their privacy. Ask for no more information than you need, and ask respectfully for that information. Give respondents the option of refusing to answer any question that makes them uncomfortable, and honor any promises you make about how you will use the data you gather.

COMPILING A PRELIMINARY BIBLIOGRAPHY

As you begin locating sources of possible value for your paper, you should be careful to record certain essential information about the books and articles you have discovered. You will need this information in order to compile a preliminary bibliography. For books, record the full title, the full name of the author or authors, the city of publication, the publisher, and the date of publication. If you are using a particular part of a book, be sure to record the pages in question. And if you are using an article or a story included in an anthology edited by someone other than the author of the material you are using, make the distinction between the author and title of the selection and the editor and title of the volume. When you have located articles in periodicals, record the author(s) of the article, the title of the article, the title of the journal in which it was published, the volume number, the issue number (if there is one), the date of the issue, and the pages between which the article can be found. (For examples of bibliographic form, see pages 76–86.)

One way to compile a preliminary bibliography is to use a set of 3 × 5 index cards, recording each source on a separate card. This involves a little more trouble than jotting references down on whatever paper you have at hand, but it will be to your ultimate advantage. As your research progresses, you can easily eliminate any sources that you were unable to obtain—or any that you have rejected as inappropriate. This method will make it easier to arrange your sources in the order required for your formal bibliography at the end of your finished paper. Some researchers prefer to use a computer notebook; others work directly from computer printouts of sources located during their search. Whatever method you use, be sure to keep accurate records. No one enjoys discovering a failure to record an important reference—especially if this discovery comes after the paper is written and shortly before it must be handed in.

Figure 16 shows a sample bibliography of sources discovered from the search illustrated earlier, on the relationship between drug use and

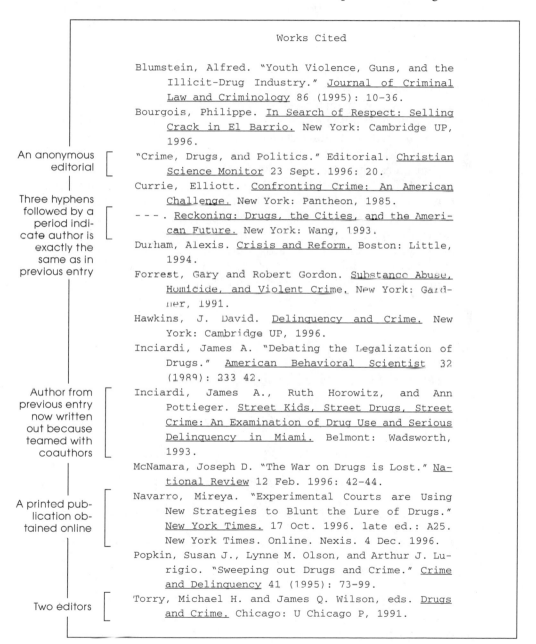

Works Cited

Blumstein, Alfred. "Youth Violence, Guns, and the Illicit-Drug Industry." Journal of Criminal Law and Criminology 86 (1995): 10–36.

Bourgois, Philippe. In Search of Respect: Selling Crack in El Barrio. New York: Cambridge UP, 1996.

An anonymous editorial
"Crime, Drugs, and Politics." Editorial. Christian Science Monitor 23 Sept. 1996: 20.

Currie, Elliott. Confronting Crime: An American Challenge. New York: Pantheon, 1985.

Three hyphens followed by a period indicate author is exactly the same as in previous entry
- - - . Reckoning: Drugs, the Cities, and the American Future. New York: Wang, 1993.

Durham, Alexis. Crisis and Reform. Boston: Little, 1994.

Forrest, Gary and Robert Gordon. Substance Abuse, Homicide, and Violent Crime. New York: Gardner, 1991.

Hawkins, J. David. Delinquency and Crime. New York: Cambridge UP, 1996.

Inciardi, James A. "Debating the Legalization of Drugs." American Behavioral Scientist 32 (1989): 233 42.

Author from previous entry now written out because teamed with coauthors
Inciardi, James A., Ruth Horowitz, and Ann Pottieger. Street Kids, Street Drugs, Street Crime: An Examination of Drug Use and Serious Delinquency in Miami. Belmont: Wadsworth, 1993.

McNamara, Joseph D. "The War on Drugs is Lost." National Review 12 Feb. 1996: 42–44.

A printed publication obtained online
Navarro, Mireya. "Experimental Courts are Using New Strategies to Blunt the Lure of Drugs." New York Times. 17 Oct. 1996. late ed.: A25. New York Times. Online. Nexis. 4 Dec. 1996.

Popkin, Susan J., Lynne M. Olson, and Arthur J. Lurigio. "Sweeping out Drugs and Crime." Crime and Delinquency 41 (1995): 73–99.

Two editors
Torry, Michael H. and James Q. Wilson, eds. Drugs and Crime. Chicago: U Chicago P, 1991.

FIGURE 16
An MLA-style bibliography

crime. It is titled and arranged according to the conventions recommended by the Modern Language Association introduced in Part 2, "Working with Sources." Note the significance of the title, "Works Cited." A bibliography for a researched paper should consist only of works that are actually cited.

For additional information on MLA-style documentation, see pages 72–74 and 76–81.

TAKING NOTES

Note taking is essential to research. Unfortunately, few researchers can tell in advance exactly what material they will want to include in their final paper. Especially during the early stages of your research, you may record information that will seem unnecessary when you have become more expert on your topic and have a clear thesis. So you will probably have to discard some of your notes when you are ready to write your paper.

By using a note card system, you allow for flexibility when you are ready to move from research to composition. The odds are against discovering material in the exact order in which you will want to use it. By spreading out your note cards on a desk or table, you can study how they best fit together. You can arrange and rearrange the cards until you have them in a meaningful sequence. This system only works, however, when you have the self-restraint to limit yourself to recording one fact, one idea, or one quotation on each

---

Prison as Deterrent

(Currie 161)

"But prison may not only fail to deter; it may make matters worse. The overuse of incarceration may strengthen the links between street and prison and help to cement users' and dealer's identity as members of an oppositional drug culture, while simultaneously shutting them off from the prospect of successfully participating in the economy outside the prison."

FIGURE 17
Sample note card

card, as shown in Figure 17. Many of your cards will have a lot of empty space that you may be tempted to fill. Don't. As soon as you decide to put two ideas on the same card, you have made an editorial decision that you may later regret. The cost of a set of note cards is minimal compared to the amount of time you must invest in research and writing.

Sorting your note cards is also one of the easiest ways to determine whether you have enough material to write a good paper. If your notes fall into a half-dozen different categories, your research might lack focus. In this case, do some more research, concentrating on the category that interests you the most. If, on the other hand, your notes fall into a clear pattern, you may be ready to start writing. The point at which you move from research into writing will depend not only on your notes but also on the length of the paper you have in mind: Long papers usually involve more research than short papers. If you classify your notes every few days during the process of doing your research, you will be in a position to judge when you have taken as many notes as you need.

ORGANIZING A RESEARCHED PAPER

If you have used a note card system, you may be able to dispense with an outline and compose your first draft by working directly from your notes—assuming that you have sorted them carefully and arranged them into an easily understandable sequence. At some point, however, most writers find it useful to outline the ideas they plan to cover. Anyone who lacks experience in writing long papers is especially likely to benefit from taking the trouble to prepare an outline. Depending on your writing process, you can outline before attempting to write or after you have completed a first draft.

The patterns discussed in Part 1 for classical arrangement and Rogerian argument (pages 17–21) can be adopted for researched papers of almost any length. Another possibility is to employ a standard formal outline:

    I. Major idea
        A. Supporting idea
            1. Minor idea
                a. Supporting detail
                b. Supporting detail
            2. Minor idea
        B. Supporting idea
    II. Major idea

And so forth. Subdivisions only make sense when there are at least two categories—otherwise there would be no need to subdivide. Roman numeral I usually implies the existence of Roman numeral II, and supporting idea A implies the existence of supporting idea B. Formal outlines are usually parallel, with each part in balance with the others.

Your outline may consist of complete sentences or simply a list of topics, but you should follow consistently whichever system you choose. The extent to which you benefit from an outline is usually determined by the amount of effort you devote to preparing it. The more developed your outline, the more likely you are to have thought your essay through and considered how it can be best organized. Your outline may show you that you have much to say about one part of your paper and little about another. This could result in a lopsided paper when the parts are supposed to be of equal importance. In this case, your outline may lead you to do some additional research to obtain more information for the part of the paper that looks as if it is going to be weak. Or you may decide to rethink your essay and draft another outline, narrowing your paper to the discussion of the part that had most interested you. Either of these decisions would make it easier for you to write a well-organized paper by reducing the risk of introducing ideas you could not pursue.

Many writers prefer to work with less formal outlines. Two widely used alternatives to a formal outline are *listing* and *mapping*. When organizing a paper by listing, writers simply make a list of the various points they want to make without worrying about Roman numerals or indention. They then number the points on the list in the order they plan to discuss them. When mapping, writers create circles or blocks on a page, starting with their main idea. A different idea is noted in each circle or block, and then lines are drawn to connect ideas that are related. There is no single method that works equally well for all writers. Unless you are specifically instructed to complete a certain type of outline, practice whatever kind of outlining works best for you.

You should remember that an outline is not an end in itself; it is only a device to help you write a good paper. You can rewrite an outline much more easily than you can rewrite a paper, so do not think of an outline as some sort of fixed contract that you must honor at all cost. Be prepared to rework any outline that does not help you to write better.

WRITING A RESEARCHED PAPER

When planning a researched paper, you should allow ample time for drafting and revising. Ideas often evolve during the writing process. Even if you have extensive notes, you may discover that you lack information to support a claim that occurred to you when you sat down to write. You would then need to do some more research or modify your claim. The first draft may also include paragraphs that do not relate to the focus of your paper, and these will need to be removed once you realize that they do not fit. Cutting and adding are normal in the writing process, so do not be discouraged if you need to make changes.

One of the challenges involved in writing a researched paper is the need to integrate source material into a work that remains distinctively your own. Many papers suffer because they include too many long quotations or because quotations (be they long or short) seem arbitrarily placed. Make sure that any quotations in your paper fit smoothly within the essay as a whole: Provide transitions that link quotations to whatever has come before them. As a general rule, anything worth quoting at length requires some discussion. After you have quoted someone, you should usually include some analysis or commentary that will make the significance of the quotation clear. Let your readers know how you would like them to respond to the material that you are citing. Identify what you agree with and what you question.

To help keep your paper your own, try to avoid using long quotations. Quote only what you need most, and edit long quotations whenever possible. Use the ellipsis (. . .) to indicate that you have omitted a word or phrase within a sentence, leaving a space before and after each period. (Add a fourth period with no space before it when the ellipsis follows a completed sentence.) When editing quotations in this way, make sure that they remain clear and grammatical. If the addition of an extra word or two would help make the quotation more easily understandable, you can make an editorial interpolation by enclosing the inserted material within square brackets [ ]. If your keyboard does not have brackets, you can draw them in by hand.

Remember also that sources do not need to be quoted in order to be cited. As noted in Part 2 (pages 64–66), paraphrasing and summarizing are important writing skills. When revising your paper, use these skills whenever possible. They can help you to avoid writing a paper that sounds like nothing more than one quotation after another, or using quotations that are so heavily edited that readers start wondering about what you have cut out. When you put another writer's ideas into your own words (being careful, of course, to provide proper documentation), you are demonstrating that you have control over your material. And by doing so, you can often make your paper more readable.

Above all else, remember that you are a writer as well as an investigator. Although research is essential to the process of writing a researched paper, there is more to the researched paper than research alone. Almost all researched papers require that you have a thesis about your topic, and that thesis should be distinctively your own. Unless specifically instructed otherwise, you should think of papers that use information drawn from sources as *arguments*—arguments that are informed and supported by evidence you have discovered through research.

PREPARING YOUR FINAL DRAFT

After investing considerable time in researching, drafting, and revising your paper, be sure to allow sufficient time for editing your final draft. If you rush this stage of the process, the work you submit for evaluation may not adequately reflect the investment of time you gave to the project as a whole. Unless instructed otherwise, you can be guided by the rules in the following checklist.

A CHECKLIST FOR MANUSCRIPT FORM

1. Papers should be typed or word-processed. Use nonerasable 8½-by-11-inch white paper (one side only). Double-space all lines, leaving a margin of one inch on all sides. If word-processing, use a printer that will produce well-defined letters.
2. In the upper left corner of page 1, or on a separate title page, include the following information: your name, your instructor's name, the course and section number, and the date the essay is submitted.
3. Number each page in the upper right corner, ½-inch from the top. If using MLA-style documentation, type your last name immediately before the page number. If using APA-style documentation, type a shortened version of the title (one or two words) before the number.
4. Make sure that you consistently follow a documentation style that is acceptable to your instructor, and give credit to all of your sources.
5. Any quotation of more than four lines in an MLA-style paper, or more than forty words in an APA-style paper, should be set off from the rest of the text. Begin a new line, indenting one inch (or ten spaces) to form the left margin of the quotation. The indention means that you are quoting, so additional quotation marks are unnecessary in this case (except for quotations within the quotation).
6. Proofread your paper carefully. Typographical errors or careless mistakes in spelling or grammar can cause your audience to lose confidence in you. If your instructor allows ink corrections, make them as neatly as you can. Redo any page that has numerous or lengthy corrections.
7. If you have word-processed your paper, be sure to separate pages that have been printed on a continuous sheet. Whether your work is word-processed or typed, use a paper clip to bind the pages together.

PART 4

SOURCES FOR ARGUMENT

SECTION 1

SURFING THE WEB:
WHO CONTROLS INFORMATION?

JON KATZ

THE RIGHTS OF KIDS IN
THE DIGITAL AGE

What happens when a world of information, much of it potentially disturbing to children, becomes accessible from the home computer tucked in the corner of a child's bedroom? Should children be denied access to pornography and adult discussion groups? Or should they be free to learn how to make their own decisions regarding the responsible use of technology? In the following argument, first published in a 1996 issue of *Wired* magazine, Jon Katz argues that children have a moral right to information. Drawing on the work of John Locke, a seventeenth-century philosopher whose ideas influenced the founders of our country, Katz structures his argument like the U.S. Constitution by dividing it into a series of "articles." Katz is a contributing editor of *Wired* and the author of *Virtuous Reality* (1997). Address: jdkatz@aol.com

Article I
Children Lead the Revolution

Children are at the epicenter of the information revolution, ground zero of the digital world. They helped build it, and they understand it as well or better than anyone. Not only is the digital world making the younger more sophisticated, altering their ideas of what culture and literacy are, it is connecting them to one another, providing them with a new sense of political self. Children in the digital age are neither unseen nor unheard; in fact, they are seen and heard more than ever. They occupy a new kind of cultural space. They're citizens of a new order, founders of the Digital Nation.

2   After centuries of sometimes benign, sometimes brutal, oppression and regulation, kids are moving out from under our pious control, finding one another via the great hive that is the Net. As digital communications flash through the most heavily fortified borders and ricochet around the world independent of governments and censors, so can children for the first time reach past the suffocating boundaries of social convention, past their elders' rigid notions of what is good for them. Children will never be the same; nor will the rest of us.

The young are the last significant social entity in America perceived to be under the total control of others. Although in recent years society has finally moved to protect kids against exploitation and physical abuse, they make up the only group in our so-called democracy with no inherent political rights, no voice in the political process. Teenagers in particular, so close to adulthood, are subjected to sometimes intolerable controls over almost every aspect of their lives.

4   In part, that's because fears for children are manifold, ranging from real danger (assault, molestation, kidnapping) to such perceived—but often unprovable—perils as the alleged damage caused by violent or pornographic imagery, the addictive nature of some new technology, the supposed loss of civilization and culture.

In some parts of America, particularly amid the urban underclass where violence and economic hardship are epidemic, those fears for children seem not only valid, but understated. But for middle-class families that consume much of this controversial popular culture, such fears seem misplaced, exaggerated, invoked mostly to regain control of a society changing faster than our ability to comprehend it.

6   The idea that children are moving beyond our absolute control may be the bitterest pill for many to swallow in the digital era. The need to protect children is reflexive, visceral, instinctive. All the harder, then, to change.

Article II
A New Social Contract

Three centuries ago, a stunning new idea was introduced to the world: No one has the right of absolute control over others. People have the inherent right to some measure of freedom. Rules should be agreed upon, not imposed. Although this notion has become our most cherished political value, in the 17th century it existed in practice nowhere on the planet. When it did spread, slowly, it was first applied to men, usually white men. Bit by bloody bit, the idea has encompassed other groups, but it has yet to be applied at all to children.

8   John Locke, the 17th-century English philosopher and essayist, is most remembered for that influential political argument: People have some say in the way they are governed. Locke preached that people naturally possess certain rights—life, liberty, and property. Rulers, he wrote, derive their power only from the consent of the people they rule. Government, then, is essentially a Social Contract: subjects give up certain freedoms and submit to the authority of government in return for just rule, the safeguarding of what is rightfully theirs. The ruler holds power only so long as he uses it justly. If that sounds familiar, it's because Locke's intellectual fingerprints are all over the Declaration of Independence and the Constitution.

Locke's contract requires mutual responsibility. If the government violates the trust placed in it by the people, if rulers "endeavor to take away and destroy the power of the people or to reduce them to slavery," then government forfeits the power the people have placed in it. An arbitrary or destructive ruler who does not respect his subjects' rights is "justly to be esteemed the common enemy and pest of mankind and is to be treated accordingly."

10   The idea of a Social Contract emphasizing mutual responsibility rather than arbitrary power seems especially relevant to the rights of children and the extent of parental authority, particularly in the midst of our raging civil war over culture and media.

Children are being subjected to an intense wave of censorship and control—V-Chips, blocking software, ratings systems on everything from movies and music to computer games. Cultural conservatives like Bob Dole and William Bennett* are forging a national political movement out of their desire to put cultural blinders on the young. President Clinton has enthusiastically embraced the idea that parents should have the right to block kids' TV programs. In this struggle, the young are largely alone; few political, educational, or social entities have lent support or defense.

12   Locke challenged the belief, widespread then and now, that the power of parents over children is "absolute." In his *Two Treatises on Government* and the essay "Some Thoughts Concerning Education," Locke argued for the moral education of children rather than the arbitrary imposition of rules. Children, like adults, were entitled to some measure of freedom because that was appropriate to their status as rational human beings. Parents' authority should not be severe or arbitrary, he wrote, but used only for the

---

* For an argument by William Bennett, see pp. 199–201.

help, instruction, and preservation of their offspring. It is eventually to be relinquished.

The adult world seized on Locke's basic concepts of individual liberty and over time established political and legal rights. The French and American Revolutions transformed the politics of the world in ways that are still being played out today. But children have lived almost completely outside these notions—and for understandable reasons. Children's rights are, in fact, vastly more complicated.

14   Any sort of legislated political emancipation for the young is almost out of the question. Children are unlikely to win the sweeping legal protections granted other minorities. But some of the most powerful movements in our political history—civil rights, feminism, gay emancipation—were moral as well as legal struggles. With children, the idea of expanded freedom also begins as a moral issue.

The lives of children are far too complex to generalize about. Degrees of maturity, emotional stability, rates of development and learning, and the level of parents' patience, thoughtfulness, and resources vary too widely to set forth strict rules. Five-year-olds aren't like 15-year-olds. And when it comes to culture, at least, boys are often not like girls.

16   But that's why the notion that all children possess some basic rights in the digital age is critical. Their choices ought not to be left completely to the often arbitrary and sometimes ignorant whims and fancies of individual educators, religious leaders, or parents, any more than people ought to be subject to the total control of kings. Parents who thoughtlessly ban access to online culture or lyrics they don't like or understand, or parents who exaggerate and distort the dangers from violent and pornographic imagery are acting out of their own anxiety and arrogance, imposing brute authority. Rather than preparing kids for the world they'll have to live in, these parents insist on preparing them for a world that no longer exists.

The young have a moral right of access to the machinery and content of media and culture. It's their universal language. It's their means of attaining modern literacy, which in the next millennium will surely be defined as the ability to access information, rather than to regurgitate the names of the presidents. It may mean the difference between economic well-being and economic hardship.

18   Blocking, censoring, and banning should be the last resort in dealing with children, not the first. Particularly if children have been given the chance to develop a moral and responsible ethic and are willing—as in Locke's notion of the Social Contract—to meet their responsibilities.

Article III
The Responsible Child

The cultural disputes between children and their families cannot be solved by extending the legal system into the home. No legislator can define every circumstance in which a child is entitled to assume more responsibility for his or her decisions. And wildly varying family values make it difficult to spell out universal rights.

20 But we as adults and parents can start to understand what a new Social Contract with children looks like—beginning with the notion of the Responsible Child. He or she is a teenager, or almost one, who meets certain criteria:

• She works to the best of her ability in school. She's reasonably responsible about her education and functions successfully in a classroom.

• She's socially responsible. She avoids drug and alcohol abuse and understands the health dangers of smoking.

• She does not harass, steal from, or otherwise harm people, including siblings, friends, fellow students.

• She carries her weight at home. She does the tasks and chores she has agreed on or has been assigned to do.

The Responsible Child is not the embodiment of some utopian vision; she can at times be difficult, rebellious, obnoxious, moody. But she makes a good-faith effort to resolve differences rationally and verbally. Saintliness is not required.

Article IV
The Moral Foundation

22 The Responsible Child does not appear miraculously but emerges as a result of years of preparation and education. Her conscience and sense of responsibility don't spontaneously form at the legal age of adulthood. They are built into her life early through thoughtful parenting and a complex series of relationships.

The vast literature on children and child psychology contains arguments about every conceivable child-rearing issue. But respected experts conclude nearly unanimously that dominant character traits don't just appear during the teen years. They get formed much earlier, from the interactions and environment provided since infancy.

24 If parents spend time with their children, form strong attachments with them, teach them morals, live moral lives, discourage and punish immoral behavior, and treat their children in a moral way, then the moral issues their children face later are much more likely to be resolved.

As parents define permissible behavior and limits, as they explain them again and again, the child gradually incorporates these rules into her own reflexive behavior. This becomes the formation of conscience and individual value systems.

26 The idea that a TV show or a lyric can transform a healthy, connected, grounded child into a dangerous monster is absurd, an irrational affront not only to science but to common sense and to what we know about children in our own lives. It is primarily the invention of politicians (who use it to frighten or rally supporters), of powerful religious groups (that can't teach dogma to the young without control), and of journalism (which sees

new media and new culture as menaces to its own once-powerful and highly profitable position in American society).

As powerful as they are, media and culture—or the sometimes offensive imagery transmitted by them—can't form our children's value systems or provide the building blocks of conscience. Only we can do that.

Article V
The Rights of Children

28   The Responsible Child has certain inalienable rights, not conferred at the caprice of arbitrary authority, but recognized by a just society as inherently belonging to every person. As we enter the digital age, this recognition is inevitable, a powerful idea that will bring children into the vast community of people who have, or are battling for, some control over their lives.

• Children have the right to be respected, to be accorded the same sensitivity that other disenfranchised minorities have grudgingly been granted by the rest of society. They should not be viewed as property or as helpless to participate in the decisions affecting their lives.

• Children should not be branded ignorant or inadequate because their educational, cultural, or social agenda is different from that of previous generations. They have the right to help redefine what education, literacy, and civic-mindedness are.

• Children have a right to two-way communications with the politicians, clergy, and educational leaders who claim to know what is best for them. Children have a right to help shape discussions about their moral lives.

• Children of various socioeconomic levels ought to have equal exposure to the new technologies—multimedia, cable channels, the Net—that deliver information, education, and culture. They have a right to have new media and technology included in their school curricula.

• Children who meet their personal and educational responsibilities ought to have nearly unrestricted access to their culture—particularly if they demonstrate an ability to maintain balance in their lives.

• Children have the right to assemble online, to form groups, and to communicate with like-minded communities through Web sites and homepages, online services, e-mail, and the range of possibilities created by the Net.

• Children have a right to challenge the use of blocking software and other technologies, like the V-Chip, that arbitrarily deny them choice, exposure to ideas, and freedom of speech.

Children's rights are not synonymous with permissiveness. Scholars of childhood agree that children need clear boundaries and occasional discipline. But if children have the opportunity from an early age to make informed decisions about themselves—what to eat, when to sleep, what to wear—they will be able to take a measure of control of their cultural lives by their teens.

30   These rights are not a gift conferred out of the goodness of our hearts, but the fulfillment of the most basic responsibility of parents: to prepare children for the world they will live in.

Article VI
Negotiating the Social Contract

How would a Social Contract about media and culture—a truce between adults and children—work?

32   The model envisioned by Locke applies eerily well to kids. By definition, a contract is agreed upon, not imposed. Its power comes not from arbitrary authority but from a moral base, a desire to do the right thing for everyone, to respect and understand the rights and needs of all parties. Parents and children would both have to want an agreement that ratifies the children's rights and makes responsible parents yield some of their power while feeling safe about it.

The rational adult has to begin by accepting that censorship and arbitrary controls don't work, that he or she has to thrash out a shared value system with his or her children. Attempting to censor children can undermine authority and values rather than affirming them. Since most older children and their friends can circumvent almost all censorious technology, and since much of the digital world is beyond the comprehension of most parents anyway, mere authority becomes limited, sometimes meaningless. Children will learn not how to form value systems, but how their moral guardians can't make their dictums stick.

34   So, family members need to think through their own notions about children and culture. How much power and control are the elders willing to cede? A parent would spell out how much TV or online time he finds appropriate and define what else is expected from the child: domestic chores, school performance, religious obligations.

The child would spell out what access to culture she wants: which TV shows, which CDs, how much time online. And she has to specify what she's willing to do in exchange. She must agree to follow rules of safety: not giving out telephone numbers or home addresses to strangers online, and telling parents about "pornographic" contacts, such as files with sexual content. Media access is granted as a right, but it's subject to some conditions.

36   There would probably be as many different kinds of contracts as there are families. But if children meet their end of the Social Contract, then parents would concede that their children have a moral right to access the TV programs they want, the CDs they want to hear, the online services they choose and can afford. Families could begin to rely on trust, negotiation, and communication rather than phobias, conflict, and suspicion.

It has to be a good-faith contract. Parents who ask too much will lose their moral authority to make an arrangement like this. Kids willing to do too little will jeopardize it as well. Some parties will probably have to set aside their broken contracts and keep on fighting.

38   Naturally, if either side violates its agreement—if kids fail in school, harm other people, start drinking heavily—then the contract is null and void. Children who can't or won't behave rationally forfeit the right to rational understandings and will return themselves to a state of diminished freedom.

But millions of American kids who can handle a racy chat room or an episode of *NYPD Blue* won't be denied cultural freedom because of their parents' fears about the kids who can't.

Article VII
Test Case

40   As it happens, for years my own household has operated under a form of Social Contract—not that we called it that or thought much about John Locke. I have seen that it can work. My wife and I have a 14-year-old daughter, who is comfortable with my writing about her cultural rights, though not about other details of her personal life.

Believing that culture is the language and currency of her generation, we've always encouraged her to understand it. She played Nintendo, watched cable, loved the *Teenage Mutant Ninja Turtles.* Now, she watches *ER, Homicide: Life on the Street,* and *The X-Files,* plus old musicals on cable and the occasional dumb sitcom after a tough week.

42   She can see virtually any movie she wants, although sometimes there is some discussion about it. If she is shocked, upset, or otherwise uncomfortable, she feels free to leave. The Motion Picture Association of America's parental rating system is an absurd guide to what children can or cannot handle and has never been the criterion in our family. When my daughter was younger, if there were serious questions about the violence, sexual content, or emotional intensity of a movie, my wife and I would sometimes see it first, then take our daughter. The ability to tell an 8-year-old when to close her eyes is a helpful thing. Now, of course, we don't have to.

She has been online since she was 10. We have never thought of acquiring blocking software, which would be offensive and demeaning to her, but she's been taught not to pass around her name, address, or phone number—and to pass problems or unsettling experiences on to us.

44   She hasn't had many. She has encountered occasional creeps and a few disturbed people online—boys who want to talk dirty, men who want to send her explicitly sexual files—and she's learned important phrases like No and Get lost. Despite the enormous publicity those kinds of contacts generate, they have been relatively rare. She does have online friendships, few of which I know anything about.

We trust her implicitly, until she provides a reason to be regarded differently. So far, so good: she does well in school, has healthy friendships, sings in a demanding chorale, has shown little interest in violence, drugs, or alcohol. She's developed a high level of common sense and analytic thoughtfulness about the culture she uses. But new media haven't supplanted old—she reads a lot, and writes, and talks. In fact, it was she, I hereby acknowledge, who first pointed out to me that my thoughts about children's rights related directly to this John Locke guy she'd learned about in her history class.

46 I have no illusions that she is a "typical" child, if there is such a thing. As an only child, she's easier to monitor. As a middle-class family, we can provide a computer, books, and an allowance high enough to cover movie tickets.

  Still, she—and we—live very much according to Locke's idea of a Social Contract. It is understood and articulated that as long as she does as well as she's doing, she has the right to her culture and to her own rational judgments about it without interference, ridicule, or censorship.

48 We all understand that she needs to be different from us. Her culture is perhaps the most important way she has of separating, of differentiating herself from us.

  So far, the contract holds.

Article VIII
The Political Power of Children

50 Cultural conservatives, politicians, parents, teachers, adults in general—and especially journalists—have greatly underestimated just how political an issue this assault on kids' culture has become.

  In topics online, on Web sites, in countless live chats, the young vent their anger at the pious efforts of the adult world to "safeguard" them, at congressional efforts to legislate "decency" on the Internet, and to curb free speech in this freest of environments. They're generating e-mail, firing up online discussions, bordering Web pages in black.

52 This is as intensely aroused and political as kids have been since the '70s. Plus this digital generation has an organizational weapon no previous generation had: the ability to find and talk to distant allies just a modem away. Easily able to measure their own lives against others, to compare their own experience with rhetoric, these kids know their culture isn't dangerous. Their tactics, occurring almost completely out of sight of parents and beyond the consciousness of journalists and politicians, could transform the politics of the young.

  Journalists have underreported the extent to which culture is politics to young people, and how they resent suggestions that culture is rendering them stupid, indifferent, and violence-prone. Since children are almost voiceless in media and in the political debates on issues affecting them, it's not surprising that their outrage goes largely unnoticed.

54   But the traditional, hidebound press is learning the high cost of relent-
lessly patronizing and offending kids—it has alarmingly few young consumers. Politicians may soon be learning the same lesson. The battles over
new media are likely to spark youthful politicization reminiscent of the
movements launched by racial minorities, women, and gays.

        Under the noses of their guardians, the young are now linked to one
another all over the world. They already share their culture online, trading
information about new movies, TV shows, and CDs, warning one another
about viruses, sharing software and tech tips. At times, they band together
to chastise or drive out aggressive, obnoxious, or irresponsible digital peers.
They steer one another to interesting Web sites.

56   But children, perhaps more than any other oppressed minority, have
a long way to go to become politically organized. And they can't engage in
political struggle by themselves.

        By now, they should have had some help. Some online benefactor
should fund something like a Children's Digital Freedom Center, similar to
the Electronic Frontier Foundation. It could provide children with truthful
information about violence, pornography, and online safety with which
they could educate their classmates and confront ignorance and misinfor-
mation about their youth culture. It could also provide legal support to
young people penalized for free expression online, or those unfairly denied
their right of access to culture.

58   Instead, what children have received from the digital community is a
deafening yawn.

Article IX
The Hypocrisy of the Digital World

Above almost all things, the digital culture prides itself on the notion that
information should be free, that this new culture should remain unfettered
and unobstructed. Efforts at corporate and governmental control and the
promotion of so-called "decency" standards are the subject of ferocious debate online and political lobbying offline.

60   But the culture is either silent or supportive of the attempts to block
children's access. The EFF wholeheartedly supports limiting children's access to the Net and even has links from its Web site to publishers of blocking
software. Even on libertarian-minded conferencing systems like The Well,
it's mostly taken for granted that children can be denied the freedom of
speech for which everyone else is so willing to fight.

        Citizens of the Digital Nation, so quick to hit the barricades when Con-
gress attempts to cut back on their freedom of speech, seem happy to embrace
the new raft of blocking software. They seem quite willing to trade children's
rights for their own freedom of expression. Don't take us, take our kids.

62   No one in the highly sensitive and politicized adult digital world blinks
when the media cheerfully talk about blocking software as the clear alternative to censoring the Internet. No one minds when reviews recommend

programs such as Cybersitter, SurfWatch, Net Nanny, and Cyber Patrol. The very names of the programs are patronizing and demeaning.

This approach is the antithesis of trust and rational discourse between adults and children and more evidence of the growing need to protect children not from smut, but from adult abuses of power. Blocking software is noxious and potentially unlimited. Some of these programs have thousands of potentially forbidden categories, going far beyond sex and violence. Once applied, censoring and restrictions inevitably will spread into other areas that adults want to place off-limits: political topics that differ from their own values, music and movie forums that don't conform to their adult tastes, online friends that don't meet their approval, Darwinian theory.

64   Although it's being introduced in America as a means of protecting children, as this technology evolves it could easily become the tyrant's best techno-pal, offering ever more ingenious ways to control speech and thought. Some children reared on this stuff will inevitably grow up thinking that the way to deal with topics we don't like is to block them—remove them from our vision and consciousness. In any other context, defenders of free speech would be bounding off the walls.

Like the movie industry's silly ratings code, blocking software gives the illusion of control. It doesn't ensure safety since sophisticated evildoers will circumvent it even more quickly than kids. And it doesn't teach citizenship in the digital world.

66   As parents withdraw, secure in the belief that the Net Nanny will do the work they should be doing, count on this: children, many of whom helped build the digital culture, will swiftly transcend this software. They would be much better off if parents accompanied them when they first set out online, showing them what is inappropriate or dangerous.

Blocking deprives children of the opportunity to confront the realities of new culture: some of it is pornographic, violent, occasionally even dangerous. They need to master those situations in a rational, supervised way to learn how to truly protect themselves.

68   The urge to block presumes that exposure to certain topics is intrinsically dangerous. But only an infinitesimally small number of kids have been lured into potentially dangerous situations as a result of online encounters—fewer than 25, according to the National Center for Missing and Exploited Children. That's a tiny figure given the billions of online encounters.

The digital world owes it to children to defend their rights as zealously as it defends its own. So far, it has failed, betraying its own heritage and, worse, its future.

Article X
What Children Need in the 21st Century

70   Children need to get their hands on the new machines. They need equal access to the technology of culture, research, and education. Poor and working-class families have few computers compared with the affluent

middle class. And we are learning that some minority children are resisting computers as the toys of the white nerd.

But if new technology can create a gap between haves and have-nots, it can also narrow it. Cheap, portable PCTVs—televisions with computers and cable modems—would help equalize the digital revolution in a hurry. Hastening the arrival of such equal access should be the first and most pressing moral issue of the digital generation.

72   Children also need to learn to use the machinery of culture safely and responsibly. That means grasping the new rules of community in the online world, transcending the often abrasive, pointlessly combative tone that permeates many online discussions. They need to learn how to research ideas and history as well as to chat, mouth off, and download games.

Children need help in becoming civic-minded citizens of the digital age, in figuring out how to use the machinery in the service of some broader social purpose than simple entertainment. They need guidance in managing their new ability to connect instantly with other cultures. They need reminders about how to avoid the dangers of elitism and arrogance.

74   But more than anything else, it's time to extend to children the promise of the fundamental idea that Locke, Thomas Paine, Thomas Jefferson, and others introduced to the world three centuries ago: That everyone has rights. That everyone should be given as great a measure of freedom as possible. That all should get the opportunity to rise to the outer limits of their potential.

We need to teach ourselves how to trust children to make rational judgments about their own safety. We see their world as a dark and dangerous place, even as they see it as challenging, entertaining, and exciting. We patronize them in the belief that they don't have the character, common sense, or conscience to withstand the dangers of their vastly expanding cultural universe. And now we try to block them from that world.

76   We haven't got a chance. Like Locke's ideas of emancipation, children's lives are taking on a momentum of their own, moving rapidly past our anxious and fearful grasp. Their emancipation is as inevitable as our own.

Since Locke's time, democracy has inexorably advanced as monarchies and authoritarian regimes have increasingly failed. They have been undermined by new ideas riding on the back of new technologies that now extend to every corner of the world. Oppressive authority and censorship seem increasingly anachronistic amidst the porous borders of the emerging digital era.

78   The approaching millennium is more than a historical landmark. It's the right time to liberate our children from the heavy hands of history. Most of us recognize that our children are moving into a miraculous new era. They will, like everyone else, take risks and face dangers. They will also reap great rewards.

Children have the chance to reinvent communications, culture, and community. To address the problems of the new world in new ways. To do better than we did. Instead of holding them back, we should be pushing them forward. Instead of shielding them, we should take them by the hands, guide them to the gates, and cheer them on.   ❖

Questions for Meaning

1. How are children changing, according to Katz, and how do these changes affect their relationships with adults?
2. What is the meaning of Locke's "Social Contract"? How can it be applied to children?
3. Why does Katz believe that children need to be able to access information electronically?
4. How do children learn to make responsible choices?
5. How should adults respond to children who make irresponsible choices?
6. Vocabulary: epicenter (1), benign (2), visceral (6), caprice (28), dictums (33), patronizing (62), inexorably (77), anachronistic (77).

Questions about Strategy

1. Katz has organized his argument into a series of "articles" imitating the plan used by the framers of the U.S. Constitution. Does this plan work?
2. This argument is based on the idea that children have a "moral right" to access information. How does Katz go about establishing this moral right? On what other grounds could he have based his argument?
3. In Article VII, Katz writes about his daughter. To what extent is this example persuasive? Under what conditions can this "test case" be considered representative of other children?
4. Katz argues, in paragraph 63, that censorship inevitably leads to additional censorship. Is this reasoning persuasive?

MAY KADI

WELCOME TO CYBERBIA

Is access to a world of information really as empowering as computer enthusiasts seem inclined to believe? And is the Internet making people more connected to others or more isolated? These are among the questions addressed by May Kadi in this argument published in 1995 by zine h2so4. As you read, consider how Kadi would respond to the way you yourself use the computer—if you are using one at all.

> Computer networking offers the soundest basis for world peace that has yet been presented. Peace must be created on the bulwark of understanding. International computer networks will knit together the peoples of the world in bonds of mutual respect; its possibilities are vast, indeed.
>
> —*Scientific American*, June 1994

Computer bulletin board services offer up the glories of e-mail, the thought provocation of Newsgroups, the sharing of ideas implicit in public posting, and the interaction of real-time chats. The fabulous, wonderful, limitless world of Communication is just waiting for you to log on. Sure. Yeah. Right.

2   I confess, I am a dedicated cyber-junkie. It's fun. It's interesting. It takes me places where I've never been before. I sign on once a day, twice a day, three times a day, more and more; I read, I post, I live. Writing an article on the ever-expanding, ever-entertaining, ever-present world of online existence would have been easy for me. But it would have been familiar, perhaps dull; and it might have been a lie. The world does not need another article on the miracle of online reality; what we need, what I need, what this whole delirious, inter-connected, global-community of a world needs, is a little reality check.

To some extent the following scenario will be misleading. There *are* flat rate online services (Netcom for one) which offer significant connectivity for a measly 17 dollars a month. But I'm interested in the activities and behavior of the private service users who will soon comprise a vast majority of online citizens. Furthermore, let's face facts, the U.S. government by and large foots the bill for the Internet, through maintaining the structural (hardware) backbone, including, among other things, funding to major universities. As surely as the Department of Defense started this whole thing, AT&T or Ted Turner is going to end up running it so I don't think it's too unrealistic to take a look at the Net as it exists in its commercial form[1] in order to expose some of the realities lurking behind the regurgitated media rhetoric and the religious fanaticism of net junkies.

Time and Money

4   The average person, the normal human, J. Individual, has an income. Big or small, how much of J. Individual's income is going to be spent on Computer Connectivity? Does 120 dollars a month sound reasonable? Well, you may find that number a bit too steep for your pocketbook, but the brutal fact is that 120 dollars is a "reasonable" amount to spend on monthly connectivity. The major online services have a monthly service charge of approximately $15. 15 dollars to join the global community, communicate with a diverse group of people and access the world's largest repository of knowledge since the Alexandrian library* does not seem unreasonable, does it? But don't overlook the average per-hour connectivity rate of an additional $3 (which can skyrocket upwards of $10, depending on your modem speed and service). You might think that you are a crack

---

[1] techno concession: I know that the big three commercial services are not considered part of the Internet property, but they (Prodigy, CompuServe and AOL) are rapidly adding real Net access and considering AOL just bought out Netcom—well, just read the article.

*The library in Alexandria, Egypt, housed one of the most important collections of manuscripts in the ancient world. After flourishing for almost six hundred years, it was destroyed in the third century AD.

whiz with your communications software—that you are rigorous and stringent and never, ever respond to e-mail or a forum while online, that you always use your capture functions and create macros, but let me tell you that no one, and I repeat, no one, is capable of logging on this efficiently every time. 30 hours per month is a realistic estimate for online time spent by a single user engaging in activities beyond primitive e-mail. Now consider that the average, one-step-above-complete neophyte user has at least two distinct BBS accounts, and do the math: Total Monthly Cost: $120. Most likely, that's already more than the combined cost of your utility bills. How many people are prepared to double their monthly bills for the sole purpose of connectivity?

In case you think 30 hours a month is an outrageous estimate, think of it in terms of television. (OK, so you don't own a television, well, goody-for-you—imagine that you do!) 30 hours, is, quite obviously, one hour a day. That's not so much. 30 hours a month in front of a television is simply the evening news plus a weekly *Seinfeld/Frasier* hour. 30 hours a month is less time than the average car-phone owner spends on the phone while commuting. Even a conscientious geek, logging on for e-mail and the up-to-the-minute news that only the net services can provide is probably going to spend 30 hours a month online. And, let's be truthful here, 30 hours a month ignores shareware downloads, computer illiteracy, real-time chatting, interactive game playing and any serious forum following, which by nature entail a significant amount of scrolling and/or downloading time.

6   If you are really and truly going to use the net services to connect with the global community, the hourly charges are going to add up pretty quickly. Take out a piece of paper, pretend you're writing a check, and print out "One hundred and twenty dollars—" and tell me again, how diverse is the online community?

That scenario aside, let's pretend that you're single, that you don't have children, that you rarely leave the house, that you don't have a TV and that money is not an issue. Meaning, pretend for a moment that you have as much time and as much money to spend online as you damn well want. What do you actually do online?

8   Well, you download some cool shareware, you post technical questions in the computer user group forums, you check your stocks, you read the news and maybe some reviews—Hey, you've already passed that 30-hour limit! But, of course, since "computer networks make it easy to reach out and touch strangers who share a particular obsession or concern," you are participating in the online forums, discussion groups, and conferences.

Let's review the structure of forums. For the purpose of this essay, we will examine the smallest of the major user-friendly commercial services—America Online (AOL). There is no precise statistic available (at least none that the company will reveal—you have to do the research by HAND!!!) on exactly how many subject-specific discussion areas (folders) exist on AOL.

Any online service is going to have zillions of posts pertaining to computer usage (e.g., the computer games area of AOL breaks into five hundred separate topics with over 100,000 individual posts), so let's look at a less popular area: the "Lifestyles and Interests" department.

10   For starters, there are 57 initial categories within the Lifestyles and Interests area. One of these categories is Ham Radio. Ham Radio? How can there possibly be 5,909[2] separate, individual posts about Ham Radio? 5,865 postings in the Biking (and that's just bicycles, not motorcycles) category. Genealogy—22,525 posts. The Gay and Lesbian category is slightly more substantial—36,333 posts. There are five separate categories for political and issue discussion. The big catch-all topic area, The Exchange, has over 100,000 posts. Basically, service wide (on the smallest service, remember) there are over a million posts.

So, you want to communicate with other people, join the online revolution, but obviously you can't wade through everything that's being discussed—you need to decide which topics interest you, which folders to browse. Within The Exchange alone (one of 57 subdivisions within one of another 50 higher divisions) there are 1,492 separate topic-specific folders—each containing a rough average of 50 posts, but with many containing close to 400. (Note: AOL automatically empties folders when their post totals reach 400, so total post numbers do not reflect the overall historical totals for a given topic. Sometimes the posting is so frequent that the "shelf life" of a given post is no more than four weeks.)

12   So, there you are, J. Individual, ready to start interacting with folks, sharing stories and communicating. You have narrowed yourself into a single folder, three tiers down in the AOL hierarchy, and now you must choose between nearly fifteen hundred folders. Of course, once you choose a few of these folders, you will then have to read all the posts in order to catch up, be current, and not merely repeat a previous post.

A polite post is no more than two paragraphs long (a screenful of text, which obviously has a number of intellectually negative implications). Let's say you choose ten folders (out of 1,500). Each folder contains an average of 50 posts. Five hundred posts, at, say, one paragraph each, and you're now looking at the equivalent of a two-hundred-page book.

14   Enough with the stats. Let me back up a minute and present you with some very disturbing, but rational, assumptions. J. Individual wants to join the online revolution, to connect and communicate. But, J. Individual is not going to read all one million posts on AOL. (After all, J. Individual has a second online service.) Exercising choice is J. Individual's god-given right as an American, and, by gosh, J. Individual is going to make some decisions. So, J. Individual is going to ignore all the support groups—after all, J. is a

---

[2] Statistics obtained in June 1994. Most of these numbers have increased by at least 20% since that time, owing to all the Internet hoopla in the media, the consumer desire to be "wired" as painlessly as possible, and AOL's guerrilla marketing tactics.

normal, well-adjusted person, and all of J.'s friends are normal, well-adjusted individuals, what does J. need to know about alcoholism or incest victims? J. Individual is white. So, J. Individual is going to ignore all the multi-cultural folders. J. couldn't give a hoot about gender issues; does not want to discuss religion or philosophy. Ultimately, J. Individual does not engage in topics which do not interest J. Individual. So, who is J. meeting? Why, people who are *just like* J.

J. Individual has now joined the electronic community. Surfed the Net. Found some friends. *Tuned in, turned on, and geeked out.* Travelled the Information Highway and, just off to the left of that great Infobahn, J. Individual has settled into an electronic suburb.

16   Are any of us so very different from J. Individual? It's my time and my money and I am not going to waste any of it reading posts by disgruntled Robert-Bly drum-beating Men's-Movement boys who think that they should have some say over whether or not I choose to carry a child to term simply because a condom broke. I know where I stand. I'm an adult. I know what's up and I am not going to waste my money arguing with a bunch of neanderthals.

Oh yeah; I am so connected, so enlightened, so open to the opposing viewpoint. I'm out there, meeting all kinds of people from different economic backgrounds (who have $120 a month to burn), from all religions (yeah, right, like anyone actually discusses religion anymore from a user-standpoint), from all kinds of different ethnic backgrounds and with all kinds of sexual orientations (as if any of this ever comes up outside of the appropriate topic folder).

18   People are drawn to topics and folders that interest them and therefore people will only meet people who are likewise interested in the same topics in the same folders. Rarely does anyone venture into a random folder just to see what others (The Others?) are talking about. This magazine being what it is, I can assume that the average reader will most likely not be as narrow-minded as the average white collar worker out in the burbs—but still, I think you and I are participating in the wide, wide world of online existence only insofar as our already existing interests and prejudices dictate.

Basically, between the monetary constraints and the sheer number of topics and individual posts, the great Information Highway is not a place where you will enter an "amazing web of new people, places, and ideas." One does not encounter people from "all walks of life" because there are too many people and too many folders. Diversity might be out there (and personally I don't think it is), but the simple fact is that the average person will not encounter it because with one brain, one job, one partner, one family, and one life, no one has the time!

20   Just in case these arguments based on time and money aren't completely convincing, let me bring up a historical reference. Please take another look at the opening quote of this essay from *Scientific American*. Featured in their "50 Years Ago Today" column, where you read "computer networks," the original quote contained the word "television." Amusing, isn't it?

Moving beyond the practical obstacles mentioned above, let's assume that the Internet is the functional, incredible information tool that everyone says it is. Are we really prepared to use it?

Who, What, Where, When and Why?

22 School trained us to produce answers. It didn't matter if your answer was right or wrong, the fact is that you did the answering while the teacher was the one asking the questions, writing down the equations, handing out the topics. You probably think that you came up with your own questions in college. But did you? Every class has its theme, its reading list, its issues; you chose topics for papers and projects keeping within the context set by your professors and the academic environment. Again, you were given questions, perhaps more thinly disguised than the questions posed to you in fourth grade, but questions nevertheless. And you answered them. Even people focusing on independent studies and those pursuing higher degrees, still do very little asking, simply because the more you study, the more questions there seem to be, patiently waiting for you to discover and answer them.

These questions exist because any contextual reality poses questions. The context in which you exist defines the question, as much as it defines the answer. School is a limited context. Even life is a limited context. Well, life was a limited context until this Information Highway thing happened to us. Maybe you think that this Infobahn is fabulous; fabulous because all that information is out there waiting to be restructured by you into those answers. School will be easier. Life will be easier. A simple tap-tap-tap on the ol' keyboard brings those answers out of the woodwork and off the Net into the privacy of your own home.

24 But this Information Highway is a two-way street and as it brings the world into your home it brings you out into the world. In a world filled with a billion answers just waiting to be questioned, expect that you are rapidly losing a grip on your familiar context. This loss of context makes the task of formulating a coherent question next to impossible.

The questions aren't out there and they never will be. You must make them.

26 Pure information has no meaning. I would venture to assert that a pure fact has no meaning; no meaning, that is, without the context which every question implies. In less than fifteen minutes I could find out how much rain fell last year in Uzbekistan, but that fact, that answer, has no meaning for me because I don't have or imagine or know the context in which the question is meaningful.

No one ever taught me how to ask a question. I answered other people's questions, received a diploma, and now I have an education. I can tell you what I learned, and what I know. I can quantify and qualify the trivia which comprises my knowledge. But I can't do that with my ignorance. Ignorance, being traditionally "bad," is just lumped together and I have little or no skills for sorting through the vast territory of what I don't know. I have an awareness of it—but only in the sense that I am aware of what I don't know about the topics which I already know something about in the first place.

28   What I mean to say is, I don't know what I don't know about, say, miners in China because I don't know anything about China, or what kinds of minerals they have, or where the minerals are, or the nature of mining as a whole. Worse yet, I don't have a very clear sense of whether or not these would be beneficial, useful, enlightening things for me to know. I have little sense of what questions are important enough for me to ask, so I don't know what answers, what information to seek out on the Internet.

In this light, it would seem that a massive amount of self-awareness is a prerequisite for using the Internet as an information source—and very few people are remotely prepared for this task. I believe that most people would simply panic in the face of their own ignorance and entrench themselves even more firmly into the black holes of their existing beliefs and prejudices. The information is certainly out there, but whether or not any of us can actually learn anything from it remains to be seen.

Fly, Words, and Be Free

30   The issues pertaining to time, money and the fundamental usefulness of pure information are fairly straightforward when contrasted with the issues raised by e-mail. E-mail is the first hook and the last defense for the Internet and computer-mediated communication. I would like to reiterate that I am by no means a Luddite when it comes to computer technology; in fact, because of this I may be unqualified to discuss, or even grasp, the dark side of electronic communication in the form of e-mail.

The general quality of e-mail sent by one's three-dimensional[3] friends and family is short, usually funny, and almost completely devoid of thoughtful communication. I do not know if this is a result of the fact that your 3-d friends already "know" you, and therefore brief quips are somehow more revealing (as they reflect an immediate mental/emotional state) than long, factual exposés, or if this brevity is a result of the medium itself. I do not know if I, personally, will ever be able to sort this out, owing to the nature of my friends, the majority of whom are, when all is said and done (unlike myself, I might add), Writers.

32   Writers have a reverence for pen and paper which does not carry over well into ASCII.* There is no glorified history for ASCII exchange

---

[3] So sue me for being a nerd. Personally, I find referring to friends one has made outside of the cyber world as one's "real" friends, or one's "objective" friends, to be insulting and inaccurate. Certainly one's cyber friends are three-dimensional in a final sense, but the "3-d" adjective is about the only term I have come up with which doesn't carry the negative judgmental weight of other terms so over-used in European philosophy. Feel free to write me if you've got a better suggestion. Better yet, write me in the appropriate context: flox@netcom.com.

* ASCII is an abbreviation used by computer specialists for American Standard Code for Information Interchange.

and perhaps because of this fact my friends do not treat the medium as they would a handwritten letter. Ultimately, there is very little to romanticize about e-mail. There is decidedly a lack of sensuality, and perhaps some lack of realism. There is an undeniable connection between writers and their written (literally) words. This connection is transferred via a paper letter in a way that can never be transferable electronically. A handwritten letter is physically touched by both the sender and the receiver. When I receive an electronic missive, I receive only an impression of the mind, but when I receive a handwritten letter, I receive a piece, a moment, of another's physical (real?) existence; I possess, I own, that letter, those words, that moment.

Certainly there is a near-mystical utopianism to the lack of ownership of electronic words. There is probably even an evolution of untold consequences. Personally, I do not think, as so many do, that a great democracy of thought is upon us—but there is a change, as ownership slips away. While this is somewhat exciting, or at least intriguing, insofar as public communication goes, it is sad for private correspondence. To abuse a well-known philosopher, there is a leveling taking place: The Internet and the computer medium render a public posting on the nature of footwear and a private letter on the nature of one's life in the same format, and to some extent this places both on the same level. I cannot help but think that there is something negative in this.

34   Accessibility is another major issue in the e-mail/handwritten letter debate. Text sent via the Net is instantly accessible, but it is accessible only in a temporal sense. E-text is inaccessible in its lack of presence, in its lack of objective physicality. Even beyond this, the speed and omnipresence of the connection can blind one to the fact that the author/writer/friend is not physically accessible. We might think we are all connected, like an AT&T commercial, but on what level are we connecting? A handwritten letter reminds you of the writers' physical existence, and therefore reminds you of their physical absence; it reminds you that there is a critical, crucial component of their very nature which is not accessible to you; e-mail makes us forget the importance of physicality and plays into our modern belief in the importance of time.

Finally, for me, there is a subtle and terrible irony lurking within the Net: the Net, despite its speed, its exchange, ultimately reeks of stasis. In negating physical distance, the immediacy of electronic transfers devalues movement and the journey. In one minute a thought is in my head, and the next minute it is typed out, sent, read, and in your head. The exchange may be present, but the journey is imperceptible. The Infobahn hype would have us believe that this phenomenon is a fast-paced dynamic exchange, but the feeling, when you've been at it long enough, is that this exchange of ideas lacks movement. Lacking movement and the journey, to me it loses all value.

36   Maybe this is prejudice. Words are not wine, they do not necessarily require age to improve them. Furthermore, I have always hated the concept that Art comes only out of struggle and suffering. So, to say that e-mail words are

weaker somehow because of the nature, or lack, of their journey, is to romanticize the struggle. I suppose I am anthropomorphizing text too much—but I
somehow sense that one works harder to endow one's handwritten words
with a certain strength, a certain soul, simply because those things are necessary in order to survive a journey. The ease of the e-mail journey means that
your words don't need to be as well prepared, or as well equipped.

Electronic missives lack time, space, embodiment and history (in the
sense of a collection of experiences). Lacking all these things, an electronic
missive is almost in complete opposition to my existence and I can't help
but wonder what, if anything, I am communicating. ❖

Questions for Meaning

1. What limits restrict the extent to which the average person can access
   information through the Internet?
2. What is the difference between a folder and a post?
3. Why would it be "polite" to limit a post to two paragraphs, or a
   screenful of text? What would be the "intellectually negative implications" of this convention?
4. According to Kadi, why is the information superhighway more likely
   to take us to "an electronic suburb" than to a truly diverse community?
5. Why does Kadi believe that the effective use of the Internet for research requires "a massive amount of self-awareness"?
6. How is reading an electronic message different from reading a handwritten letter? Which does Kadi seem to prefer? Which do you prefer
   to receive?

Questions about Strategy

1. Consider the quotation from *Scientific American,* which Kadi cites at
   the beginning of her article and then discusses in paragraph 20. How
   useful is it, given the purpose of this argument?
2. When calculating the monthly cost of computer networking, Kadi
   imagines someone using the Internet for thirty hours a month. Does
   this estimate seem reasonable? How important is this estimate to her
   case as a whole?
3. Paragraphs 8–13 are devoted to describing how information is organized on an online service and how someone would proceed when
   searching through this information. What is the purpose of this description?
4. Kadi urges readers to "face facts." To what extent has she provided
   facts that are useful to face? Does she rely on opinion as well as fact?
5. How does Kadi present herself as an individual? What kind of limitations does she acknowledge? What role does her self-presentation
   play in her argument?

Erik Ness

BIGBROTHER@CYBERSPACE

As the world becomes increasingly wired and more transactions take place through computer networks, will much of our private lives become known to people we've never met or even thought about? And how will these strangers use the information about us that is now at their disposal? Invoking the idea of Big Brother, the totalitarian ruler in George Orwell's *1984,* Erik Ness argues that the Internet poses a potential danger to civil liberty. His argument first appeared in a 1994 issue of *The Progressive,* a monthly periodical known for advocating liberal political opinions. Ness is editor of *The Progressive Media Project.*

In its popular series of futuristic commercials, AT&T paints a liberating picture of your not-too-distant life, when the information superhighway will be an instrument of personal freedom and a servant to your worldly needs and desires. But is the future of cyberspace really so elegant, so convenient? Or does it represent a serious threat to your privacy and your freedom?

2   The information superhighway is at least a decade away for most of us, but whether you know it or not, you already exist in cyberspace—through credit and other electronic records, your phone line, and your cable television. Constitutional scholar Laurence Tribe has argued that "without further thought and awareness . . . the danger is clear and present" that the Constitution's core values will be compromised "in the dim reaches of cyberspace."

When you visit your doctor, it is increasingly likely that your medical records are kept on a computer. Many of the health-care bills introduced in Congress this year called for a national medical database to link these records. Unfortunately, law-enforcement officers could gain access to those files without even obtaining a warrant. President Nixon's henchmen had to break into Daniel Ellsberg's psychiatrist's office to pull his files. Using a national medical database, they would need only to press a button.

4   Of course, the Government already has large stores of sensitive personal information at its disposal. In July of this year, Senator John Glenn, Ohio Democrat, released Internal Revenue Service papers showing that its employees were using IRS computers to prowl through the tax files of family, friends, neighbors, and celebrities. Since 1989, the IRS says, the agency has investigated more than 1,300 of its employees for unauthorized browsing; more than 400 employees have been disciplined.

But even seemingly benign information—your address in a government computer, for example—can betray you. Chris Criner volunteers as an escort for an abortion clinic in Tustin, California. After a Saturday morning of escort work in November 1992, Criner returned home to find a note on his door reading, "Hi. We came by for coffee. We'll be back." One week later,

Operation Rescue picketed his apartment. Criner was mystified; after clinic work he always went shopping or took a different route home to shake any over-zealous pursuers.

6 Criner had noticed a new protester lately—a man scribbling notes on a clipboard. Then one protester asked about Criner's wife, a clinic worker, using her given name—not the one she was known by. On a hunch, Criner and others at the clinic filed a complaint with the California Department of Motor Vehicles and found that four of their license plates had been illegally traced within an hour of each other at the Anaheim Police Department.

A former police employee eventually confessed to intruding into the restricted files. But Criner is still chilled by the incident—particularly after the shooting deaths of two abortion providers and a clinic escort in Pensacola, Florida. "Who knows where this information went besides this one little picket group?" he wonders. "Maybe it's on a computer bulletin board somewhere, or in some militant pro-life newsletter. Should I worry about my wife getting shot in the back of the head as she walks up to our front door because they know where we live?"

8 Businesses, government officials, activists, engineers, and intellectuals are busily defining cyberspace, and with various goals. Their divergent interests meet on the National Information Infrastructure, the so-called information superhighway. This cable—capable of delivering voice, data, and video images at high speed—is eventually supposed to connect every home and business in the United States and the world to an ever-growing web of electronic services ranging from stock quotations to movies on demand. The buzzword for this change is "convergence"—the melding of telephone, computer, and television technologies into the foundation of an information economy.

The Clinton Administration, particularly Vice President Al Gore, is a self-proclaimed champion of this information age. The business world is salivating over potential profits in the information economy. Meanwhile, consumer advocates and privacy experts warn that, without proper safeguards, this potential global village could become George Orwell's *1984*.

10 The National Information Infrastructure is projected to cost between $400 billion and $700 billion. During the 1992 Presidential campaign, Gore called for a major Government role in its development, but high Federal debt has led the Administration to favor private-sector design and operation instead. This shift has placed an even bigger burden on Congressional efforts this year to restructure the nation's $170 billion telecommunications industry, consisting of local telephone companies (worth $90 billion), long-distance carriers ($60 billion), and cable television industry (worth $20 billion).

The basic goal was to allow phone and cable operators to compete with each other locally, while preventing a total monopoly of both by any one company in one area and developing a new definition of universal service. Regulators and activists alike have long been leery of allowing a monopoly of the wires going into the American home, and their apprehensions have been heightened as electronic communication and commerce increasingly become central parts of our lives.

12   But even as telephone companies and cable television were eager to compete with each other for emerging markets, their rivalry got the better of them, killing telecommunications restructuring in the Senate. "Much of this battle is over who will control the television of the future," explains Jeff Chester of the Washington-based Center for Media Education. One example, he says, was NBC's effort to create a competitor for Ted Turner's twenty-four-hour Cable News Network. John Malone, president of TCI—who has a financial stake in CNN—controlled enough of the cable market that he was able to force NBC to turn a hard-news service into a softer, infotainment-oriented channel. "Their principal focus is profit, not the currency of democracy, not the diversity of ideas," warns Chester.

"We're in real danger of having a handful of giant, global communications corporations controlling the public mind," says Chester, whose organization filed a thirty-eight-page brief with the FCC opposing last year's mega-deal between Bell Atlantic and cable giant Telecommunications, Inc. The deal broke down, but that has not slowed the pace of consolidation: In the last year, AirTouch Communication acquired U.S. West (a deal worth $13.5 billion), AT&T Corporation merged with McCaw Cellular Communications, Inc. (a $12.6 billion value), and Viacom bought Blockbuster Entertainment ($7.97 billion).

14   "There is a direct relationship between the health of our democracy and the diversity of our communications system," says Chester. "I think one reason why the body politic is so ill can be traced back to problems with the media system and the institutions which are part of it."

If we're not careful, he says, today's captive consumer of telephone and cable television will become tomorrow's totally exposed consumer. "We're turning over the info superhighway to Madison Avenue, so they can better, more effectively serve the needs of advertisers to target individuals in discrete demographic groups."

16   As if to emphasize this, no sooner had the telecommunications restructuring bill died for the year than the computer service America Online ignited a fresh battle in cyberspace when it advertised its "upscale" subscriber list in a direct-mail trade publication. "America Online members are computer and modem owners who pay up to $200 a month to enjoy hundreds of entertaining and informative services," the ad promised. "Credit-worthy— over 85 per cent pay by credit card. . . . Mail Order Buyers!"

The popular online service drew fire from Massachusetts Representative Edward Markey, chairman of the House Subcommittee on Telecommunications and Finance, who fired off a letter to America Online president Steve Case, arguing that "comprehensive privacy protections must become part of the electronic ethics of companies doing business on the information superhighway and a fundamental right of all its travelers."

18   According to David Banisar, staff attorney for the Electronic Privacy Information Center, the America Online controversy is important because commerce on the Internet is in danger of becoming more like a shopping mall than a public street. "In shopping malls, the owners can pretty much do what they want," he warns, "and those same shopping malls are going to be collecting reams, if I can use an old-fashioned term, of personal data." With more transactions taking place over the net, more personal information about you enters cyberspace. "Even if you go into a store," says Banisar, "the odds are it's going to transfer transaction information via the same superhighway to its suppliers, to its deliverers, and to its main offices."

America Online was not unique. As Case pointed out, CompuServe, another online service, had been renting its list for years. In fact, the mailing-list business is a refined industry; lists can include explicit and implicit demographic information ranging from income to political preference to your favorite television shows. But these are relatively primitive compared to what advancing computer technology could produce: complete profiles of consumers, including brand-name inclinations, credit histories, and shopping habits. Many supermarkets already use check-cashing cards that, in conjunction with computerized scanners, keep detailed records of consumer spending habits. Will your insurance company someday be able to learn whether or not you buy beer and cigarettes?

20   First Amendment rights are already at issue in cyberspace. One major concern is whether commercial online companies deserve the broad protection of telephone companies, which have no responsibility for the content of conversations on their wires, and bookstores, which are also broadly protected, or are like publishers and broadcasters, who are held accountable for libel and other transgressions.

CompuServe, the oldest and largest online service, appears to want it both ways. In 1990, an online journal called Rumorville, produced under contract for CompuServe, published allegedly defamatory remarks about a competitor, Skuttlebut. When Skuttlebut sued for libel in a New York district court, CompuServe argued that it was more like a bookstore than a publisher, and therefore subject to a different standard of libel. The court agreed, saying a "computerized database is the functional equivalent of a more traditional news vendor." Because it did not exercise control over editorial content, it was not held liable for defamation.

22   But last year, CompuServe took a different approach toward Richard Patterson, a computer programmer and CompuServe member who believes—and claimed online—that the company had infringed on his trademark. CompuServe asked a Federal court to resolve the trademark dispute, but warned Patterson that if he discussed the suit online it would sever his CompuServe access.

This contradictory strategy indicates the general confusion over what rights and privileges are accorded in the commercial online environment.

Because the services are private, they are not automatically obligated to respect constitutional rights of privacy and freedom of expression. Several years ago, Prodigy, another service, booted subscribers who tried to fight a rate hike, and censored anti-Semitic comments in online forums. Just this year, America Online closed several feminist discussion forums for fear that young girls might stumble upon adult discussions.

24   Censorship can take insidious forms online. Users do not always understand the different regions of cyberspace, which is divided into loosely overlapping sectors ranging from the commercial services to the Internet to underground bulletin boards trafficking in stolen credit card numbers. Usenet, for example, is a sprawling electronic forum with more than 8,000 discussion groups ranging from alt.fan.NoamChomsky to alt.tv-dinosaurs .barney.die.die.die.

CompuServe and America Online both offer access to Usenet, but restrict areas—largely those dealing with sexuality—that they deem objectionable. On CompuServe, you can't subscribe to a newsgroup deemed objectionable by the company unless you know the exact title. Since many people choose their newsgroups by scanning for key words, the company automatically reserves full access for the initiated. America Online does not provide access at all to what it decides are objectionable groups. Both companies promised to provide me with the list of excluded discussion groups, but did not.

26   Less-restricted portions of the net are also censored, though generally with a lighter touch. Working within established and respected community guidelines, some Usenet groups are moderated to keep discussions focused. It's easy to appreciate the utility of the policy—communication on the net is often hailed for its casual intelligence and its potential to build community. But if every keystroke of every person who had ever surfed the Net were saved in perpetuity, it would quickly drown in its own chatter.

Of more immediate concern these days is the increasingly unruly environment as new members unfamiliar with traditions flood the Net. The Internet actually began as a military research project, but when scientists discovered its usefulness for exchanging data and computer power, the National Science Foundation took over administration. It grew largely unregulated into what has been called the largest functioning anarchy, with users establishing protocols and "netiquette."

28   Within this intellectual framework of self-governance, the move toward commercialism has met vociferous resistance. Last April, the Phoenix immigration law firm of Canter & Segal advertised its services on Usenet by placing messages in thousands of forums, the vast majority of which had no relationship to immigration. While informational postings in related areas have been tolerated on Usenet, the indiscriminate Canter & Segal posting drew a furious response. Outraged "netizens" deluged the company with angry e-mail messages called "flames." Undeterred by the communal outrage, Canter & Segal ventured onto the Net again in June, drawing the ire of a Norwegian programmer who devised a search-and-destroy

program, or "cancelbot" to wipe out the firm's transmissions. As the Net becomes more crowded and contentious, the specter of vigilante censors seems quite real.

Despite the phenomenal growth of computer networks, relatively few people are actually online. Some five million subscribe to commercial services, while as many as twenty million gain access to the Internet through universities or work. Online computing has sparked such interest because it is the most likely model for the emerging information economy. In the future, your telephone, computer, and television will all be linked, and you'll gain access to everything from the latest rap video to maps of Virginia in the 1600s stored in the Library of Congress, using the kinds of graphical interfaces being pioneered by America Online and CompuServe. But while the media hype a Golden Age of democracy spurred by the free flow of information, commercial online services resemble nothing so much as the current offerings of television and newsstands: *Time, The Atlantic,* ABC, DC Comics, the *Chicago Tribune,* Associated Press, and Reuters.

30   What would it take for a publication like *The Progressive* to get online? Brian Jaffe, director of online publications for CompuServe, the country's largest commercial online service, is firm about its priorities. "We're in business to make money," he explains. "The overall tone is going to be: You have to sell me on you."

First, *The Progressive* would have to show CompuServe that it would "add value to the service" by providing the demographic makeup of the people it was planning to reach online. Second, Jaffe looks at brand-name awareness. "When you pop up in our WHAT'S NEW—our intrusive marketing area—and I see *The Progressive* is online, come visit our area, I don't know what type of emotion that's going to stir in our two-and-a-quarter million users." Finally, Jaffe looks at "comarketing opportunities"—basically, what kind of new members *The Progressive* would offer to CompuServe—an evaluation driven by circulation and demographics. "We are an extremely powerful marketing entity," says Jaffe, citing CompuServe's phenomenal growth rate of 85,000 new members a month. Next to this, *The Progressive*'s 32,000 circulation is relatively small, a factor that he says doesn't work in its favor.

32   Still, you may yet find publications like *The Progressive* available from commercial online services. "I'm never going to turn a deaf ear, because I never know when the next winner is going to come around," says Jaffe. But, he cautions, "You're right, we don't have a lot of political-type publications online. To be quite honest with you—maybe you can convince me otherwise—but it doesn't quite fit in with the publishing formula that I'm looking for in a successful online product."

The clout of these commercial services already intimidates small publications. As a staff member from one alternative periodical said after discussing its efforts to get online. "Don't say anything about us being critical of them that could hurt their willingness to sign us on in the future."

34   This clout will only increase as the Internet moves from the public to the private sector. More than half of it is now commercial in origin, and the National Science Foundation is passing management of the remainder into private hands. The Internet has thrived in part because its flat-rate pricing has made it possible for individuals and nonprofits to take full advantage of electronic communications. Eventually, the Net will abandon flat-rate pricing, which could curtail open participation as costs rise. The booming media interest in the Internet may also be more cloud than silver lining: "It's clear to me the media industries want to use the Internet as another programming channel that they control," says Chester.

While the Clinton Administration has won praise for its information-age advocacy, it has taken a beating on privacy. "The Clinton Administration has paid some lip service to privacy issues, but it's really done almost nothing," explains Dave Banisar of the Electronic Privacy Information Center.

36   Bill Clinton's first mistake was the hugely unpopular Clipper chip proposal. Clipper is a computer chip that scrambles a message using a classified mathematical function.

Users would have numerical keys to encode and decode messages, but two agencies—the Treasury Department and the National Institute of Standards and Technology—would hold copies of the keys in escrow, providing Government access as needed. Clipper was the response of law-enforcement and national-security officials who see cheap and powerful computers making it easier for criminals and spies to break the law.

38   Many cryptographers worried that Clipper, classified and developed in secret by the National Security Agency, might not be secure, and would not sufficiently protect privacy. To get your key, law officers would not have to present a warrant—they would only have to fax a request claiming they had a warrant. Safeguards against dissemination of the key and guaranteeing destruction once the order had expired were also deemed insufficient.

The keys for every Clipper chip would be available to only a handful of people, but if these individuals were corrupted, the whole system would be compromised. NSA involvement also worried some people: Had the agency built a trapdoor into the system that would allow it special access?

40   Even the Office of Technology Assessment criticized the agency's involvement in Clipper, concluding it was "part of a long-term control strategy intended to retard the general availability of 'unbreakable' or 'hard-to-break' cryptography within the United States."

Clipper has been essentially abandoned for data encryption, but is still on the table as a standard for voice encryption. Gore is currently working to develop a compromise, but has said that the White House will not yield on the proposed key escrow, though the Government would not have to be the escrow agent.

42   Clipper is only one part of vigorous efforts by the authorities to protect their eavesdropping rights. "If you think crime is bad now, just wait and

see what happens if the FBI one day is no longer able to conduct court-approved electronic surveillance," FBI director Louis Freeh told an audience last May soon after the reintroduction of his agency's Digital Telephony in Congress.

First proposed by the Bush Administration and one of the few bills successfully pushed through the last Congress by Clinton, digital telephony requires common carriers—telephone companies—to help law-enforcement officers with appropriate court orders to listen to your conversations. It would also make transactional data—who's calling whom—easily available to law-enforcement officers. To do this, the phone companies need special equipment to ensure access to their new digital switches—equipment the legislation would buy for $500 million.

44 But is this cost-effective law enforcement? Freeh testified before the Senate in March that not a single wiretap order has been hindered by advancing technology. Since the 1968 passage of wiretap legislation, there have been about 900 Federal and state wiretaps per year, costing an average of $46,492 per tap in 1992.

Why should law-abiding citizens be concerned with wiretaps, codes, and scrambled conversations? The British royal family is certainly the most public example of the hazards of unsecured communications, but Philip Zimmermann, a cryptographic-software designer, told Congress last year that technological advances made possible massive Government intrusions on privacy. "Today," Zimmermann warned, "electronic mail is gradually replacing conventional paper mail, and is soon to be the norm for everyone, not the novelty it is today.

46 "Unlike paper mail," he added, "e-mail messages are just too easy to intercept and scan for interesting key words. This can be done easily, routinely, automatically, and undetectably on a grand scale. This is analogous to drift net fishing—making a quantitative and qualitative Orwellian difference to the health of democracy."

Among the rationales for increased electronic-monitoring powers is the need to fight computer crime. Law-enforcement officials cite a burgeoning traffic in pornography, illegally copied software, and stolen credit information, but often they have been too trigger-happy in policing a world they don't fully understand. Specific targets have been computer bulletin boards, which people dial into to obtain information or to talk.

48 Police in Munroe Falls, Ohio, confiscated the $3,000 computer of Mark Lehrer, charging that kids had seen pornography on his bulletin board, Akron Anomaly. Lehrer did have some X-rated files, but access was restricted—users had to send a copy of their driver's license to get in. A few explicit photos were in common space—Lehrer claims a filing error—so local police recruited a fifteen-year-old to gain access to the files, then busted Lehrer. But with no complaints from local parents, the charge didn't stick. Police filed new charges alleging that other photos—not even available on the bulletin board, but seized with the computer—could have depicted minors.

Lacking the money for expert testimony, Lehrer entered a guilty plea to a misdemeanor charge of possessing a criminal tool—his computer. But confiscating the computer for a misfiled picture is akin to seizing a convenience store for a misfiled copy of *Penthouse*. An *Akron Beacon* editorial asked "whether the police were protecting against a child pornographer or using the intimidating power of the police and judicial system to help themselves to a nice hunk of expensive machinery."

50   Michael Elansky ran the Ware House bulletin board in West Hartford, Connecticut. Elansky was arrested in August 1993, when police found files on his bulletin board explaining in detail the construction of various explosive devices. The files had been written four years earlier by a fifteen-year-old, and contained constitutionally protected information widely available in sources ranging from chemistry textbooks to *The Anarchist Cookbook*.

Elansky's case was compounded by his previous scrapes with the law—he eventually entered guilty pleas to parole violations—but the charges relating to the bulletin board files were never dropped. Activists maintain that his arrest and detention (Elansky could not post the $500,000 bond) were a violation of First Amendment rights and do not bode well for free speech in cyberspace.

52   "I don't think it's a police conspiracy to chill the whole Net," says Banisar of such crackdowns, "but it certainly has that result." Banisar says the most closely watched legal contest in cyberspace is that of Robert Alan Thomas and his wife, Carleen, who live in Milpitas, California, where they ran the Amateur Action Bulletin Board Service. Subscribers—3,600 in the United States and Europe—paid $99 a year, using their computers to call the Amateur Action computer and download pornographic photographs, chat with other members, and order explicit videotapes.

Then a Tennessee hacker broke into the system. Disturbed by the hard-core content, the intruder alerted the Memphis authorities, who began a sting operation. The Thomases were busted and saddled with eleven Federal obscenity charges—not in California but in Tennessee, the heart of the Bible belt. For the first time a bulletin-board operator was prosecuted where the obscene material was received instead of at its point of origin. The Thomases were convicted; the case is on appeal and could end up in the Supreme Court.

54   At issue is the Supreme Court's 1973 ruling that obscenity be judged by local community standards. This time, the Court would have to answer a new question: Where are you when you're in cyberspace? "Whatever your view of looking at nudie pictures, this is pretty chilling for everybody in the rest of the country that doesn't want to be subject to Tennessee morals," says David Banisar of the Electronic Privacy Information Center. "If I wanted to be subject to Tennessee morals, I'd move to Tennessee."

Just as Al Gore is playing an important role in the National Information Infrastructure, his father helped create the interstate highway system in the 1950s. The interstate, while it ushered in an era of great prosperity, has also been blamed for the decline of the cities and the loss of services to poor and minority communities. Many advocates fear that a poorly designed information superhighway could lead to further marginalization of the underprivileged in society.

56   The big telecommunications players are at pains to promise this won't happen, and both Pacific Telesis and AT&T-McCaw have signed commitments with community groups in California to ensure that the state's minority, low-income, inner-city and disabled populations are wired into the electronic future. But a recent study of early plans for advanced communications networks by a coalition of groups (including the National Association for the Advancement of Colored People, the Consumer Federation of America, and the Center for Media Education) suggests that poor and minority neighborhoods are already becoming victims of "electronic redlining."

"Everyone is going to need affordable access to interactive communications services to ensure that the public has access to a basic range of information," explains Jeffrey Chester. He says it's conceivable that the media could evolve so that C-SPAN is the only source of information for what's going on in Congress, making a lower-cost tier of information services vital for democracy.

58   "We don't know what a Twenty-first Century version of public television will look like, but we can start thinking about it when we look at the Internet and freenet and community radio stations," he suggests. Freenets, for example, provide access to e-mail, computer databases, and the Internet in such cities as Buffalo, Cleveland, and Seattle, through libraries and other outreach programs. "Those services are not going to become a part of the information superhighway without a real public policy to ensure that they are a viable—not marginal—part of the media system," warns Chester.

Another access question raised by the information economy is that when information is bought and sold in units, you can only know as much as you can afford. The commercial databases used by large corporations, law firms, and news services are expensive. In legal cases, in particular, this puts the well-heeled at a distinct advantage. Most of the material in legal databases consists of case law and judicial decisions in the public domain, but such companies as West Publishing maintain that they own the copyright for the page numbers of the decisions, giving them an effective monopoly in the legal database market for many states and Federal courts. Furthermore, local, state, and federal Governments maintain many valuable databases which are not currently accessible to their putative owners—the general public.

60 While this is a dark rendering of tomorrow, the future of cyberspace could be a lot more promising. Activists worldwide are already using advanced computer networks to share information and coordinate strategies. And citizens across the country could instantaneously gather information from a variety of sources uncensored by the corporate media.

But the perils of the Information Age are broad. In his book, *The Cult of Information,* Theodore Roszak reminds us that information cannot replace—

and may even obscure—knowledge, insight, and wisdom. "Every mature technology brings an immediate gain followed by enormous long-term liabilities," he writes. "How things will balance out is a matter of vigilance, moral courage, and the distribution of power."

62   Consider the story of Philip Zimmermann, a software engineer who believes in "freeware"—software given away to help people better use their computers. In 1991, Zimmermann released an encryption program called Pretty Good Privacy (PGP) to help protect electronic mail; since then it has spread all over the world. On the day that Boris Yeltsin went to war against his own parliament, Zimmermann received an e-mail message from Latvia: "Phil I wish you to know: Let it never be, but if dictatorship takes over Russia your PGP is widespread from Baltic to Far East now and will help democratic people if necessary. Thanks." But despite the worldwide availability of PGP and other encryption tools, this technology is still controlled by national-security interests. The U.S. Customs Service is currently investigating how PGP was exported.

    Testifying last year before the House Subcommittee for Economic Policy, Trade, and the Environment, Zimmermann worried that "some elements of the Government" were intent on denying citizens their privacy. "This is unsettling because in a democracy, it is possible for bad people to occasionally get elected—sometimes very bad people," said Zimmermann. "Normally, a well-functioning democracy has ways to remove these people from power. But the wrong technology infrastructure could allow such a future government to watch every move anyone makes to oppose it. It could very well be the last government we ever elect." ❖

Questions for Meaning

1. What is the relationship between privacy and democracy? How has the information superhighway made privacy more difficult to preserve?
2. Who has a stake in defining cyberspace? How might their goals differ?
3. Why have so many people been able to gain relatively easy access to the Internet?
4. Who is at risk in the electronic future? Who might be denied access to advanced communications networks?
5. Will all information become available electronically, or is some information unlikely to go online?
6. Vocabulary: convergence (8), demographic (15), defamation (21), insidious (24), vociferous (28), cryptographers (38), encryption (41), rendering (60).

Questions about Strategy

1. Consider the picture of the information superhighway with which Ness opens his essay—a picture that he then challenges. Does it fairly state a commonly held view?

2. What kind of political values does Ness invoke in this argument? What do these values reveal about the audience for whom he originally wrote?
3. How does Ness expect readers to respond to the question at the end of paragraph 19? What are the implications of this answer?
4. Ness ends his argument by suggesting that American democracy is at risk. Within the context of this essay, does this claim seem plausible?

NANCY WILLARD

ⓝPORNOGRAPHY ON THE INTERNET

Can the problem of pornography on the Internet be resolved through technology, or is it part of a larger social problem that must be addressed in our own homes and communities? Nancy Willard, author of *The Cyberethics Reader* (1996), published the following editorial on an Internet home page in 1995, attaching the following note: "I just completed this article and submitted it to our local newspaper as a guest editorial—don't know whether they will run it. As will be evident, it is addressed to those who might not have an in-depth understanding of Internet technology and the issues around pornography. I hope that it provides some helpful ideas for your thinking and discussions with people in your community." Address: nwillard@ordata.com

The issue of pornography on the Internet has received much attention lately. Unfortunately, some of the media coverage has been misleading, the technical issues are confusing, accurate information is sparse, and the issue is being sensationalized by some politicians.

2   On one hand, the extent of the problem has been greatly overexaggerated. Within the scope of all of the incredible resources that are available through the Internet, pornography is a tiny portion and quite easy to avoid. The Internet provides access to a vast amount of information and communication that is highly beneficial to our society. The Internet is not a place to be feared or avoided.

On the other hand, pornography on the Internet is clearly a problem that we must find a way to resolve. A disturbingly high amount of this pornography is not erotica, but sexual violence—images and text that glorify the sadistic sexual torture of women and the exploitation of children. It is depraved, warped, vile. While there are legitimate concerns about the extent to which government ought to dictate what people can read and see, there are limits to acceptability and much of this stuff crosses the limits. Just because some depraved individuals have the ability through new technologies to more freely share their depravity, does not mean that we, in the name of free speech, have the obligation to provide them with a conduit to our homes and communities.

4   Imposing government control through new laws will be extremely difficult. Internet technology is called open systems technology and it is just that, open and virtually impossible to control. A popular saying on the Internet is "the Internet interprets censorship as damage and routes around it." The Internet is also global, so whatever laws that might be passed in the U.S. will not have any effect beyond our borders.

Some technical background may be helpful to your understanding. There are two basic ways that you can access pornography on the Internet. Some pornography is stored on remote computers that are located somewhere on the Internet, anywhere in the world. To get to this material you either use Telnet, which allows you to login to the remote computer or you use FTP or World Wide Web to send commands to the remote computer telling it to send selected material to you.

6   The other way that pornography is transmitted is through USENET newsgroups. Newsgroups are global discussion groups that cover a wide range of topics. The newsgroup data is transmitted throughout the world. The data is downloaded by your Internet provider and is stored on their computer in a revolving manner—new data comes in, the old data moves off. The pornography is found in a hierarchy of newsgroups called "alt.sex"— alt.sex.bestiality, alt.sex.pedophilia, etc. The pornography is in the form of both text and images.

While the number of alt.sex newsgroups is small, the amount of computer data traffic they account for is high. It is estimated that 20–22% of the USENET newsgroup data feed—the data being downloaded into the local computer—is pornography. A significant portion of the alt.sex images are "teasers" that are posted as advertisements for commercial BBSs that sell pornography images. Studies on the use of the Internet have consistently shown that several of the alt.sex newsgroups are among the most popular newsgroups.

8   An Internet provider has the ability to select which newsgroups they will download. My local Internet provider does not download the alt.sex newsgroups because of the drain it would place on his resources and because his clientele are businesspeople. Schools that provide Internet access also do not download the pornographic newsgroups. Schools also block access to any known remote pornography sites and monitor students when they are accessing the Internet.

Congressional action is pending that addresses this issue. The Senate is acting in a reactionary fashion and has proposed legislation that is considered by many people to be unconstitutional and unworkable in the Internet environment—but it makes for good public posturing. The House appears to be backing legislation that instructs the Department of Justice to do more research and propose some legal and enforceable solutions. Hopefully, the House legislation will prevail. What is not needed at this time is legislation that is ill considered and quite likely to be rejected by the courts. The issues are complex and we need to take some time to fully understand them.

10   New software is coming on the market that can assist in blocking access. The software prevents access to the alt.sex newsgroups and to any of the known remote sites that host pornography. Obviously, since new sites are always being found or being established, the list of blocked sites must be kept updated.

But there are many unanswered questions. A partial list includes: Who is going to be responsible for making decisions about what is or is not pornography? How do we decide what should be allowed but only for adult access (erotica) and what is totally beyond the bounds of acceptability (sexual violence)? Should discussion groups related to gay and lesbian issues or safe sex be inaccessible to minors? Should all of these decisions be made in the home with no role for government or does government have some responsibility with respect to the regulation of materials that are truly unacceptable or the safety of minors? Should you impose liability on a system administrator who may not have actual knowledge that pornography has been placed on their system? The current legal test for pornography includes reference to "community standards." Whose community—where the material is located or where the recipient lives? Should our universities—tax-supported institutions—be downloading pornography on systems that are established to support education and research objectives? How do we limit the transmission of truly objectionable material, while preserving open expression?

12   Most of the recent attention has been focused on the issue of preventing access by minors. But clearly the problem is much more than this. Sexual violence is the fastest growing violent crime in the U.S. Family violence and child abuse are destroying the lives of many innocent people. Being able to restrict your 14-year-old daughter's access to pornography will not address the kinds of attitudes or physical abuse she may be exposed to in the "real world."

As a society we must recognize and address the fact that there are a significant number of people, primarily men, who believe that the sexual abuse and exploitation of women and children is acceptable behavior.

14   What is becoming ever more clear throughout this debate is that laws and technical fixes will only provide partial answers. What is lacking is the most significant potential restraint, namely moral and ethical values enforced by individual and organizational conscience and social rebuke. What is required is that we, as a society, and as individuals in society, internalize a set of values that embody a higher level of respect for others. This issue will not be resolved without each of us taking responsibility for our actions and calling upon other individuals and organizations within our realm of influence to also demonstrate responsible behavior.

So where can you start?

16   With yourself. Look closely inside, what are your values? Do you treat other people with respect? Do you stand up for what you know is right and

challenge what you know is wrong? Do you rely on what other people think or tell you to think or do you have an internal value system that guides your actions? Are your actions consistent with your words?

If you are a man, what is your opinion of women? Do you treat the women, your wife, your partner, your co-workers, with respect? Do you engage in sex primarily for mutual enjoyment or primarily for your own physical satisfaction? Have you ever forced or pressured a woman to engage in sex when she was not interested? What are your thoughts about young women?

18   If you are a woman, do you respect yourself enough to be assertive about your rights and needs? Or do you give in to keep the peace?

With your family. Do you talk about values with your children and are your actions in accordance with your words? Do you demonstrate to them on a daily basis your respect for others, your respect for them, and your respect for yourself? Do you expect them to obey you because you are the "boss" (external control) or do you assist them in learning how to make appropriate decisions for themselves (internal control)? Do you avoid so-called entertainment that is violent or prurient in nature and do you discuss with your children why such material is not acceptable? Do you allow your children to demonstrate lack of respect or violence towards others?

20   In your community. Are you respectful of all people regardless of their gender, color, race, religion, physical status, or sexual preference? Do you speak up when you are concerned about the actions of individuals or organizations in your community? Do you contribute time and money to those organizations that are seeking to make your community a better place for all to live in? Do you work to ensure that the children in your community have the opportunity to grow up in a happy and healthy environment? Do you support your schools and ensure that they have sufficient resources to accomplish their very vital tasks?

In cyberspace. Have you selected an Internet or online services provider that is acting responsibly and is exerting reasonable editorial control? Has the provider provided you with information and services to assist you in protecting your children from danger or from access to inappropriate material? Does the provider respond promptly to any concerns you may have? Does the provider use its resources to provide access to material that is unacceptable (i.e., is your money going to support access to the alt.sex newsgroups)? Have you taken the time to discuss with your children the dangers they may face in cyberspace and how to protect themselves and how you expect they will conduct themselves online? Have you taken the time to have your children show you the sites on the Internet that excite them and introduce you to their online friends? Do you, yourself, avoid materials that promote sexual or other forms of violence? Do you behave responsibly, respectfully, and demonstrate good netiquette, while you are online? ❖

Questions for Meaning

1. Why does Willard believe that fears about the availability of pornography on the Internet are exaggerated?
2. How does Willard distinguish between "pornography" and "erotica"? Why might it be useful to make this distinction?
3. Why is government censorship unlikely to eliminate pornography from the Internet?
4. How does Willard want readers to respond to the availability of pornography on the Internet? What does she recommend we do?
5. Vocabulary: conduit (3), pedophilia (6), reactionary (9), downloading (11), prurient (19).

Questions about Strategy

1. How does Willard establish her reason for writing? Why is it useful for her to make this reason clear?
2. In paragraph 11, Willard raises a series of questions that she does not answer. What does she achieve by raising these questions?
3. According to Willard (in paragraph 13), "we must recognize and address the fact that there are a significant number of people, primarily men, who believe that the sexual abuse and exploitation of women and children is acceptable behavior." What does Willard gain by calling attention to gender? Would her statement be more persuasive, or less, if she eliminated the reference to men?
4. How useful is the advice with which Willard concludes her argument? Does her essay persuade you to follow this advice?

ONE STUDENT'S ASSIGNMENT

Write an argument focused on whether access to the Internet should be restricted, either by the government or by service providers, in order to protect users from pornography and other disturbing material. When searching for information, consult both the World Wide Web and printed material available in the university library. Follow the plan for classical arrangement: Begin by catching the attention of your audience, then provide background information on your subject, indicate your position, provide proof for your position, respond to views different from your own, and conclude by summarizing your main points. Use MLA-style documentation, and include a list of works cited.

Regulation of the Internet
B. J. Nodzon

It's one o'clock in the morning, and you have a sociology paper discussing sexually transmitted diseases due at 8:00 A.M. Other assignments consumed your time; consequently, you failed to conduct any research beyond what was available in your textbook. You still need more current, in-depth information, but the library is closed at this late hour. As you panic over this dilemma, it hits you: the Internet. You quickly start your computer and log onto the University's system only to find that your search cannot be conducted because you used the word *sexually.* Frantically, you call a friend who lives off-campus and ask him to conduct a search on his computer, which uses a different service provider. Your friend exhausts every possible search engine for information on STDs; however, the material is restricted.

2   This scenario could easily occur since many universities block a number of entries into the Internet (Goldman 112). Many high schools also limit access to reduce the possibility of students encountering offensive material. Access to Internet information outside of universities and schools has been threatened since the U.S. Senate narrowly passed the Communications Decency Act. The Act has been called unconstitutional because its vague language apparently bans classic pieces of literature and prohibits certain topics for discussion groups. Other attempts to regulate the Internet have been made by service providers. For example, CompuServ blocked access to 200 newsgroups because of complaints from the German government about obscene content (Burton 5). Similarly, fearful that young girls might accidentally discover sexually explicit discussions, America Online dropped a number of feminist discussion forums (Ness 142). These acts have caused great debate about who should regulate the Internet—if it should be regulated at all.

Certainly, some material on the Internet is not suitable for children to view; however, this does not mean the material should be banned. I believe free speech and freedom of information should be embraced on the Internet; neither the government nor the global service providers should regulate or censor the content of the Internet. The only acceptable type of regulation is local self-regulation conducted by parents who want to monitor their children's access and by universities and schools that do not want students to use school computers for accessing nonacademic material. To help minimize illegal activity on the Internet, current obscenity and liability laws need only an amendment that will cover digital and computer networks (Burton 6).

4   The hypothetical scenario described earlier demonstrates the need for access to updated information during all hours of the day. With updated information, students and researchers can learn more about their topics and can provide their readers with current information. Even a good library cannot provide as much current material as the Internet can. Through accessible information on the

Internet, students and researchers who are pressed for time will no longer be constricted by the hours of the library or the limits of its collection. The Internet also assists people in the American workforce. For instance, doctors can obtain updated medical information and view reports from other physicians around the country, and businesspeople can search for financial and stock information. All of these people utilize the Internet's advancements in the accessing and distribution of information—and no one can accurately predict what information will need to be consulted in the future.

The new technology of the Internet also helps Americans practice our historically important right to free speech. People now have a new medium to view a wide range of opinions and ideas, which helps them discover, learn, and formulate their own opinions on important issues. Even people with established ideas need to examine opposing viewpoints in order to evolve or embrace new ideas. Through the global reaches of the Internet, people have an opportunity to research controversial issues and become more informed, active participants in national and international society.

6   Some people argue that the federal government should apply legislation prohibiting offensive material on the Internet. However, the global reaches of the Internet make any form of government legislation difficult to enforce. "(M)aterial prohibited in one country can be stored on a server in another and then accessed from the first and . . . , at present, there is little that governments can do about this" (Burton 6). International legislation is also unworkable because each country holds different standards when considering offensive material.

Since international legislation is impossible, many people suggest that global service providers should regulate the Internet. However, this causes many of the same concerns expressed with government legislation because service providers cannot prohibit access to material deemed offensive in a specific country. Once again, this causes problems because different standards prevail in different countries. Furthermore, with the power to regulate the Internet, service providers have the opportunity to block material for self-serving purposes. Hypothetically, America Online could block a discussion group that criticizes the increased prices of the service. This type of control violates free speech and places too much responsibility on the server.

8   Service providers have a legitimate concern that they might be found guilty of distributing offensive material over the Internet. Unfortunately, many service providers overcompensate by blocking material and discussion groups that are perfectly legal. However, the Supreme Court's decision in *Smith v. California* illustrates the Court's belief that distributors of large amounts of information

should not be held liable for any random amounts of offensive material contained therein (Goldman 1099). Furthermore, the Electronic Communications Privacy Act of 1986 gives systems operators a legal reason not to know the content of the files on their bulletin boards. The Act states that a system operator is not entitled to divulge data contained in an electronic communication service to any outside source (Goldman 1100–1101). Service providers are also not guilty of distribution because the people who access the offensive material are actively seeking it. Systems operators merely make the material available for users to take (Goldman 1099). Therefore, service providers cannot be held liable and should not make themselves responsible for the content of the Internet.

I agree that service providers should not ignore users' complaints about offensive material. If someone notifies the service provider about offensive or illegal material on the Internet, then the service provider is obligated to notify the FCC. I also concede that there are legitimate reasons why service providers can prohibit material from the Internet. For instance, many operators are forced to shut down web pages and discussion groups because of viruses or systems overload. These are acceptable reasons to block access to material on the Internet. However, the content of a web page or discussion group should never be the reason for a service provider to block access.

10   I am sympathetic to many people's concerns about the welfare of children and what they might encounter on the Internet. Children should not be exposed to or accidentally stumble upon material unsuitable for their age. Therefore, special programs, such as NetNanny, CyberSitter, and SurfWatch, can be utilized by parents to prohibit content that may be unsuitable for their children (Burton 10). This type of regulation begins with the user and does not require regulation from the government or service providers. This local regulation by individuals will not interfere with the millions of other Internet users and will help protect children.

I also understand the schools' and universities' wish to limit access to nonacademic material on the Internet. Some aspects of the Internet are unsuitable in an academic environment and may cause extra strain on the local system. Therefore, future software will almost certainly be designed for universities to restrict access from school facilities. The standards and type of regulation will be decided by each university and will not interfere with the millions of other Internet users.

12   The wish to regulate the Internet is valid. However, how we regulate the Internet could change our ideas of free speech and freedom of information. Regulation by a single government or by a single global service provider is impossible due to the global reaches of the Internet. Strict regulation of the Internet is also

potentially unconstitutional in America because it could violate our constitutional guarantee of free speech. Current obscenity laws will sufficiently govern the Internet; however, some offensive, yet legal, material will still circulate on it. Therefore, current software and soon-to-be-developed programs can be utilized by parents and universities to block unsuitable material. Regulation standards must be set locally, or our freedom of speech and information will be compromised.

Works Cited

Burton, Paul. "Content on the Internet: Free or Fettered?" Online. Internet. 12 Apr. 1996. Available FTP:http://www.dis.strath.ac.uk/people/paul /CIL96.html

Goldman, Robert F. "Put Another Log on the Fire, There's a Chill on the Internet: The Effect of Applying Current Anti-Obscenity Laws to Online Communications." Georgia Law Review. 29 (1995): 1075–1120.

Ness, Erik. "BigBrother@cyberspace." The Informed Argument. Brief ed. Ed. Robert K. Miller. Fort Worth: Harcourt, 1999. 138–148.

SUGGESTIONS FOR WRITING

1. In response to the argument by Jon Katz, write a Bill of Rights for parents.
2. Drawing on the argument by Nancy Willard, write an argument focused on eliminating pornography from the Internet.
3. Write an essay defining "obscenity."
4. Drawing on Kadi and Ness, write an essay describing problems on the information superhighway.
5. Kadi describes herself as a "cyber-junkie." Write an essay defining what this term means to you.
6. Interview the systems operator at your school or workplace and then report what you learn about the nature of the computer system you access when at school or at work.
7. Using three different search engines, do research on regulating the Internet and then write an essay comparing your results.
8. Visit a high school in your area and interview students and teachers about the quality of the school's computer resources. What kind of computer instruction is available there? Write an evaluation of how well students at the school are being prepared to access information electronically.
9. Write an essay in which you teach how to find information on the Internet. Assume that your audience can get access to a network but has never previously used a computer for anything besides word processing. Technology makes this audience nervous, so try to be reassuring.

Collaborative Project

Investigate how much information about the members of your writing team is available to anyone with access to a computer and your Social Security numbers, phone numbers, driver's license numbers, medical record numbers, or electronic addresses. Check such sources as the records office at your school, the personnel department of your employer, the Department of Motor Vehicles, your banks, and a credit bureau. If you receive unsolicited catalogs in the mail, find out how these companies got your mailing address. Report your findings in an essay focused on the nature of privacy in an electronic age.

SECTION 2

SEXUAL HARASSMENT: DEFINING THE BOUNDARIES

ANNE B. FISHER

ⓥ SEXUAL HARASSMENT: WHAT TO DO?

How should businesses respond to the problem of sexual harassment in the workplace? And what does "sexual harassment" mean? Anne B. Fisher explores these and other questions in the following 1993 article from *Fortune* magazine, a well-respected business monthly. As you read, note what Fisher reports about the law and how it is changing.

Tailhook. New rules on college campuses against romances between professors and students. A controversial book that purports to tell the real story of Anita Hill and Clarence Thomas. And of course that staple of late-night-TV jokes, Senator Bob Packwood.* In the shift and glimmer of the media kaleidoscope, sexual harassment is a constant glinting shard.

2   Yet no headline-making subject in recent memory has stirred so much confusion. No doubt you've read your company's policy statement and, from just under its surface, you feel the legal eagles' gimlet stare. But what does sexual harassment really mean? Managers of both sexes are sifting through the past and fretting about next week. Was it all right to say I liked her dress? Is it okay to ask him out to lunch to talk about that project? Should I just stop touching anybody, even if it's only a congratulatory pat on the back? For that big client meeting in Houston, wouldn't it be less risky to fly out with Frank than with Francine? Or, for female managers, vice versa?

If you think you've got reason to worry, you probably don't; the ones who do are usually unaware they have a problem. But right in your own organization, maybe even in your own department, your hallway, your pod, somebody may be so befuddled and self-destructive as to miss the point entirely. Sexual harassment is not really about sex. It's about power—more to the point, the abuse of power.

Blanket statement

* Senator Bob Packwood of Oregon was accused of sexually harassing many of the women who worked in his office. He was widely criticized and eventually resigned from office after the Senate Ethics Committee voted to expel him.

4   Imagine it this way. Suppose one of your most senior and valued people has a little problem. Great producer, terrific salesperson, meets every goal, exceeds every guideline, but, well, there's this one glitch: He steals things. Every time he leaves an office he takes something with him—a pen, a coffee mug, a book, some change that was lying around. He's been at it a long time, can't seem to help it and, anyway, he's a good guy, a *great* guy. You're his boss. What are you going to do when he walks off with somebody's $3,000 note-book computer? That's grand larceny, and the victim is hopping mad.

For more and more managers these days, the analogy fits. Let's sup-pose the fellow isn't stealing material things but rather chipping away at the human dignity and professional self-respect of other people. Can't seem to resist patting fannies and whispering innuendoes. Told a subordinate he'd like to negotiate her raise at the local No-Tell Motel. Cornered a female col-league and loudly compared her physical attributes with those of the cur-rent Playmate of the Month. All the time he's producing great stuff. But the whispering behind his back is getting louder; the troops are murmuring about calling the lawyers and human resources people. What do you do with this guy? (Alas, despite a much publicized $1 million jury award in May to a male plaintiff harassed by his female boss in Los Angeles, harassers are, in nine cases out of ten, guys.)

6   Talk to him, of course. If that doesn't work, and odds are it won't, turn him in to the human resources person in charge of these matters. And do it pronto. Otherwise you could be liable along with your employer. Un-solicited, unwelcome, and downright extortionate sexual demands are as illegal as stealing computers. So are purposeful and repeated efforts to intimidate colleagues by transforming the office into a remake of *Animal House*—what the law calls "hostile environment" harassment. He who steals my briefcase, to paraphrase Shakespeare, steals trash. But the loss of some-one's dignity, productivity, and eagerness to come to work in the morning is a theft not only from the person robbed of it, but from the company too.

Sexual harassment is not a compliment on anyone's wardrobe or a friendly pat on the shoulder. It is not the occasional tasteless remark or care-less quip. It is not even asking someone for a date the second time, when she's already said no once. To stand up in court, a harassment charge must rest on either a persistent and calculated pattern of antisocial behavior or a single *quid pro quo*—"You'll never get anywhere in this company unless you sleep with me"—that is so egregious as to leave no room for misinterpretation.

8   The courts have recognized sexual harassment as an offense under Title VII since 1977. But the number of complaints filed with the Equal Em-ployment Opportunity Commission has nearly doubled in the past five years, to 10,532 in 1992. It's debatable whether that rise occurred because instances of harassment increased or whether events like the Hill–Thomas hearings encouraged people who had long remained silent to speak up. The EEOC doesn't keep a record of how many cases end up in litigation; many are settled on the courthouse steps. One thing is certain. The consequences for corporations are costly.

Research by Freada Klein Associates, a workplace-diversity consulting firm in Cambridge, Massachusetts, shows that 90 percent of Fortune 500 companies have dealt with sexual harassment complaints. More than a third have been sued at least once, and about a quarter have been sued over and over again. Klein estimates that the problem costs the average large corporation $6.7 million a year.

10   Bettina Plevan, an attorney at Proskauer Rose Goetz & Mendelsohn in New York City, specializes in defending companies against sexual harassment lawsuits. She says employers spend an average of $200,000 on each complaint that is investigated in-house and found to be valid, whether or not it ever gets to court. Richard Hafets, a labor lawyer at Piper & Marbury in Baltimore, believes sexual harassment could be tomorrow's asbestos, costing American business $1 billion in fees and damages in the next five years.

But the costs of sexual harassment go well beyond anything that can be measured on a profit-and-loss statement. Women, often still treated like interlopers in the office, say they feel vulnerable to the myriad subtle—and not so subtle—sexual power trips some men use to keep them in their place. At an Aetna Life & Casualty golfing party last September, four executives vented their resentment of female managers' presence at what had traditionally been an all-male event. Their mildest offense—and the only one we're halfway willing to describe in a magazine your kids might see—was calling women executives "sluts." In response Aetna demoted two of the men and asked the two others to resign.

12   Jeannine Sandstrom, a senior vice president of the executive recruiting firm Lee Hecht Harrison in Dallas, knows of instances where harassers were caught because they sent X-rated messages to their victims via voice mail or e-mail. Marvels Sandstrom: "How self-destructive do you have to be to do something like this, knowing how easy it is to trace?"

In most cases harassment is more subtle—and far more difficult to prove. As agonizing as it may be, women have an obligation to speak up and tell someone who is hounding them to stop it. Although federal law defines sexual harassment as "unwelcome" behavior, the courts say it doesn't count as such unless the offender knows it's unwelcome. Yet a 1991 study by two professors at the University of St. Thomas in St. Paul, Minnesota, revealed that, among women in a nationwide survey who said they had been victims of sexual harassment, only 34 percent told the harasser to knock it off; just 2 percent filed a formal complaint.

14   With the economy in its current shaky state, many women may be too fearful of losing their jobs to speak up. Or they may be reluctant to be seen as whiners, either by their peers or by the people above them. But if a woman wants to file a grievance, it's important to be able to prove that she told the perpetrator to back off. Some experts suggest tape-recording the conversation or sending a registered letter (return receipt requested) detailing the offending behavior and declaring it not OK. This helps in any follow-up by human resources or legal staff, even in cases where witnesses or other direct proof of the harassment are available.

As for men, the majority of whom wouldn't dream of harassing anybody, they are terrified of being falsely accused—with some reason. "What I'm seeing lately is that companies are overreacting, and accusers are believed on the basis of very little evidence or none at all," says Ellen Wagner, an attorney and author who specializes in labor law. "And the ultimate punishment, termination, is a first resort rather than a last one."

16   Consider the case of Louis Kestenbaum. From 1977 to 1984, Kestenbaum was vice president in charge of guest operations at a secluded ranch and spa that Pennzoil operated in northern New Mexico. In January 1984, someone wrote an anonymous letter to Pennzoil's top management accusing Kestenbaum of sexual harassment and other misdeeds. Kestenbaum denied the allegations but was fired anyway. He sued Pennzoil and won $500,000 in damages for wrongful discharge. The reason? Pennzoil's in-house investigator admitted in court that she had relied on rumor and innuendo in compiling the sexual-harassment report that got Kestenbaum the ax. "No attempt was made to evaluate the credibility of the persons interviewed," wrote the judge.

Both sexes sometimes feel they're stumbling around in a minefield, lost in enemy territory without a helicopter. What makes the terrain so treacherous is that people have an inconvenient way of seeing the same behavior quite differently. Margaret Regan is a Towers Perrin partner who has conducted a senior-management training program called Respect at Work for dozens of corporations. She points out that some of what might look like sexual harassment is in reality an innocent error arising from past experience. "My favorite example is when we ask a group of men and women, "How many times is it all right to ask someone out after they've said no once?" says Regan. "In one class I led, one of the men said, 'Ten.' The women were appalled. They said, '*Ten times?* No way! Twice is enough!' "

18   It turned out, when he got a chance to explain his answer, that the offending fellow had to ask 10 or 12 times before the girl of his dreams agreed to go to the senior prom with him in 1959. It worked out fine: They've been married for 32 years. "Naturally ten times seemed reasonable to him," says Regan. "So much of what people think about these things comes from stuff they grew up with—and just never had any reason to question."

Consultants who design sexual harassment workshops, and managers who have attended them, agree on one thing: The best training gives participants a chance to talk to each other, instead of just listening to a lecture or watching a film. In classes where men and women are asked to compare their impressions of the same hypothetical situation, real revelations can occur.

20   Perhaps not surprisingly, Aetna has stepped up its training program since the infamous golfing incident last fall. Anthony Guerriero, 34, a pension consultant at the company, took the course in January. He says, "The guys in the class were absolutely not resistant to it, not at all. In fact, it's a relief to have someone spell out exactly what sexual harassment is. The men in my session were all saying, 'It's about time.' "

Male managers aren't the only ones who benefit from the classes. Women are sometimes startled to find how widely their perceptions differ from those of other women. Janet Kalas, 45, director of Medicare administration at Aetna, has 300 people reporting to her. "What startled me about the training was how tolerant I am," she says. In one group-discussion exercise, the instructor described an imaginary scenario in which a male and a female colleague, both married to others, are out of town on business. Late in the evening, they're still working on a client presentation for the next morning, and they decide to finish it in the female manager's hotel room. Recalls Kalas, "My reaction was, Well, that's practical. What's the big deal? But other people, men and women both, were saying, 'My gosh, don't do that, it's like an *invitation* to this guy.' I was surprised."

22   Towers Perrin recently queried executives at 600 major U.S. companies and found that about half planned to increase the amount of sexual harassment training they give managers and employees. A dozen or so big corporations have already built shining reputations among consultants and researchers for the quality, creativity, and overall earnestness of their training programs. Among them: Du Pont, Federal Express, General Mills, Levi-Strauss, Merck, and Syntex. But will they talk about what they're doing? Not a chance. "Nobody likes to acknowledge that this problem even exists," says Robert Steed, who runs a consulting firm in Westchester County, New York, that specializes in sexual-harassment training. "It makes people queasy. So their view is, the less said the better." Adds a public relations manager at a Fortune 500 company: "The general feeling is, what if we get written up somewhere as having this terrific training program—and then we get sued a week later? In other words, no comment."

For a company's policy to do any good, much less be taken seriously in a courtroom, employees have to understand it. Barbara Spyridon Pope, the Navy assistant secretary who almost single-handedly exposed the Tailhook scandal, recently established a consulting firm in Washington, D.C., to advise corporate clients on how to communicate their sexual-harassment guidelines to the troops. Her surveys show that 60 percent to 90 percent of U.S. workers know there is a policy but haven't the foggiest what it says. "Having a policy is fine, but by itself it isn't enough," says Pope. "The Navy had a policy too."

24   Sitting people down to discuss their differences on this issue is more than a therapeutic parlor game. Case law over the past decade has established that a company with a well-defined anti-sexual-harassment stance can escape liability for hostile-environment harassment. No wonder, then, that you keep getting all those policy memos and invitations to sign up for workshops. But to prevail in court, companies must also have clear procedures for handling complaints when they arise. Typically, employers choose an impartial ombudsperson, usually in the human resources department, to hear and investigate charges before the lawyers get into the act. If the complaint seems legitimate, the company must then take what the judge in a pivotal 1986 case, *Hunter* v. *Allis-Chalmers,* called "immediate and appropriate action."

Depending on the circumstances, this might range from transferring the harassed or the harasser to a different department, to docking the harasser a couple of weeks' pay, to firing the guilty party outright.

This fall the Supreme Court will hear *Harris* v. *Forklift Systems,* its first sexual harassment case since 1986. The suit was filed by Teresa Harris, who left her job at a Nashville truck-leasing company after months of crude remarks and propositions from the firm's president. The matter was dismissed by a federal judge in Tennessee and ended up in federal appeals court in Cincinnati, where the dismissal was upheld. Reason: Ms. Harris had not proven that she was psychologically damaged by her boss's behavior.

26   If psychological damage becomes the new standard in harassment cases, which is what the high court has agreed to decide, plaintiffs will have a far harder time winning. Says Anne Clark, an attorney for the National Organization for Women: "You shouldn't have to suffer a nervous breakdown before you can make a claim." Lawyers who represent companies reply that a decision in favor of the psychological-damage standard would cut down on frivolous suits. To which working women are apt to say: "Frivolous? Nobody in her right mind would have her name dragged through the dirt over a frivolous charge!"

No matter how the court rules, managers and employees would do well to keep their own responsibilities in mind. For actual or potential harassers that means: Watch it, buster. For women, it means: Speak up. For their bosses, the best advice is: Get help. Says Susan Crawford, a partner at Holtzmann Wise & Shepard in Palo Alto, California: "I've found that managers too often are reluctant to refer a complaint to human resources. Instead they try to handle it themselves. But bosses need to see that this is a complicated issue with a lot of pitfalls, and it is not a sign of failure on their part to say, 'Hey, I need help with this. I'm not the expert here.' " The people in your company who really know where all the pitfalls are—and who will try to be fair to everybody—are not in your department. They are probably upstairs somewhere. Call them.

28   For all the seriousness of the issue, it would be a great pity if men and women got to the point of giving up on workplace friendships altogether—a point some men say privately they've already reached. Remember Rob, Buddy, and Sally on the old *Dick Van Dyke Show?* Okay, it was way back in the supposedly benighted early Sixties, but those three were a great professional team, and they were pals. For men and women in corporate America, there could be far worse role models. It will be a sad day, if it ever comes, when people are too nervous to ask a pal out for a drink.   ❖

Questions for Meaning

1. According to Fisher, what is sexual harassment ultimately about?
2. What quotation from Shakespeare is paraphrased in paragraph 6?
3. If a woman is being harassed by a man, why is it important that she make it clear to him that she finds his behavior objectionable?

4. What kind of training is most likely to help men and women avoid harassment in the workplace?
5. Why is it advantageous for companies to have clearly defined harassment policies?
6. Vocabulary: gimlet (2), innuendoes (5), extortionate (6), quip (7), egregious (7), interlopers (11), myriad (11), infamous (20), ombudsperson (24), pivotal (24), benighted (28).

Questions about Strategy

1. Consider the analogy in paragraph 4. Fisher states that it works for many managers. Does it work for you?
2. What is the implication of the statistics quoted in paragraph 13?
3. How reputable are the sources cited in this article?
4. How appropriate is the allusion in paragraph 28? Who is most likely to understand it? What does this allusion reveal about Fisher's sense of audience?

ELLEN FRANKEL PAUL

BARED BUTTOCKS AND FEDERAL CASES

What kinds of legal protection can people expect from behavior they find offensive? According to Ellen Frankel Paul, "A distinction must be restored between morally offensive behavior and behavior that causes serious harm." As you read her article, note the distinction that she makes. Paul teaches political science at Bowling Green State University. Her books include *Property Rights and Eminent Domain* (1987) and *Equality and Gender: The Comparable Worth Debate* (1988). The following article was first published in *Society* in 1991.

Women in American society are victims of sexual harassment in alarming proportions. Sexual harassment is an inevitable corollary to class exploitation; as capitalists exploit workers, so do males in positions of authority exploit their female subordinates. Male professors, supervisors, and apartment managers in ever increasing numbers take advantage of the financial dependence and vulnerability of women to extract sexual concessions.

2 These are the assertions that commonly begin discussions of sexual harassment. For reasons that will be adumbrated below, dissent from the prevailing view is long overdue. Three recent episodes will serve to frame this disagreement.

  Valerie Craig, an employee of Y & Y Snacks, Inc., joined several co-workers and her supervisor for drinks after work one day in July of 1978.

Her supervisor drove her home and proposed that they become more intimately acquainted. She refused his invitation for sexual relations, whereupon he said that he would "get even" with her. Ten days after the incident she was fired from her job. She soon filed a complaint of sexual harassment with the Equal Employment Opportunity Commission (EEOC), and the case wound its way through the courts. Craig prevailed, the company was held liable for damages, and she received back pay, reinstatement, and an order prohibiting Y & Y from taking reprisals against her in the future.

4   Carol Zabowicz, one of only two female forklift operators in a West Bend Co. warehouse, charged that her co-workers over a four-year period from 1978–1982 sexually harassed her by such acts as: asking her whether she was wearing a bra; two of the men exposing their buttocks between ten and twenty times; a male co-worker grabbing his crotch and making obscene suggestions or growling; subjecting her to offensive and abusive language; and exhibiting obscene drawings with her initials on them. Zabowicz began to show symptoms of physical and psychological stress, necessitating several medical leaves, and she filed a sexual-harassment complaint with the EEOC. The district court judge remarked that "the sustained, malicious, and brutal harassment meted out . . . was more than merely unreasonable; it was malevolent and outrageous." The company knew of the harassment and took corrective action only after the employee filed a complaint with the EEOC. The company, was, therefore, held liable, and Zabowicz was awarded back pay for the period of her medical absence, and a judgment that her rights were violated under the Civil Rights Act of 1964.

On September 17, 1990, Lisa Olson, a sports reporter for *The Boston Herald,* charged five football players of the just-defeated New England Patriots with sexual harassment with making sexually suggestive and offensive remarks to her when she entered their locker room to conduct a post-game interview. The incident amounted to nothing short of "mind rape," according to Olson. After vociferous lamentations in the media, the National Football League fined the team and its players $25,000 each. The National Organization for Women called for a boycott of Remington electric shavers because the owner of the company, Victor Kiam, also owns the Patriots and allegedly displayed insufficient sensitivity at the time when the episode occurred.

6   All these incidents are indisputably disturbing. In an ideal world—one needless to say far different from the one that we inhabit or are ever likely to inhabit—women would not be subjected to such treatment in the course of their work. Women, and men as well, would be accorded respect by co-workers and supervisors, their feelings would be taken into account, and their dignity would be left intact. For women to expect reverential treatment in the workplace is utopian, yet they should not have to tolerate outrageous, offensive sexual overtures and threats as they go about earning a living.

One question that needs to be pondered is: What kinds of undesired sexual behavior should women be protected against by law? That is, what kind of actions are deemed so outrageous and violate a woman's rights to such extent that the law should intervene, and what actions should be considered inconveniences of life, to be morally condemned but not adjudicated? A subsidiary question concerns the type of legal remedy appropriate for the wrongs that do require redress. Before directly addressing these questions, it might be useful to diffuse some of the hyperbole adhering to the sexual-harassment issue.

8   Surveys are one source of this hyperbole. If their results are accepted at face value, they lead to the conclusion that women are disproportionately victims of legions of sexual harassers. A poll by the Albuquerque *Tribune* found that nearly 80 percent of the respondents reported that they or someone they knew had been victims of sexual harassment. The Merit Systems Protection Board determined that 42 percent of the women (and 14 percent of men) working for the federal government had experienced some form of unwanted sexual attention between 1985 and 1987, with unwanted "sexual teasing" identified as the most prevalent form. A Defense Department survey found that 64 percent of women in the military (and 17 percent of the men) suffered "uninvited and unwanted sexual attention" within the previous year. The United Methodist Church established that 77 percent of its clergywomen experienced incidents of sexual harassment, with 41 percent of these naming a pastor or colleague as the perpetrator, and 31 percent mentioning church social functions as the setting.

A few caveats concerning polls in general, and these sorts of polls in particular, are worth considering. Pollsters looking for a particular social ill tend to find it, usually in gargantuan proportions. (What fate would lie in store for a pollster who concluded that child abuse, or wife beating, or mistreatment of the elderly had dwindled to the point of negligibility!) Sexual harassment is a notoriously ill-defined and almost infinitely expandable concept, including everything from rape to unwelcome neck massaging, discomfiture upon witnessing sexual overtures directed at others, yelling at and blowing smoke in the ears of female subordinates, and displays of pornographic pictures in the workplace. Defining sexual harassment, as the United Methodists did, as "any sexually related behavior that is unwelcome, offensive or which fails to respect the rights of others," the concept is broad enough to include everything from "unsolicited suggestive looks or leers [or] pressures for dates" to "actual sexual assaults or rapes." Categorizing everything from rape to "looks" as sexual harassment makes us all victims, a state of affairs satisfying to radical feminists, but not very useful for distinguishing serious injuries from the merely trivial.

10   Yet, even if the surveys exaggerate the extent of sexual harassment, however defined, what they do reflect is a great deal of tension between the sexes. As women in ever increasing numbers entered the workplace in

the last two decades, as the women's movement challenged alleged male hegemony and exploitation with ever greater intemperance, and as women entered previously all-male preserves from the board rooms to the coal pits, it is lamentable, but should not be surprising, that this tension sometimes takes sexual form. Not that sexual harassment on the job, in the university, and in other settings is a trivial or insignificant matter, but a sense of proportion needs to be restored and, even more importantly, distinctions need to be made. In other words, sexual harassment must be de-ideologized. Statements that paint nearly all women as victims and all men and their patriarchal, capitalist system as perpetrators, are ideological fantasy. Ideology blurs the distinction between being injured—being a genuine victim—and merely being offended. An example is this statement by Catharine A. MacKinnon, a law professor and feminist activist:

> Sexual harassment perpetuates the interlocked structure by which women have been kept sexually in thrall to men and at the bottom of the labor market. Two forces of American society converge: men's control over women's sexuality and capital's control over employees' work lives. Women historically have been required to exchange sexual services for material survival, in one form or another. Prostitution and marriage as well as sexual harassment in different ways institutionalize this arrangement.

Such hyperbole needs to be diffused and distinctions need to be drawn. Rape, a nonconsensual invasion of a person's body, is a crime clear and simple. It is a violation of the right to the physical integrity of the body (the right to life, as John Locke or Thomas Jefferson would have put it). Criminal law should and does prohibit rape. Whether it is useful to call rape "sexual harassment" is doubtful, for it makes the latter concept overly broad while trivializing the former.

12 Intimidation in the workplace of the kind that befell Valerie Craig— that is, extortion of sexual favors by a supervisor from a subordinate by threatening to penalize, fire, or fail to reward—is what the courts term *quid pro quo** sexual harassment. Since the mid-1970s, the federal courts have treated this type of sexual harassment as a form of sex discrimination in employment proscribed under Title VII of the Civil Rights Act of 1964. A plaintiff who prevails against an employer may receive such equitable remedies as reinstatement and back pay, and the court can order the company to prepare and disseminate a policy against sexual harassment. Current law places principal liability on the company, not the harassing supervisor, even when higher management is unaware of the harassment and, thus, cannot take any steps to prevent it.

Quid pro quo sexual harassment is morally objectionable and analogous to extortion: The harasser extorts property (i.e., use of the

---

* Latin for "one thing in return for another."

woman's body) through the leverage of fear for her job. The victim of such behavior should have legal recourse, but serious reservations can be held about rectifying these injustices through the blunt instrument of Title VII: In egregious cases the victim is left less than whole (for back pay will not compensate her for ancillary losses), and no prospects for punitive damages are offered to deter would-be harassers. Even more distressing about Title VII is the fact that the primary target of litigation is not the actual harasser, but rather the employer. This places a double burden on a company. The employer is swindled by the supervisor because he spent his time pursuing sexual gratification and thereby impairing the efficiency of the workplace by mismanaging his subordinates, and the employer must endure lengthy and expensive litigation, pay damages, and suffer loss to its reputation. It would be fairer to both the company and the victim to treat sexual harassment as a tort—that is, as a private wrong or injury for which the court can assess damages. Employers should be held vicariously liable only when they know of an employee's behavior and do not try to redress it.

14 As for the workplace harassment endured by Carol Zabowicz—the bared buttocks, obscene portraits, etc.—that too should be legally redressable. Presently, such incidents also fall under the umbrella of Title VII, and are termed hostile environment sexual harassment, a category accepted later than *quid pro quo* and with some judicial reluctance. The main problem with this category is that it has proven too elastic: cases have reached the courts based on everything from off-color jokes to unwanted, persistent sexual advances by co-workers. A new tort of sexual harassment would handle these cases better. Only instances above a certain threshold of egregiousness or outrageousness would be actionable. In other words, the behavior that the plaintiff found offensive would also have to be offensive to the proverbial "reasonable man" of the tort law. That is, the behavior would have to be objectively injurious rather than merely subjectively offensive. The defendant would be the actual harasser not the company, unless it knew about the problem and failed to act. Victims of scatological jokes, leers, unwanted offers of dates, and other sexual annoyances would no longer have their day in court.

A distinction must be restored between morally offensive behavior and behavior that causes serious harm. Only the latter should fall under the jurisdiction of criminal or tort law. Do we really want legislators and judges delving into our most intimate private lives, deciding when a look is a leer, and when a leer is a Civil Rights Act offense? Do we really want courts deciding, as one recently did, whether a school principal's disparaging remarks about a female school district administrator was sexual harassment and, hence, a breach of Title VII, or merely the act of a spurned and vengeful lover? Do we want judges settling disputes such as the one that arose at a car dealership after a female employee turned down a male co-worker's offer of a date and his colleagues retaliated by calling her offensive names and embarrassing her in front of customers? Or another case in which a female shipyard worker complained of an "offensive working environment" because of the prevalence of pornographic material on the docks? Do we want the state to prevent or compensate us for any behavior that someone might find offensive? Should people have a legally enforceable right not to be offended by others? At some point, the price for such protection is the loss of both liberty and privacy rights.

16   Workplaces are breeding grounds of envy, personal grudges, infatuation, and jilted loves, and beneath a fairly high threshold of outrageousness, these travails should be either suffered in silence, complained of to higher management, or left behind as one seeks other employment. No one, female or male, can expect to enjoy a working environment that is perfectly stress-free, or to be treated always and by everyone with kindness and respect. To the extent that sympathetic judges have encouraged women to seek monetary compensation for slights and annoyances, they have not done them a great service. Women need to develop a thick skin in order to survive and prosper in the workforce. It is patronizing to think that they need to be recompensed by male judges for seeing a few pornographic pictures on a wall. By their efforts to extend sexual-harassment charges to even the most trivial behavior, the radical feminists send a message that women are not resilient enough to ignore the run-of-the-mill, churlish provocation from male co-workers. It is difficult to imagine a suit by a longshoreman complaining of mental stress due to the display of nude male centerfolds by female co-workers. Women cannot expect to have it both ways: equality where convenient, but special dispensations when the going gets rough. Equality has its price and that price may include unwelcome sexual advances, irritating and even intimidating sexual jests, and lewd and obnoxious colleagues.

Egregious acts—sexual harassment per se—must be legally redressable. Lesser but not trivial offenses, whether at the workplace or in other more social settings, should be considered moral lapses for which the offending party receives opprobrium, disciplinary warnings, or penalties, depending on the setting and the severity. Trivial offenses, dirty jokes, sexual overtures, and sexual innuendoes do make many women feel intensely discomfited, but, unless they become outrageous through persistence or content, these too should be taken as part of life's annoyances. The perpetrators should be either endured, ignored, rebuked, or avoided, as circumstances and personal inclination dictate. Whether Lisa Olson's experience in the locker room of the Boston Patriots falls into the second or third category is debatable. The media circus triggered by the incident was certainly out of proportion to the event.

18   As the presence of women on road gangs, construction crews, and oil rigs becomes a fact of life, the animosities and tensions of this transition period are likely to abate gradually. Meanwhile, women should "lighten up," and even dispense a few risqué barbs of their own, a sure way of taking the fun out of it for offensive male bores.   ❖

Questions for Meaning

1. Explain the analogy in paragraph 1. What parallel can be drawn between sexual harassment and "class exploitation"?
2. Which of the cases discussed in paragraphs 3 through 5 are clearly illegal in Paul's view?
3. Why is Paul skeptical of statistics gathered by pollsters?
4. According to Paul, why has sexual harassment in the workplace become evident?
5. Why does Paul question prosecuting sexual harassment cases under Title VII of the Civil Rights Act of 1964?
6. On what grounds does Paul argue that women should be prepared to accept a degree of inappropriate behavior in the workplace?
7. Vocabulary: corollary (1), adumbrated (2), malevolent (4), vociferous (5), hyperbole (8), hegemony (10), patriarchal (10), proscribed (12), extortion (13), egregious (13), scatological (14), churlish (16), opprobrium (17).

Questions about Strategy

1. Paul opens her argument with the views she challenges. What is the advantage of this strategy?
2. Does Paul treat sexual harassment lightly, or does she recognize that women have cause for concern?
3. Consider paragraphs 8 and 9. How effectively does Paul challenge statistics showing a high rate of sexual harassment?
4. In paragraph 15, Paul asks, "Do we want the state to prevent or compensate us for any behavior that someone might find offensive?" What answer does she expect to this question? Has she brought you to the point where you are prepared to give it?

HARSH LUTHAR AND ANTHONY TOWNSEND

MAN HANDLING

"Man Handling" was first published in *The National Review,* a monthly magazine known for advocating politically conservative positions. When it appeared there in 1995, Harsh Luthar was an assistant professor of management at Bryant College and Anthony Townsend was an assistant professor of management at the University of Nevada, Las Vegas. As you read, consider how helpful their ideas would be for people preparing to supervise other people in the workplace.

Although a popular success, *Disclosure* was derided by feminists who considered its premise—sexual harassment of a man by a woman—silly at best,

dangerous at worst. After all, everyone knows sexual harassment is something a man does to a woman. That assumption is reflected in the Equal Employment Opportunity Commission's guidelines on sexual harassment,
where the harasser is always a "he" and the victim a "she." You have to refer to
a footnote to verify that the law, in theory, protects men as well as women.

2   Most of the published research on sexual harassment agrees: women
are victims; men are harassers. In surveys, some 40 per cent of women report being harassed at work, compared to a negligible proportion of men.
When men do report harassment, their harassers are often other men.

But these indicators may not give us an accurate picture of what is
going on. To begin with, the leading sexual-harassment researchers are feminist ideologues who are mainly concerned with finding evidence of patriarchal oppression. They design their studies accordingly: most of the research
does not even include male subjects.

4   More to the point, most men would not recognize sexual harassment if
it hit them in the face. Ask a number of men if they have been harassed, and
nine out of ten, will say, "No, but I'd like to be." Men generally do not consider teasing, sexual jokes, and lewd innuendoes from female co-workers
harassment; they are not upset by the kinds of comments and incidents that
have brought female plaintiffs millions of dollars in awards for "hostile environment" claims. In a recent lawsuit against the Jenny Craig diet organization by several male employees, one of the plaintiffs said he initially liked it
when the women he worked with told him he had a nice body. He and the
others did not file suit until they were denied promotions, were assigned to
poor sales territories, or were terminated from the organization. After ex-
amining their complaint, the Massachusetts Commission Against Discrimination found probable cause of gender bias in the organization's actions
against the men.

Since men are not sensitive to harassing behavior that women (or at
least feminists) construe as harassment, it's not surprising that they are not
filing many harassment complaints. Consider a scenario. A young man
gets a job as an assistant manager in a bank. His boss, a member of the National Association of Bank Women, often talks about the importance of
mentoring young women and complains that men have created a glass
ceiling that oppresses female managers. Her coffee mug is emblazoned
with an anti-male statement. To top it off, she and the other women who
work in the branch often tell dirty jokes in which men are portrayed
derogatorily. There's little question that this man is the victim of a "hostile
environment," one that may well interfere with his ability to perform his
duties. But if you ask him whether he has been sexually harassed, he will
probably say no.

6   To get beyond this barrier, male subjects in harassment surveys should
be asked not whether they have been sexually harassed but whether certain
kinds of behavior have occurred. When we ask male undergraduates if they
have ever been sexually harassed by a female instructor, almost all of them
say no. But when we ask if they have experienced specific types of treatment

in a female instructor's classroom, such as derogatory or off-color comments about men, some 60 per cent of them report such incidents.

As for "sleep with me or else" harassment—the kind dramatized in *Disclosure*—we are starting to see court cases indicating that some men (and women) have been pressured into sex by a predatory female boss. There is every reason to believe that more such cases will appear as more women assume positions of power.

8　　Yet most people still snicker about female harassment of males. Several men who claimed to have been sexually harassed appeared recently on *Donahue*. Between the host's eye rolling and the audience's derision, you would have though these men were reporting encounters with UFOs. Sometimes even juries do not take the subject seriously. In a 1991 case in Michigan, the jury agreed that a man had endured repeated fondling by his female co-workers but awarded him only $100 in damages. Compare that to the hundreds of thousands of dollars regularly awarded to female plaintiffs.

⌐Men are doubly penalized by the current alarm about sexual harassment. On the one hand, they are weakened in any office encounter with a woman because she always holds the harassment trump card. On the other hand, the current interpretation of harassment law gives women license to say and do things in the workplace to which men cannot respond in kind. There is an open hostility toward men in many workplaces, and no one is rushing to document or change it.⌐

10　　Business, which should have an interest in finding out the truth, has instead swallowed whole the received wisdom on sexual harassment and acted on it swiftly and thoroughly. Companies spend millions of dollars on "harassment training," hoping that putting employees through these programs will stave off potential problems or at least inoculate them against major liability. Although some of the harassment training is of passable quality (given the flawed evidence on which it is based), too much of the training results in resentment by male employees and "over-empowerment" of female employees. In a recent case, a group of male air-traffic controllers filed charges against the Federal Aviation Administration, claiming they were forced to observe photos of male sex organs and let female participants fondle them during harassment training.

Sexually harassed men face skepticism from both sides of the political spectrum. On the Left, no one is seriously challenging the anti-male feminist paradigm. On the Right, commentators have cautioned that men should not succumb to the harassment hysteria. Yet conservatives in particular should take a more active interest in setting the record straight, given the costs and public-policy ramifications of current erroneous theories.

Workplace Tensions

12　The current approach to sexual harassment has clearly hurt working relationships between men and women. Men are retreating to the safety of their offices, avoiding private contact with female co-workers, and carefully censoring their speech. Although the evidence has not yet been collected, it seems likely that male harassment victims, like their female counterparts, are more likely to be absent from work, to be less productive, and to leave the organization. In addition, men confronted by a sexually hostile environment may lash out against female co-workers, thereby prompting sexual-harassment complaints.

Trying to document a large, invisible mass of harassed men in the work force, however, does not mean advocating a new set of entitlements. On the contrary, recognizing that women are also harassers will help control the hysteria. Public policy, judicial interpretation, and popular sentiment have been swayed by statistics fraught with paradigmatic prejudice and methodological error. It is time for responsible researchers to begin an objective reexamination of the way that men and women treat each other at work. If the research shows that both men and women are experiencing harassment, then judicial remedy and public policy can be adjusted, and the idea of a harassing class and a victim class can be discarded.

14   It may also be time to reconsider the extent to which government can or should try to assure a comfortable working environment. People often receive treatment at work they do not like. The problem may lie in how the individual interprets the treatment.

Differing male and female interpretations of harassing behavior led the federal courts to establish the "reasonable woman" standard in 1991. This codified what we have known all along: men and women see things differently. According to the ruling, behavior that a man considers acceptable can constitute harassment if it is offensive to a "reasonable woman." In other words, decades of evolving feminist theory have led us back to a Victorian vision of woman; she cannot endure what a man can and must be protected.

16   Most of the outcry over sexual harassment is not about bosses demanding sex but about men doing and saying things that some women find offensive. Perhaps women are behaving just as offensively, but men have learned to live with it. The real answer to the "hostile environment" problem may be that women should learn to live with it too.⏋ ❖

Questions for Meaning

1. According to this article, how do men and women differ in their response to sexual harassment?
2. Why do the authors believe that men are "doubly penalized" by current attitudes toward sexual harassment?
3. How does sexual harassment affect performance in the workplace?
4. On what grounds do Luthar and Townsend object to businesses training employees to avoid sexual harassment?
5. Vocabulary: derided (1), innuendoes (4), construe (5), paradigm (11), ramifications (11).

Questions about Strategy

1. How useful is the opening allusion to *Disclosure*, a film that appeared shortly before this article was first published? Do the authors provide sufficient information so that you can understand what this film was about if you were not already familiar with it?
2. The authors claim that "leading sexual-harassment researchers are feminist ideologues." What evidence do they provide to support this claim?
3. Consider the scenario described in paragraph 5. Is it believable?
4. How would you describe the tone of this argument?

KINGSLEY R. BROWNE

TITLE VII AS CENSORSHIP: HOSTILE-ENVIRONMENT HARASSMENT AND THE FIRST AMENDMENT

Arguments of considerable length and complexity appear regularly in law journals, as legal scholars argue on behalf of new interpretations of the law, clarify prevailing interpretations, or demonstrate the need for new rulings. Kingsley R. Browne teaches law at Wayne State University, and "Title VII as Censorship" is part of a much longer argument he published in the *Ohio State Law Journal* in 1991. In order to make this work more accessible for college students, the seventy-four footnotes In the following version have been edited down, with Browne's permission, from 408 in the original version. Even so, you may find Browne's work challenging because of the extensive research upon which it draws. As you prepare to read, note how the argument is divided into separate sections and plan to read one section at a time.

I. Introduction

"Women do not belong in the medical profession; they should stay home and make babies!" Is such a statement occurring in the workplace a constitutionally protected expression of a currently unfashionable social view, or is it sexual harassment in violation of Title VII of the Civil Rights Act of 1964? If it violates Title VII, is Title VII to that extent inconsistent with the First Amendment? Many courts and commentators have addressed the first question—that is, the contours of "hostile environment" harassment—but few have acknowledged the possibility of constitutional protection for such statements. The purpose of this Article is to examine the extent to which the broad definition of "hostile work environment" adopted by the courts in harassment cases establishes a content-based—even viewpoint-based—restriction of expression that is inconsistent with contemporary First Amendment jurisprudence. To the extent that it does establish such a restriction Title VII must be given a narrowing construction in order to avoid a finding of invalidity.

2   Recent attention to the First Amendment implications of racist and sexist speech has focused largely on attempts by colleges and universities to regulate such speech and the application of general tort doctrine to such speech. It is not surprising that scholars have been particularly interested in regulation of speech in their own bailiwick. Yet the amount of attention paid university policies prohibiting racist and sexist speech seems out of proportion to their global importance since these policies seem to be the product of a temporary aberration that would burn itself out probably sooner than later even without any kind of legal intervention. Like the Indianapolis anti-pornography ordinance, regulation of offensive speech on campus probably generates far more expression than it regulates. Moreover, when legal intervention did occur, in the form of *Doe v. University of Michigan*[1] and *American Booksellers Ass'n v. Hudnut,*[2] the courts' responses were sure and decisive: the First Amendment prohibits regulation of racist and sexist speech on the basis of the viewpoint expressed.

In contrast with the immediate rejection of regulation of campus speech and pornography that was deemed to convey a "wrongheaded" view about women, regulation of offensive speech in the workplace has been proceeding apace virtually without comment for well over a decade. Although it has resulted in suppression of a vast amount of expression, objections from the traditional defenders of free speech have not been forthcoming. An optimist might suggest that the concern over free speech in the academy is simply the opening skirmish in a broader battle to challenge regulation of offensive speech everywhere; the champions of the First Amendment are simply attempting to get their own house in order before taking on the rest of the world. The indications are otherwise, however. Even the *Doe* court suggested that "speech which creates a hostile or abusive working environment on the basis of race or sex" is unprotected by the First Amendment.[3] It is difficult to avoid the conclusion that some who would protect the speech of students and faculty but not the speech of workers possess an elitist perspective that simply values the former group of speakers more than the latter. The lack of value of the speech of workers seems to be based upon one or more of the following opinions: (1) when workers speak they do not convey ideas; (2) ideas are not important to workers; (3) the ideas of workers are not important to us. These judgments can form no part of a First Amendment jurisprudence.

4   Regulation of speech in the workplace that is deemed "harassing" is pervasive. The Guidelines of the Equal Employment Opportunity Commission provide the most commonly accepted definition of "sexual harassment," a definition that courts have adapted to fit cases of racial harassment as well: "verbal or physical conduct of a sexual nature [that] has the purpose or effect of unreasonably interfering with an individual's

work performance or creating an intimidating, hostile, or offensive work environment,"[4] Although the Guidelines purport to regulate only "verbal or physical *conduct*," the concept of "verbal conduct" has no obvious meaning, and courts have consistently interpreted it to mean "verbal expression." Relying on the EEOC's definition of hostile-environment harassment, courts, both state and federal, have found employers liable for "conduct" ranging from clearly unprotected forcible sexual assault and other unwanted sexual touching to "obscene propositions," sexual vulgarity (including "off color" jokes) and "sexist" remarks, some of which are almost certainly protected by the First Amendment. Similarly, racial jokes, slurs, and other statements deemed derogatory to minorities have served as the basis for claims of racial harassment.

The restrictions on expression created by harassment regulation are not merely incidental; indeed, courts have recognized that the very purpose of the law is to "prevent . . . bigots from expressing their opinions in a way that abuses or offends their co-workers."[5] Moreover, protected expression[6] is often a substantial, if not the primary, basis for imposing liability. That is, the trier of fact is offended by the implicit or explicit message of the expression—for example, that women should be sexual playthings for men, that women (or blacks) do not belong in the workplace, or that they should hold an inferior position in our society. Yet, the right to express one's social views is generally considered to be at or near the core of the First Amendment's protection of free expression.

6   A broad definition of sexual and racial harassment necessarily delegates broad powers to courts to determine matters of taste and humor, and the vagueness of the definition of "harassment" leaves those subject to regulation without clear notice of what is permitted and what is forbidden. The inescapable result is a substantial chilling effect on expression. Holding employers liable for the offensive speech of their employees exacerbates that chilling effect, because fear of litigation and liability creates a powerful incentive for employers—which in the private sector are not subject to the constraints of the First Amendment—to censor the speech of their employees. Employers have responded to these incentives by substantially overregulating the speech of their employees.

Although with only one apparent exception[7] no reported harassment decision has imposed liability solely on the basis of arguably protected expression, it does not follow that hostile-environment claims therefore pose little threat to First Amendment rights. First, when protected expression is excluded from the liability calculus, the remaining unprotected expression or conduct, though of a harassing nature, may not be sufficiently severe or pervasive on its own to support a judgment. Second, even if sufficient unprotected conduct or expression is present so that a trier of fact *could* find against the defendant, a risk that liability may be imposed based in part on protected speech is intolerable under the First Amendment. Third, under the doctrine of overbreadth, a legal scheme that reaches a substantial amount of protected speech cannot be applied to reach even unprotected expression.[8] Therefore, evidence of protected speech should not be admitted at trial to support a claim of hostile environment.

8   The First Amendment does not insulate all speech from legal regulation, but in order for speech to be regulated on the basis of content, it must fall within some recognized exception to the First Amendment—such as defamation, obscenity, or "fighting words"—or a new exception must be recognized. Although some "harassing speech"[9] falls neatly within existing exceptions, much does not, and the Title VII standard is sufficiently broad that it covers both protected and unprotected speech. . . .

II. The Theory of Harassment Under Title VII

Title VII expressly prohibits neither sexual nor racial harassment. Instead, it generally provides that it is an unlawful employment practice for an employer "to discriminate against any individual with respect to his compensation, terms, conditions, or privileges of employment because of such individual's race, color, religion, sex, or national origin."[10] Nonetheless, courts have identified two forms of sexual harassment that violate Title VII—"*quid pro quo*" and "hostile work environment" harassment. "*Quid pro quo*" harassment typically involves a claim that an employee, usually female, was required to submit to sexual advances as a condition of receiving job benefits or that her failure to submit to such advances resulted in a tangible job detriment, such as discharge or failure to receive a promotion. "Hostile work environment" harassment involves the claim that the workplace is so "polluted" with sexual hostility toward women—or racial hostility to other races—that it discriminatorily alters the "terms and conditions of employment" within the meaning of the statute.[11] The hostility may be expressed either through conduct or through speech. The focus of this Article is limited to hostile-environment harassment and then only to the extent that the hostile environment is created in whole or in part by expression.[12]

10   The first case to recognize a hostile-environment theory under Title VII was a race case. In *Rogers v. EEOC,* Judge Goldberg stated:

> [E]mployees' psychological as well as economic fringes are statutorily entitled to protection from employer abuse, and . . . the phrase "terms, conditions, or privileges of employment" in Section 703 is an expansive concept which sweeps within its protective ambit the practice of creating a working environment heavily charged with ethnic or racial discrimination.[13]

Numerous cases since *Rogers* have relied upon this broad conception of the phrase "terms, conditions, or privileges of employment" to hold that a racially or sexually hostile atmosphere violates Title VII even absent any discrimination in wages, job assignments, or other tangible benefits, and *Rogers* was a major impulse behind the EEOC's promulgation of its Guidelines. In *Meritor Savings Bank, FSB v. Vinson,* the Supreme Court, in recognizing a cause of action for sexual harassment leading to non-economic injury, quoted the EEOC Guidelines approvingly, stating that in adopting those Guidelines, "the EEOC drew upon a substantial body of judicial decisions and EEOC precedent holding that Title VII affords employees the right to work in an environment free from discriminatory intimidation, ridicule, and insult."[14] The Court announced that "a requirement that a man or woman run a gauntlet of sexual abuse in return for the privilege of being allowed to work and make a living can be as demeaning and disconcerting as the harshest of racial epithets."[15] The Court emphasized, however, that "not all workplace conduct that may be described as 'harassment' affects a 'term, condition, or privilege' of employment within the meaning of Title VII."[16] Rather, for harassment to be actionable under Title VII, "it must be sufficiently severe or pervasive 'to alter the conditions of [the victim's] employment and create an abusive working environment.' "[17] The Court in *Vinson* had no trouble finding sufficient allegations of hostile environment, because the plaintiff alleged that she had been forcibly raped.

The reported cases reveal that the definitions of sexual and racial harassment under Title VII are at the same time broader and narrower than the conventional definition of "harassment," which generally connotes a pattern of conduct aimed at a particular person and intended to annoy. The statutory definition is broader in that expression can constitute "harassment" even when it is not directed toward the plaintiff and not intended to annoy, and narrower in that it includes only harassment based upon protected status and, even then, only harassment that is sufficiently severe or pervasive as to alter the terms and conditions of employment.

12   Although some courts have stated that a plaintiff must show a "pattern of harassment," rather than "a few isolated incidents," others have expressly rejected that distinction and suggested that the plaintiff "need not prove that the instances of alleged harassment were related in either time or type,"[18] and others have suggested that it is error for a court to conclude that harassment did not exist simply because very few incidents were alleged.[19] Conduct need not be overtly sexual or racial to be actionable; other hostile conduct directed against the victim because of the victim's race or sex is also prohibited.

Ironically, though couched in terms of discriminatory treatment, the real claim in many harassment cases is that the work atmosphere did *not* change in response to the addition of women (or minorities) to the environment. The rationale is that conduct that appears harmless to men may be offensive to women, although such reasoning seems inconsistent, at least superficially, with the view that Title VII "rejects the notion of 'romantic paternalism' towards women."[20] For example, the court in *Andrews v. City of Philadelphia*[21] rejected the argument that the environment was not a hostile one because "a police station need not be run like a day care center," stating that neither should it have "the ambience of a nineteenth-century military barracks," although an all-male police station having such an ambience would certainly not violate Title VII. The court also noted that although men might find the obscenity and pornography that pervaded the work-place "harmless and innocent," women might well "feel otherwise," and such expression may be "highly offensive to a woman who seeks to deal with her fellow employees and clients with professional dignity and without the bar-rier of sexual differentiation and abuse." As a consequence, a locker room atmosphere that was perfectly legal before the entry of women into the job becomes illegal thereafter.

14   The extent to which courts will be willing to pursue the above logic remains to be seen. Suppose, for example, an employer had a policy of im-posing discipline against any employee who used profanity in front of a woman. The assumption that women as a group may be more offended by profanity than men as a group seems like just the sort of stereotype that Title VII was intended to erase. Just as it may be empirically true that women as a group are more offended by profanity than men, it also may be empirically true that women as a group are more nurturant than men, but courts have interpreted Title VII to prohibit reliance on the latter general-ization, and it is unclear why the two generalizations should enjoy a differ-ent status.

     Because harassment claims rest upon a discrimination theory, a num-ber of courts have suggested that where sexual conduct is equally offensive to males and females there is no actionable harassment. Similarly, where su-pervisors are abusive to all employees, many courts have rejected racial and sexual harassment claims. Other courts have allowed such claims, however, where the harassment of the plaintiff took a sexual or racial form. The latter cases seem inconsistent with the underlying theory of Title VII harassment, which is that the employee suffers an adverse working environment because of race or sex. A supervisor who refers to subordinates by terms such as "dumb bastard," "dumb bitch," "fat bastard," "red-headed bastard," and "black bastard" cannot fairly be said to have discriminated against the woman and the black in favor of the fat, dumb, and red-headed employees. All were subjected to an abusive environment, and unless the black and the woman would have been spared the abuse but for their race and sex, they are not victims of discrimination. By similar reasoning, when harassment is directed against an individual because of a personal grudge, it should not be actionable even if it takes a racial or sexual form, though the cases come out the other way. Conversely, of course, where the harassment does not take a sexual or racial form but is aimed at the victim because of the victim's race or sex, harassment on the prohibited basis exists.

16   The Supreme Court has not yet wholly defined the extent of an em-ployer's liability for harassment by its employees. In *quid pro quo* cases, which by definition involve supervisory employees, courts generally apply automatic vicarious liability on the theory that such behavior is like any other form of prohibited discrimination, where the employer is liable irre-spective of whether it knew of the particular discriminatory conduct by one of its agents or had a policy against it.[22] The scope of employer liability for hostile-environment harassment is not as well settled and may depend

upon whether the harasser is a supervisor or a co-worker. Although the EEOC Guidelines provide that an employer is automatically liable in all cases of sexual harassment,[23] the Supreme Court in *Vinson* rejected that standard.[24] The Court declined, however, to articulate any standard in its place, although it did suggest that courts should look to general agency principles and consider the following factors: (1) whether the employer has a policy prohibiting sexual harassment; (2) whether the policy was communicated to employees; (3) whether the employer had notice of the harassment; and (4) whether the employer's response upon learning of the harassment was adequate.[25] However, the Court noted that "absence of notice to an employer does not necessarily insulate that employer from liability."[26] Courts since *Vinson* are split on whether notice is required in supervisor cases, but in cases involving co-workers most courts have required that the plaintiff show that the employer knew or should have known of the harassment and failed to take adequate remedial steps.[27] There is no need, however, for the employee to show that the failure of the employer to remedy the situation was discriminatory. An employer that routinely tells employees to work out their problems with their co-workers is liable for harassment if it applies the same rule to complaints of harassment.

Reported decisions under Title VII have found a wide variety of speech to constitute or contribute to a sexually or racially hostile working environment. In many of the cases discussed below, additional facts contributed to the decision. The point of the illustrations is not that only protected expression was involved or that the ultimate conclusions by the courts were necessarily wrong. Rather, the examples show that pure expression plays a large role in many of the decisions, a conclusion having substantial First Amendment implications.

III. Title VII as a Viewpoint-Based Restriction on Expression

18 Expression contributing to harassment claims comes in a variety of forms. While much of it is exceedingly crude and probably outside the protection of the First Amendment, some is merely uncivil, some at most insensitive, and some perhaps wholly harmless. As the description of the cases below reveals, speech that is only arguably sexist, sexual, or racist may form the basis for a claim of harassment. Central to a finding of unlawful harassment is often a conclusion by the court that the message is "offensive," "inappropriate," or even "morally wrong." Even if the employer ultimately prevails in such cases, it must incur a high cost in litigation fees for declining to regulate the speech of employees. Because the underlying objection to sexist or sexual speech and to racist speech* is sometimes different, the two forms of harassment will be considered separately. . . .

There are two primary messages conveyed by the expression that leads to sexual harassment complaints. The first is a message of unwelcomeness

* This abridged version of Browne's argument does not include his discussion of racist speech.

or hostility; expressions that women do not belong in the workplace or scornful or derisive statements about women would fall in this class. The second is a message that the harasser views the plaintiff in particular or women in general in a sexual light. For sake of discussion, the former will be called the "hostility message," while the latter will be called the "sexuality message."

20   Many sexual harassment cases have involved the use of "bad words" of a sexual nature. Crude or otherwise inappropriate language referring to or addressing women is commonly present in hostile-environment cases, though it is not generally by itself enough to establish a claim of harassment. The terms complained of are primarily of two kinds, and they convey both of the above-described messages: (1) the "hostility message" is conveyed by terms of derision, such as "broad," "bitch," and "cunt;"[28] and (2) the "sexuality message" is conveyed by terms of "endearment," such as "honey,"[29] "sweetie," and "tiger." The complained-of terms may refer to women in general, particular women other than the plaintiff, or they may refer to the plaintiff herself and be addressed either to her or to others while referring to her.

At least with respect to the most vulgar expressions, arguably it is just the use of "indecent" words—words that are "beyond the pale" of what can be spoken in polite society—that is being regulated. That, of course, would justify viewing the most vulgar terms as contributing to a hostile environment, but it would not justify reliance on milder terms, such as "broad." But Title VII is not a "clean language act,"[30] and bad language conveying no idea is not the target of the harassment cases. Thus, the court in *State v. Human Rights Commission*,[31] distinguished between "gender-specific" terms, such as "cunt," "bitch," "twat," and "raggin' it"—which constitute "conduct of a sexual nature"—and "general sexual" terms, such as "fuck" and "motherfucker" used as expletives, which do not. The court held that a supervisor's reference to women's physical appearance and his reference to women by "gender-specific" derogatory terms constituted sexual harassment because it was an "expression of animosity" toward women.[32] The finding of harassment was not based primarily on one-to-one expressions of hostility by the supervisor toward the employee, but instead on the general disrespect he showed women in his conversations with others.

22   More explicit expressions of "Neanderthal" attitudes toward women have also been held to support a claim of hostile environment. Thus, in *Lipsett v. University of Puerto Rico*,[33] a female medical resident claimed that one of her fellow residents told her that women should not become surgeons "because they need too much time to bathe, to go to the bathroom, to apply makeup, and to get dressed," and she frequently heard other comments to the effect that women did not belong in surgery.[34] Although these statements were "not explicitly *sexual*," the court concluded that they were "charged with anti-female animus" because they "challenged their capacity as women to be surgeons" and "questioned the legitimacy of their being in the Program at all."[35] As a result, they could contribute to the hostile environment. Rejecting the defendant's argument that many of the comments

were jokes, the court observed that "[b]elittling comments about a person's ability to perform, on the basis of that person's sex, are not funny."[36]

Plaintiffs in sexual harassment cases also frequently challenge the exhibition of written or pictorial material that they believe is demeaning or mocking toward women. Pin-ups or "girlie magazines" in the workplace have been the subject of innumerable sexual harassment claims.[37] The conflicting approaches to the problem of sexually oriented displays are revealed by the majority and dissenting opinions in *Rabidue v. Osceola Refining Co.*[38] The majority rejected a claim that was based upon anti-female language and pin-ups, stating:

> The sexually oriented poster displays had a *de minimis* effect on the plaintiff's work environment when considered in the context of a society that condones and publicly features and commercially exploits open displays of written and pictorial erotica at the newsstands, on prime-time television, at the cinema, and in other public places.[39]

24   On the other hand, Judge Keith's frequently cited dissent would have found that the alleged harasser's "misogynous language" combined with the pin-ups constituted a Title VII violation because they "evoke and confirm the debilitating norms by which women are primarily and contemptuously valued as objects of male sexual fantasy."[40] In the dissent's view, the "precise purpose" of Title VII was to prevent sexual jokes, conversations, and literature from "poisoning the work environment."[41] Two of the displays that Judge Keith seemed to find particularly reprehensible were a poster showing a woman in a supine position with a golf ball on her breasts and a man standing over her, golf club in hand, yelling "Fore" and a supervisor's desk plaque declaring "Even male chauvinist pigs need love."[42]

The message restricted by exclusion of pin-ups is the "sexuality message." Kathryn Abrams describes that message as follows:

> Pornography on an employer's wall or desk communicates a message about the way he views women, a view strikingly at odds with the way women wish to be viewed in the workplace. Depending on the material in question, it may communicate that women should be objects of sexual aggression, that they are submissive slaves to male desires, or that their most salient and desirable attributes are sexual. Any of these images may communicate to male coworkers that it is acceptable to view women in a predominantly sexual way.[43]

26   The very recent case of *Robinson v. Jacksonville Shipyards, Inc.,*[44] which adopted the view of both the *Rabidue* dissent and the Abrams article, was apparently the first reported decision to impose liability for sexual harassment based entirely on the pervasive presence of sexually oriented magazines, pin-up pictures—such as *Playboy* foldouts and tool-company calendars—and "sexually demeaning remarks and jokes" by male coworkers; the plaintiff complained of neither physical assaults nor sexual propositions.[45] Some of

the pictures were posted on walls in public view, but included within the category of sexually harassing behavior were incidents where male employees were simply reading the offending magazines in the workplace[46] or carrying them in their back pockets.[47] The court rejected the suggestion of *Rabidue* that sexually oriented pictures and comments standing alone cannot form the basis for Title VII liability, stating that "[e]xcluding some forms of offensive conduct as a matter of law is not consistent with the factually oriented approach" required by Title VII.[48]

A desire not to be viewed as a "sex object" also underlies the objection to sexual propositions in the workplace. Sexual harassment cases have often involved sexual propositions of varying degrees of vulgarity. For example, in *Continental Can Co. v. State*,[49] an employee's coworkers told her how they could "make her feel sexually" and that they could make her want to leave her husband.[50] In another case, male workers told dirty jokes, suggested that plaintiff participate in a sexually explicit home video, and one worker suggested that she "sit on [his] face."[51] In yet another, the plaintiff alleged that the message, "How about a little head?" appeared on the screen of her computer terminal.[52] Although sometimes the advances are crude and explicit, that is not always the case. For example, in *Zowayyed v. Lowen Co.*, the plaintiff alleged that the company president wrote a note to her reading, "You have very playful eyes. Do you play?" and the next day said to her, "If you don't bait the hook, you can't catch the fish."[53] Sometimes the assertion goes beyond what the alleged harasser has said to what the harasser is thinking. Thus, plaintiffs in sexual harassment cases have relied on both the tone of voice[54] and the look on a face.

28   A recent Ninth Circuit case held that the plaintiff had established a prima facie case of sexual harassment based on what can only be described as a pathetic romantic overture by a coworker.[55] The accused harasser, a revenue agent of the Internal Revenue Service named Gray, had asked the plaintiff, a fellow agent, out for a drink after work. The plaintiff declined but suggested that they have lunch the following week. The next week, Gray asked the plaintiff out for lunch, but she declined. The following week, Gray handed the plaintiff a note stating:

> I cried over you last night and I'm totally drained today. I have never been in such constant term oil [sic]. Thank you for talking with me. I could not stand to feel your hatred for another day.[56]

Plaintiff left the room and asked a male coworker to tell Gray that she was not interested in him and to leave her alone. The next week, Gray sent plaintiff a three-page letter stating in part:

> I know that you are worth knowing with or without sex. . . . Leaving aside the hassles and disasters of recent weeks. I have enjoyed you so much over these past few months. Watching you. Experiencing you from O so far away. Admiring your style and elan. . . . Don't you think it odd that two people

who have never even talked together, alone, are striking off such intense sparks . . . I will [write] another letter in the near future.[57]

The letter also said, "I am obligated to you so much that if you want me to leave you alone I will. . . . If you want me to forget you entirely, I can not do that."[58] The Ninth Circuit reversed the district court's grant of summary judgment, rejecting the lower court's conclusion that the incident was "isolated and genuinely trivial"[59] and holding that "Gray's conduct was sufficiently severe and pervasive to alter the conditions of [plaintiff's] employment and create an abusive working environment."[60]

Not all cases involve statements of views about women in general; sometimes the displays are more focused. For example, a female firefighter established a claim of sexual harassment based in large part upon the appearance of "blatant sexual mockery" in the form of graffiti and cartoons on the communal bulletin boards and living space of the firehouse.[61] A display that the court seemed to find among the more offensive was a cartoon posted in the firehouse depicting a woman firefighter at a men's urinal,[62] though the message seems quite "political" in the context of a fire department under orders to set positions aside for women.[63] The term "political" is used here and throughout the Article in its broad sense—that is, pertaining to matters of social policy. Speech expressing views about matters of social policy—such as the proper role of the races and sexes—should be considered political in the same sense that speech advocating nondiscriminatory treatment should be. The most obvious interpretation of the *Berkman* cartoon is that it is a negative comment on the notion of sexual integration of the fire department.

30   The importance of an anti-female message in harassment cases is starkly revealed by *Goluszek v. Smith*,[64] in which a male plaintiff claimed that male coworkers had harassed him. The plaintiff was an unsophisticated man who apparently was quite sensitive to comments about sex. His coworkers showed him pictures of nude women, told him they would get him "fucked," and poked him in the buttocks with a stick,[65] all conduct that most courts would find constituted sexual harassment if directed toward women. Although the court acknowledged that Goluszek was harassed because he was a male,[66] it held that the harassment was not actionable under Title VII. Unlike this case, said the court, in a valid Title VII harassment case, "the offender is saying by words or actions that the victim is inferior because of the victim's sex."[67] Because Goluszek was a male in a male-dominated environment, the court reasoned that the harassment could not have embodied the message that he was inferior because of his sex. . . .

VIII. Conclusion

The impulse to censor is a powerful one, and it has been given free rein under Title VII. Not only has "targeted vilification" been regulated, but much less harmful and less invidiously motivated expression has been restricted as well.

That so much speech has been stifled without substantial outcry is in large measure a reflection of the powerful current consensus against racism and sexism. But it is precisely when a powerful consensus exists that the censorial impulse is most dangerous and, ironically, least necessary. The primary risk of censorship in our society today is not from a government fearful of challenge, but from majorities seeking to establish an orthodoxy for all society. When the orthodoxy is one of "equality," that risk is at its highest.

32   The definition of "harassment" contained in the EEOC Guidelines and applied by the courts, combined with vicarious employer liability, creates a substantial chilling effect on discussion in the workplace of matters even tangentially dealing with sex and race. Acting pursuant to those Guidelines, courts have displayed remarkably little discernment among examples of expression. Once they have been labelled as racist or sexist, all such expression has been deemed regulable. Although much of the speech that has been described in this Article arguably may be regulated through appropriately narrow and specific legislation that is viewpoint neutral, the Guidelines are not the appropriate vehicle, and, in fact, are so vague and so overbroad that they may not be applied even to unprotected speech consistent with the Constitution.

The current approach to regulation of offensive speech is directly contrary to the traditional notion that noxious ideas should be countered through juxtaposition with good ideas in the hope that the bad ideas will lose out in the marketplace of ideas. To a degree perhaps unprecedented, the current attempt to stifle offensive speech can be viewed as an attempt to achieve not only an egalitarian orthodoxy of speech and action but an orthodoxy of thought itself. Consider, for example, prohibitions against employees' having sexually explicit pictures on the inside of their lockers or their reading *Playboy* (or worse) in the workplace. The justification for such regulation is not that women of delicate sensibilities might see the material and be shocked by it. Rather, the basis for the prohibition is that some people, mostly women, are offended by what the employee is thinking while he is looking at the pictures; they are offended by the way he "views"—that is, "thinks about"—women.

34   An apparently growing number of academics and judges explicitly defend limitations of expression on the ground that restricting expression will modify beliefs. Thus, Delgado states, "a tort for racist speech will discourage such speech, establish a new public conscience, and ultimately change attitudes."[68] It should not be concluded that the censorship advocated is solely for protection of the target; Delgado seeks also to protect the speaker. In a passage reminiscent of the Soviet attempt to label political dissidents mentally ill, he argues: "Bigotry harms the individuals who harbor it by reinforcing rigid thinking, thereby dulling their moral and social senses and possibly leading to a 'mildly . . . paranoid' mentality."[69]

The "thought-control" rationale for restricting expression is not confined to academic commentary. A similar justification for limitation of speech was provided by the Sixth Circuit in *Davis v. Monsanto Chemical*

Co.:[70] "By informing people that the expression of racist or sexist attitudes in public is unacceptable, people may eventually learn that such views are undesirable in private, as well. Thus, Title VII may advance the goal of eliminating prejudices and biases in our society." Thus is the "freedom to think as you will and to speak as you think," so celebrated by Justice Brandeis,[71] converted to a duty to think as you are told and to speak as you are told to think.

36 It is but a small step from requiring a person to refrain from expressing beliefs in the hope that he will cease to hold them to requiring a person to express beliefs in the hope that he will begin to hold them. If the state may justify a prohibition on a person's saying "blacks are inferior" by pointing to the effect of the prohibition on a person's beliefs, the state should have equivalent power to require that a person affirm a belief in racial equality on the ground that repeated affirmation will cause the person to come to believe it, and, once having come to believe it, to conform his actions to his newly acquired beliefs. Thus, the state could require as a condition of holding public employment—or attending public school—that an applicant sign an "equality oath," affirming a belief in the equality of the races and sexes.

In addition to its Orwellian overtones, the assumption that beliefs can be altered by forbidding expression is probably wrong. As Paul Chevigny has suggested in the context of the debate over pornography regulation, propaganda—whether in the form of "anti-female" pornography or racist expression—appeals only to those whose systems of belief make them receptive to the representations.[72] Suppressing pornography (or racist speech) is "beside the point in a cognitive world where we can interpret new experience only through existing patterns."[73] The only effective method of altering a worldview that is deemed pernicious is to provide a persuasive response—that is, "more speech." "Shut up!" is not a persuasive response.

38 Although the contrary is sometimes asserted, challenging censorship is not to cast one's lot with those censored or to minimize the substance of the opinions of those urging censorship. Instead, it is to accept the fundamental *constitutional* truth that the government may not establish a fundamental *moral* truth through suppression of expression. Probably everyone reading this Article would agree that the world would be a better place without much of the expression that is described in the harassment cases. It does not follow, however, that the world would be a better place if elimination of such expression is compelled by the threat of governmental sanctions. Persuasion that the offensive views are wrong or that they not be expressed where they are unwelcome is a far better solution than "silence coerced by law—the argument of force in its worst form."[74] ❖

Notes

1. 721 F. Supp. 852 (E.D. Mich. 1989) (striking down the University of Michigan offensive-speech policy).
2. 771 F.2d 323, 331 (7th Cir. 1985). *aff'd,* 475 U.S. 1001 (1986) (striking down the Indianapolis anti-pornography ordinance).

3. Doe v. University of Michigan, 721 F. Supp. 852, 863 (E.D. Mich. 1989).
4. 29 C.F.R. § 1604.11(a)(3). Because the EEOC lacks the authority to promulgate substantive regulations, the Guidelines lack the force of law. However, federal courts, including the Supreme Court, have uniformly relied upon them, *see, e.g.,* Meritor Sav.
   Bank, F.S.B. v. Vinson, 477 U.S. 57, 65 (1986), and many state statutes and regulations have adopted the EEOC language, *see, e.g.,* ILL. REV. STAT. ch. 68, § 2–101(E);
   MICH. COMP. LAWS § 37.2103(h).
5. Davis v. Monsanto Chemical Co., 858 F.2d 345, 350 (6th Cir. 1988), *cert. denied,* 109
   S. Ct. 3166 (1989). Andrews v. City of Philadelphia, 895 F.2d 1469, 1486 (3d Cir.
   1990) (quoting *Davis,* 858 F.2d 345).
6. The terms "protected expression" and "protected speech" are used in this Article
   because they are commonly used in the literature. There is, of course, no expression that is protected or unprotected under all circumstances. A political speech
   may be prohibited by regulations prohibiting noise in an intensive-care unit, and
   obscenity may not be prohibited by a law that distinguishes among obscene expressions based upon their political content. Thus, it may actually be more meaningful to speak in terms of "prohibited regulation" than in terms of "protected
   speech."
7. Robinson v. Jacksonville Shipyards, Inc., 1991 U.S. Dist. LEXIS 794 (M.D. Fla. 1991).
8. Broadrick v. Oklahoma, 413 U.S. 601, 615 (1973).
9. The term "harassing speech" is used to describe speech that courts have held to contribute to a finding of harassment under Title VII, without regard to whether the
   speech by itself would be actionable or whether the speaker intended to annoy the
   listener.
10. 42 U.S.C. § 2000c.
11. The distinction between the two kinds of harassment is not always clear, and some
    courts have criticized attempts to draw such distinctions. For example, in Mitchell v.
    OsAir, Inc., 629 F. Supp. 636, 643 (N.D. Ohio 1986), the court, referring to a hostile
    environment, stated that "[t]he threat of loss of work explicit in the quid pro quo
    may only be implicit without being any less coercive."
12. A somewhat different form of hostile-environment claim is that consensual sexual
    relationships of other persons create an offensive sexually charged environment. In
    Broderick v. Ruder, 685 F. Supp. 1269, 1280 (D.D.C. 1988), the court held that the
    plaintiff proved a sexually hostile work environment by demonstrating the existence
    of pervasive consensual sexual conduct in the office. *See also* Drinkwater v. Union
    Carbide Corp., 904 F.2d 853, 862 (3d Cir. 1990) (acknowledging the theory, but re-
    jecting the argument because there was no evidence that romantic relationships were
    "flaunted" or prevalent).
13. 454 F.2d 234, 238 (5th Cir. 1971), *cert. denied,* 406 U.S. 957 (1972).
14. 477 U.S. 57, 65 (1986). *See also* Scott v. Sears, Roebuck & Co., 798 F.2d 210, 213 (7th
    Cir. 1986) ("After *Meritor* there is no mistaking the acceptability of the EEOC defini-
    tion (and verbiage) found at § 1604.11(a)").
15. 477 U.S. at 67 (quoting Henson v. City of Dundee, 682 F.2d 897, 902 (11th Cir.
    1982)).
16. 477 U.S. at 67 (citing Rogers v. EEOC, 454 F.2d 234, 238 (5th Cir. 1971) ("mere ut-
    terance of an ethnic or racial epithet which engenders offensive feelings in an em-
    ployee" would not affect the conditions of employment to sufficiently significant
    degree to violate Title VII)), *cert. denied,* 406 U.S. 957 (1972); Henson v. City of
    Dundee, 682 F.2d at 904 (quoting *Rogers,* 454 F.2d 234).
17. 477 U.S. at 67 (quoting Henson v. City of Dundee, 682 F.2d at 904). *See also* Ander-
    son v. Chicago Housing Authority, 1988 U.S. Dist. LEXIS 14454, *20 (N.D. Ill. 1988)
    (rejecting claim based on "a few isolated incidents of sexual harassment" on ground
    that it was not enough to characterize workplace as "abusive working environment").
18. Davis v. Monsanto Chem. Co., 858 F.2d 345, 349 (6th Cir. 1988), *cert. denied,* 109 S.
    Ct. 3166 (1989). *See also* Waltman v. Int'l. Paper Co., 875 F.2d 468, 475 (5th Cir.

1989) ("focus is whether [plaintiff] was subjected to recurring acts of discrimination, not whether a given individual harassed [plaintiff] recurrently.").

19. King v. Board of Regents, 898 F.2d 533, 537 (7th Cir. 1990) ("although a single act can be enough, . . . generally repeated incidents create a stronger claim of hostile environment, with the strength of the claim depending on the number of incidents and the intensity of each incident"); Vance v. Southern Bell Tel. & Tel. Co., 863 F.2d 1503, 1510 (11th Cir. 1989) ("the determination of whether the defendant's conduct is sufficiently 'severe or pervasive' to constitute racial harassment does not turn solely on the number of incidents alleged by plaintiff.").

20. United States v. City of Buffalo, 457 F. Supp. 612, 629 (W.D.N.Y. 1978) (quoting Rosen v. Public Serv. Elec. & Gas Co., 328 F. Supp. 454, 464 (D.C. N.J. (1990)). *See also* Note, *Sexual Harassment and Title VII: A Better Solution,* 30 B.C. L. REV. 1071 (1989) (arguing that sexual harassment is not really discrimination and urging enactment of separate sexual harassment legislation).

21. 895 F.2d 1469, 1486 (3d Cir. 1990).

22. Lipsett v. University of Puerto Rico, 864 F.2d 881, 901 (1st Cir. 1988); Sparks v. Pilot Freight Carriers, Inc., 830 F.2d 1554, 1564 n.22 (11th Cir. 1987); Horn v. Duke Homes, Div. of Windsor Mobile Homes, Inc., 755 F.2d 599, 605 (7th Cir. 1985); Katz v. Dole, 709 F.2d 251, 256 n.6 (4th Cir. 1983); McCalla v. Ellis, 180 Mich. App. 372, 379–80, 446 N.W.2d 904, 909 (1989).

23. 29 C.F.R. § 1604.11(c).

24. 477 U.S. 59, 72 (1986).

25. *Id.* at 71–72.

26. *Id.* at 72.

27. *Lipsett* at 902 (1st Cir. 1988); Davis v. Monsanto Chem. Co., 858 F.2d 345, 349 (6th Cir. 1988).

28. Some words, primarily those relating to female sexual anatomy, may actually convey a dual message by showing contempt for women by equating them with their sex organs.

29. Robinson v. Jacksonville Shipyards, Inc., 1991 U.S. Dist. LEXIS 794, at *27 (M.D. Fla. 1991).

30. Katz v. Dole, 709 F.2d 251, 256 (4th Cir. 1983).

31. 178 Ill. App. 3d 1033, 1046, 534 N.E.2d 161, 170 (1989).

32. *Id.* at 1049, 534 N.E.2d at 171. Comments similar to those in this case were not considered enough to create a hostile environment by the court in Rabidue v. Osceola Ref. Co., 805 F.2d 611 (6th Cir. 1986), *cert. denied,* 481 U.S. 1041 (1987).

33. 864 F.2d 881 (1st Cir. 1988).

34. *Id.* at 887. Another supervisory resident justified his assigning plaintiff menial tasks by asserting that women should not be surgeons because they could not be relied upon while they were menstruating or, as he put it, "in heat." *Id. See also* Arnold v. City of Seminole, 614 F. Supp. 853, 862–63 (N.D. Okla. 1985) (comments that women are not fit to become police officers; picture of a nude woman posted on a locker door with words "Do women make good cops—No - No - No.").

35. 864 F.2d at 905 (emphasis in original).

36. *Id.* at 906.

37. Andrews v. City of Philadelphia, 895 F.2d 1469, 1472 (3d Cir. 1990) ("pornographic" pictures of women were displayed in the locker room on the inside of a locker that was generally kept open); Waltman v. International Paper Co., 875 F.2d 468, 471 (5th Cir. 1989) (sexually oriented calendars on walls and in lockers); Bennett v. Corroon & Black Corp., 845 F.2d 104, 105 (5th Cir. 1988) (presence of "obscene cartoons" bearing plaintiff's name), *cert. denied,* 489 U.S. 1020 (1989); Lipsett v. University of Puerto Rico, 864 F.2d 881 (1st Cir. 1988) (*Playboy* centerfolds displayed by male residents in rest facility); Rabidue v. Osceola Ref. Co., 805 F.2d 611 (6th Cir. 1986), *cert. denied,* 481 U.S. 1041 (1987); Sanchez v. City of Miami Beach, 720 F. Supp. 974, 977 n.9 (S.D. Fla. 1989) ("various pictures from *Playboy, Penthouse,* and other publications were posted

in the station."); Robinson v. Jacksonville Shipyards, Inc., 1991 U.S. Dist. LEXIS 794 (M.D. Fla. 1991) ("allegation that the pervasive presence of pornography in the workplace is offensive to female employees generally and plaintiff in particular."); Barbetta v. Chemlawn Servs. Corp., 669 F. Supp. 569 (W.D.N.Y. 1987) (presence of "pornographic" magazines and sexually oriented pictures and calendars); Brown v. City of Guthrie, 1980 WL 380, *3 (W.D. Okla. 1980) (presence of magazines containing photographs of nude women in police dispatcher's desk for policemen to look at during their spare time).

38. 805 F.2d 611 (6th Cir. 1986), *cert. denied,* 481 U.S. 1041 (1987).

39. *Id.* at 622.

40. *Id.* at 627 (Keith, J., dissenting). Barbetta v. Chemlawn Servs. Corp., 669 F. Supp. 569, 573 (W.D.N.Y. 1987) (explicitly rejecting *Rabidue* majority opinion and adopting position of *Rabidue* dissent that "sexual posters and anti-female language can seriously affect the psychological well-being of the reasonable woman and interfere with her ability to perform her job," *id.* at 573 n.2 (quoting *Rabidue,* 805 F.2d at 627 (Keith, J., dissenting)), and may "create an atmosphere in which women are viewed as men's sexual playthings," *Barbetta,* 669 F. Supp. at 573); Robinson v. Jacksonville Shipyards, Inc., 1991 U.S. Dist. LEXIS 794 (M.D. Fla. 1988) ("To the extent that *Rabidue* holds that some forms of abusive, anti-female behavior must be tolerated in the work environment because the behavior is prominent in society at large, the case conflicts with the established law in this Circuit") (citation omitted).

41. 805 F.2d at 626.

42. Rabidue v. Osceola Ref. Co., 805 F.2d at 624 (Keith, J., dissenting). (M.D. Fla. 1991) (Title VII prohibits speech that is "disproportionately more offensive or demeaning to one sex . . . because it conveys the message that they do not belong, that they are welcome in the workplace only if they will subvert their identities to the sexual stereotypes prevalent in that environment").

43. Abrams, *Gender Discrimination and the Transformation of Workplace Norms,* 42 VAND. L. REV. 1183, 1212 n.118 (1989). Abrams' categorical assertion that the message of pornography is "strikingly at odds with the way women wish to be viewed in the workplace" seems overbroad and based not on an empirical judgment that all women object to being viewed in a sexual manner in the workplace, but rather on the normative judgment that women *should* object. Moreover, not all women object to pornographic materials, even in the workplace, and many who do object do so on grounds having nothing to do with views of "sexual subordination."

44. 1991 U.S. Dist. LEXIS 794 (M.D. Fla. 1991).

45. *Id.* at 90.

46. *Id.* at 18, 25.

47. *Id.* at 37.

48. *Id.* at 120–23. The court also examined, albeit superficially, the argument that the first amendment imposes limits on the kind of activity that can be the subject of sexual harassment claims. *Id.* at 154–62.

49. 297 N.W.2d 241, 245 (Minn. 1980).

50. *Id.* at 245. One coworker told her that "he wished slavery days would return so that he could sexually train her and she would be his bitch." *Id.* at 246. Coworkers also told her that women who worked at factories were "tramps." *Id.*

51. Egger v. Local 76, Plumbers & Pipefitters Union, 644 F. Supp. 795, 797 n.3, 799 (D. Mass. 1986).

52. Monge v. Superior Court, 176 Cal. App. 3d 503, 507, 222 Cal. Rptr. 64, 65 (1986).

53. 735 F. Supp. 1497, 1499 (D. Kan. 1990). *See also* Scott v. Sears, Roebuck & Co., 798 F.2d 210, 211 (7th Cir. 1986) (plaintiff alleged that she had been "propositioned," which turned out on deposition to mean that the alleged harasser had asked to take her to a restaurant for drinks after work; not sufficient to create actionable hostile environment).

54. Andrews v. City of Philadelphia, 895 F.2d 1469, 1474 (3d Cir. 1990) (plaintiff asserted that alleged harasser spoke to her in "seductive tones").

55. Ellison v. Brady, 924 F.2d 872 (9th Cir. 1991).
56. *Id.* at 874.
57. *Id.* at 874 n.1.
58. *Id.* Shortly thereafter, Gray transferred to a different office, but almost immediately filed a union grievance requesting a return to his original office. The IRS and the union settled the grievance by allowing Gray to retransfer, provided he spend four more months in the new office and promise not to bother the plaintiff. When plaintiff learned that Gray was returning, she filed a charge of sexual harassment.
59. *Id.* at 876.
60. *Id.* at 878.
61. Berkman v. New York, 580 F. Supp. 226, 231 (E.D.N.Y. 1983), *aff'd,* 755 F.2d 913 (2d Cir. 1985).
62. *Berkman,* 580 F. Supp. at 232 n.7.
63. *Id.* at 228.
64. 697 F. Supp. 1452 (N.D. Ill. 1988).
65. *Id.* at 1454.
66. *Id.* at 1456. The court also noted that if Goluszek were a woman, defendant would have taken action to stop the harassment. *Id.*
67. *Id.*
68. *Professor Delgado Replies,* at 595. R. George Wright suggests a similar justification: "Assuming that legal restraints on legal speech deter racist speech, genuine social gains may result. Enforced behavioral change, in the form of avoiding racist speech, may tend to produce genuine attitudinal change, as persons bring their attitudes into line with their non-racist speech."

Wright, at 23–24. Mari Matsuda also would justify regulation on the basis of its impact on beliefs: "Racism as an acquired set of behaviors can be dis-acquired, and law is the means by which the state typically provides incentives for changes in behavior." Matsuda, at 2361.
69. Delgado, at 140. Delgado also argues: "[b]igotry, and thus the attendant expression of racism, stifles, rather than furthers, the moral and social growth of the individual who harbors it." *Id.* at 176.

Of course, if all it took to justify regulation of speech was a determination that it "stifles . . . the moral and social growth of the individual," we could limit expression of any ideas that we did not value. Some might argue that Marxism stifles the moral and social growth of the individual, while others might argue that laissez-faire capitalism does the same. Educators across the country believe that Bart Simpson stifles the moral and social growth of the individual, although the Neilsen ratings suggest that a substantial segment of the population either does not agree or does not care. *See A Giant Case of Simpsonitis,* Chicago *Tribune,* Style Section, at 12 (June 13, 1990).
70. 858 F.2d 345, 350 (6th Cir. 1988).
71. Whitney v. California, 274 U.S. 357, 375 (1927) (Brandeis, J., concurring).
72. Chevigny, *Pornography and Cognition: A Reply to Cass Sunstein,* 1989 DUKE L.J. 420, 432.
73. *Id.*
74. Whitney v. California, 274 U.S. 357, 375–76 (1927) (Brandeis, J., concurring).

Questions for Meaning

1. Why is the First Amendment relevant to the discussion of sexual harassment in the workplace?
2. In paragraph 13, what does the term "romantic paternalism" mean?
3. According to Browne, what are the two main messages conveyed by sexual harassment complaints?

4. Consider the cartoon described in paragraph 29. Why could a cartoon like this be considered "political"? If defined as political speech, would the cartoon be allowed to remain or would it have to be removed?

5. Given the risk of litigation, how are employers most likely to frame regulations governing speech at work?

6. How much free speech should men and women enjoy in the workplace? Does Browne support any restrictions on speech at work?

7. Vocabulary: aberration (2), exacerbates (6), ambience (13), empirically (14), vicarious (16), animus (22), reprehensible (24), plaintiff (26), actionable (30), discernment (32).

Questions about Strategy

1. How do you respond to the questions Browne poses at the beginning of his opening paragraph? Does your response suit Browne's purpose in raising these questions?

2. Browne opens his argument by contrasting attempts to regulate speech on college campuses with attempts to do so in the workplace. What does this contrast establish, and why is it useful for Browne's purpose?

3. Compare the examples in paragraphs 27 and 28. Do they seem equally serious? What does Browne achieve by using these examples?

4. How sympathetic is Browne to the kind of speech he wants to protect? Does he ever concede that unregulated speech can be harmful?

5. In his conclusion (paragraph 36), Browne claims, "It is but a small step from requiring a person to refrain from expressing beliefs in the hope that he will cease to hold them to requiring a person to express beliefs in the hope that he will begin to hold them." Do you agree?

ONE STUDENT'S ASSIGNMENT

Drawing on material in *The Informed Argument,* Brief Edition, and at least two additional sources, write a synthesis of articles on sexual harassment in the workplace. When writing, imagine an audience that consists either of managers who need to be briefed on the principal issues in the debate over harassment in the workplace, or of employees who need to decide what kind of behavior is appropriate at work. Use APA-style documentation.

What Managers Need to Know: A Synthesis of Arguments
Concerning Sexual Harassment in the Workplace
Jessica Cozzens

Sexual harassment is one of the most controversial topics currently facing the American workforce. In fact, a study performed in 1986 suggests: "Unwanted sexual attention may be the single most widespread occupational hazard in the workplace today" (Riger, 1991, p. 497). An additional study performed in 1988 indicates that 42% of all the women surveyed "reported that they had experienced some form of unwanted and uninvited sexual attention . . ." (Riger, 1991, p. 497). In 1992 the Equal Opportunity Employment Commission reported that the number of complaints filed within a five-year period had doubled (Fisher, 1993, p. 160). Unfortunately, these statistics only serve to fuel the growing controversy regarding sexual harassment in the workforce.

2   On one hand we have individuals such as Fisher (1993), Hill (1995), and Riger (1991), who define sexual harassment in traditional terms where women, in nine cases out of ten (Fisher, 1993, p. 160), are the victims, often afraid to stand up for their rights and then abused when they do come forward. Studies conducted in 1982 and 1992 show that only 2–3% of harassment victims actually file complaints through formal channels (Fisher, 1993; Riger, 1991). Furthermore, Fisher (1993) reported that only 34% of the victims surveyed felt confident enough to confront the offender and request that the offensive action be terminated (p. 161). A study conducted in 1988 among Federal workers found that 33% of those who filed formal complaints claimed that it "made things worse" (Riger, 1991, p. 502). When these victims finally do confront their harassers, they are often met with further abuse and ridicule. The Hill–Thomas hearings of 1991 can be offered as an example. During the course of the hearings Anita Hill was portrayed as "prudish yet lewd, easily duped yet shrewd and ambitious, fantasizing yet calculating, pathetic yet evil" (Hill, 1995, p. 275), a view quite different from how Anita Hill sees herself. Fisher (1993) points out that these conflicts are often fueled by the simple fact that individuals often see certain types of behavior quite differently. Riger (1991) takes this issue a step further in claiming that these conflicting viewpoints are primarily gender-based; men and women tend to have very different ways of looking at the world.

On the other side of the spectrum are individuals such as Browne (1991), Paul (1991), and Luthar and Townsend (1995), who believe that the sexual harassment controversy has been blown out of proportion. They believe that in order to make it into the court system the "behavior would have to be objectively injurious rather than merely subjectively offensive" (Paul, 1991, p. 169). These advocates are calling for a distinction "between morally offensive behavior and behavior that causes serious harm" (Paul, 1991, p. 169). Browne (1991) emphasizes that the constitutional right to free speech should not be jeopardized by sexual harassment litigation. Luthar and Townsend (1995) agree, pointing out that women often find men's behavior offensive and claim that "the real answer to the 'hostile environment' problem [a basis for harassment suits] may be that women should learn to live with it too" (p. 174). Paul (1991) adds only that women should "lighten up, and even dispense a few risqué barbs of their own" (p. 170).

4   Title VII of the Civil Rights Act as well as the guidelines from the Equal Employment Opportunity Commission provide the foundation for sexual harassment cases today. They provide for two types of sexual harassment: *Quid pro quo,* which is equivalent to "Sleep with me, or else," and conduct that "has the purpose or effect of unreasonably interfering with an individual's work performance or creating an intimidating, hostile, or offensive working environment" (Riger, 1991, p. 498). While there is universal consensus regarding quid pro quo harassment, other types of abuse are more difficult to address. In order to interpret the standards defining a hostile working environment, courts have devised the "reasonable person rule," which basically asks whether a reasonable person would be offended by the behavior in question (Browne, 1991; Luthar & Townsend, 1995; Riger, 1991). The question then becomes: What is a reasonable person, and how is this different for men and women? Riger believes that "Men tend to find sexual overtures from women at work to be flattering, whereas women find similar approaches from men to be insulting" (p. 499). She believes that these problems stem from imbalances in the workforce and wants to promote "gender equity within organizations" (Riger, 1991, p. 503), eliminating the need for employers to distinguish between a "reasonable man" and a "reasonable woman." Luthar and Townsend (1995) dislike the reasonable woman theory, feeling that it has "led us back to a Victorian vision of woman; she cannot endure what a man can and must be protected" (p. 174). Browne (1991) and Paul (1991) both question the practicality of Title VII itself, and argue that *quid pro quo* places an unfair burden on the employer to prevent the offensive action. Paul also argues against Title VII, maintaining that monetary compensation does not compensate the victim for his or her mental distress.

Employer responsibility is one of the central themes within the sexual harassment debate. Title VII currently provides that the burden of protection actually falls on the employer (Browne, 1991; Fisher, 1993; Paul, 1991; Riger, 1991). Both Fisher (1993) and Riger (1991) stress that, for their own protection, employers are expected to not only develop and aggressively enforce an aggressive sexual harassment policy, but also promote an extensive education program clearly defining the policy. Luthar and Townsend (1995), however, question the value of such education programs. Furthermore, Browne (1991) believes that employers are virtually coerced into overregulating free speech in an attempt to protect themselves from liability. This overregulation often leads directly to violations of the First Amendment's guarantee of freedom of expression. Rather than the current system of penalizing

Enviomnt

the employer, or Riger's proposal of increased education and clearly defined policies, Browne (1991) maintains that the world is not made a better place through elimination of free expression with employer threats or government sanctions. Instead, Browne proposes that the only solution is to persuade the offender that his or her views are wrong, thereby preserving the constitutional rights of the general public. Paul (1991) takes quite a different approach and proposes that sexual harassment should be treated by the courts as a tort, or a personal injury. If sexual harassment is treated as a tort, employers would no longer be held liable for an employee's actions unless they were aware of the harassment and failed to act on their knowledge. Furthermore, harassers would be held personally responsible for damages assessed by the courts, perhaps thereby deterring potential harassers (Paul, 1991).

6   It is clear that there will be no easy solution to end this debate. Whether the courts continue to uphold the *quid pro quo* and hostile work environment premises, or one day declare sexual harassment to be a tort, it is unlikely that an absolute consensus will ever be reached. One thing both sides can agree on, however, is that this debate has led to increased pressure and tension in offices around the country. Men and women everywhere admit to withdrawing from the social work environment for fear of committing an unforgivable and potentially prosecutable social blunder, a trend which, if continued, can only result in a further lowering of the work morale across America.

References

Browne, K. R. (1991). Title VII as censorship: Hostile-environment harassment and the first amendment. In R. Miller (Ed.), The informed argument (brief ed.) (pp. 175–191). Fort Worth: Harcourt.

Fisher, A. B. (1993). Sexual harassment: What to do? In R. Miller (Ed.), The informed argument (brief ed.) (pp. 159–164). Fort Worth: Harcourt.

Hill, A. (1995). Marriage and patronage in the empowerment and disempowerment of African American women. In A. Hill & E. Jordan (Eds.), Race, gender, and power in America: The legacy of the Hill-Thomas hearings (pp. 271–291). New York: Oxford University Press.

Luthar, H., & Townsend, A. (1995). Man handling. In R. Miller (Ed.), The informed argument (brief ed.) (pp. 171–174). Fort Worth: Harcourt.

Paul, E. F. (1991). Bared buttocks and federal cases. In R. Miller (Ed.), The informed argument (brief ed.) (pp. 165–170). Fort Worth: Harcourt.

Riger, S. (1991). Gender dilemmas in sexual harassment policies and procedures. American Psychologist, 46, 497–505.

SUGGESTIONS FOR WRITING

1. Draw on your knowledge of your own gender and write an essay explaining what you think "the other gender" most needs to understand about sexual harassment.

2. Does your school or workplace have a policy against sexual harass- ment? If so, obtain a copy and write an evaluation of it.
3. Drawing on the articles by Anne B. Fisher and Ellen Frankel Paul, write a grievance procedure for sexual harassment in the workplace.
4. Write an essay comparing "Bared Buttocks and Federal Cases" with "Man Handling." On what points do the authors of these arguments seem to agree? How do their arguments differ in terms of structure and tone?
5. Reread the argument by Harsh Luthar and Anthony Townsend and write a response to it.
6. Write an argument defining how much freedom of speech people should enjoy in the workplace.
7. Do research on the confirmation hearings of Clarence Thomas in 1991, and then write an essay focused on whether the evidence you have dis- covered indicates that Anita Hill was sexually harassed by Thomas.
8. Obtain the full version of Kingsley R. Browne's "Title VII as Censor- ship: Hostile-Environment Harassment and the First Amendment." Write a summary of those parts (IV–VII) omitted from the abridged version published in this book.
9. Research recent cases involving sexual harassment in the military, and make a written recommendation for how this problem should be treated.

COLLABORATIVE PROJECT

Write a code of conduct that defines acceptable behavior when persons are trying to initiate a personal relationship with someone they have met at work or in class. Indicate also the behavior that is unacceptable. Be sure to consider the views of people of different gender and different sex- ual orientation, as well as other cultural differences such as age, race, and social class. Include specific recommendations for how someone can clearly indicate that personal overtures are unwelcome.

SECTION 3

SAME-GENDER MARRIAGE: WHAT IS A FAMILY?

ANDREW SULLIVAN

SIMPLE EQUALITY

A graduate of Oxford and Harvard universities, Andrew Sullivan has been a leading advocate of same-gender marriage. From 1991 to 1996, he was editor of *The New Republic,* a widely respected magazine with a liberal editorial policy. In 1995, he published *Virtually Normal; An Argument about Homosexuality,* a book described by the *New York Times* as a "model of civil discourse." The following argument was first published that same year. As you read, note how Sullivan treats marriage as a civil rights issue.

"A state cannot deem a class of persons a stranger to its laws," declared the Supreme Court recently.

2   It was a monumental statement. Gay men and lesbians, the conservative court said, are no longer strangers in America.

They are citizens, entitled, like everyone else, to equal protection—no special rights, but simple equality.

4   For the first time in Supreme Court history, gay men and women were seen not as some powerful lobby trying to subvert America, but as the people we truly are—the sons and daughters of countless mothers and fathers, with all the weaknesses and strengths and hopes of everybody else.

And what we seek is not some special place in America but merely to be a full and equal part of America, to give back to our society without being forced to lie or hide or live as second-class citizens.

6   That is why marriage is so central to our hopes. People ask us why we want the right to marry, but the answer is obvious. It's the same reason anyone wants the right to marry.

At some point in our lives, some of us are lucky enough to meet the person we truly love. And we want to commit to that person in front of our family and country for the rest of our lives.

8 It's the most simple, the most natural, the most human instinct in the world. How could anyone seek to oppose that?

Yes, at first blush, it seems like a radical proposal, but, when you think about it some more, it's actually the opposite. Throughout American history, to be sure, marriage has been between a man and a woman, and in many ways our society is built upon that institution.

10 But none of that need change in the slightest. After all, no one is seeking to take away anybody's right to marry, and no one is seeking to force any church to change any doctrine in any way. Particular religious arguments against same-sex marriage are rightly debated within the churches and faiths themselves.

That is not the issue here: There is a separation between church and state in this country. We are asking only that when the government gives out civil marriage licenses, those of us who are gay should be treated like anybody else.

12 Of course, some argue that marriage is by definition between a man and a woman. But for centuries, marriage was by definition a contract in which the wife was her husband's legal property. And we changed that. For centuries, marriage was by definition between two people of the same race.

And we changed that. We changed these things because we recognized that human dignity is the same whether you are a man or a woman, black or white. And no one has any more of a choice to be gay than to be black or white or male or female.

14 Some say that marriage is only about raising children, but we let childless heterosexual couples be married (Bob and Elizabeth Dole, Pat and Shelley Buchanan, for instance). Why should gay couples be treated differently?

Others fear that there is no logical difference between allowing same-sex marriage and sanctioning polygamy and other horrors. But the issue of whether to sanction multiple spouses (gay or straight) is completely separate from whether, in the existing institution between two unrelated adults, the government should discriminate between its citizens.

16 This is, in fact, if only Bill Bennett* could see it, a deeply conservative cause. It seeks to change no one else's rights or marriages in any way. It seeks merely to promote monogamy, fidelity and the disciplines of family life among people who have long been cast to the margins of society.

And what could be a more conservative project than that? Why indeed would any conservative seek to oppose those very family values for gay people that he or she supports for everybody else? Except, of course, to make gay men and lesbians strangers in their own country, to forbid them ever to come home. ❖

---

* A counterargument by Bennett begins on p. 199.

Questions for Meaning

1. According to Sullivan, why do gay men and lesbians want to be able to legally marry their partners?
2. What does Sullivan mean when he writes, in paragraph 11, "There is a separation between church and state in this country"? Where does this "separation" come from?
3. Why does Sullivan believe that his support for same-gender marriage is "deeply conservative"?
4. In his conclusion, Sullivan appeals to "family values." How would you define such values?

Questions about Strategy

1. To begin an essay with a quotation is a common writing strategy. What does Sullivan achieve by opening with the specific quotation he chose?
2. Consider how Sullivan defines homosexuals, in paragraph 4, as "the sons and daughters of countless mothers and fathers, with all the weaknesses and strengths and hopes of everybody else." To what kind of values is this definition designed to appeal?
3. How does Sullivan respond to opponents of same-gender marriage?
4. How does the last sentence of this argument help to unify it?

WILLIAM J. BENNETT

AN HONORABLE ESTATE

A former Secretary of Education, William Bennett has also served as Chairman of the National Endowment for the Humanities and as Director of the Office of National Drug Control Policy. He has a PhD from the University of Texas as well as a law degree from Harvard, and he speaks frequently on behalf of conservative causes. "An Honorable Estate" is an editor's title for the following argument, which was first published in 1996 as part of a debate with Andrew Sullivan (pages 197–198), which was distributed by the *New York Times* to newspapers around the country. As you read, note how Bennett appeals to traditional values.

There are at least two key issues that divide proponents and opponents of same-sex marriage.

2 The first is whether legally recognizing same-sex unions would strengthen or weaken the institution.

The second has to do with the basic understanding of marriage itself.

4   The advocates of same-sex marriage say that they seek to strengthen and celebrate marriage. That may be what some intend.

But I am certain that it will not be the reality.

6   Consider: The legal union of same-sex couples would shatter the conventional definition of marriage,⎟change the rules which govern behavior, endorse practices which are completely antithetical to the tenets of all of the world's major religions,⎟send conflicting signals about marriage and sexuality, particularly to the young, and obscure marriage's enormously consequential function—procreation and child-rearing.

Broadening the definition of marriage to include same-sex unions would stretch it almost beyond recognition—and new attempts to expand the definition still further would surely follow.

8   On what principled ground can Andrew Sullivan exclude others who most desperately want what he wants: legal recognition and social acceptance?

Why on earth would Sullivan exclude from marriage a bisexual who wants to marry two other people?⎟After all, exclusion would be a denial of that person's sexuality. The same holds true of a father and daughter who want to marry. Or two sisters.⎟

10   Or men who want (consensual) polygamous arrangements. Sullivan may think some of these arrangements are unwise. But having employed sexual relativism in his own defense, he has effectively lost the capacity to draw any lines and make moral distinctions.

Forsaking all others is an essential component of marriage. Obviously it is not always honored in practice. But it is the ideal to which we rightly aspire, and in most marriages the ideal is in fact the norm.

12   Many advocates of same-sex marriage simply do not share this ideal; promiscuity among homosexual males is well known.

Sullivan himself has written that gay male relationships are served by the "openness of the contract" and that homosexuals should resist allowing their "varied and complicated lives" to be flattened into a "single, moralistic model."

14   But that "single, moralistic model" has served society exceedingly well. The burden of proof ought to be on those who propose untested arrangements for our most important institution.

A second key difference I have with Sullivan goes to the very heart of marriage itself. I believe that marriage is not an arbitrary construct which can be redefined simply by those who lay claim to it.

16   It is an honorable estate, instituted of God and built on moral, religious, sexual and human realities. Marriage is based on a natural teleology, on the different, complementary nature of men and women—and how they refine, support, encourage and complete one another.

It is the institution through which we propagate, nurture, educate and sustain our species.

18   That we have to engage in this debate at all is an indication of how steep our moral slide has been.

Worse, those who defend the traditional understanding of marriage are routinely referred to (though not to my knowledge by Sullivan) as "homophobes," "gay-bashers," "intolerant" and "bigoted." Can one defend an honorable, 4,000-year-old tradition and not be called these names?

20   This is a large, tolerant, diverse country. In America people are free to do as they wish, within broad parameters. It is also a country in sore need of shoring up some of its most crucial institutions: marriage and the family, schools, neighborhoods, communities.

But marriage and family are the greatest of these. That is why they are elevated and revered. We should keep them so.   ❖

Questions for Meaning

1. According to Bennett, what are the main issues in the debate over same-gender marriage?
2. On what grounds does Bennett object to same-gender marriage?
3. What does Bennett mean, in paragraph 10, by "sexual relativism"?
4. How does Bennett define marriage?

Questions about Strategy

1. What does Bennett achieve in paragraph 6 by appealing to "the tenets of all of the world's major religions"? Is there any risk to this strategy?
2. How does Bennett characterize gay men, and how does this characterization serve his purpose?
3.. In paragraph 18, Bennett claims, "That we have to engage in this debate at all is an indication of how steep our moral slide has been." Does this claim help his argument?
4. Objecting to words like "homophobes" and "intolerant," Bennett asks, "Can one defend an honorable, 4,000-year-old tradition and not be called these names?" How does he expect readers to answer this question? Judging from his essay, would it be unfair to apply such language to Bennett?

FENTON JOHNSON

WEDDED TO AN ILLUSION

This argument was the cover story of *Harper's* magazine in November 1996—the national election year during which Congress passed the Defense of Marriage Act, a bill that defined marriage as the union of a man and a woman. Johnson draws attention to this legislation but then focuses on the meaning of marriage, the persons it benefits, and how it might work better in the future. As you read, note how Johnson combines scholarship and personal experience when arguing for a new understanding of marriage. If you are interested in learning more about his experience, read his memoir *Geography of the Heart* (1996).

Last summer, when American politicians underwent yet another of their periodic convulsions over the status of gays and lesbians, I found myself pondering the evolving history of marriage. In response to the possible recognition of same-gender marriages by the state of Hawaii, Congress overwhelmingly passed the Defense of Marriage Act, which reserves federal benefits and rights for male-female couples and permits states not to recognize same-gender marriages performed in other states. Sponsored in the House of Representatives by Bob Barr (three marriages) and endorsed by then Senator Bob Dole (two marriages), the bill was called "gay baiting" by the White House and "unnecessary" by President Clinton (he of the colorful personal life), who signed it nonetheless in late September. The law might appear to be only so much election-year positioning and counter-positioning, but long after this year's political season is forgotten, we will be agonizing over the questions implicit in the legislation. As a married, straight friend cracked to me, "If marriage needs Congress to defend it, then we know we're in trouble."

2   *Marriage.* What does it mean these days? Peau de soie, illusion veil, old, new, borrowed, blue? Can it mean the same thing to a heterosexual couple, raised to consider it the pinnacle of emotional fulfillment, as to a same-gender couple, the most conventional of whom must find the label "married" awkward? Can it mean the same thing to a young lesbian—out since her teens, occasionally bisexual, wanting a child, planning a career—as to me, a forty-plus shell-shocked AIDS widower? And in an era of no-fault divorce, can it mean to any of us what it meant to our parents?

The unacceptability of gay marriages may have bloomed with sudden propitiousness on the agendas of Clinton and Dole, but the issue has been steadily moving into the legal conversation across the last twenty-five years. In 1991 three Hawaiian couples—two lesbian, one gay-male—sued the state over the denial of their applications for marriage licenses; on principle, a heterosexual ACLU attorney took the case. Two years later, to everyone's amazement, the Hawaii Supreme Court ruled, in *Baehr* v. *Lewin,* that the state's denial of licenses violated the Hawaii constitution's equal-rights protections. The court took care to note that the sexual orientation of the plaintiffs was irrelevant. At issue instead was discrimination based on gender: the state discriminates by offering benefits (including income tax, worker's compensation, retirement, welfare, and spousal support) to married men and women that it denies to exclusively male or female couples.

4   This is no minor point. What the court ruled on in Hawaii was not *gay* marriage but simply *marriage:* whether the union of two people of the same gender qualifies for the benefits the state offers to mixed-gender couples, no matter if the spouses marry for love or children or Social Security benefits, no matter if they are gay or straight or celibate—in other words, all those reasons, good and bad, for which men and women now marry.

The Hawaii justices remanded the case to a lower court, challenging the attorney general to justify gender discrimination in marriage benefits. The plaintiffs' attorneys currently expect the State Supreme Court to allow the issuance of marriage licenses to same-gender couples by late 1997, though more litigation seems as likely, given the determination and financing of the opposition. If the state court acts as the plaintiffs anticipate, the matter will surely reach the federal level. Contrary to widespread reporting and rhetoric, Article IV of the U.S. Constitution does not necessarily require states to recognize marriages performed in other states; interstate recognition of marriage remains largely unexplored legal terrain.[1] If a couple marries in Hawaii, then moves to New York or Georgia, can those states refuse to recognize the marriage? Under the Defense of Marriage Act, the answer is yes, though some legal experts argue that states already have this right, while other experts contend that the act is unconstitutional. Either way the issue invokes a resonant precedent: as recently as 1967, sixteen states refused to recognize mixed-race marriages legally performed elsewhere. Those antimiscegenation laws were struck down that same year by the U.S. Supreme Court in *Loving* v. *Virginia,* a landmark case that the Hawaii court cited at length in *Baehr* v. *Lewin.*

6   At stake first and foremost are the rights of gays and lesbians to assume the state-conferred benefits of marriage. The assumption of these rights is controversial enough, but *Baehr* has still larger implications for an institution that has historically served as the foundation of a male-dominated society. It's instructive to recall that in the late 1970s Phyllis Schlafly and her anti–Equal Rights Amendment (ERA) allies predicted that the codification of the equality of women and men, as embodied in a federal ERA, would lead to gay marriage, presumably because they felt that to codify the equality of women and men would undermine the values upon which traditional marriage rests. The federal amendment failed, but Hawaii (along with several other states) adopted its own ERA; and here we are, just as Schlafly predicted—right in the place, I argue, where we ought to be. For this is the profound and scary and exhilarating fact: to assume the equality of women and men is to demand rethinking the institution that more than any other defines how men and women relate.

---

[1] States have always established their own standards for the recognition of marriage; no consistent, nationwide definition of marriage has ever existed. Currently, a few states (e.g., Pennsylvania) still recognize common-law marriages, though for such marriages to be recognized in a non-common-law state, participants must usually submit to some official procedure. Some states allow first cousins to marry, some do not, and the minimum age for legal marriage varies from state to state, as does the recognition of such contracts across state lines.

Marriage has always been an evolving institution, bent and shaped by the historical moment and the needs and demands of its participants. The Romans recognized the phenomenon we call "falling in love," but they considered it a hindrance to the establishment of stable households. Marriages certified by the state had their foundations not in religion or romance but in pragmatics—e.g., the joining of socially prominent households. Divorce was acceptable, and women were generally powerless to influence its outcome; the early Catholic Church restricted divorce partly as a means of protecting women and children from easy abandonment.

8   At the beginning of the thirteenth century, facing schisms and heresies, and seeking to consolidate its power, the Catholic Church institutionalized marriage, confirming it as a sacrament and requiring that a priest officiate—a crucial step in the intrusion of organized religion into what had previously been a private transaction. Several centuries later, the conception of "family" began to be transformed from an extended feudal unit that often included cousins, servants, and even neighbors to a tightly knit nuclear unit composed of parents and children and headed by a man. With marriage as its cornerstone, this idealized unit forms the foundation for virtually all American legislation concerning the family.

Throughout these developments, one aspect of marriage remained consistent: even as women were idealized, they were widely regarded as chattel—part of the husband's personal property; marriage was state certification of that ownership. With the women's suffrage movement came a growing acceptance of the equality of women and men, along with the principle that the individual's happiness is of equal or greater importance than the honoring of social norms, including the marriage contract. Divorce became both common and accepted, to the point that even the woman who marries into wealth gains little economic security (absent a good lawyer or a prenuptial agreement).

10   Women have arguably gotten the worst of both worlds: Men may more easily leave their wives, but women are nowhere near achieving earning parity, so that now they must cope with economic insecurity as well as the fear of being dumped. For every woman who revels in freedom and the income from a fulfilling career, many more face supporting themselves and often their children on welfare or at a low salary with few benefits and no job security, dependent on child support or alimony often in arrears. No wonder that almost a third of babies are now born out of wedlock, a figure that has risen consistently since the 1950s. Some of these mothers (more than a few of them lesbians) are building matriarchal families, but many are giving birth to unplanned and probably unwanted children. Whether by design or by happenstance, these unmarried women are the primary force in changing the profile of the family; any discussion about contemporary marriage that excludes them is pointless.

Both our culture and its couples are searching for some new thinking, informed by the understanding that what is at stake is our perception of the marriage contract and women's role in defining it. Understandably, advocates of same-gender marriage have shied away from territory so daunting, focusing on the narrower civil-rights issues—the need to extend, as required by our American commitment to equal treatment before the law, the invitation to another class of people to participate in the same troubled ritual, with one tangible result being a bonanza for attorneys specializing in gay divorce.

12   That fight is important, but in the long run the exclusive focus on civil rights minimizes the positive implications of the social transformation lesbians and gays are helping to bring about. For centuries gay and lesbian couples, along with significant numbers of unmarried heterosexuals, have formed and maintained relationships outside legislative and social approval that have endured persecution and duress for this simple reason: love. This is not to downplay the importance of the marriage license, which comes with rights and responsibilities without which gays and lesbians will never be considered full signatories to the social contract; nor is it to imply that these relationships are perfect. It is rather to point out the nature of gay couples' particular gift, the reward of those lucky enough to be given the wits and courage to survive in the face of adversity. Many of us know as much or more about partnering than those who have fallen into it as a given, who may live unaware of the degree to which their partnerships depend on the support of conventions—including the woman's acceptance of the man's primacy.

    Baehr v. *Lewin* represents the logical culmination of generations of challenge, by feminists joined later by gay and lesbian activists, to an institution once almost exclusively shaped by gender roles and organized religion. As such, it presents a historic opportunity to reexamine the performance and practice of the institution on which so many of our hopes, rituals, and assumptions are based; to reconsider what we are institutionalizing and why.

14   Seeking to provide a legally defensible justification for limiting benefits to mixed-gender marriages, the Hawaii attorney general, after years of research, has thus far only confirmed this insurmountable reality: if one subscribes to the principles that government should not serve specific religious agendas and that it should not discriminate on the basis of gender, there is no logical reason to limit marriage benefits to mixed-gender couples. Opponents of same-gender marriage argue that it contradicts the essential purpose of the institution, which is procreation; but the state does not ask prospective mixed-gender spouses if they intend to have children, and the law grants a childless married couple the same rights and benefits as their most prolific married neighbors. Invoking the nation's Judeo-Christian heritage is no help; even if one believes that Christians and Jews should dictate government policy, a few of the more liberal denominations have already endorsed same-gender marriage, and the issue is under serious debate in

mainstream churches.[2] How may the state take sides in a theological debate, especially when the parties to the debate are so internally divided? In 1978, the Supreme Court established in *Zablocki* v. *Redhail* that a citizen's right to marry is so fundamental that it cannot be denied even to individuals who have demonstrated that they are inadequate to the task. Given that the law guarantees the right of deadbeat dads and most prison inmates to marry, what could be the logic for denying that right to two men or two women who are maintaining a stable, responsible household?

The strongest argument against same-gender marriage is not logical but arbitrary: Society must have unambiguous definitions to which it turns when faced with conflicts between the desires of its citizens and the interests of its larger community. Marriage is a union between a man and a woman because that is how most people define the word, however unjust this may be for same-gender couples who wish to avail themselves of its rights.

16   Advocates of same-gender marriage respond that "the interests of the larger community" is an evolving concept. That an institution embodies social norms does not render it immune to change—slavery was once socially accepted, just as mixed-race marriages were widely forbidden and divorce an irreparable stigma. The rebuttal is accurate, but it evades the question of where the state draws the line in balancing individual needs and desires against the maintenance of community norms. Why should the state endorse same-gender couples but not (as opponents of same-gender marriage argue will result) polygamists or child spouses? The question is now more pressing because of the prevailing sense of accelerated cultural breakdown, wherein nothing seems secure, not even the definition of . . . well, marriage.

Surely the triumph of Reaganomics and corporate bottom-line thinking is more responsible for this breakdown of the social contract than the efforts of an ostracized minority to stabilize its communities. In any case, marriage and the family began their transformation long before the gay civil-rights movement. By 1975, only six years after the Stonewall rebellion that marked the first widespread public emergence of lesbians and gays, half of all marriages ended in divorce. But in uncertain times people search for scapegoats, and unless gays and lesbians can make a convincing case for the positive impact of our relationships, we are not likely to persuade any but the already converted.

18 Tellingly enough, male writers have been more passionate than women in their attachment to traditional marriage forms. Among gay male writers, Andrew Sullivan *(Virtually Normal)* and William Eskridge Jr. *(The Case for*

---

[2] Many gay Protestant congregations, Reform Jews, Unitarians, and a number of Quaker congregations have endorsed and/or performed same-gender marriage. Presbyterians recently passed a resolution urging the national office to explore the feasibility of filing friend-of-the-court briefs "in favor of giving civil rights to same-sex partners," and the Episcopal Church is studying the blessing of same-sex unions. In addition, Hawaii's Buddhist bishops have announced their support of same-gender marriage.

Same-Sex Marriage) have written excellent supporting arguments.[3] Both consider legalization of same-gender marriage a means toward encouraging same-gender couples to model themselves on heterosexual marriage.

Sullivan makes an eloquent case for gay marriage but gives only a nod to the high failure rate of heterosexual marriages. Eskridge is sensitive to the women's issues inherent in marriage, but like Sullivan he endorses the institution as it exists, albeit alongside other options for partnering. Along the way he endorses the myth that marriage conveys the means to control extramarital sexual behavior to men (or women) otherwise unlikely to achieve such control, as well as the myth that gay men are more promiscuous than their straight counterparts.[4] More discouraging is Eskridge's acceptance of the assumption that sexual desire is the beast lurking in our social jungle, whose containment is a prerequisite for a moral civilization (he subtitles his book *From Sexual Liberty to Civilized Commitment,* epitomizing in a phrase the puritanical impulse to make bachelorhood equivalent to moral lassitude, where all sexual expression outside wedlock is morally tainted).

20   That sexuality and morality are intimately linked I take as a given; one loses sight of this connection at the risk of one's self-respect and, by extension, one's ability to love others. We are surrounded by evidence of that loss of respect, particularly in television and advertising, whose relentless promotion of amoral heterosexual sex is surely the greatest factor in breaking down public and private morality. But to presume that morality follows on marriage is to ignore centuries of evidence that each is very much possible without the other.

Among heterosexual male writers, even the most intelligent dwell in fantasy logic; when they arrive at a difficult point they invoke God (an unanswering authority), or homophobic bombast, or both. James Q. Wilson, management and public policy professor at UCLA, is among the more reasonable, but even he attacks (with no apparent irony) the "overeducated," whom he accuses of "mounting a utilitarian assault on the family." As the ninth of nine children of a rural, blue-collar family whose parents (married forty-seven years) sacrificed a great deal to educate their children, I note that the only "overeducated" people I have met are those who take as gospel the rules they have been taught rather than open their eyes to the reality in which they live, who witness love and yet deny its full expression.

22   Not all men and women fall into marriage unconscious of role models, of course. But it's hard work to avoid a form shouted at all of us daily in a million ways, whereas for same-gender partnerships to fall into that form requires deliberate denial. For same-gender relationships to endure, the

---

[3] By contrast, *Virtual Equality,* lesbian activist Urvashi Vaid's 440-page treatment of gay and lesbian civil rights, mentions same-gender marriage only glancingly, by way of offering a generalized endorsement.

[4] Since great numbers of gay men remain partly or wholly in the closet, there's no accurate way to measure or compare gay male and straight male experiences. But generalizations about gay male life based on behavior in bars and sex clubs are surely no more accurate than generalizations about heterosexual male behavior drawn from visiting America's red-light districts.

partners have to figure out that we are required to make them up as we go along. This does not mean that we are always adequate to the task, which is why my friend Frederick Hertz, an Oakland attorney specializing in same-gender partnerships, originally opposed same-gender marriage. "Marriage as it exists imposes a legal partnership on people that is seldom in sync with how they think about their relationship," he tells me. "Marriage is designed to take care of dependent spouses, people who stay home to take care of the children, as well as to compensate for economic inequalities between genders. The idea of supporting a spouse for the rest of his or her life is totally contrary to the way most people nowadays think." Hertz (a partner in a fourteen-year relationship) resists the "couple-ism" that he perceives arising among gays and lesbians because he believes it imitates a heterosexual world in which women whose partners die or abandon them are left with almost no social support. "I talk to straight divorced women in their forties and fifties," he says. "They have a lack of self-worth that's devastating. My single gay friends have a hard enough time—imagine what things would be like for them if marriage were the norm."

Then the realities of working with gay and lesbian couples struggling without social approval brought Hertz to an uneasy support of the battle for same-gender marriage rights. Unlike most advocates, however, he qualifies his endorsement by adding that "while we're working for gay-marriage rights we should also be talking about issues of economic and emotional dependency among couples. . . . A partner can contribute emotional support to a relationship that is as valuable to its sustenance as an economic contribution. We need to find legal ways to protect those dependent spouses." To that end Hertz argues for a variety of state-endorsed domestic-partnership arrangements in addition to marriage, noting that although such categories may create a kind of second-class relationship, they're a step toward the state offering options that reflect contemporary life. "I want to go to the marriage bureau and have options among ways of getting married," he says. "I want the social acceptance of marriage but with options that are more appropriate for the range of couples' experiences—including same-gender childless couples."

24   In other words, rather than attempt to conform same-gender couplings to an institution so deeply rooted in sexism, why not consider ways of incorporating stability and egalitarianism into new models of marriage? Rather than consider the control of sexual behavior as a primary goal of marriage, why not leave issues of monogamy to the individuals and focus instead on marriage as the primary (though not the only) means whereby two people help each other and their dependents through life?

Invoking the feminist writer Martha Fineman, American University law professor Nancy Polikoff argues that organizing society around sexually connected people is wrong; the more central units are dependents and their caretakers. Extrapolating from this thinking, one can imagine the state requiring that couples, regardless of gender, take steps toward attaining the benefits currently attached to marriage. Under this model the state might restrict the most significant of marriage's current benefits to those couples who demonstrate stability. The government might then get out of the marriage-certification business altogether; Hawaii governor Ben Cayetano, among others, has suggested as much. Government-conferred benefits currently reserved for married couples would instead be allocated as rewards for behavior that contributes to social stability. Tax breaks would be awarded, regardless of marital status, to stable lower- and middle-income households financially responsible for children, the elderly, or the handicapped. Other state- or federally conferred privileges—such as residency for foreign spouses, veteran's benefits, tax-free transfer of property, and the right to joint adoption—would be reserved for couples who had demonstrated the ability to sustain a household over two to five years. The decision to assume the label "marriage" would be left to the individuals involved, who might or might not seek ratification of their decision by a priest or minister or rabbi. The motivation behind such changes would be not to eliminate marriage but to encourage and sustain stable households, while leaving the definition and sustenance of marriage to the partners involved, along with their community of relatives, friends, and—if they so choose—churches.

26   In the most profound relationship I have known, my partner and I followed a pattern typical of an enduring gay male relationship. We wrangled over monogamy, ultimately deciding to permit safe sex outside the relationship. In fact, he never acted on that permission; I acted on it exactly once, in an incident we discussed the next day. We were bound not by sexual exclusivity but by trust, mutual support, and fidelity—in a word, love, only one manifestation of which is monogamy.

    Polikoff tells of another model, unconventional by the standards of the larger culture but common among gay and lesbian communities: A friend died of breast cancer; her blood family arrived for the funeral. "They were astounded to discover that their daughter had a group of people who were a family—somebody had organized a schedule, somebody brought food every night," she says. "In some ways it was the absence of marriage as a dominant institution that created space for the development of a family defined in much broader ways." I find it difficult to imagine either of these relationships—mine or that described by Polikoff—developing in the presence of marriage as practiced by most of our forebears; easier to imagine our experiences influencing the evolution of marriage to a more encompassing, compassionate place.

28   Earlier I called myself an "AIDS widower," but I was playing fast and loose with words; I can't be a widower, since my partner and I were never married. He was the only child of Holocaust survivors, and he taught me, an HIV-negative man preoccupied with the future, the lessons his parents had taught him: the value of living fully in the present and the power of love.

    He fell ill while we were traveling in France, during what we knew would be our last vacation. After checking him into a Paris hospital, I had to sneak past the staff to be at his side; each time they ordered me out, until finally they told me they would call the police. Faced with the threat of violence, I left the room. He died alone as I paced the hall outside his door, frantic to be at his side but with no recourse—I was, after all, only his friend.

30 At a dinner party not long ago I asked a mix of gay and heterosexual guests to name ways society might better support the survival of gay and lesbian relationships. A beat of silence followed, then someone piped up: "You mean, the survival of *any* relationships." Everyone agreed that all relationships are under stress, that their dissolution had become an accepted, possibly assumed part of the status quo.

The question is not, as opponents would have us believe, will marriage survive the legalization of same-gender partnerships? Instead, the questions are how do society and the state support stable households in a world where the composition of families is changing, and how might same-gender relationships contribute to that end?

32 Denied access to marriage, lesbians and gays inevitably idealize it, but given the abuse the dominant culture has heaped on the institution, maybe it could use a little glamour. In my more hopeful moments, I think gays and lesbians might help revitalize and reconceptualize marriage by popularizing the concept of rich, whole, productive couplings based less on the regulation of sexual behavior and the maintenance of gender roles than on the formation of mutually respectful partnerships. *Baehr* v. *Lewin* presents us with a chance to conceive of a different way of coupling, but only if we recognize and act on its implications. Otherwise the extension (if achieved) to same-gender couples of the marital status quo will represent a landmark civil-rights victory but a subcultural defeat in its failure to incorporate into the culture at large lessons learned by generations of women and men—lesbian or gay or straight—who built and sustained and fought for partnerships outside the bounds of conventional gender roles.

In *Word Is Out*, a 1977 documentary portraying lesbian and gay lives, comedienne Pat Bond described butch and femme role-playing among lesbians in the 1950s, roles as unvarying as those of Ozzie and Harriet. "Relationships that lasted twenty or thirty years were role-playing," she says. "At least in that role-playing you knew the rules, you at least knew your mother and father and you knew what they did and you tried to do the same thing. . . . Now you say, 'Okay, I'm not butch or femme, I'm just me.' Well, who the hell is me? What do I do? How am I to behave?"

34 To heterosexuals who feel as if the marriage debate is pulling the rug of certainty from beneath them, I say, Welcome to the club. Gays' and lesbians' construction of community—which is to say, identity—is the logical culmination of the American democratic experiment, which provides its citizens with an open playing field on which each of us has a responsibility to define and then respect his or her boundaries and rules. Human nature being what it is, the American scene abounds with stories of people unable, unwilling, or

uninterested in meeting that challenge—people who fare better within a package of predetermined rules and boundaries. For those people (so long as they are straight), traditional marriage and roles remain. But for the questioning mind and heart, the debate surrounding marriage is only the latest intrusion of ambiguity into the artificially ordered world of Western thinking.

And Western culture has never tolerated ambiguity. The Romans placed their faith in the state; the Christians, in God; the rationalists, in reason and science. But in marked contrast to Eastern religions and philosophy, all have in common their search for a constant governing structure, a kind of unified field theory for the workings of the heart. The emergence of gays and lesbians from the closet (a movement born of Western religious and rationalist thinking) is only one among many developments that reveal the futility of that search—how it inevitably arrives at the enigma that lies at the heart of being.

36   But the rules are so comforting and comfortable! And it is easier to oppress some so that others might live in certainty, ignoring the reality that the mystery of love and life and death is really grander and more glorious than human beings can grasp, much less legislate.   ❖

Questions for Meaning

1. Why is it significant that the Hawaii Supreme Court focused its decision on gender rather than sexual orientation?
2. According to Johnson, why has marriage benefited men more than women? Why does he believe same-gender marriage will foster more equality between men and women?
3. What's wrong, in Johnson's view, with considering same-gender marriage solely as a civil rights issue? What other issues does he want people to consider?
4. Why might some gay and lesbian couples hesitate to marry even if they are deeply committed to each other?
5. The federal government currently extends tax benefits to married couples simply because they are married. Who should be entitled to such benefits, according to Johnson?
6. Vocabulary: propitiousness (3), remanded (5), pragmatics (7), schisms (8), chattel (9), denominations (14), epitomizing (19), lassitude (19), extrapolating (25), enigma (35).

Questions about Strategy

1. Why does Johnson cite the number of times the House sponsor and the Senate endorser of the Defense of Marriage Act have been married? Is he making an ad hominem argument or pointing to a real inconsistency?

2. Does Johnson ever recognize arguments that can be made against same-gender marriage? How fairly does he treat people with whom he disagrees?
3. Johnson draws on personal experience at several points in this essay. How successfully has he incorporated his own experience into his argument?
4. In paragraph 31, Johnson seeks to redefine the debate over same-gender marriage. What happens if you agree with the way he has re-defined the question?
5. The last four paragraphs of this essay contrast ambiguity with certainty. Why does Johnson try to persuade readers to accept living with ambiguity? How effective is this conclusion?

Jean Bethke Elshtain

ACCEPTING LIMITS

Centennial Professor of Political Science at Vanderbilt University, Jean Bethke Elshtain has written extensively on American culture for many years. Her books on the family include *The Family in Political Thought* (1982) and *Rebuilding the Nest: A New Commitment to the American Family* (1990). Her most recent works include *Democracy on Trial* (1995) and *Augustine and the Limits of Politics* (1995). This argument was first published in 1991 as part of a discussion in *Commonweal.* As you read, note how Elshtain defines the purpose of marriage and the state's responsibility to protect it.

Every society embraces an image of a body politic. This complex symbolism incorporates visions and reflections on who is inside and who is outside; on what counts as order and disorder; on what is cherished and what is despised. This imagery is fluid but not, I will argue, entirely up for grabs. For without some continuity in our imagery and concern, we confront a deepening nihilism. In a world of ever-more transgressive enthusiasms, the individual—the self—is more, not less, in thrall to whatever may be the reigning ethos. Ours is a culture whose reigning ethic is surely individualism and freedom. Great and good things have come from this stress on freedom and from the insistence that there are things that cannot and must not be done for me and to me in the name of some overarching collective. It is, therefore, unsurprising that anything that comes before us in the name of "rights" and "freedom" enjoys a *prima facie** power, something akin to political grace.

* Latin for "at first appearance."

2 But perhaps we have reached the breaking point. When Madonna proclaims, in all sincerity, that mock masturbation before tens of thousands is "freedom of expression" on a par, presumably, with the right to petition, assemble, and protest, something seems a bit out of whack—distorted, quirky, not-quite-right. I thought about this sort of thing a lot when I listened to the stories of the "Mothers of the Disappeared" in Argentina and to their invocation of the language of "human rights" as a fundamental immunity—the right not to be tortured and "disappeared." I don't believe there is a slippery slope from queasiness at, if not repudiation of, public sexual acts for profit, orchestrated masturbation, say, and putting free speech as a fundamental right of free citizens in peril. I don't think the body politic has to be nude and sexually voracious—getting, consuming, demanding pleasure. That is a symbolism that courts nihilism and privatism (however publicly it may be trumpeted) because it repudiates intergenerational, familial, and communal contexts and believes history and tradition are useful only to be trashed. Our culture panders to what social critic John O'Neill calls the "libidinal body," the body that titillates and ravishes and is best embodied as young, thin, antimaternal, calculating, and disconnected. Make no mistake about it: much of the move to imagery of the entitled self and the aspirations to which it gives rise are specifically, deeply, and troublingly antinatal—hostile to the regenerative female body and to the symbolism of social regeneration to which this body is necessarily linked and has, historically, given rise.

  Don't get me wrong: not every female body must be a regenerative body. At stake here is not mandating and coercing the lives of individuals but pondering the fate of a society that, more and more, repudiates generativity as an animating image in favor of aspiration without limit of the contractual and "wanting" self. One symbol and reality of the latter is the search for intrusive intervention in human reproducing coming from those able to command the resources of genetic engineers and medical reproduction experts, also, therefore, those who have more clout over what gets lifted up as our culture's dominant sense of itself. One finds more and more the demand that babies can and must be made whenever the want is there. This demandingness, this transformation of human procreation into a technical operation, promotes a project Oliver O'Donovan calls "scientific self-transcendence." The technologizing of birth is antiregenerative, linked as it is to a refusal to accept any natural limits. What technology "can do," and the law permits, we seem ready to embrace. Our ethics rushes to catch up with the rampant rush of our forged and incited desires.

4 These brief reflections are needed to frame my equally brief comments on the legality, or not, of homosexual marriage. I have long favored domestic partnership possibilities—ways to regularize and stabilize commitments and relationships. But marriage is not, and never has been, primarily about two people—it is and always has been about the possibility of generativity. Although in any given instance, a marriage might not have led to the raising of a family, whether through choice or often unhappy recognition of, and final reconciliation to, the infertility of one or another spouse, the symbolism of

marriage-family as social regenesis is fused in our centuries-old experience with marriage ritual, regulation, and persistence.

The point of criticism and contention runs: in defending the family as framed within a horizon of intergenerationality, one privileges a restrictive ideal of sexual and intimate relations. There are within our society, as I already noted, those who believe this society can and should stay equally open to all alternative arrangements, treating "life-styles" as so many identical peas in a pod. To be sure, families in modernity coexist with those who live another way, whether heterosexual and homosexual unions that are by choice or by definition childless; communalists who diminish individual parental authority in favor of the preeminence of the group; and so on.

6   But the recognition and acceptance of plural possibilities does not mean each alternative is equal to every other with reference to specific social goods. No social order has ever existed that did not endorse certain activities and practices as preferable to others. Ethically responsible challenges to our terms of exclusion and inclusion push toward a loosening but not a wholesale negation in our normative endorsement of intergenerational family life. Those excluded by, or who exclude themselves from, the familial intergenerational ideal, should not be denied social space for their own practices. And it is possible that if what were at stake were, say, seeking out and identifying those creations of self that enhance an aesthetic construction of life and sensibility, the romantic bohemian or rebel would get higher marks than the Smith family of Remont, Nebraska. Nevertheless, we should be cautious about going too far in the direction of a wholly untrammeled pluralism lest we become so vapid that we are no longer capable of distinguishing between the moral weightiness of, say, polishing one's Porsche and sitting up all night with an ill child. The intergenerational family, as symbolism of social regenesis, as tough and compelling reality, as defining moral norm, remains central and critical in nurturing recognitions of human frailty, mortality, and finitude and in inculcating moral limits and constraints. To resolve the untidiness of our public and private relations by either reaffirming unambiguously a set of unitary, authoritative norms or eliminating all such norms as arbitrary is to jeopardize the social goods that democratic and familial authority, paradoxical in relation to one another, promise—to men and women as parents and citizens and to their children.   ❖

Questions for Meaning

1. According to Elshtain, what values now seem most important in the United States?
2. Why is Elshtain willing for gay and lesbian couples to be recognized as "domestic partners" but not as married couples?

3. What is the meaning of the "libidinal body," and why does Elshtain believe this concept is relevant to the issue of gay marriage?
4. Why does Elshtain believe that a distinction can be made between recognizing different alternatives and giving equal consideration to each?
5. Vocabulary: nihilism (1), transgressive (1), thrall (1), voracious (2), antinatal (2), generativity (4), pluralism (6), vapid (6), inculcating (6).

Questions about Strategy

1. What is Elshtain's purpose in contrasting a Madonna concert with Argentine mothers who waged a public protest against a military dictatorship?
2. Why does Elshtain discuss the ethics of human reproduction before addressing the question of gay marriage?
3. Does Elshtain make any concessions to readers who have values different from her own?
4. In paragraph 6, consider how Elshtain contrasts the life of a "romantic bohemian" with "the Smith family of Remont, Nebraska" and "the moral weightiness of, say, polishing one's Porsche and sitting up all night with an ill child." Do these contrasts help her argument?

ONE STUDENT'S ASSIGNMENT

Recognizing that there are sharply divided opinions on the subject of same-gender marriage, write a Rogerian argument that will help conflicting parties find common ground. Your essay should demonstrate that you have paid close attention to views different from your own and have considered why they deserve to be taken seriously. Introduce your own views only after you have given fair consideration to the ideas of people you hope to persuade. Draw not only on the sources gathered in *The Informed Argument,* Brief Edition, but also on additional research. Use MLA-style documentation.

Speak Now or Forever Hold the Past
Dana Simonson

My parents eloped 25 years ago last June. To them, it was their best and only option; they were in love. My parents are *still* in love and married, even though my mother's parents objected to the marriage. After coming to understand their deep commitment, my grandparents became supportive of my parents' marriage. Like most Americans, they realize that faithfulness in relationships promotes healthy living and that marriage is the clearest way for couples to confirm their commitment to each other alone. However, not all Americans enjoy the same opportunities to marry. In the past, my grandparents—and others of their generation—may not have considered men marrying men and women marrying women, but the time has come to discuss this possibility.

2   Opponents of same-gender marriage often cite personal religious beliefs, arguing that marriage is primarily a religious institution. "It is an honorable estate, instituted of God and built on moral, religious, sexual and human realities" from which homosexuals should be excluded because "the legal union of same-sex couples . . . endorse[s] practices which are completely antithetical to the tenets of all of the world's major religions" (W. Bennett 200). They assert that gays and lesbians can, indeed, be married, only not to a person of the same gender. I also perceive that they have a concern that homosexuals are trying to achieve special rights and privileges and that allowing them to marry would cause "a radical deconstruction of the institution [of marriage]" (Schiffren 21). Moreover, many people are concerned about the place of children in same-gender marriages, believing that heterosexuality "is critical for raising healthy children and transmitting the values that are the basis of our culture" (Schiffren 21).

     I commend these citizens for upholding their religious ideals, since individuals tend to lose hope if they do not believe in values which endure. Opponents of same-gender marriage also reveal a concern for fairness insomuch as a certain group of people may be aspiring for special privileges from which others might be excluded. I also share the concern for the future of children involved in same-gender marriages. Above all, I agree with the concern that the government has a responsibility to provide a healthy society.

4   Nevertheless, I propose that the marriage decision belongs to individual citizens. Couples who are publicly ready to commit themselves to fidelity should have the authority to make their own decisions. My main interest is that insofar as Americans do not equally share the *option* of marriage, we are creating a divided society. This separation is worsening because "in uncertain times people search for scapegoats" (Johnson 206).

     The convictions held by those opposed to same-gender marriage, understandable though they are, restrict the rights of others. Although these citizens have a right to their religious beliefs, they do not have the right to impose these beliefs on others. Heterosexual couples can be legally married even if they are not religious. Why should not homosexual couples—many of whom are religious—enjoy the same opportunity? Today we are discussing the civil, not religious, right of same-gender couples to marry the individuals they love.

6   Same-gender couples are recommending equality rather than special privileges. "[W]hat we seek is not some special place in America but merely to be a full and equal part of America, to give back to our society without being forced to lie or hide or live as second-class citizens" (Sullivan 197). Married, same-gender couples would indeed receive benefits equal to, but no greater than, those of heterosexual couples. We would all be subject to the same marriage laws, such as a consenting adult age limit, prohibition of polygamy, and required child support.

Without the option of marriage, same-gender couples might encounter financial stress because of unshared health insurance, retirement and inheritance benefits, and the inability to file joint income taxes. Why should any couple, with or without children, suffer financially after they are not allowed the right to marriage? Financial stress might also hurt the children of same-gender couples, possibly depriving them of college-education savings.

8   Many would agree that raising children within a marriage is not only a great struggle, but also an immense privilege. To take part in this experience, some couples choose to adopt children. As marriage is fulfilling in itself, other married, heterosexual couples choose not to have children. Like heterosexual couples, each homosexual couple will have to make their own decision. In fact, many same-gender couples have already made the decision to raise children, but these families do not enjoy the full protection and rights they deserve; marriage often leads to higher social acceptance of a couple's children. The possible stigma children face because their parents cannot be married is damaging.

In order to have a healthy society, same-gender couples need to have the option of marriage. Couples themselves would benefit through control of their lives. Also, the children of couples would gain security as part of a socially recognized, stable family unit because their parents are married. Moreover, we would all partake in the benefits because "Society has a vested interest in stable, committed relationships" (Hartinger 682). Most important is the knowledge that marriage should be based on love; since all humans are capable of love, we are all eligible for marriage. Rather than realizing and accepting change, "it is easier to oppress some so that others might live in certainty, ignoring the reality that the mystery of love and life and death is really grander and more glorious than human beings can grasp, much less legislate" (Johnson 211). Not all couples in love will choose to be married, but we should all have the option.

10   If we put forth the imaginary effort to understand a same-gender couple who wishes to be married, would we not be supportive of their commitment? One writer in a same-gender relationship inspires us to put forth the effort, "I know that to

understand a life that is different from the life lived by most people takes time—and an open mind" (L. Bennett 32). It took my grandparents two years to accept my parents' marriage. Although my grandfather has since passed away, my grandmother helped organize my parents' 25th anniversary party last summer. Today, my grandmother also understands and is supportive of her grandson's same-gender relationship. In defense of their love and their struggle for the equal right for same-gender couples to be married, my grandmother spoke out, "They're no different than you or me . . . they have a kitchen and cook together." Times have changed, and my grandmother exclaimed, "They even have a cappuccino maker!"

Works Cited

Bennett, Lisa. "Why Can't We Get Married?" Mademoiselle Oct. 1996: 32.

Bennett, William. "An Honorable Estate." The Informed Argument. Brief ed. Ed. Robert K. Miller. Fort Worth: Harcourt, 1999. 199–201.

Hartinger, Brent. "A Case for Gay Marriage." Commonweal 22 Nov. 1991: 681–683.

Johnson, Fenton. "Wedded to an Illusion." The Informed Argument. Brief ed. Ed. Robert K. Miller. Fort Worth: Harcourt, 1999. 201–211.

Schiffren, Lisa. "Gay Marriage, an Oxymoron." New York Times 23 Mar. 1996, nat. ed., sec. 1:21.

Sullivan, Andrew. "Simple Equality." The Informed Argument. Brief ed. Ed. Robert K. Miller. Fort Worth: Harcourt, 1999. 197–198.

SUGGESTIONS FOR WRITING

1. Should anyone in love be able to get married? Write an argument on behalf of what you believe a successful marriage requires.

2. How important is the sexual orientation of parents? Write an essay defining what you think parents should offer their children.

3. Andrew Sullivan argues that conservatives should support same-gender marriage; William Bennett argues that they should not. Write an essay defining what it means to be a conservative.

4. Imagine that you have been asked to moderate the debate between Andrew Sullivan and William Bennett, whose arguments have been included in this section. Write an essay designed to help them heal their differences.

5. Write an argument for or against the legalization of same-gender marriage in your state.

6. Drawing on the essay by Fenton Johnson, and other sources if you wish, write a paper about how marriage between men and women has changed during the twentieth century.

7. Should couples live together before they get married, or do such arrangements weaken the institution of marriage? Write an argument for or against cohabitation.

8. Write an essay defining "domestic partnership."
9. Should American corporations extend benefits to domestic partners as well as to spouses? Write an essay about how you think businesses should respond to employees who are partnered to someone of their own gender.
10. Imagine that a close friend has just come out to you, revealing that she is in love with another woman. You were shocked when she told you, and you didn't know what to say. Now, feeling that you let your friend down, you decide to write her a letter explaining your response. Write a letter that will both convey your beliefs and preserve your friendship.

COLLABORATIVE PROJECT

Interview a diverse group of people to learn what they think of marriage. Try to include married couples, couples who are living together without being married, couples who are dating but not living together, and both single men and single women. Be sure to include people of different ages and different cultural backgrounds—as well as people who are heterosexual, homosexual, or bisexual—so that you can gather a range of views. If possible, interview people, such as clergy and social workers, who are experienced in counseling couples. Then write a report that provides an analysis of the data you have gathered.

SECTION 4

IMMIGRATION: WHO GETS TO BECOME AN AMERICAN?

EMMA LAZARUS

THE NEW COLOSSUS

Emma Lazarus (1849–1887) was a Russian-born poet who settled in New York. Her works include *Admetus and Other Poems* (1871), *Alide* (1874), *Songs of the Semite* (1882), and *By the Waters of Babylon* (1887). But of all her works, none is so famous as her sonnet to the Statue of Liberty. Now carved on the statue's pedestal, the poem was first published in 1883. As you read it, note the pattern with which lines are rhymed.

1   Not like the brazen giant of Greek fame,
With conquering limbs astride from land to land;
Here at our sea-washed, sunset gates shall stand
A mighty woman with a torch, whose flame
5   Is the imprisoned lightning, and her name
Mother of Exiles. From her beacon-hand
Glows world-wide welcome; her mild eyes command
The air-bridged harbor that twin cities frame.
"Keep, ancient lands, your storied pomp!" cries she
10   With silent lips. "Give me your tired, your poor,
Your huddled masses yearning to breathe free,
The wretched refuse of your teeming shore.
Send these, the homeless, tempest-tost to me,
I lift my lamp beside the golden door!"

Questions for Meaning

1. Lazarus calls her poem "The New Colossus" and begins by contrasting the Statue of Liberty with "the brazen giant of Greek fame." To what is she alluding?
2. Although the Statue of Liberty is on the American east coast, Lazarus associates it with "sunset gates." From what point of view would New York be associated with the setting sun rather than the rising sun?

3. In the final line, Lazarus makes "golden door" a metaphor for New York harbor. In what sense then can arrival in America be seen as reaching a "golden door"?

4. Vocabulary: astride (line 2), beacon (line 6), pomp (line 9), teeming (line 12).

Questions about Strategy

1. Lazarus composed her poem as a sonnet: a fourteen-line poem expressing a complete thought written with a fixed number of stressed and unstressed syllables in each line and divided into an octave (eight lines) and a sextet (six lines). In this form, the end of the first line rhymes with the end of the fourth, fifth and eighth lines; the second line rhymes with the third, sixth, and seventh; and, in the sextet, two new sounds are introduced, with every other line rhyming. Does her use of this poetic form contribute to the argument made by the poem?

2. In line 6, Lazarus renames the Statue of Liberty. The statue's actual name is "Liberty Enlightening the World." Lazarus calls it "Mother of Exiles." How do these names differ, and how does the change reveal the poet's purpose in this poem?

 PETER BRIMELOW

A NATION OF IMMIGRANTS

Born and educated in Great Britain, Peter Brimelow now lives and works in the United States. His books include *The Patriot Game: Canada and the Canadian Question Revisited* (1986) and *The Wall Street Game* (1988). "A Nation of Immigrants" is an editor's title for the following short excerpt from a long, controversial article on immigration that Brimelow published in *National Review* in 1992. Founded by William F. Buckley Jr., *National Review* is a monthly magazine that reflects politically conservative opinions.

Everyone has seen a speeded-up film of the cloudscape. What appears to the naked eye to be a panorama of almost immobile grandeur writhes into wild life. Vast patterns of soaring, swooping movement are suddenly discernible. Great towering cumulo-nimbus formations boil up out of nowhere, dominating the sky in a way that would be terrifying if it were not, in real life, so gradual that we are barely aware that anything is going on.

2   This is a perfect metaphor for the development of the American nation. America, of course, is exceptional. What is exceptional about it, however, is not the way in which it was created, but the speed.

"*We are a nation of immigrants.*" No discussion of U.S. immigration policy gets far without someone making this helpful remark. As an immigrant myself, I always pause respectfully. You never know. Maybe this is what they're taught to chant in schools nowadays, a sort of multicultural Pledge of Allegiance.

4   But it secretly amuses me. Do they really think other nations sprouted up out of the ground? ("Autochthonous" is the classical Greek word.) The truth is that *all* nations are nations of immigrants. But the process is usually so slow and historic that people overlook it. They mistake for mountains what are merely clouds.

This is obvious in the case of the British Isles, from which the largest single proportion of Americans are still derived. You can see it in the place-names. Within a few miles of my parents' home in the north of England, the names are Roman (Chester, derived from the Latin for camp), Saxon (anything ending in *-ton*, town, like Oxton), Viking (*-by*, farm, like Irby), and Norman French (Delamere). At times, these successive waves of peoples were clearly living cheek by jowl. Thus among these place-names is Wallesey, Anglo-Saxon for "Island of the Welsh"—Welsh being derived from the word used by low-German speakers for foreigners wherever they met them, from Wallonia to Wallachia. This corner of the English coast continued as home to some of the pre-Roman Celtic stock, not all of whom were driven west into Wales proper as was once supposed.

6   The English language that America speaks today (or at least spoke until the post-1965 fashion for bilingual education) reflects the fact that the peoples of Britain merged, eventually; their separate contributions can still be traced in it. Every nation in Europe went through the same process. Even the famously homogeneous Japanese show the signs of ethnically distinct waves of prehistoric immigration.

But merging takes time. After the Norman Conquest in 1066, it was nearly three hundred years before the invaders were assimilated to the point where court proceedings in London were again heard in English. And it was nearly nine centuries before there was any further large-scale immigration into the British Isles—the Caribbean and Asian influx after World War II.

8   Except in America. Here the process of merging has been uniquely rapid. Thus about 7 million Germans have immigrated to the U.S. since the beginning of the nineteenth century. Their influence has been profound—to my British eye it accounts for the odd American habit of getting up in the morning and starting work. About 50 million Americans told the 1980 Census that they were wholly or partly of German descent. But only 1.6 million spoke German in their homes.

So all nations are made up of immigrants. But what is a nation—the end-product of all this merging? This brings us into a territory where words are weapons, exactly as George Orwell pointed out years ago. "Nation"—as suggested by its Latin root *nascere,* to be born—intrinsically implies a link by blood. A nation is an extended family. The merging process through which all nations pass is not merely cultural, but to a considerable extent biological, through intermarriage.

10   Liberal commentators, for various reasons, find this deeply distressing. They regularly denounce appeals to common ethnicity as "nativism" or "tribalism." Ironically, when I studied African history in college, my politically correct tutor deprecated any reference to "tribes." These small, primitive, and incoherent groupings should, he said, be dignified as "nations." Which suggests a useful definition: tribalism/nativism is nationalism of which liberals disapprove.

American political debate on this point is hampered by a peculiar difficulty. American editors are convinced that the term "state" will confuse readers unless reserved exclusively for the component parts of the United States—New York, California, etc. So when talking about sovereign political structures, where the British would use "state," the Germans "*Staat,*" and the French "*l'état,*" journalists here are compelled to use the word "nation." Thus in the late 1980s it was common to see references to "the nation of Yugoslavia," when Yugoslavia's problem was precisely that it was not a nation at all, but a state that contained several different small but fierce nations— Croats, Serbs, etc. (In my constructive way, I've been trying to introduce, as an alternative to "state," the word "polity"—defined by Webster as "a politically organized unit." But it's quite hopeless. Editors always confuse it with "policy.")

12   This definitional difficulty explains one of the regular entertainments of U.S. politics: uproar because someone has unguardedly described America as a "Christian nation." Of course, in the sense that the vast majority of Americans are Christians, this is nothing less than the plain truth. It is not in the least incompatible with a secular *state* (polity).

But the difficulty over the N-word has a more serious consequence: it means that American commentators are losing sight of the concept of the "nation-state"—a sovereign structure that is the political expression of a specific ethno-cultural group. Yet the nation-state was one of the crucial inventions of the modern age. Mass literacy, education, and mobility put a premium on the unifying effect of cultural and ethnic homogeneity. None of the great pre-modern multinational empires have survived. (The Brussels bureaucracy may be trying to create another, but it has a long way to go.)*

14   This is why Ben Wattenberg is able to get away with talking about a "Universal Nation." On its face, this is a contradiction in terms. It's possible, as Wattenberg variously implies, that he means the diverse immigrant groups will eventually intermarry, producing what he calls, quoting the English poet John Masefield a "wondrous race." Or that they will at least be assimilated by American culture, which, while globally dominant, is hardly "universal." But meanwhile there are hard questions. What language is this

---

* Brussels is the administrative site of the European Community, which governs the Common Market, among other responsibilities.

"universal nation" going to speak? How is it going to avoid ethnic strife? dual loyalties? collapsing like the Tower of Babel? Wattenberg is not asked to reconcile these questions, although he is not unaware of them, because in American political discourse the ideal of an American nation-state is in eclipse.

Ironically, the same weaknesses were apparent in the rather similar concept of "cultural pluralism" invented by Horace M. Kallen at the height of the last great immigration debate, before the Quota Acts of the 1920s. Kallen, like many of today's pro-immigration enthusiasts, reacted unconditionally against the cause for "Americanization" that the 1880-to-1920 immigrant wave provoked. He argued that any unitary American nationality had already been dissipated by immigration (sound familiar?). Instead, he said the U.S. had become merely a political state (polity) containing a number of different nationalities.

16   Kallen left the practical implications of this vision "woefully undeveloped" (in the words of the *Harvard Encyclopedia of American Ethnic Groups*). It eventually evolved into a vague approval of tolerance, which was basically how Americans had always treated immigrant groups anyway—an extension, not coincidentally, of how the English built the British nation.

But in one respect, Kallenism is very much alive: he argued that authentic Americanism was what he called "the American Idea." This amounted to an almost religious idealization of "democracy," which again was left undeveloped but which appeared to have as much to do with non-discrimination and equal protection under the law as with elections. Today, a messianic concern for global "democracy" is being suggested to conservatives as an appropriate objective for U.S. foreign policy.

18   And Kallenism underlies the second helpful remark that someone always makes in any discussion of U.S. immigration policy: "*America isn't a nation like the other nations—it's an idea.*"

Once more, this American exceptionalism is really more a matter of degree than of kind. Many other nations have some sort of ideational reinforcement. Quite often it is religious, such as Poland's Roman Catholicism; sometimes cultural, such as France's ineffable Frenchness. And occasionally it is political. Thus—again not coincidentally—the English used to talk about what might be described as the "English Idea": English liberties, their rights as Englishmen, and so on. Americans used to know immediately what this meant. As Jesse Chickering wrote in 1848 of his diverse fellow-Americans: "English laws and institutions, adapted to the circumstances of the country, have been adopted here. . . . The tendency of things is to mold the whole into one people, whose leading characteristics are English, formed on American soil."

20   What is unusual in the present debate, however, is that Americans are now being urged to abandon the bonds of a common ethnicity and instead to trust entirely to ideology to hold together their state (polity). This

is an extraordinary experiment, like suddenly replacing all the blood in a patient's body. History suggests little reason to suppose it will succeed. Christendom and Islam have long ago been sundered by national quarrels. More recently, the much-touted "Soviet Man," the creation of much tougher ideologists using much rougher methods than anything yet seen in the U.S., has turned out to be a Russian, Ukrainian, or Kazakh after all.

Which is why Shakespeare has King Henry V say, before the battle of Agincourt, not "we defenders of international law and the dynastic principle as it applies to my right to inherit the throne of France," but

We few, we happy few, we band of brothers.

However, although intellectuals may have decided that America is not a nation but an idea, the news has not reached the American people—especially that significant minority who sternly tell the Census Bureau their ethnicity is "American." (They seem mostly to be of British origin, many generations back.) And it would have been considered absurd throughout most of American history.

22   John Jay in *The Federalist Papers* wrote that Americans were "one united people, a people descended from the same ancestors, speaking the same language, professing the same religion, attached to the same principles of government, very similar in their manners and customs." Some hundred years later, Theodore Roosevelt in his *Winning of the West* traced the "perfectly continuous history" of the Anglo-Saxons from King Alfred to George Washington. He presented the settling of the lands beyond the Alleghenies as "the crowning and greatest achievement" of "the spread of the English-speaking peoples," which—though personally a liberal on racial matters—he saw in explicit terms: "it is of incalculable importance that America, Australia, and Siberia should pass out of the hands of their red, black, and yellow aboriginal owners, and become the heritage of the dominant world races."

Roosevelt himself was an example of ethnicities merging to produce this new nation. He thanked God—he teased his friend Rudyard Kipling—that there was "not a drop of British blood" in him. But that did not stop him from identifying with Anglo-Saxons or from becoming a passionate advocate of an assimilationist Americanism, which crossed ethnic lines and was ultimately to cross racial lines.

24   And it is important to note that, at the height of the last great immigration wave, Kallen and his allies totally failed to persuade Americans that they were no longer a nation. Quite the contrary: once convinced that their nationhood was threatened by continued massive immigration, Americans changed the public policies that made it possible. While the national-origins quotas were being legislated, President Calvin Coolidge put it unflinchingly: "America must be kept American."

Everyone knew what he meant. ❖

Questions for Meaning

1. Why does Brimelow question the value of asserting that the United States is a nation of immigrants?
2. How does Brimelow distinguish between "nation" and "state"? Why does he believe that the distinction is important?
3. According to Brimelow, how has the debate over immigration changed? Why is he concerned about this change?
4. In paragraph 21, Brimelow alludes to the battle of Agincourt. When was this battle fought? Who won? And why was this outcome significant?
5. Vocabulary: writhes (1), discernible (1), homogeneous (6), deprecated (10), sundered (20), incalculable (22).

Questions for Strategy

1. How effective is the comparison Brimelow makes between a speeded-up film of clouds and the development of American history?
2. How would you describe the tone of this article? Can you point to specific lines that support your view?
3. Consider paragraphs 22 and 23. Has Brimelow strengthened his case by appealing to American figures of historical importance? Has he left himself open to counterargument?
4. Brimelow concludes by stating that "everyone" knew what it meant to be American back in the 1920s. What is Brimelow implying here? How does this implication affect you?

DENISE TOPOLNICKI

 # MAKING IT BIG IN AMERICA

This argument first appeared in a 1995 issue of *Money,* a magazine that frequently publishes success stories and other articles focused on how to generate and preserve personal wealth. As you read, note how staff writer Denise Topolnicki draws attention to numerous individuals who seem to represent the American dream that financial success comes to those who are unafraid of opportunity and prepared to work hard.

A lot of the angry Californians who helped pass Proposition 187—to deny costly welfare, health care and public education to undocumented aliens—probably had someone like Hilda Pacheco in mind when they pulled the lever in November. Pacheco, 32, entered the state illegally from Mexico in 1978, never finished high school and is the single mother of two children. People like her, the argument goes, are draining $2.3 billion a year from

California's strained health care, prison and education systems while also filling some of the relatively few jobs available in the state's recessionary economy. What's more, they lack the skills ever to contribute as much as they will take. *People like her should go home.*

2   Such anti-immigrant sentiments echo well beyond California's borders today. Arizona, California, Florida, New Jersey and Texas are suing the federal government for a collective $14 billion—the states' estimate of their outlay to support, educate, hospitalize and imprison illegal aliens. In Washington, the Commission on Immigration Reform, headed by former Democratic Rep. Barbara Jordan, urged Congress to create a national registry of legal workers, effectively barring jobs from the estimated 200,000 to 300,000 undocumented immigrants each year. And the new Republican majority in Congress has gone further, threatening to cut off welfare benefits even for legal immigrants, except for refugees and those over age 75.

Before you reach your own conclusion about these initiatives, you may want to learn more about people like Hilda Pacheco. What you discover may not conform to the talk radio image of immigrants as leeches. Rather than being a drag on the economy, Pacheco—like most immigrants—is making it in America. She has never been on welfare, has attained legal status and has elevated herself from a subminimum-wage job at a hamburger stand 16 years ago to her current $50,000-a-year managerial position at a worker-training firm. "I'm sure that illegals pay more taxes than they get credit for," Pacheco says.

4   With immigrants entering the U.S. at a rate of 1 million a year, foreign-born residents—legal and illegal—now represent 8.5% of the U.S. population, nearly twice the percentage (4.7%) in 1970. And in California, where fully 40% of recent immigrants settle, 22% of the population was born outside the U.S. Still, foreign-born residents today make up a much smaller portion of the U.S. population than they did following the great wave of immigration at the start of the century, when foreign-born residents peaked at 15%.

People who criticize today's immigrants, however, contend that as a whole, the current newcomers are fundamentally different from the 13 million Eastern and Southern Europeans who immigrated to the U.S. in the first half of this century. They surely are different in at least one sense: Just 38% of today's arrivals are white, compared with 88% of those who came before 1960. Critics also argue that our high-tech economy now demands brains, not brawn, which means poorly educated and unsophisticated immigrants have little hope of following their predecessors into the middle class.

6   If you look at the research on immigrants, however, you'll find that much of the pessimism is unwarranted. Contrary to what many Americans believe:

• The vast majority of today's immigrants—legal and illegal—are doing well, or at least striving to pave the way for their children to live better lives. Figures from the Census Bureau reveal that immigrants who arrived in the

U.S. before 1980 actually boast higher average household incomes ($40,900) than all native-born Americans ($37,300).

   • Few immigrants come here to get on welfare. In reality, working-age, nonrefugee immigrants are less likely than their native-born counterparts to be on the dole.

   • Immigrant children aren't gobbling up precious educational dollars, either. In fact, only 4% of the $227 billion we spend to educate our children is spent educating legal immigrant children and just 2% is spent on the estimated 648,000 kids who are here illegally.

   • Immigrants are not long-term drains on our economy. Yes, the estimated 3.8 million illegal immigrants cost us about $2 billion a year, chiefly because many work in low-wage jobs and often don't pay income taxes. But over time, immigrants become productive. As a group, the foreign-born pay $25 billion to $30 billion a year *more* in taxes than they consume in government services, says the Urban Institute.

   Like yesterday's immigrants, the newcomers choose America because it offers a chance to prosper. Jeffrey S. Passel, the Urban Institute's director of immigration research and policy, is optimistic about their prospects. "The very act of pulling up stakes and moving to a foreign country indicates that you have initiative and want to better yourself," he says.

8   The successes of today's immigrants hold lessons for us all, whether our ancestors came here on the Mayflower, in slave ships, on a turn-of-the-century steamer or on a jetliner.

Jobs, Not Welfare

Immigration's foes are fond of pointing out that 9% of immigrant households collect cash welfare benefits, compared with only 7% of households headed by native-born Americans. But that single statistic paints a misleading picture. Welfare use is high almost exclusively among legal refugees from war-torn or Communist countries, including Cambodia (50% of all households), Laos (46%), Vietnam (26%), the former Soviet Union (17%) and Cuba (16%). Unlike other immigrants, these favored refugees are immediately entitled to public assistance. As a result, 16% of the refugees, in contrast to only 3% of other immigrants, who came here during the 1980s, get public aid.

10   The notion that illegal immigrants come to the U.S. to obtain welfare benefits is a myth. Illegals already are barred from all public assistance except for emergency medical care under Medicaid, and the women, infants and children (WIC) nutrition program. Further, even a legal immigrant who goes on the dole during his five years in the U.S. risks deportation. Though few actually get the boot, the law still acts as a deterrent because an immigrant on welfare would have difficulty getting the approvals necessary to sponsor relatives for residency in the U.S., which is a prime goal for many immigrants.

Thirty-two-year-old Iraji Khiar reflects the prevalent immigrant attitude toward welfare. He fled war-torn Ethiopia in 1977 and spent the next 10 years with family friends in the Sudan before being sponsored for U.S. entry by a cousin who had come a few years earlier. But when Khiar arrived in San Diego in 1987, he couldn't locate his relative, and in order to survive, he accepted the Catholic Church's help in signing him up for welfare—for all of four weeks. At that point, Khiar refused further aid, insisting that he wanted to earn his keep "with my own sweat." He began working as a high school janitor at $7.75 an hour and attending classes toward an associate's degree in business administration from San Diego City College. He later went into the food business with another cousin and her brother. Today the trio typically work 141 hours a week at the Maryam Sambussa Factory, which bakes savory East African pastries, and the Sphinx International Restaurant, which serves up a multiethnic stew of East African and African American foods. The Sphinx features African and American music—when it's not karaoke night.

The Dream Is Alive

12   Academics have found that the longer immigrants are here, the more likely they are to have obtained two staples of the American dream: a home and their own business. For example, among immigrants who have lived here five to nine years, 44% own their own homes. That figure rises to 55% after at least 10 years.

Some scholars believe that immigrants eventually pull ahead of natives in the income race because their work habits aren't constricted by our notions of the typical eight-hour workday. Further, a willingness to strike out on their own has allowed many immigrants to earn more money sooner than they would have in the corporate world, given their often limited command of English. Overall, the same portion (7%) of immigrants as native-born Americans are self-employed, and both groups of entrepreneurs earn, on average, about $30,000 a year. Yet for some ethnic groups, self-employment rates are significantly higher, particularly for Koreans (18%) and Iranians (12%). Immigrants also are well represented in highly skilled professional and technical jobs. Two of every 10 U.S. physicians are foreign-born, for example, as is one in eight engineers.

14   Nevertheless, some immigration experts argue that immigrants who arrived here *after* 1980 will never do as well as natives because they're more likely than their predecessors to have come from Third World nations. Only time will tell whether recent immigrants' median household income of $31,100 will rise. Still, a closer look at the facts reveals that these newcomers aren't as disadvantaged as they first appear. Explains University of Texas sociologist Frank D. Bean: "To say that today's immigrants are of lower quality than their predecessors puts an unfair onus on them. They actually have more education than immigrants who came here 20

years ago." Indeed, between 1970 and 1990, the percentage of immigrants with college degrees climbed from 19% to 27%. Meanwhile, the portion of immigrants who dropped out of high school fell to 37% from 48%. (By comparison, 15% of native-born Americans are high school dropouts and 27% are college graduates.) Nearly half (47%) of African immigrants hold college degrees.

Even if you assume that most immigrants who lack college degrees will never earn much in today's demanding job market, it's wrong to presume that they won't become taxpayers or that their children will get stuck in low-wage jobs. As Michigan State sociologist Ruben C. Rumbaut, an expert on recent immigrants, reminds us: "At the turn of the century, many people argued that the U.S. was attracting immigrants who had little education and few job skills. But the fact that you came here as a peasant didn't mean that your children would forever be part of the unwashed underclass."

Immigrant Kids: Moving to the Head of the Class

16 The widely held belief that most immigrant kids demand to be taught in their native languages indefinitely is also dead wrong, as is the notion that we are spending a ton of money on bilingual education. Federal spending on bilingual education, adjusted for inflation, actually *fell* 48% during the 1980s, despite a 50% increase in the number of public school children with limited proficiency in English. In addition, studies show that English is the language of choice for the children of immigrants, no matter what their nationality. The experience of the Rev. Nancy C. Moore, senior pastor of Faith United Presbyterian Church in Los Angeles' predominantly Hispanic Highland Park neighborhood, is instructive. Since most of the 72 children who signed up for Sunday School two years ago were Hispanic, Mrs. Moore decided to assign two teachers to each classroom, one who spoke English, another who spoke Spanish. She dropped the plan, however, when she discovered that 69 of the kids already knew English and that the three who didn't wanted to be taught in their adopted language, not their parents' tongue.

There's also plenty of evidence that immigrants' children are performing well academically, despite poverty, poorly educated parents and discrimination—problems often associated with underachievement in native-born Americans. Even children who missed years of school while detained in refugee camps abroad do amazingly well. In one study, for example, University of Michigan researchers tracked 536 Vietnamese, Laotian and Chinese-Vietnamese children who attended public schools in low-income sections of Boston, Chicago, Houston, Orange County, Calif., and Seattle during the early 1980s. Most were B students, more than a quarter regularly got A's, and only 4% had grade point averages at or below C. They also did better than average on a standardized achievement test: in math, an impressive 27% ranked in the top 10% nationwide.

18 Why do these kids remind us of Horatio Alger rather than Bart Simpson? Because their parents preached a mantra that has served immigrants

for generations: Control your destiny through education. The kids, in turn, relish the chance to learn; in their homelands, education is generally reserved for the wealthy. As a result, families gather around their kitchen tables on weeknights, with older children expected to assist younger siblings. The University of Michigan researchers found that, on average, immigrant grade school students studied two hours and five minutes a night, while high school kids hit the books three hours and 10 minutes. The typical American junior or senior high school student studies only an hour and a half per day. Unfortunately, other researchers have found that when immigrant kids' grades falter, it is often because of overassimilation into American culture. In other words, the longer they live here, the more television they watch and the less homework they do—results that reflect more poorly on us than them.

Another myth: Success is limited to Asian kids. A study of Salvadoran, Guatemalan and Nicaraguan illegals who attended overcrowded, violence-plagued schools in the San Francisco area found that they were the academic stars of otherwise dismal institutions. Although two-thirds of the 50 Central American students surveyed worked 15 to 30 hours a week to supplement their families' income, half made the honor roll.

20   The most astonishing achievements, however, belong to the Hmong, people who were subsistence farmers and CIA operatives in the mountains of northern Laos during the Vietnam War. Many adult Hmong are not literate even in their native language, and a disturbing three-quarters of their households are on welfare. Yet studies of Hmong schoolkids in San Diego and St. Paul conducted during the past four years reveal that they earn better grades than native-born white children. Ruben Rumbaut is still haunted by one San Diego teenager he interviewed a few years ago. The girl's mother had died giving birth to her eighth child; her father remarried and had six more children. In the U.S., the family of 16, joined by the girl's maternal grandparents, squeezed into two apartments. The girl was responsible for keeping house, so she usually couldn't start studying until midnight. Yet she scored 1216 on the SAT (the national average is 902). Muses Rumbaut: "Whenever I think of that girl, I know it's unwise to make pronouncements about the future success of immigrants' children simply by looking at aggregate census data on recent immigrants' education and income."

Yet despite immigrant accomplishments, some Americans seem determined to keep whispering: *No matter what, they'll never be real Americans.* They'll keep their strange customs, congregate in ethnic enclaves, and as their numbers and economic well-being increase, they will demand political power.

22   And if they do, well, they won't be very much unlike the largely unschooled, ragtag ethnic tribes that landed on our shores three or four generations ago and still insist on clinging to such rituals as polka dancing, playing boccie and marching in the St. Patrick's Day parade. Aren't we better off for having let them in? ❖

Questions for Meaning

1. What do the statistics in paragraph 4 reveal about U.S. history in the twentieth century?
2. According to this argument, how are today's immigrants affecting the U.S. economy?
3. What factors can explain the financial success of many of today's immigrants?
4. What would be the purpose of establishing a national registry of legal workers?
5. Vocabulary: unwarranted (6), dole (10), median (14), onus (14), mantra (18), falter (18), aggregate (20).

Questions about Strategy

1. What does Topolnicki achieve by opening with the example of Hilda Pacheco?
2. Where does Topolnicki recognize the views of people who question the value of today's immigrants? How effectively does she respond to these concerns?
3. How credible are the sources cited in this argument?
4. This essay concludes with a rhetorical question. How does the author expect readers to answer this question? Is this a reasonable expectation?

GEORGE J. BORJAS

THE NEW ECONOMICS OF IMMIGRATION

A professor of Economics at the University of California at San Diego, George J. Borjas has emerged as a prominent voice in public debate over American immigration policy. His books include *Hispanics in the U.S. Economy* (1985), *Friends or Strangers: The Impact of Immigrants on the U.S. Economy* (1990), and *Immigration and the Work Force* (1992). In the following argument, first published by the *Atlantic Monthly* in 1996, Borjas discusses the effects of recent immigration on the economy as a whole and argues that immigration is making some Americans richer and others poorer.

The United States is on the verge of another great debate over immigration. Thus far the focus of this still-inchoate debate has been on illegal immigration or welfare benefits to legal immigrants, not on the larger issue of the character and consequences of the current high levels of legal immigration. Economic factors by themselves should not and will not decide the outcome of this debate. But they will play an important role. Economics helps us to frame answerable questions about immigration: Who gains by it? Who loses? And in light of the answers to these questions, what should U.S. immigration policy be?

2   There have been two major shifts in immigration policy in this century. In the twenties the United States began to limit the number of immigrants admitted and established the national-origins quota system, an allocation scheme that awarded entry visas mainly on the basis of national origin and that favored Germany and the United Kingdom. This system was repealed in 1965, and family reunification became the central goal of immigration policy, with entry visas being awarded mainly to applicants who had relatives already residing in the United States.

The social, demographic, and economic changes initiated by the 1965 legislation have been truly historic. The number of immigrants began to rise rapidly. As recently as the 1950s only about 250,000 immigrants entered the country annually; by the 1990s the United States was admitting more than 800,000 legal immigrants a year, and some 300,000 aliens entered and stayed in the country illegally. The 1965 legislation also led to a momentous shift in the ethnic composition of the population. Although people of European origin dominated the immigrant flow from the country's founding until the 1950s, only about 10 percent of those admitted in the 1980s were of European origin. It is now estimated that non-Hispanic whites may form a minority of the population soon after 2050. More troubling is that immigration has been linked to the increase in income inequality observed since the 1980s, and to an increase in the costs of maintaining the programs that make up the welfare state.

4   These economic and demographic changes have fueled the incipient debate over immigration policy. For the most part, the weapons of choice in this debate are statistics produced by economic research, with all sides marshaling facts and evidence that support particular policy goals. In this essay I ask a simple question: What does economic research imply about the kind of immigration policy that the United States should pursue?

A Formula for Admission

Every immigration policy must resolve two distinct issues: how many immigrants the country should admit and what kinds of people they should be.

6   It is useful to view immigration policy as a formula that gives points to visa applicants on the basis of various characteristics and then sets a passing grade. The variables in the formula determine what kinds of people will be let into the country, and the passing grade determines how many will be let into the country. Current policy uses a formula that has one overriding variable: whether the visa applicant has a family member already residing in the United States. An applicant who has a relative in the country gets 100 points, passes the test, and is admitted. An applicant who does not gets 0 points, fails the test, and cannot immigrate legally.

Of course, this is a simplistic summary of current policy. There are a lot of bells and whistles in the immigration statutes (which are said to be only slightly less complex than the tax code). In fact the number of points a person gets may depend on whether the sponsor is a U.S. citizen or a permanent resident, and whether the family connection is a close one (such as a parent, a spouse, or a child) or a more distant one (a sibling). Such nuances help to determine the speed with which the visa is granted. A limited number of visas are given to refugees. Some are also distributed on the basis of skill characteristics, but these go to only seven percent of immigrants.

8   Although the United States does not officially admit to using a point system in awarding entry visas, other countries proudly display their formulas on the Internet. A comparison of these point systems reveals that the United States is exceptional in using essentially one variable. Canada, Australia, and New Zealand have more-complex formulas that include an applicant's educational background, occupation, English-language proficiency, and age along with family connections.

Sometimes a host country awards points to people who are willing to pay the visa's stated price. Canada, for example, has granted entry to virtually anyone who would invest at least $250,000 in a Canadian business. Although this "visas-for-sale" policy is a favorite proposal of economists (if we have a market for butter, why not also a market for visas?), it is not taken very seriously in the political debate, perhaps because policymakers feel a repugnance against what may be perceived as a market for human beings. I will therefore discuss the implications of economic research only for policies in which points are awarded on the basis of socioeconomic characteristics, not exchanged for dollars.

What Have We Learned?

10   The academic literature investigating the economic impact of immigration on the United States has grown rapidly in the past decade. The assumptions that long dominated discussion of the costs and benefits of immigration were replaced during the 1980s by a number of new questions, issues, and perceptions.

Consider the received wisdom of the early 1980s. The studies available suggested that even though immigrants arrived at an economic disadvantage, their opportunities improved rapidly over time. Within a decade or two of immigrants' arrival their earnings would overtake the earnings of natives of comparable socioeconomic background. The evidence also suggested that immigrants did no harm to native employment opportunities, and were less likely to receive welfare assistance than natives. Finally, the children of immigrants were even more successful than their parents. The empirical evidence, therefore, painted a very optimistic picture of the contribution that immigrants made to the American economy.

12   In the past ten years this picture has altered radically. New research has established a number of points.

• The relative skills of successive immigrant waves have declined over much of the postwar period. In 1970, for example, the latest immigrant arrivals on average had 0.4 fewer years of schooling and earned 17 percent less than natives. By 1990 the most recently arrived immigrants had 1.3 fewer years of schooling and earned 32 percent less than natives.

• Because the newest immigrant waves start out at such an economic disadvantage, and because the rate of economic assimilation is not very rapid, the earnings of the newest arrivals may never reach parity with the earnings of natives. Recent arrivals will probably earn 20 percent less than natives throughout much of their working lives.

• The large-scale migration of less-skilled workers has done harm to the economic opportunities of less-skilled natives. Immigration may account for perhaps a third of the recent decline in the relative wages of less-educated native workers.

• The new immigrants are more likely to receive welfare assistance than earlier immigrants, and also more likely to do so than natives: 21 percent of immigrant households participate in some means-tested social-assistance program (such as cash benefits, Medicaid, or food stamps), as compared with 14 percent of native households.

• The increasing welfare dependency in the immigrant population suggests that immigration may create a substantial fiscal burden on the most-affected localities and states.

• There are economic benefits to be gained from immigration. These arise because certain skills that immigrants bring into the country complement those of the native population. However, these economic benefits are small—perhaps on the order of $7 billion annually.

• There exists a strong correlation between the skills of immigrants and the skills of their American-born children, so that the huge skill differentials observed among today's foreign-born groups will almost certainly become tomorrow's differences among American-born ethnic groups. In effect, immigration has set the stage for sizable ethnic differences in skills and socioeconomic outcomes, which are sure to be the focus of intense attention in the next century.

The United States is only beginning to observe the economic consequences of the historic changes in the numbers, national origins, and skills of immigrants admitted over the past three decades. Regardless of how immigration policy changes in the near future, we have already set in motion circumstances that will surely alter the economic prospects of native workers and the costs of social-insurance programs not only in our generation but for our children and grandchildren as well.

Whose Interests Will We Serve?

14   If economic research is to play a productive role in the immigration debate, research findings should help us to devise the formula that determines admission into the United States. We need to decide what variables are to be

used to award points to applicants, and what is to be the passing grade. Before we can resolve these issues, however, we have to address a difficult philosophical question: What should the United States try to accomplish with its immigration policy?

The answer to this question is far from obvious, even when the question is posed in purely economic terms. We can think of the world as composed of three distinct groups: people born in the United States (natives), immigrants, and people who remain in other countries. Whose economic welfare should the United States try to improve when setting policy—that of natives, of immigrants, of the rest of the world, or of some combination of the three? The formula implied by economic research depends on whose interests the United States cares most about.

16   Different political, economic, and moral arguments can be made in favor of each of the three groups. I think that most participants in the U.S. policy debate attach the greatest (and perhaps the only) weight to the well-being of natives. This is not surprising. Natives dominate the market for political ideas in the United States, and most proposals for immigration reform will unavoidably reflect the self-interest and concerns of native voters.

Immigration almost always improves the well-being of the immigrants. If they don't find themselves better off after they enter the United States, they are free to go back or to try their luck elsewhere—and, indeed, some do. A few observers attach great weight to the fact that many of the "huddled masses" now live in relative comfort.

18   As for the vast populations that remain in the source countries, they are affected by U.S. immigration policy in a number of ways. Most directly, the policy choices made by the United States may drain particular skills and abilities from the labor markets of source countries. A brain drain slows economic growth in the source countries, as the entrepreneurs and skilled workers who are most likely to spur growth move to greener pastures. Similarly, the principles of free trade suggest that world output would be largest if there were no national borders to interfere with the free movement of people. A policy that restricts workers from moving across borders unavoidably leads to a smaller world economy, to the detriment of many source countries.

The three groups may therefore have conflicting interests, and economics cannot tell us whose interests matter most. The weight that we attach to each of the three groups depends on our values and ideology. For the sake of argument I will assume a political consensus that the objective of immigration policy is to improve the economic well-being of the native population.

20   Beyond that, we have to specify which dimension of native economic well-being we care most about: per capita income or distribution of income. As we shall see, immigration raises per capita income in the native population, but this does not mean that all natives gain equally. In fact, some natives are likely to see their incomes greatly reduced. We must therefore be able to judge an immigration policy in terms of its impact on two different economic dimensions: the size of the economic pie (which economists call

"efficiency") and how the pie is sliced ("distribution"). The relative weights that we attach to efficiency and distribution again depend on our values and ideology, and economics provides no guidance on how to rank the two.

For the most part, economists take a very narrow approach: policies that increase the size of the pie are typically considered to be better policies, regardless of their impact on the distribution of wealth in society. We shall begin our construction of an immigration policy by taking this narrow approach. In other words, let's assume that immigration policy has a single and well-defined purpose: to maximize the size of the economic pie available to the native population of the United States. We shall return to the distributional issues raised by immigration policy later on.

The Economic Case for Immigration

22 To see how natives gain from immigration, let's first think about how the United States gains from foreign trade. When we import toys made by cheap Chinese labor, workers in the American toy industry undoubtedly suffer wage cuts and perhaps even lose their jobs. These losses, however, are more than offset by the benefits accruing to consumers, who enjoy the lower prices induced by additional competition. An important lesson from this exercise, worth remembering when we look at the gains from immigration, is that for there to be gains from foreign trade for the economy as a whole, some sectors of the economy must lose.

Consider the analogous argument for immigration. Immigrants increase the number of workers in the economy. Because they create additional competition in the labor market, the wages of native workers fall. At the same time, however, native-owned firms gain, because they can hire workers at lower wages; and many native consumers gain because lower labor costs lead to cheaper goods and services. The gains accruing to those who consume immigrants' services exceed the losses suffered by native workers, and hence society as a whole is better off.

24 Immigration therefore has two distinct consequences. The size of the economic pie increases. And a redistribution of income is induced, from native workers who compete with immigrant labor to those who use immigrants' services.

The standard economic model of the labor market suggests that the net gain from immigration is small. The United States now has more than 20 million foreign-born residents, making up slightly less than 10 percent of the population. I have estimated that native workers lose about $133 billion a year as a result of this immigration (or 1.9 percent of the gross domestic product in a $7 trillion economy), mainly because immigrants drive down wages. However, employers—from the owners of large agricultural enterprises to people who hire household help—gain on the order of $140 billion (or 2.0 percent of GDP*). The net gain, which I call the immigration

* GDP is an abbreviation used by economists for gross domestic product.

surplus, is only about $7 billion. Thus the increase in the per capita income of natives is small—less than $30 a year. But the small size of this increase masks a substantial redistribution of wealth.

26   My calculation used the textbook model of a competitive labor market: wages and employment are determined in a free market that balances the desires of people looking for work with the needs of firms looking for workers. In this framework an increase in the number of workers reduces wages in the economy—immigrants join natives in the competition for jobs and bid down wages in the process. There is a lot of disagreement over how much native wages fall when immigrants enter the labor market. Nevertheless, a great deal of empirical research in economics, often unrelated to the question of immigration, concludes that a 10 percent increase in the number of workers lowers wages by about three percent.

    If we accept this finding, we can argue as follows: We know that about 70 percent of GDP accrues to workers (with the rest going to the owners of companies), and that natives make up slightly more than 90 percent of the population. Therefore, native workers take home about 63 percent of GDP in the form of wages and salaries. If the 10 percent increase in the number of workers due to immigration has lowered wages by three percent, the share of GDP accruing to native workers has fallen by 1.9 percentage points (or 0.63×0.03). Thus my conclusion that in a $7 trillion economy native earnings drop by $133 billion.

28   Those lost earnings do not vanish into thin air. They represent an income transfer from workers to users of immigrants' services—the employers of immigrants and the consumers who buy the goods and services produced by immigrants. These winners get to pocket the $133 billion—and then some, because the goods produced by immigrant workers generate additional profits for employers. Under the assumption that a 10 percent increase in the number of workers reduces wages by three percent, it turns out that the winners get a windfall totaling $140 billion. Hence the $7 billion immigration surplus.

    We can quibble about assumptions, but the rigor of economic theory suggests that this nitpicking may not alter our conclusions much. For example, one could argue—and many do—that immigrants do not reduce the earnings of native workers. If we wished to believe this, however, we would also be forced to conclude that natives do not benefit from immigration at all. If wages do not fall, there are no savings in employers' payrolls and no cost savings to be passed on to native consumers. Remember the lesson from the foreign-trade example: no pain, no gain.

30   One could also argue that immigration has reduced the earnings of natives very substantially—by, say, 10 percent. The immigration surplus would then be about $25 billion annually. The net gain from immigration, therefore, remains small even with an unrealistically high estimate of the impact of immigration on native earnings. Imagine what U.S. policy would look like today if our earnings had fallen by 10 percent as a result of past immigration.

The immigration surplus has to be balanced against the cost of providing services to the immigrant population. Immigrants have high rates
of welfare recipiency. Estimates of the fiscal impact of immigration (that
is, of the difference between the taxes paid by immigrants and the cost of
services provided to them) vary widely. Some studies claim that immigrants pay $25–30 billion more in taxes than they take out of the system,
while other studies blame them for a fiscal burden of more than $40 bil-
lion on natives.

32   It is doubtful that either of these statistics accurately reflects the gap
between taxes paid and the cost of services provided. Studies that claim a
beneficial fiscal impact tend to assume that immigrants do not increase the
cost of most government programs other than education and welfare. Even
though we do not know by how much immigrants increase the cost of police protection, maintaining roads and national parks, and so forth, we do
know that it costs more to provide these services to an ever larger population. However, studies that claim a large fiscal burden often overstate the
costs of immigration and understate the taxes paid. As a result, estimates of
the fiscal impact of immigration should be viewed with suspicion. Nevertheless, because the immigration surplus is around $7 billion, the net bene-
fit from immigration after accounting for the fiscal impact is very small,
and could conceivably be a net loss.

How Many and Whom Should We Admit?

In principle, we should admit immigrants whenever their economic contribution (to native well-being) will exceed the costs of providing social
services to them. We are not, though, in a position to make this calculation
with any reasonable degree of confidence. In fact, no mainstream study has
ever attempted to suggest, purely on the basis of the empirical evidence,
how many immigrants should be admitted.

34   This unfortunate lack of guidance from economic research has, I believe, led to sudden and remarkable swings in policy proposals. As recently
as 1990 Congress legislated an increase in the number of legal immigrants
of about 175,000 people annually. Last year the Commission on Immigration Reform, headed by Barbara Jordan, recommended that legal immigration be cut by about 240,000 people a year—a proposal that was
immediately supported by President Clinton. (The Clinton Administration,
however, successfully resisted congressional efforts to follow up on the commission's recommendations.)

Although we do not know how many immigrants to admit, simple
economics and common sense suggest that the magic number should not be
an immutable constant regardless of economic conditions in the United
States. A good case can be made for linking immigration to the business
cycle: admit more immigrants when the economy is strong and the unemployment rate is low, and cut back on immigration when the economy is
weak and the unemployment rate is high.

36   Economic research also suggests that the United States may be better off if its policy of awarding entry visas favors skilled workers. Skilled immigrants earn more than less-skilled immigrants, and hence pay more in taxes, and they are less likely to use welfare and other social services.

Depending on how the skills of immigrants compare with the skills of natives, immigrants also affect the productivity of the native work force and of native-owned companies. Skilled native workers, for example, have much to gain when less-skilled workers enter the United States: they can devote all their efforts to jobs that use their skills effectively while immigrants provide cheap labor for service jobs. These gains, however, come at a cost. The jobs of less-skilled natives are now at risk, and these natives will suffer a reduction in their earnings. Nonetheless, it does not seem far-fetched to assume that the American work force, particularly in comparison with the work forces of many source countries, is composed primarily of skilled workers. Thus the typical American worker would seem to gain from unskilled immigration.

38   How does immigration affect companies' profits? Companies that use less-skilled workers on the production line gain from the immigration of the less-skilled, who reduce the earnings of less-skilled workers in favor of increasing profits. However, other companies—perhaps even most—might be better off with skilled immigrants. Many studies in economics suggest that skilled labor is better suited to the machines that are now used widely in the production process. Most companies would therefore gain more if the immigrant flow were composed of skilled workers.

Most workers prefer unskilled immigrants, whereas most companies prefer skilled immigrants. This conflict can be resolved only by measuring how much native workers gain from unskilled immigration and how much companies gain from skilled immigration, and comparing the two. Although there is a lot of uncertainty in the academic literature, we do know that the productivity of capital is very responsive to an influx of skilled workers. The large increase in the profits of the typical company, and the corresponding reduction in the cost of goods produced by skilled workers, suggest that the United States might be better off with a policy favoring skilled immigrants.

40   The gains from skilled immigration will be even larger if immigrants have "external effects" on the productivity of natives. One could argue, for example, that immigrants may bring knowledge, skills, and abilities that natives lack, and that natives might somehow pick up this know-how by interacting with immigrants. It seems reasonable to suspect that the value of these external effects would be greater if natives interact with highly skilled immigrants. This increase in the human capital of natives might offset—and perhaps even reverse—the harm that immigration does to the wages of competing workers.

Although such effects now play a popular role in economic theory, there is little empirical evidence supporting their existence, let alone measuring their magnitude. I find it difficult to imagine that interaction with immigrants entering an economy as large as that of the United States could have a measurable effect. Nevertheless, if external effects exist, they reinforce the argument that the United States would gain most from skilled immigrants.

Efficiency versus Distribution

42   Participants in the immigration debate routinely use the results of economic research to frame the discussion and to suggest policy solutions. Perhaps the most important contributions of this research are the insights that immigration entails both gains and losses for the native population, that the winners and the losers are typically different groups, and that policy parameters can be set in ways that attempt to maximize gains and minimize losses. If the objective of immigration policy is to increase the per capita income of the native population, the evidence suggests that immigration policy should encourage the entry of skilled workers. It is important to remember, however, that even though the immigration of skilled workers would be beneficial for the United States as a whole, the gains and losses would be concentrated in particular subgroups of the population.

As we have seen, the net gains from current immigration are small, so it is unlikely that these gains can play a crucial role in the policy debate. Economic research teaches a very valuable lesson: the economic impact of immigration is essentially distributional. Current immigration redistributes wealth from unskilled workers, whose wages are lowered by immigrants, to skilled workers and owners of companies that buy immigrants' services, and from taxpayers who bear the burden of paying for the social services used by immigrants to consumers who use the goods and services produced by immigrants.

44   Distributional issues drive the political debate over many social policies, and immigration policy is no exception. The debate over immigration policy is not a debate over whether the entire country is made better off by immigration—the gains from immigration seem much too small, and could even be outweighed by the costs of providing increased social services. Immigration changes how the economic pie is sliced up—and this fact goes a long way toward explaining why the debate over how many and what kinds of immigrants to admit is best viewed as a tug-of-war between those who gain from immigration and those who lose from it.

History has taught us that immigration policy changes rarely, but when it does, it changes drastically. Can economic research play a role in finding a better policy? I believe it can, but there are dangers ahead. Although the pendulum seems to be swinging to the restrictionist side (with ever louder calls for a complete closing of our borders), a greater danger to the national interest may be the few economic groups that gain much from immigration. They seem indifferent to the costs that immigration imposes on other segments of society, and they have considerable financial incentives to keep the current policy in place. The harmful effects of immigration will not go away simply because some people do not wish to see them. In the short run these groups may simply delay the day of reckoning. Their potential long-run impact, however, is much more perilous: the longer the delay, the greater the chances that when immigration policy finally changes, it will undergo a seismic shift—one that, as in the twenties, may come close to shutting down the border and preventing Americans from enjoying the benefits that a well-designed immigration policy can bestow on the United States. ❖

Questions for Meaning

1. What two major shifts in twentieth-century immigration policy are identified by Borjas?
2. What basic issues must be considered when determining immigration policy?
3. According to Borjas, who is most likely to gain from the immigration of low-skilled workers and who is most likely to suffer?
4. Why is Borjas concerned with both the size of the "economic pie" and the way it is sliced? What would be the effect of an immigration policy that focused on only one of these concerns?
5. What kind of immigration does Borjas favor? Does he make any specific recommendations?
6. Vocabulary: inchoate (1), demographic (3), incipient (4), repugnance (9), empirical (11), assimilation (12), parity (12), correlation (12), detriment (18), accrues (27), immutable (35), entails (42), parameters (42), seismic (45).

Questions about Strategy

1. Consider the summary of immigration policy in paragraph 6, a summary that Borjas calls "simplistic" in paragraph 7. To what extent does paragraph 7 improve the summary? What is the advantage of beginning with a simplification and then admitting complications? What are the risks of this strategy?
2. How reliable is the evidence Borjas provides to support his case? Does he provide sufficient evidence to be convincing?
3. In paragraph 9, Borjas makes an assumption that is important for the rest of his argument. Is this assumption reasonable? Is anyone likely to disagree?
4. How effective is the analogy, in paragraphs 22–23, between immigration and foreign trade?
5. Does Borjas ever respond to arguments that could be made against his own?
6. What assumptions has Borjas made about his audience? Does he explain economic concepts so that they can be understood by readers who lack his expertise, or does he envision an audience of his peers?

ONE STUDENT'S ASSIGNMENT

Drawing on recent data, revise the student essay on immigration that appears in the Fourth edition of *The Informed Argument*.* Discuss your plans with the author of that essay, and share drafts with him as you revise. The final essay should be a collaborative effort that satisfies both of you.

Another Look at the Economics of Immigration
Janelle Anderson and Christopher J. Lovrien

America has long been called a nation of immigrants. It has been said so many times that it has become a cliché. Yet the fact remains, the United States' 200-year rise from newborn to superpower was made possible largely because of the skills and ambitions of immigrants. Chinese immigrants helped build the railroads that were essential to our country's economic growth. Italian stone masons helped create many of our most important public buildings. Andrew Carnegie, one of the greatest philanthropists in our history, was born in Scotland, and, more recently, Irish-Americans like the Kennedys have provided vital national leadership. It is not surprising then that our current Secretary of State, Madeleine Albright, was born in Czechoslovakia. Immigrants have long brought vitality to this nation and that is why we should continue to encourage legal immigration.

2   However, many Americans seem to want immigration to be restricted. Barbara Jordan, the head of the Commission on Immigration Reform, recommended that immigration "be curbed by 240,000 people a year" (Borjas 239). As the economy took a downturn in the early 1990s and unemployment rose, some cried out that immigrants were taking jobs from low-skilled Americans. While this may be true in the short term, immigrants positively affect the economy in the long run. More immigrants means not only more workers but also more consumers. In economic terms, this means an increase in demand and the creation of more jobs. Economists will tell you that the number of jobs in an economy is not finite. Although research shows that less-skilled native workers' employment opportunities may be slightly reduced when immigrants enter a local labor market (Borjas 238), immigrants are still consumers. Additionally, immigrants can bring special skills that complement natives' skills.

---

* Christopher J. Lovrien wrote the essay published in the Fourth Edition when he was my student in 1994. I wanted to keep Chris's argument when preparing a new edition of the book but saw that his argument needed updating. Janelle Anderson took the same course with me in 1996, when this new edition was being prepared. Knowing that Janelle and Chris were in frequent communication, I offered them this assignment as a collaborative project.—Robert K. Miller

Another concern about the influx of immigrants is the extra burden they are said to place on the welfare system. This concern is understandable in light of the deficit and the ongoing debate on cutting social programs. It is argued that the government spends federal funds not only on those who come in legally, but also on those who enter illegally. This is not the case, however; illegal immigrants are already banned from assistance except in the case of emergency medical assistance (Topolnicki 228). Welfare benefits that immigrants do receive are awarded almost exclusively to political refugees. The truth is that immigrants pay $25–30 billion more in taxes than they use in government services (Topolnicki 228). Quite simply, most immigrants are not leeching off the system. Even though an immigrant, particularly a political refugee, may need and receive welfare when she enters America, this does not necessarily mean a continued dependence on welfare. While some immigrants do receive welfare benefits, most contribute more money to social programs through taxes than they withdraw through government assistance.

4   So what should the U.S. policy on immigration be? We should be conscious that immigration is a tremendous tool for improving our country. Americans should also keep in mind that, with the exception of Native Americans, everyone in this country has descended from immigrants. If earlier family members had not been allowed to immigrate to the United States, our citizens would not be able to call America "home" today. If we allow, or even seek out immigrants, especially skilled immigrants, the government can direct immigration to help strengthen the United States.

The first step is to ensure that the government knows who is entering the country. This means illegal immigration must be curbed. The best way to do this is to increase legal immigration. Currently, the government allows between 800,000 and one million immigrants to legally enter the country each year. It is estimated that another 300,000 enter illegally. Statistics show that when legal immigration is cut, illegal immigration generally increases. Increasing the quota of legal immigrants could decrease the number entering illegally.[1] The same number of people would be entering the country, but the government would have more control over who they are. A higher quota of legal immigrants would mean we could allow more people with special skills and education to enter the country.

6   Immigrants who are educated and have special skills are an asset to the United States. All immigrants are an asset to the country because they are consumers, but those with education and special skills are particularly beneficial to America. Economic research shows that our country will be better off favoring entry of skilled workers. These skilled immigrants generally are able to get higher-paying jobs, and therefore pay more in taxes. Also, these immigrants

do not need to use welfare or any other social services (Borjas 240). The immigrants who have come to the United States since 1980 actually have more education than the immigrants who came here before 1980. Today, 27 percent of the immigrants have college degrees when they arrive. Two out of every ten U.S. physicians are foreign-born, as is one out of every eight engineers (Topolnicki 229). There is no doubt in our minds that these people constitute an asset for the United States. They are the people who are living out the American Dream. After they have lived here for ten years, 55 percent of the immigrants own their own homes (Topolnicki 229). This is the ultimate example of what the American Dream is about: bettering oneself and the country.

Looking at the history of opposition to immigration, we see some interesting trends. There seems to always have been those who felt that certain immigrants were going to ruin the country. When the Germans began immigration to America, some "ethnic" Americans said they would cause the breakdown of America. In fact, the country became stronger. When the potato famine drove a wave of Irish immigrants to America, some Americans (including some of the new German-Americans) said they would ruin the country. They were wrong. The country became stronger and the Irish-Americans eventually flourished despite initial prejudice toward them. With history as a precedent, why is there any reason to believe that this new wave of immigrants will be anything but good for America? People argue that these new immigrants are "different" from the 13 million Eastern and Southern Europeans who immigrated to the United States in the first half of the twentieth century. This is true in one sense only: Of today's Immigrants, only 38 percent are white; 88 percent of those who came before 1960 were white (Topolnicki 227). We certainly hope the value of new immigrants is not being judged on the basis of skin-color prejudices. When people like Peter Brimelow say that large-scale immigration will cause America to lose its culture, they fail to realize that American culture has not only been immensely enriched by other ethnic cultures, but these "other cultures" are the basis for what Americans call our culture.

8   Why are immigrants to America often able to do so well in their new country and add so much to it? In no small part, it's because of their character. Immigrants must be ambitious enough to leave their native country. As Jeffrey S. Passel, director of the Urban Institute's immigration research and policy, says, "The very act of pulling up stakes and moving to a foreign country indicates that you have initiative and want to better yourself" (qtd. in Topolnicki 228). By increasing legal immigration and selecting skilled people, we can make sure that we do get well-educated and highly ambitious people who are the most likely to prosper in society and to benefit it.

This proposal is in no way saying that we must restrict immigration only to those who are already affluent or skilled. The current immigration policy recognizes the importance of reunifying families, and this should continue. The United States also accepts those who have been politically oppressed. We must continue to do this for obvious humane reasons. But even in the case of political refugees, the government must realize and be selective about who is coming into the country. In the case of political refugees, the government will be able to help them initially so they can begin to realize the American Dream for themselves.

10   America has had a long history of welcoming talented immigrants. Legal immigrants are taxpayers and consumers. Therefore, immigrants help our country not only by expanding its culture but also by contributing new skills that help America's economy. The next great physicist might very well be arriving in New York or San Francisco right now, and whether she is European, Asian, or African, we hope the border guards will not send her away.   ❖

Notes

¹ This argument has been advanced by Gary S. Becker, winner of the 1992 Nobel Prize in economics. See "Illegal Immigration: How to Turn the Tide," Business Week 22 Feb. 1993: 24. Becker's article can also be found in The Informed Argument. 5th ed. Ed. Robert K. Miller. Fort Worth: Harcourt, 1998. 217–218.

Suggestions for Writing

1. Is the United States "a nation of immigrants"? Does our country have a special responsibility to accept "huddled masses yearning to breathe free"? Write an essay focused on how traditional American values—as you define them—should determine our immigration policy.
2. Topolnicki and Borjas both focus on the economic consequences of immigration. Drawing on these sources, write an argument for or against the belief that immigration causes harm to the American economy.
3. Research the procedures followed by the U.S. Immigration and Naturalization Service when determining who gets to immigrate legally to the United States, and write an essay that summarizes what you discover.
4. Is U.S. immigration policy racist? Write an essay attempting to answer this question. Draw on information provided by Brimelow and do additional research if necessary.
5. Write an essay comparing U.S. and Canadian immigration laws.
6. Write an argument for or against increasing the number of legal immigrants from Mexico.
7. How should the American government respond when illegal immigrants arrive safely in America after a dangerous voyage? Should these

aliens be returned to the country from which they fled? Or should they be allowed to remain within the United States?

8. Write an essay defining the meaning of asylum and the extent to which the United States should accept foreigners seeking political asylum. Draw on at least three sources that you have discovered on your own.

COLLABORATIVE PROJECT

Interview immigrants living in your own community as well as any local officials who have responsibility for immigrants. Evaluate whether new arrivals are being treated fairly in your area. Then write a report that summarizes what you have discovered and recommends any changes that you believe are necessary.

SECTION 5

NATIONAL PARKS: WHAT IS THEIR FUTURE?

James Duffus

A REPORT FROM THE GENERAL ACCOUNTING OFFICE

When members of Congress and other influential members of the federal government need information, they can turn not only to their staffs but to the General Accounting Office, a nonpartisan branch of the federal bureaucracy charged with responsibility for keeping track of expenditures and evaluating how dollars are spent. This 1995 report was requested by the Senate Committee on Energy and Natural Resources and the House Subcommittee on National Parks, Forests, and Lands. At that time, James Duffus was Director of National Resources Management at the General Accounting Office and was responsible for the report issued in his name. As you read, note how the report includes information that can be useful to policy makers but does not specifically recommend how that information should be used.

Purpose

In recent years, concern has grown over the health of America's national parks, which now serve more than 270 million visitors a year. These parks contain many of the country's most significant natural areas and historic sites. In response to several congressional requesters, GAO reviewed the National Park Service's efforts at meeting its dual missions of serving visitors and protecting the natural and cultural resources entrusted to it. The review focused on determining (1) what, if any, deterioration in visitor services or park resources is occurring at the 12 park units that GAO visited; (2) what factors contribute to any degradation of visitor services and parks' natural and cultural resources; and (3) what choices are available to help deal with identified problems.

Background

2 The Department of the Interior's National Park Service manages 368 park units that together cover more than 80 million acres. Thirty-one of those units have been added in the last 10 years. The units are diverse in size and purpose, ranging from large natural areas to battlefields and monuments. Balancing the dual objectives of providing for the public's enjoyment and preserving the resources for future generations has long shaped the debate about how best to manage the system.

GAO's review focused on 12 park units: 4 national parks, 2 historic parks and 1 historic site, 2 monuments, 1 battlefield, 1 recreation area, and 1 seashore. Chosen for the diversity they present in size, type, and geographic location, these units represent a cross section of units in the system.

Results in Brief

4 There is cause for concern about the health of national parks for both visitor services and resource management. The overall level of visitor services was deteriorating at most of the park units that GAO reviewed. Services were being cut back, and the condition of many trails, campgrounds, and other facilities was declining. Trends in resource management were less clear because most park managers lacked sufficient data to determine the overall condition of their parks' natural and cultural resources. In some cases, parks lacked an inventory of the resources under their protection.

Two factors particularly affected the level of visitor services and the management of park resources. These were (1) additional operating requirements placed on parks by laws and administrative requirements and (2) increased visitation, which drives up the parks' operating costs. These two factors seriously eroded funding increases since the mid-1980s.

6 The national park system is at a crossroads. While the system continues to grow, conditions at the parks have been declining, and the dollar amount of the maintenance backlog has jumped from $1.9 billion in 1988 to over $4 billion today. Dealing with this situation involves making difficult choices about how parks are funded and managed. These choices call for efforts on the part of the Park Service, the administration, and the Congress and center on one or more of the following: (1) increasing the amount of financial resources going to the parks, (2) limiting or reducing the number of units in the park system, and (3) reducing the level of visitor services. Additionally, the Park Service should be able to stretch available resources by operating more efficiently and continuing to improve its financial management and performance measurement systems.

Principal Findings

Eleven of the 12 parks in GAO's review had cut visitor services. For example, at Shenandoah National Park in Virginia, programs to help visitors understand the park's natural and scenic aspects were cut by more than 80 percent from 1987 to 1993. At Padre Island National Seashore in Texas, no lifeguards were on duty along the beach during the summer of 1994 for the first time in 20 years. Such cutbacks can affect the visitors' safety and health as well as their enjoyment of and access to a park's amenities.

8   In addition, at those parks with significant cultural resources, the condition of these resources was generally declining. For example, at Ellis Island in New York, the nation's only museum devoted exclusively to immigration, 32 of 36 historic buildings have seriously deteriorated, and according to park officials, about two-thirds of these buildings could be lost within 5 years if not stabilized. In some parks, the location and the status of cultural resources—primarily archeological—were largely unknown. For example, at Hopewell Furnace National Historic Site—an 850-acre park in Pennsylvania that depicts part of the nation's early industrial development—the Park Service has never performed a complete archeological survey of the park to identify and inventory all its cultural resources.

Likewise, officials at large natural parks, such as Yosemite and Glacier, knew little about the condition of many natural resources. At Yosemite, for example, officials knew little about the condition of birds, fish, and such mammals as badgers, river otters, and wolverines. The Park Service has not systematically collected scientific data to inventory its natural resources or monitor changes in their condition over time. As a result, the agency cannot now determine whether the overall condition of many key natural resources is improving, deteriorating, or remaining constant.

10   Park Service policy directs that park management be based on knowledge of the parks' cultural and natural resources and their condition. The Park Service's lack of progress in addressing this decades-old concern is threatening its ability to preserve and protect the resources entrusted to it.

Two Main Factors Contribute to the Current Situation

Although many parks have received operating budget increases since 1985, laws, administrative rules, and other policy changes have given parks many additional operating requirements. While not disagreeing with the merits of these requirements, park managers said that the requirements affected the availability of funds for visitor services and resource management activities because parks often had not received enough funds to cover the entire cost of compliance and managers therefore had to use funds from existing operating budgets. For example, in fiscal year 1994, Yosemite spent $42,000 to meet several Occupational Safety and Health Act requirements and $80,000 to identify and remove hazardous waste. The park did not receive additional funds to cover this $122,000 expense. Officials also cited required cost-of-living increases and employer retirement contributions that were not accompanied by sufficient additional funds to pay for them. Because salaries and benefits constitute such a large percentage of a park's budget—in most cases, over 75 percent for the parks in GAO's review—nearly any such increase can have a major impact.

12   Increased visitation was the second main factor eroding the parks' ability to keep up with visitor and resource needs. Eight of the 12 parks that GAO reviewed experienced increased visitation since 1985; the average increase was 26 percent. At some parks, the substantial increase in visitation has driven up costs for such activities as waste disposal, general maintenance and supplies, utilities, and employee overtime. Moreover, the expanded length of the tourist season at many parks requires providing at least minimal visitor services for longer periods. To address this need, some parks have cut back on the scope and amount of services available during the peak season.

Choices for Addressing Park Conditions Center on Three Alternatives

If current circumstances continue, further deterioration in park conditions is likely. Choices to deal with this situation center on three alternatives: (1) increasing the amount of financial resources going to the parks, (2) limiting or reducing the number of units in the park system, and (3) reducing the level of visitor services.

14   One alternative to address the deteriorating conditions is to increase the amount of financial resources available to the parks. While increased appropriations are one source of dollars, they are unlikely in today's tight fiscal climate. Other revenue sources are potentially available, including increased park entrance and other user fees, higher returns from in-park concessioners, and funds from partnership agreements with nonfederal entities. Less than 8 percent of the system's annual operating budget is currently generated through such means. However, for parks to benefit from such changes, the increased revenues would need to stay within the park system and not be returned to the U.S. Treasury, as now occurs. Imposing or increasing fees may also affect park visitation and use, a consequence that would need to be considered.

A second alternative would limit or perhaps even cut back the number of units in the national park system. As the system keeps growing, associated infrastructure and development needs will also increase, putting more park units in competition for the limited federal funding available. While not an answer to all the current problems, limiting or cutting back park units until conditions could be adequately addressed would help ease the Park Service's financial pressures.

16   A third alternative would reduce the visitor services provided by the parks to more closely match the level of services that can be realistically accomplished with available resources. This could include, for example, limiting operations of fewer hours per day and fewer days per year, limiting the number of visitors, or perhaps temporarily closing some facilities to public use.

The Park Service Can Better Focus Resources

Previous work by GAO and the Department of the Interior's Inspector General has shown that the Park Service lacks (1) necessary financial and program data on its operations, (2) adequate internal controls on how its funds are spent, and (3) performance measures on what is being accomplished with the money being spent. Currently, the Park Service is taking corrective actions to resolve its problems with financial data and internal controls and is in the process of developing performance measurement systems. While these actions alone will probably not be sufficient to meet all of the Park Service's funding needs, they should increase efficiency so that the Park Service can do more under current funding levels.

Recommendations

18   GAO is making no recommendations in this report.

Agency Comments and GAO's Evaluation

GAO provided a draft of this report to National Park Service officials for their review and comment. On July 13, 1995, GAO met with Park Service officials—including the Park Service's Director and Associate Directors of Administration and Professional Services—to obtain their comments. Overall, the officials agreed with the factual content and conclusions of the report. They suggested several technical clarifications throughout the report and provided updated information. Changes to the report were made as appropriate. The officials also offered several comments relating to the alternatives to deal with the problems identified in the report. Park Service officials said that increased appropriations was an alternative that was not delineated in the report. GAO agrees that it is an alternative, but an unlikely one in today's tight fiscal climate. The report was revised to reflect this comment. Park Service officials also commented that private capital is another alternative. GAO agrees and believes that this point is included in the report's discussion of more entrepreneurial management by park managers.

20   Park Service officials further commented that increasing fees at national parks would not make the system self-sufficient, although they support the need for increased fees. They also said that there may be some units for which fees should not be charged because of their national significance. GAO agrees that increasing fees will not solve all of the parks' financial problems. GAO also recognizes that charging fees may be undesirable or infeasible for some units. The report has been revised to reflect both points. Park Service officials also commented on the alternative of limiting or reducing the number of park units. They said that there is no evidence that the addition of new units has affected the amount of resources for existing units. GAO believes that given the current tight fiscal climate, future growth in appropriations is unlikely; accordingly, new units would be competing for available funds.   ❖

Questions for Meaning

1. What is the dual mission of the National Park Service? What potential conflict is there between these two elements of its mission?
2. What sites did the GAO investigate for this report, and why were these sites selected?
3. What factors have been affecting the quality of services and management in our national parks? What evidence is there that the park system is under strain?
4. According to its own policy, how should the Park Service determine the way parks are managed? Is the Service honoring its policy?
5. If the federal government decides to halt further deterioration in park conditions, what options does it have, according to this report? In your opinion, which of these options is most feasible?

Questions about Strategy

1. How does Duffus establish the focus of this report? Is this focus appropriate for a report from the General Accounting Office? Are any management issues excluded by this focus?
2. How would you describe the tone of this report? Is it appropriate for its original audience and purpose?
3. Although this report finds problems within the administration of the National Park Service, it makes no specific recommendations. What does this decision reveal? Can any recommendations be inferred from this report?
4. This report concludes with a statement describing a meeting between representatives of the General Accounting Service and the National Park Service. What did this meeting accomplish? What does Duffus accomplish by putting this information in his report?

TERRY L. ANDERSON

IT'S TIME TO PRIVATIZE

It is becoming increasingly apparent that our national parks system is under strain. One problem is the popularity of the parks: the more people visit them, the more congested they become and the more damage can be done. Another problem is that park administrators have lacked sufficient funding to make necessary repairs and maintain adequate services. What, then, can be done to save the parks at a time when federal dollars are becoming harder to come by? As the title of the following argument suggests, Terry L. Anderson believes that entrepreneurs can make the park system more self-sufficient. Anderson is Executive Director of the Political Economy Research Center in Bozeman,

Montana. He first published "It's Time to Privatize" in the May 1996 issue of *The World & I.*

Bumper-to-bumper traffic on Yellowstone's deteriorating roads. Closed gates at Yosemite. A 10-year wait to float through the Grand Canyon. Overcrowding of our national parks cannot be debated.

2   One way to deal with this problem is to increase the entry fees and reinvest them directly into improved management. As it is now, visitors to national parks pay almost nothing, and taxpayers, not users, bear the costs. Until that changes, we will have overcrowding and inadequate visitor service.

Low fees inevitably lead to overuse. A family of four in a Winnebago pays only $10 for a seven-day permit to visit Yellowstone, or 36 cents per person per day for use of a national treasure. With the price so low, people visit more often and stay longer than they would otherwise. Traffic congestion is commonplace, campgrounds fill up in early morning, and muddy trails erode from heavy use.

4   Low fees also mean woefully inadequate budgets. Yellowstone, the "crown jewel" of our park system, has 2.2 million acres and 3 million visitors. Yet its budget for operations is only $17 million, shameful for a park of its size, and its backlog of capital improvements exceeds $250 million.

Environmentalists often accuse commodity users such as logging companies and miners of "feeding at the government trough" through subsidies. But recreational subsidies are far worse. In fiscal year 1994, fees collected for all recreation on federal lands were only 10 percent of what the agencies spent on recreation.

6   Yellowstone Park took in only about $1.30 per visitor in 1993 but spent $6.00. Given the amount tourists spend on transportation, meals, and lodging, it is safe to say that a trip to a national park like Yellowstone is worth far more than $1.30 per person! Visitors are getting something for nothing—the definition of a subsidy.

It was not always this way, as the history of Yellowstone illustrates, and it does not have to be that way in the future.

8   The common folklore is that Yellowstone was the brainchild of far-sighted conservationists. According to the story, as they sat around one of the first campfires in the park, they pledged that these wonders of nature—the geysers, the hot springs, the geological formations that they had just explored—should be protected forever.

But the reality is quite different. Profits spawned the world's first national park. The owners of the Northern Pacific Railroad saw the tourism potential of Yellowstone. They financed the expeditions that collected information about the area and lobbied Congress to set aside the area as a park—and to do it fast, before homesteaders cut the timber or carved up the park into small tourist attractions.

10   As one railroad official put it, "We do not want to see the Falls of the Yellowstone driving the loom of a cotton factory, or the great geysers boiling pork for some gigantic packing-house, but in all the native majesty and

grandeur." Because railroads had monopolies on transportation to the West and were able to take control of internal facilities, they were the driving force behind not only Yellowstone but also the Grand Canyon, Mount Rainier, and many of the other early parks.

Railroads initially wanted low or no entry fees, so they could charge the maximum for train tickets, stagecoach rides, and hotel facilities. But they also understood the importance of limiting congestion. For example, stagecoach departures were staggered to minimize dust.

12   The first meaningful entry fees for our national parks came when personal automobiles were allowed into the parks. Such fees undoubtedly were supported by railroads as a way of limiting competition. And indeed, with the first entry fees for Yellowstone set at $100 in today's dollar, some tourists would have thought twice about visiting the park.

Despite such high fees, enough people were still willing to pay so that national parks were self-sufficient. In 1917, the first year of the National Park Service's existence, fees collected in the major parks such as Yellowstone, Yosemite, Grand Canyon, and Mount Rainier exceeded operating costs.

14   At that time, entrance fees went to a special treasury account with no congressional oversight. The only role for Congress was to provide additional appropriations when capital improvement funds were needed. But this didn't last long. Congress wanted control of the agency, and controlling the purse strings was the best way. By 1918 legislation was passed requiring that all monies go to the general fund. Not surprisingly, revenues fell, because the National Park Service had little interest in collecting them.

Even so, there was support for the idea that the user should pay. As Secretary of Interior Harold Ickes put it in 1939, "Those who actually visit the national parks and monuments should make small contributions to their upkeep for the services those visitors receive which are not received by other citizens who do not visit the parks but who contribute to the support of these parks."

16   In recent years Congress has altered the fee structure for use of federal lands, in some cases raising fees and in others lowering them. Legislation enacted in 1959 required all federal agencies to set "a reasonable charge" for their services. But in 1978, when the Park Service faced large budget cuts and responded with proposals to increase fees, Congress passed a moratorium that froze fees.

In 1982, the federal Office of Management and Budget put pressure on the Park Service to obtain at least 25 percent of its operation and maintenance funds from fees. Unfortunately, such fee revenues were offset by reduced budget appropriations so the Park Service had little incentive to collect the fees.

18   Most recently, Congress allowed the Park Service to keep a share of fees to cover the costs of collection. As a result, collections went up, but the extra revenues only cover the costs of collection and do not provide better services for park visitors.

HOW THE PARKS CAN BE SAVED

🏕 Raise fees and allow managers to use those fees for improving visitor services.

🏕 Allow alternative sources of incomes. In Texas, park managers generate revenues from dances, weddings, bird-watching tours, and nature seminars.

🏕 Cut dependency on Washington bureaucracy and handouts.

The bottom line from the history of fees is that the taxpayer heavily subsidizes the national parks. This "welfare" system for funding national parks guarantees overcrowding and underfunding, and it focuses entrepreneurial talents on Washington rather than on the ground.

20   Because budgets are enacted by congressional committees, Park Service officials pay more attention to politicians than to visitors. The number of visitors, not the quality of visits, becomes the *raison d'être* for the Park Service. The absurdity of this approach is illustrated by the fact that commuters using Rock Creek Parkway, a major arterial highway through Washington, D.C., used to be counted as national park visitors because the Park Service managed that land!

To make the park experience better for visitors, we need to raise fees and allow managers to use those fees for improving visitor services. Such a step could switch on entrepreneurship within the Park Service. Suddenly, the focus would be on quality, not quantity.

22   A study by Donald Leal of PERC, a think tank in Bozeman, Montana, suggests the positive results that could occur. Leal compared state and federal timber management of lands that are similar or even adjacent. He found that the state of Montana made $2 for every dollar it spent for timber management on state-owned lands, while the Forest Service lost $0.50 for every dollar it spent on timber operations on national forests in Montana. Measures of environmental quality also show that state forests were better managed over the long haul. Why the difference?

Revenues from Montana's state forests help fund public schools. Hence parents, teachers, and school administrators become "majority stockholders" who care about the bottom line. In contrast, most revenues from national forests drain into the general treasury abyss in Washington. Hence, the Forest Service has little incentive to be economically responsible.

24   Some state park systems are also self-supporting. While national parks are severely subsidized, state parks in New Hampshire and Ver-

mont earn sufficient revenues to cover expenses, and Texas state parks are moving in that direction. Because the parks are "profit centers," the managers are entrepreneurs. Their revenues depend on satisfied visitors, so they have an incentive to give the customer a quality experience.

In Texas, for example, park managers generate revenues from dances, weddings, bird-watching tours, nature seminars, and "Christmas in the parks." On just 500,000 acres, one-fourth the area of Yellowstone, Texas parks generate $25 million annually, compared with Yellowstone's $3 million. As one Texas park manager put it, "We were so limited by bureaucracy, but now, the sky is the limit."

26   There are several reasons why the time is right to move the Washington bureaucracy toward allowing greater self-sufficiency for the national parks. First, our national parks and their visitors are not getting what they deserve. Many people pass through the gates, but the quality of the experience is diminished by overcrowding.

Second, these days people are willing to pay to enjoy the outdoors. Large private landowners recognize this and are earning profits from recreation. For example, the International Paper Company leases land to 2,100 hunting clubs and rents small parcels where families can park their trailers and enjoy the outdoors. Private fund drives for the parks also indicate a willingness to pay. The Glacier National Park Association, for example, has started a "Backcountry Preservation Fund," asking for private contributions to fund projects that protect natural resources.

28   Finally, budgets are tight and likely to get tighter. In this fiscal setting, user fees become the only way to adequately fund the national parks.

From Yellowstone to the Grand Canyon, entrepreneurship was the original driving force behind the national park system. Restructuring the incentives by making users pay and linking each park's expenditures to gate receipts can rekindle that entrepreneurship for the sake of our national parks and their visitors. By resisting reform in the name of democracy and equal access, we are only delaying the day of reckoning. It's time to stop subsidizing our national parks to death.   ❖

Questions for Meaning

1. How does Anderson define "subsidy"? Why does he believe that visitors to our national parks are being subsidized?
2. Where did entrance fees for the parks go in 1917? What changed in 1918? What has been the consequence of this change?
3. Why has timber management in Montana been more profitable on state land than on national forests in that state?
4. What recommendations does Anderson make for reforming the administration of our national parks?
5. Why does Anderson believe that the time is right for a change in park management?

Questions about Strategy

1. Consider the sequence of sentences in Anderson's opening paragraph. Do the first three sentences provide sufficient evidence for the conclusion reached in the fourth?
2. In paragraphs 8–11, Anderson contrasts what he calls "folklore" and "reality." What advantage is there to devoting more space, in this case, to "reality"? Are you convinced that this version of "reality" is historically accurate?
3. Illustrating how park managers can make parks profitable, Anderson devotes paragraph 25 to describing the administration of parks in Texas. Does this example help his argument?
4. In his conclusion, Anderson contrasts "entrepreneurship" with "resisting reform in the name of democracy and equal access." How would you paraphrase this conflict? What kind of readers are likely to respond positively to a conflict defined in these terms?

DAVE FOREMAN

MISSING LINKS

Although we frequently think of our national parks and wilderness areas in terms of how well they serve our own needs, environmentalists urge us to consider how this land can be used to preserve wildlife. Dave Foreman, director of the Sierra Club and chairman of the Wildlands Project, is also the author of *Confessions of an Eco-Warrior* (1991) and coauthor of *The Big Outside* (1992). He first published this argument in a 1995 issue of *Sierra*. As you read, note how he points to positive achievements and emphasizes a proposal for positive change instead of dwelling on the failures of the past.

Field biologists, with their stubbornly insistent focus on the minutiae of the living world, are unlikely people to be scaring the bejesus out of us.

2 But they were the first to see, beginning back in the 1970s, that populations of myriad species were declining and ecosystems were collapsing around the world. Tropical rainforests were falling to saw and torch. Ocean fish stocks were crashing. Coral reefs were dying. Elephants, rhinos, gorillas, tigers, and other "charismatic megafauna" were being slaughtered. Frogs everywhere were vanishing. The losses were occurring in oceans and on the highest peaks, in deserts and in rivers, in tropical rainforests and arctic tundra.

Michael Soulé, a population biologist who founded the Society for Conservation Biology, and Harvard's famed entomologist E. O. Wilson pieced together these disturbing anecdotes and bits of data. By studying the fossil record, they knew that during 500 million years of terrestrial evolution there had been five great extinctions. The last occurred 65 million years ago when the dinosaurs disappeared.

4   Wilson, Soulé, and company calculated that the current rate of extinction is as much as 10,000 times the normal background rate documented in the fossil record. That discovery hit with the subtlety of a comet striking Earth: we are presiding over the sixth great extinction in the planet's history.

Wilson warns that one-third of all species on Earth could die out in the next 40 years. Soulé says that the only large mammals remaining after the year 2000 will be those that humans consciously choose to protect. "For all practical purposes," he says, "the evolution of new species of large vertebrates has come to a screeching halt."

6   Alas, this biological meltdown can't be blamed on something as simple as stray cosmic detritus. Instead, responsibility sits squarely on the shoulders of 5.5 billion eating, manufacturing, warring, breeding, and real-estate-developing humans.

The damage done in the United States is particularly well documented. According to a National Biological Service study released early this year, ecosystems covering half the area of the 48 contiguous states are endangered or threatened. The longleaf-pine ecosystem, for example, once the dominant vegetation of the coastal plain from Virginia to Texas and covering more than 60 million acres, remains only in tiny remnants. Ninety-nine percent of the native grassland of California has been lost. There has been a 90 percent loss of riparian ecosystems in Arizona and New Mexico. Of the 261 types of ecosystems in the United States, 58 have declined by 85 percent or more and 38 by 70 to 84 percent.

8   If the United States had completely ignored its public lands, it might simply be getting what it deserved. But that's not the case. National parks and designated wilderness areas in this country make up the world's finest nature-reserve system. When President Clinton signed into law the California Desert Protection Act in 1994, the acreage of federally designated wilderness carved out of our public lands soared to more than 100 million acres, nearly half of which are outside Alaska. The acreage of the national park system jumped to almost 90 million, more than one-third in the Lower 48. That is much more than I thought we would ever protect when I enlisted in the wilderness wars a quarter-century ago.

But that's still not enough for Reed Noss, editor of the widely cited scientific journal *Conservation Biology* and one of the National Biological Service report's authors, who claims "we're not just losing single species here and there, we're losing entire assemblages of species and their habitats."

10   How is it that we have lost so many species while we have protected so much?

The answer, environmental historians tell us, lies in the goals, arguments, and processes used to establish wilderness areas and national parks over the last century. In his epochal study, *National Parks: The American Experience* (University of Nebraska, 1979), Alfred Runte discusses the arguments crafted to support establishment of the early national parks. Foremost was what Runte terms "monumentalism," the preservation of inspirational scenic grandeur like the Grand Canyon or Yosemite Valley, and the protection of curiosities of nature like Yellowstone's hot pots and geysers. Later proposals for national parks had to measure up to the scenic quality of a Mt. Rainier or a Crater Lake. Even the spectacular Olympic Mountains were initially denied national park status because they weren't deemed up to snuff.

12   A second argument for new national parks was based on what Runte calls "worthless lands." Areas proposed for protection, conservationists argued, were unsuitable for agriculture, mining, grazing, logging, and other productive uses. Yellowstone could be set aside because no one in his right mind would try to grow corn there; no one wanted to mine the glaciers of Mt. Rainier or log the sheer cliffs of the Grand Canyon. The worthless-lands argument often led park advocates to agree to boundaries gerrymandered around economically valuable forests eyed by timber interests, or simply to leave out such lands in the first place. Where parks were designated over the objections of extractive industries (such as at Kings Canyon, which was coveted as a reservoir site by California's Central Valley farmers), protection prevailed only because of the dogged efforts of the Sierra Club and allied groups.

When the great conservationist Aldo Leopold and others suggested that wilderness areas be protected in the national forests in the 1920s and '30s, they adapted the monumentalism and worthless-lands arguments with great success. The Forest Service's enthusiasm for Leopold's wilderness idea was, in fact, partly an attempt to head off the Park Service's raid on the more scenic chunks of the national forests. Wilderness advocates also used utilitarian arguments in their campaigns: the Adirondack Preserve in New York was set aside to protect the watershed for booming New York City, and the first forest reserves in the West were established to protect watersheds near towns and agricultural regions.

14   The most common argument for designating wilderness areas, though, touted their recreational values. Leopold, who railed against "Ford dust" in the backcountry, wanted to preserve scenic areas suitable for roadless pack trips of two weeks' duration. Bob Marshall expanded the recreational theme, defending wild areas as "reservoirs of freedom and inspiration" for those willing to hike the trails and climb the peaks.

In the final analysis, though, most national parks and wilderness areas were (and are) decreed because they had friends. Conservationists know that the way to protect an area is to develop a constituency for it. We rally support for wilderness designation by giving people slide shows, taking them into the area, and urging them to write letters, lobby, or even put

Largest remaining roadless areas in the contiguous United States. The map above shows roadless areas of more than 100,000 acres in the West and 50,000 acres in the East. There are more than 385 such areas in the continental United States, ranging from Idaho's 3.3-million-acre "River of No Return" area to Vermont's 50,000-acre Meachum Swamp. But the 10 percent of the Lower 48 that remains wild is shrinking by 2 million acres a year.

their bodies on the line in protest. If we're lucky, and not too many concessions are made to resource industries, we end up with wilderness that we can be proud of. The result is that wilderness areas tend to be spectacularly scenic, rugged enough to thwart resource exploitation (or simply lacking valuable timber and minerals altogether), and popular for non-motorized recreation.

16   But there's one problem: that's not necessarily what wildlife needs.

It's important to note that ecological integrity has always been at least a minor goal and argument in wilderness and national-park advocacy. In the 1920s and '30s, the Ecological Society of America and the American Society of Mammalogists developed proposals for ecological reserves on the public lands. Aldo Leopold was a pioneer in the sciences of wildlife management and ecology, and argued for wilderness areas as ecological baselines. Even the Forest Service applied ecosystem thinking when it recommended areas for wilderness in its second Roadless Area Review and Evaluation (RARE II) in the late 1970s. Somehow, though, professional biologists and advocates for wilderness preservation drifted apart—far enough so that the Forest Service now lumps its wilderness program under its division of recreation.

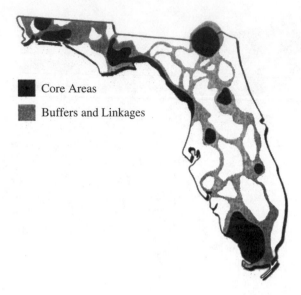

Core Areas

Buffers and Linkages

Panther paths. To protect wildlife in the nation's fastest-growing state, Florida agencies adopted and refined Reed Noss' core-and-buffer nature-reserve scheme. Using computer mapping, they identified biodiversity hot spots on nearly 5 million acres. If these are added to the state's 7 million acres of protected lands, the black bear and the panther may have a fighting chance. Florida is now working with landowners to protect strategic areas and has appropriated $3.2 billion to purchase key lands by the year 2000.

18 It took news of a global biological meltdown to shake up both biology and conservation. Biology could no longer be removed from activism. Conservation could no longer be just about outdoor museums and back-packing parks. Biologists and conservationists all began to understand that species can't be brought back from the brink of extinction one by one. Nature reserves had to protect entire ecosystems, guarding the flow and dance of evolution.

For insight, conservation biologists drew on an obscure corner of population biology called "island biogeography." In the 1960s, E. O. Wilson and Robert MacArthur studied colonization and extinction rates in oceanic islands like the Hawaiian chain. They hoped to devise a mathematical formula for the number of species that an island can hold, based on factors such as the island's size and its distance from the mainland.

20 They also looked at islands, places like Borneo or Vancouver, that were once part of nearby continents. When the glaciers melted 10,000 years ago and the sea level rose, these high spots were cut off from the mainland. Over the years, continental islands invariably lose species of plants and animals that remain on their parent continents, a process called "relaxation."

Certain generalities jumped out at the researchers. The first species to vanish from continental islands are the big ones—the tigers and elephants. The larger the island, the slower the rate at which species disappear. The farther an island is from the mainland, the more species it loses; the closer, the fewer. If an island is isolated, it loses more species than one in an archipelago.

22   In 1985, ecologist William Newmark looked at a map of the western United States and realized that its national parks were also islands. The smaller the park and the more isolated it was from other wildlands, the more species it had lost. The first to go had been the large wide-ranging creatures: gray wolf, grizzly bear, wolverine. Relaxation had occurred, and was still occurring. Newmark predicted that all national parks would continue to lose species. Even a big protected area like Yellowstone isn't large enough to maintain viable populations of the largest wide-ranging mammals. Only the complex of national parks in the Canadian Rockies is substantial enough to ensure their survival.

While Newmark was applying island biogeography to national parks, Reed Noss and Larry Harris at the University of Florida were studying the state's endangered panther and its threatened black bear, hoping to design nature reserves for these species that were more than outdoor museums. A small, isolated group of bears or panthers faces two threats. Because it has few members, inbreeding can lead to genetic defects. And a small population is more vulnerable to extinction ("winking out" in ecological jargon) than a larger one. If the animals are isolated, their habitat can't be recolonized by nearby members of the species. But if habitats are connected so that animals can move between them—even as little as one horny adolescent every ten years—then inbreeding is thwarted and a habitat can be recolonized.

24   Noss and Harris designed a nature-reserve system for Florida consisting of core reserves surrounded by buffer zones and linked by habitat corridors. Over the past decade this visionary application of conservation biology has been refined by the state of Florida, and now state agencies and The Nature Conservancy are using it to set priorities for land acquisition and protection of key areas. Once a pie-in-the-sky proposal, a conservation-biology-based reserve system is now the master plan for land protection in Florida.

Ecosystem theory has caused biologists to rethink the way they viewed large carnivores, too. Scientists had always considered the biggest animals perched atop the food chain to be sovereign species whose condition had little effect on the well-being of the flora and fauna down below. Until the 1930s, in fact, the National Park Service used guns, traps, and poison to exterminate wolves and mountain lions from Yellowstone and other parks. Early in his career, even Aldo Leopold beat the drum for killing predators.

26   Today, biologists know that lions and bears and wolves are ecologically essential to entire systems. For example, the eastern United States is overrun with white-tailed deer, which devastate trees with their excess foraging. If

allowed to return, wolves and mountain lions would move deer from their concentrated wintering yards and reduce their numbers, thereby allowing the forest to return to more natural patterns of succession and species composition.

Even songbirds suffer when wolves and cougars disappear. The decline in populations of migrant neotropical songbirds such as warblers, thrushes, and flycatchers as a result of forest fragmentation in Central and North America is well documented. But the collapse is also partly attributable to the absence of large carnivores. Cougars and gray wolves don't eat warblers or their eggs, but raccoons, foxes, and possums do, and the cougars and wolves eat these midsize predators. When the big guys were hunted out, the populations of the middling guys exploded—with dire results for the birds.

28   In addition to being critical players in various eat-or-be-eaten schemes, large carnivores are valuable as "umbrella" species. Simply put, if enough habitat is protected to maintain viable populations of large mammals like wolverines or jaguars, then most of the other species in the region will also be protected.

A final piece in conservation biology's big-picture puzzle is the importance of natural disturbances to various ecosystems. To be viable, habitats must be large enough to absorb major natural disturbances (known as "stochastic events" in ecologist lingo). When Yellowstone burned in 1988, there was a great hue and cry over the imagined destruction. But ecologists tell us that the fire was natural and beneficial. Because Yellowstone covers 2 million acres and is surrounded by several million acres more of national-forest wilderness, the extensive fires affected only a portion of the total reserve area.

30   Things didn't turn out so well when The Nature Conservancy's Cathedral Pines Preserve in Connecticut was hammered by tornadoes in 1989. In this tiny patch of remnant old-growth white-pine forest, 70 percent of the trees were knocked flat, devastating the entire ecosystem. Had the tornadoes ripped through a forest of hundreds of thousands of acres, they instead would have played a positive role by opening up small sections of the forest to new growth.

Conservation biology's central tenets are not hard to grasp. For a natural habitat to be viable (and for a conservation strategy to succeed) there is a handful of general rules: bigger is better; a single large habitat is usually better than several small, isolated ones; large native carnivores are better than none; intact habitat is preferable to artificially disturbed habitat; and connected habitats are usually better than fragmented ones.

32   Too often, wilderness areas and national parks in the United States fail to qualify as viable habitat. They are pretty, yet unproductive. For the most part, the richer deep forests, rolling grasslands, and fertile river valleys on which a disproportionate number of rare and endangered species depend have passed into private ownership or been released for development. To make matters worse, the elimination of large carnivores, control of natural

fire, and livestock grazing have degraded even our largest and most remote parks and wilderness areas.

Conservation biologists tell us we must go beyond our current national park, wildlife refuge, and wilderness area systems. What's needed are large wilderness cores, buffer zones, and biological corridors. The cores would be managed to protect and, where necessary, restore native biological diversity and natural processes. Wilderness recreation is compatible with these areas, as long as ecological considerations come first. Surrounding the cores would be buffer zones where increasing levels of compatible human activity would be allowed as one moved away from the center. Corridors would provide secure routes between cores, enabling wide-ranging plant and animal species to disperse and facilitating genetic exchange between populations.

34 Existing wilderness areas, national parks, and other federal and state reserves are the building blocks for this ecologically based network. While rarely extensive enough to protect habitat in and of themselves, these fragmented wildland chunks preserve imperiled and sensitive species. Had today's parks and wilderness areas not been protected through the tireless efforts of wilderness conservationists over the years, these species would be much more in danger than they are today, if they existed at all.

In the northern Rockies, groups such as the Alliance for the Wild Rockies and the Greater Yellowstone Coalition have been working to turn fragmented wildlands into viable habitat. They reckon that if Yellowstone isn't large enough to maintain healthy populations of grizzlies and wolverines, then we need to link the park with larger areas.

36 At a minimum that means treating the national forests around the park as integral to the park itself. Even grander ideas would link Yellowstone with the vast wilderness areas of central Idaho, the Glacier National Park/Bob Marshall Wilderness complex in northern Montana, and on into Canada.

These efforts produced the most expansive ecosystem-based legislation ever proposed in the United States. The Northern Rockies Ecosystem Protection Act (NREPA) would designate 20 million acres of new wilderness areas and identify essential corridors between them. The bill, endorsed by the Sierra Club, currently has 35 cosponsors.

38 Through its Critical Ecoregions Program, the Sierra Club is applying ecosystem principles to other large landscapes across North America. . . . But conservation biology's tenets can also be applied on a traditional scale. Across the country, activists are helping shape the next generation of national-forest management plans. They are identifying habitat for sensitive species, remnants of national forest, and travel corridors for wide-ranging species. They can then champion the creation of wildlife linkages and expansion of existing wilderness areas into ecologically rich habitats. In many places, they'll be able to make the case that roads be closed to protect sensitive ecosystems, that once-present species like wolves and mountain lions be reintroduced, and that damaged watersheds be restored.

But it gets even wilder.

40   In late 1991 a small group of scientists and activists married conservation biology and conservation activism on the grandest and most visionary
scale yet. The Wildlands Project has set itself the all-encompassing goal of
designing science-based reserve networks that will protect and restore the
ecological richness and native biodiversity of North America from Alaska to
Panama.

        At a time when legislators are handing out private rights to public
lands like candy, such visions may seem like delusions. Congress is dominated by zealots who would tear down decades of conservation policy and
open public lands to the exploiters Teddy Roosevelt fought almost a century
ago. Senator Slade Gorton (R-Wash.) does the bidding of the timber industry in trying to gut the Endangered Species Act; just across the hall Representative Billy Tauzin (D-La.) unleashes lies and demagoguery against
wetlands protection and the Clean Water Act. Lurching through the Contract With America checklist, Congress threatens wilderness in the Arctic
National Wildlife Refuge, in the Northern Rockies, and in the slickrock
canyons of Utah. Even the national parks aren't safe from legislators who
know the price of everything and the value of nothing.

42   An understanding of conservation biology and a vision of ecologically
designed wilderness cores, corridors, and buffer zones can help stop the war
being waged on the environment. First, conservation policies and arguments
are strengthened by a grounding in sound science. Second, a big-picture
view allows activists to see that they are not isolated, that their campaigns to
protect local wildlands fit into a national, even continental plan.

        And it is no small benefit that a vision of wilderness recovery allows us
to show what conservationists are *for.* Too often, activists are dismissed as
negative, whining doomsayers. By developing long-term proposals for
wilderness, we say, "Here is our vision for what North America should look
like. Civilization and wilderness can coexist. By acting responsibly with respect for the land, we can become a better people."

44   A management plan that treats Florida as an ecological whole, a federal bill that crosses borders to protect wildlands throughout the northern
Rockies, and a continent-wide proposal like The Wildlands Project's wrest
the fundamental debate from those who would gladly plunder our natural
heritage. Do we have the generosity of spirit, the greatness of heart to share
the land with other species? I think we do.   ❖

Questions for Meaning

1. What is the significance of the research by Michael Soulé and E. O.
    Wilson? What are the implications of this research for policies deter-
    mining the management of national parks and other public lands?
2. What types of land were originally set aside as wilderness areas and
    national parks? What values support this kind of thinking?
3. What does Foreman mean by "ecological integrity"?

4. How can national parks be defined as "islands"? What does "island bio-geography" indicate will happen to animals living in these "islands"?
5. What are the basic principles of conservation biology? What kind of changes would be necessary to honor these principles in resource management?
6. Vocabulary: myriad (2), entomologist (3), detritus (6), contiguous (7), riparian (7), epochal (11), extractive (12), utilitarian (13), archipelago (21), viable (22), carnivores (25), tenets (31), integral (36), wrest (44).

Questions about Strategy

1. Although his argument is focused on the future of publicly held land in the United States, Foreman begins by referring to tropical rainforests, elephants, and gorillas. What does this strategy accomplish?
2. How credible is the evidence presented in this argument?
3. Why does Foreman believe conservationists must argue for projects they support instead of simply arguing against what they oppose? How successfully does his own argument illustrate this approach?
4. What values does Foreman appeal to in his conclusion? What does he accomplish by appealing specifically to these values at the end of his argument?

WILLIAM CRONON

THE TROUBLE WITH WILDERNESS

William Cronon is Frederick Jackson Turner Professor of History, Geography, and Environmental Studies at the University of Wisconsin. His works on environmental history include *Changes in the Land: Colonists, and the Ecology of New England* (1983), *Nature's Metropolis: Chicago and the Great West* (1991), and *Uncommon Ground: Toward Reinventing Nature* (1995). In the following essay, Cronon explores the meaning of "wilderness," showing how this concept has changed during the past two centuries. A careful scholar, Cronon included forty-three footnotes when he published this essay in *Uncommon Ground*—notes providing documentation and additional discussion. These notes have been omitted from the version reprinted here in order to conserve space. As you read, note how Cronon's reservations about prevailing attitudes toward "wilderness" are linked to his concern about the quality of the environment as a whole.

The time has come to rethink wilderness.

2   This will seem a heretical claim to many environmentalists, since the idea of wilderness has for decades been a fundamental tenet—indeed, a passion—of the environmental movement, especially in the United States. For many Americans wilderness stands as the last remaining place where civilization, that all too human disease, has not fully infected the earth. It is an island in the polluted sea of urban-industrial modernity, the one place we can turn for escape from our own too-muchness. Seen in this way, wilderness presents itself as the best antidote to our human selves, a refuge we must somehow recover if we hope to save the planet. As Henry David Thoreau* once famously declared, "In Wildness is the preservation of the World."

But is it? The more one knows of its peculiar history, the more one realizes that wilderness is not quite what it seems. Far from being the one place on earth that stands apart from humanity, it is quite profoundly a human creation—indeed, the creation of very particular human cultures at very particular moments in human history. It is not a pristine sanctuary where the last remnant of an untouched, endangered, but still transcendent nature can for at least a little while longer be encountered without the contaminating taint of civilization. Instead, it is a product of that civilization, and could hardly be contaminated by the very stuff of which it is made. Wilderness hides its unnaturalness behind a mask that is all the more beguiling because it seems so natural. As we gaze into the mirror it holds up for us, we too easily imagine that what we behold is Nature when in fact we see the reflection of our own unexamined longings and desires. For this reason, we mistake ourselves when we suppose that wilderness can be the solution to our culture's problematic relationships with the nonhuman world, for wilderness is itself no small part of the problem.

4   To assert the unnaturalness of so natural a place will no doubt seem absurd or even perverse to many readers, so let me hasten to add that the nonhuman world we encounter in wilderness is far from being merely our own invention. I celebrate with others who love wilderness the beauty and power of the things it contains. Each of us who has spent time there can conjure images and sensations that seem all the more hauntingly real for having engraved themselves so indelibly on our memories. Such memories may be uniquely our own, but they are also familiar enough to be instantly recognizable to others. Remember this? The torrents of mist shoot out from the base of a great waterfall in the depths of a Sierra canyon, the tiny droplets cooling your face as you listen to the roar of the water and gaze up toward the sky through a rainbow that hovers just out of reach. Remember this too: looking out across a desert canyon in the evening air, the only sound a lone raven calling in the distance, the rock walls dropping away into

---

* Henry David Thoreau (1817–1862) was an American naturalist, political activist, and writer. His account of living simply in the woods near Walden Pond has moved many generations of readers.

a chasm so deep that its bottom all but vanishes as you squint into the amber light of the setting sun. And this: the moment beside the trail as you sit on a sandstone ledge, your boots damp with the morning dew while you take in the rich smell of the pines, and the small red fox—or maybe for you it was a raccoon or a coyote or a deer—that suddenly ambles across your path, stopping for a long moment to gaze in your direction with cautious indifference before continuing on its way. Remember the feelings of such moments, and you will know as well as I do that you were in the presence of something irreducibly nonhuman, something profoundly Other than yourself. Wilderness is made of that too.

And yet: what brought each of us to the places where such memories became possible is entirely a cultural invention. Go back 250 years in American and European history, and you do not find nearly so many people wandering around remote corners of the planet looking for what today we would call "the wilderness experience." As late as the eighteenth century, the most common usage of the word "wilderness" in the English language referred to landscapes that generally carried adjectives far different from the ones they attract today. To be a wilderness then was to be "deserted," "savage," "desolate," "barren"—in short, a "waste," the word's nearest synonym. Its connotations were anything but positive, and the emotion one was most likely to feel in its presence was "bewilderment"—or terror.

6   Many of the word's strongest associations then were biblical, for it is used over and over again in the King James Version to refer to places on the margins of civilization where it is all too easy to lose oneself in moral confusion and despair. The wilderness was where Moses had wandered with his people for forty years, and where they had nearly abandoned their God to worship a golden idol. "For Pharaoh will say of the Children of Israel," we read in Exodus, "they are entangled in the land, the wilderness hath shut them in." The wilderness was where Christ had struggled with the devil and endured his temptations: "And immediately the Spirit driveth him into the wilderness. And he was there in the wilderness for forty days tempted of Satan; and was with the wild beasts; and the angels ministered unto him." The "delicious Paradise" of John Milton's Eden* was surrounded by "a steep wilderness, whose hairy sides / Access denied" to all who sought entry. When Adam and Eve were driven from that garden, the world they entered was a wilderness that only their labor and pain could redeem. Wilderness, in short, was a place to which one came only against one's will, and always in fear and trembling. Whatever value it might have arose solely from the possibility that it might be "reclaimed" and turned toward human ends— planted as a garden, say, or a city upon a hill. In its raw state, it had little or nothing to offer civilized men and women.

But by the end of the nineteenth century, all this had changed. The wastelands that had once seemed worthless had for some people come to

---

* One of the greatest of all English poets, John Milton (1608–1674) describes Eden in *Paradise Lost*.

seem almost beyond price. That Thoreau in 1862 could declare wildness to be the preservation of the world suggests the sea change that was going on. Wilderness had once been the antithesis of all that was orderly and good— it had been the darkness, one might say, on the far side of the garden wall— and yet now it was frequently likened to Eden itself. When John Muir arrived in the Sierra Nevada in 1869, he would declare, "No description of Heaven that I have ever heard or read of seems half so fine." He was hardly alone in expressing such emotions. One by one, various corners of the American map came to be designated as sites whose wild beauty was so spectacular that a growing number of citizens had to visit and see them for themselves. Niagara Falls was the first to undergo this transformation, but it was soon followed by the Catskills, the Adirondacks, Yosemite, Yellowstone, and others. Yosemite was deeded by the U.S. government to the state of California in 1864 as the nation's first wildland park, and Yellowstone became the first true national park in 1872.

8   By the first decade of the twentieth century, in the single most famous episode in American conservation history, a national debate had exploded over whether the city of San Francisco should be permitted to augment its water supply by damming the Tuolumne River in Hetch Hetchy valley, well within the boundaries of Yosemite National Park. The dam was eventually built, but what today seems no less significant is that so many people fought to prevent its completion. Even as the fight was being lost, Hetch Hetchy became the battle cry of an emerging movement to preserve wilderness. Fifty years earlier, such opposition would have been unthinkable. Few would have questioned the merits of "reclaiming" a wasteland like this in order to put it to human use. Now the defenders of Hetch Hetchy attracted widespread national attention by portraying such an act not as improvement or progress but as desecration and vandalism. Lest one doubt that the old biblical metaphors had been turned completely on their heads, listen to John Muir attack the dam's defenders. "Their arguments," he wrote, "are curiously like those of the devil, devised for the destruction of the first garden—so much of the very best Eden fruit going to waste; so much of the best Tuolumne water and Tuolumne scenery going to waste." For Muir and the growing number of Americans who shared his views, Satan's home had become God's own temple.

The sources of this rather astonishing transformation were many, but for the purposes of this essay they can be gathered under two broad headings: the sublime and the frontier. Of the two, the sublime is the older and more pervasive cultural construct, being one of the most important expressions of that broad transatlantic movement we today label as romanticism; the frontier is more peculiarly American, though it too had its European antecedents and parallels. The two converged to remake wilderness in their own image, freighting it with moral values and cultural symbols that it carries to this day. Indeed, it is not too much to say that the modern environmental movement is itself a grandchild of romanticism and post-frontier

Thomas Cole, *Expulsion from the Garden of Eden,* 1827–28. (Gift of Mrs. Maxim Karolik for the M. and M. Karolik Collection of American Paintings, 1815–1865, courtesy Museum of Fine Arts, Boston)

idcology, which is why it is no accident that so much environmentalist discourse takes its bearings from the wilderness these intellectual movements helped create. Although wilderness may today seem to be just one environmental concern among many, it in fact serves as the foundation for a long list of other such concerns that on their face seem quite remote from it. That is why its influence is so pervasive and, potentially, so insidious.

10   To gain such remarkable influence, the concept of wilderness had to become loaded with some of the deepest core values of the culture that created and idealized it: it had to become sacred. This possibility had been present in wilderness even in the days when it had been a place of spiritual danger and moral temptation. If Satan was there, then so was Christ, who had found angels as well as wild beasts during His sojourn in the desert. In the wilderness the boundaries between human and nonhuman, between natural and supernatural, had always seemed less certain than elsewhere. This was why the early Christian saints and mystics had often emulated Christ's desert retreat as they sought to experience for themselves the visions and spiritual testing He had endured. One might meet devils and run the risk of losing one's soul in such a place, but one might also meet God. For some that possibility was worth almost any price.

By the eighteenth century this sense of the wilderness as a landscape where the supernatural lay just beneath the surface was expressed in the doctrine of the *sublime,* a word whose modern usage has been so watered down by commercial hype and tourist advertising that it retains only a dim echo of its former power. In the theories of Edmund Burke, Immanuel Kant, William Gilpin,* and others, sublime landscapes were those rare places on earth where one had more chance than elsewhere to glimpse the face of God. Romantics had a clear notion of where one could be most sure of having this experience. Although God might, of course, choose to show Himself anywhere, He would most often be found in those vast, powerful landscapes where one could not help feeling insignificant and being reminded of one's own mortality. Where were these sublime places? The eighteenth-century catalog of their locations feels very familiar, for we still see and value landscapes as it taught us to do. God was on the mountaintop, in the chasm, in the waterfall, in the thundercloud, in the rainbow, in the sunset. One has only to think of the sites that Americans chose for their first national parks—Yellowstone, Yosemite, Grand Canyon, Rainier, Zion—to realize that virtually all of them fit one or more of these categories. Less sublime landscapes simply did not appear worthy of such protection; not until the 1940s, for instance, would the first swamp be honored in Everglades National Park, and to this day there is no national park in the grasslands.

12   Among the best proofs that one had entered a sublime landscape was the emotion it evoked. For the early romantic writers and artists who first began to celebrate it, the sublime was far from being a pleasurable experience. The classic description is that of William Wordsworth[†] as he recounted climbing the Alps and crossing the Simplon Pass in his autobiographical poem *The Prelude.* There, surrounded by crags and waterfalls, the poet felt himself literally to be in the presence of the divine—and experienced an emotion remarkably close to terror:

> The immeasurable height
> Of woods decaying, never to be decayed,
> The stationary blasts of waterfalls,
> And in the narrow rent at every turn
> Winds thwarting winds, bewildered and forlorn,
> The torrents shooting from the clear blue sky,
> The rocks that muttered close upon our ears,
> Black drizzling crags that spake by the way-side
> As if a voice were in them, the sick sight
> And giddy prospect of the raving stream,

---

* Edmund Burke (1729–1797), English statesman and author; Immanuel Kant (1724–1804), German philosopher; and William Gilpin (1724–1804), English travel writer and essayist, all fostered new ways of viewing the natural world.

[†] Like other Romantic poets, William Wordsworth (1770–1850) celebrated the beauty and power of nature in his work.

> The unfettered clouds and region of the Heavens,
> Tumult and peace, the darkness and the light—
> Were all like workings of one mind, the features
> Of the same face, blossoms upon one tree;
> Characters of the great Apocalypse,
> The types and symbols of Eternity,
> Of first, and last, and midst, and without end.

This was no casual stroll in the mountains, no simple sojourn in the gentle lap of nonhuman nature. What Wordsworth described was nothing less than a religious experience, akin to that of the Old Testament prophets as they conversed with their wrathful God. The symbols he detected in this wilderness landscape were more supernatural than natural, and they inspired more awe and dismay than joy or pleasure. No mere mortal was meant to linger long in such a place, so it was with considerable relief that Wordsworth and his companion made their way back down from the peaks to the sheltering valleys.

Lest you suspect that this view of the sublime was limited to timid Europeans who lacked the American know-how for feeling at home in the wilderness, remember Henry David Thoreau's 1846 climb of Mount Katahdin, in Maine. Although Thoreau is regarded by many today as one of the great American celebrators of wilderness, his emotions about Katahdin were no less ambivalent than Wordsworth's about the Alps.

> It was vast, Titanic, and such as man never inhabits. Some part of the beholder, even some vital part, seems to escape through the loose grating of his ribs as he ascends. He is more lone than you can imagine. . . . Vast, Titanic, inhuman Nature has got him at disadvantage, caught him alone, and pilfers him of some of his divine faculty. She does not smile on him as in the plains. She seems to say sternly, why came ye here before your time? This ground is not prepared for you. Is it not enough that I smile in the valleys? I have never made this soil for thy feet, this air for thy breathing, these rocks for thy neighbors. I cannot pity nor fondle thee here, but forever relentlessly drive thee hence to where I *am* kind. Why seek me where I have not called thee, and then complain because you find me but a stepmother?

This is surely not the way a modern backpacker or nature lover would describe Maine's most famous mountain, but that is because Thoreau's description owes as much to Wordsworth and other romantic contemporaries as to the rocks and clouds of Katahdin itself. His words took the physical mountain on which he stood and transmuted it into an icon of the sublime: a symbol of God's presence on earth. The power and the glory of that icon were such that only a prophet might gaze on it for long. In effect, romantics like Thoreau joined Moses and the children of Israel in Exodus when "they looked toward the wilderness, and behold, the glory of the Lord appeared in the cloud."

14   But even as it came to embody the awesome power of the sublime, wilderness was also being tamed—not just by those who were building settlements in its midst but also by those who most celebrated its inhuman beauty. By the second half of the nineteenth century, the terrible awe that Wordsworth and Thoreau regarded as the appropriately pious stance to adopt in the presence of their mountaintop God was giving way to a much more comfortable, almost sentimental demeanor. As more and more tourists sought out the wilderness as a spectacle to be looked at and enjoyed for its great beauty, the sublime in effect became domesticated. The wilderness was still sacred, but the religious sentiments it evoked were more those of a pleasant parish church than those of a grand cathedral or a harsh desert retreat. The writer who best captures this late romantic sense of a domesticated sublime is undoubtedly John Muir, whose descriptions of Yosemite and the Sierra Nevada reflect none of the anxiety or terror one finds in earlier writers. Here he is, for instance, sketching on North Dome in Yosemite Valley:

> No pain here, no dull empty hours, no fear of the past, no fear of the future. These blessed mountains are so compactly filled with God's beauty, no petty personal hope or experience has room to be. Drinking this champagne water is pure pleasure, so is breathing the living air, and every movement of limbs is pleasure, while the body seems to feel beauty when exposed to it as it feels the campfire or sunshine, entering not by the eyes alone, but equally through all one's flesh like radiant heat, making a passionate ecstatic pleasure glow not explainable.

The emotions Muir describes in Yosemite could hardly be more different from Thoreau's on Katahdin or Wordsworth's on the Simplon Pass. Yet all three men are participating in the same cultural tradition and contributing to the same myth: the mountain as cathedral. The three may differ in the way they choose to express their piety—Wordsworth favoring an awe-filled bewilderment, Thoreau a stern loneliness, Muir a welcome ecstasy—but they agree completely about the church in which they prefer to worship. Muir's closing words on North Dome diverge from his older contemporaries only in mood, not in their ultimate content:

> Perched like a fly on this Yosemite dome, I gaze and sketch and bask, oftentimes settling down into dumb admiration without definite hope of ever learning much, yet with the longing, unresting effort that lies at the door of hope, humbly prostrate before the vast display of God's power, and eager to offer self-denial and renunciation with eternal toil to learn any lesson in the divine manuscript.

Muir's "divine manuscript" and Wordsworth's "Characters of the great Apocalypse" were in fact pages from the same holy book. The sublime wilderness had ceased to be a place of satanic temptation and become instead a sacred temple, much as it continues to be for those who love it today.

16   But the romantic sublime was not the only cultural movement that helped transform wilderness into a sacred American icon during the nineteenth century. No less important was the powerful romantic attraction of primitivism, dating back at least to Rousseau*—the belief that the best antidote to the ills of an overly refined and civilized modern world was a return to simpler, more primitive living. In the United States, this was embodied most strikingly in the national myth of the frontier. The historian Frederick Jackson Turner wrote in 1893 the classic academic statement of this myth, but it had been part of American cultural traditions for well over a century. As Turner described the process, easterners and European immigrants, in moving to the wild unsettled lands of the frontier, shed the trappings of civilization, rediscovered their primitive racial energies, reinvented direct democratic institutions, and thereby reinfused themselves with a vigor, an independence, and a creativity that were the source of American democracy and national character. Seen in this way, wild country became a place not just of religious redemption but of national renewal, the quintessential location for experiencing what it meant to be an American.

One of Turner's most provocative claims was that by the 1890s the frontier was passing away. Never again would "such gifts of free land offer themselves" to the American people. "The frontier has gone," he declared, "and with its going has closed the first period of American history." Built into the frontier myth from its very beginning was the notion that this crucible of American identity was temporary and would pass away. Those who have celebrated the frontier have almost always looked backward as they did so, mourning an older, simpler, truer world that is about to disappear forever. That world and all of its attractions, Turner said, depended on free land—on wilderness. Thus, in the myth of the vanishing frontier lay the seeds of wilderness preservation in the United States, for if wild land had been so crucial in the making of the nation, then surely one must save its last remnants as monuments to the American past—and as an insurance policy to protect its future. It is no accident that the movement to set aside national parks and wilderness areas began to gain real momentum at precisely the time that laments about the passing frontier reached their peak. To protect wilderness was in a very real sense to protect the nation's most sacred myth of origin.

18   Among the core elements of the frontier myth was the powerful sense among certain groups of Americans that wilderness was the last bastion of rugged individualism. Turner tended to stress communitarian themes when writing frontier history, asserting that Americans in primitive conditions had been forced to band together with their neighbors to form communities and democratic institutions. For other writers, however, frontier democracy for communities was less compelling than frontier freedom for individuals. By fleeing to the outer margins of settled land and society—so the story

---

* The French philosopher, Jean Jacques Rousseau (1712–1778), argued that human beings were essentially good in a primitive state but become corrupted by social influences.

ran—an individual could escape the confining strictures of civilized life. The mood among writers who celebrated frontier individualism was almost always nostalgic; they lamented not just a lost way of life but the passing of the heroic men who had embodied that life. Thus Owen Wister in the introduction to his classic 1902 novel *The Virginian* could write of "a vanished world" in which "the horseman, the cow-puncher, the last romantic figure upon our soil" rode only "in his historic yesterday" and would "never come again." For Wister, the cowboy was a man who gave his word and kept it ("Wall Street would have found him behind the times"), who did not talk lewdly to women ("Newport would have thought him old-fashioned"), who worked and played hard, and whose "ungoverned hours did not unman him." Theodore Roosevelt wrote with much the same nostalgic fervor about the "fine, manly qualities" of the "wild rough-rider of the plains." No one could be more heroically masculine, thought Roosevelt, or more at home in the western wilderness:

> There he passes his days, there he does his life-work, there, when he meets death, he faces it as he has faced many other evils, with quiet, uncomplaining fortitude. Brave, hospitable, hardy, and adventurous, he is the grim pioneer of our race; he prepares the way for the civilization from before whose face he must himself disappear. Hard and dangerous though his existence is, it has yet a wild attraction that strongly draws to it his bold, free spirit.

This nostalgia for a passing frontier way of life inevitably implied ambivalence, if not downright hostility, toward modernity and all that it represented. If one saw the wild lands of the frontier as freer, truer, and more natural than other, more modern places, then one was also inclined to see the cities and factories of urban-industrial civilization as confining, false, and artificial. Owen Wister looked at the post-frontier "transition" that had followed "the horseman of the plains," and did not like what he saw: "a shapeless state, a condition of men and manners as unlovely as is that moment in the year when winter is gone and spring not come, and the face of Nature is ugly." In the eyes of writers who shared Wister's distaste for modernity, civilization contaminated its inhabitants and absorbed them into the faceless, collective, contemptible life of the crowd. For all of its troubles and dangers, and despite the fact that it must pass away, the frontier had been a better place. If civilization was to be redeemed, it would be by men like the Virginian who could retain their frontier virtues even as they made the transition to post-frontier life.

20   The mythic frontier individualist was almost always masculine in gender: here, in the wilderness, a man could be a real man, the rugged individual he was meant to be before civilization sapped his energy and

threatened his masculinity. Wister's contemptuous remarks about Wall Street and Newport suggest what he and many others of his generation believed—that the comforts and seductions of civilized life were especially insidious for men, who all too easily became emasculated by the femininizing tendencies of civilization. More often than not, men who felt this way came, like Wister and Roosevelt, from elite class backgrounds. The curious result was that frontier nostalgia became an important vehicle for expressing a peculiarly bourgeois form of antimodernism. The very men who most benefited from urban-industrial capitalism were among those who believed they must escape its debilitating effects. If the frontier was passing, then men who had the means to do so should preserve for themselves some remnant of its wild landscape so that they might enjoy the regeneration and renewal that came from sleeping under the stars, participating in blood sports, and living off the land. The frontier might be gone, but the frontier experience could still be had if only wilderness were preserved.

Thus the decades following the Civil War saw more and more of the nation's wealthiest citizens seeking out wilderness for themselves. The elite passion for wild land took many forms: enormous estates in the Adirondacks and elsewhere (disingenuously called "camps" despite their many servants and amenities), cattle ranches for would-be rough riders on the Great Plains, guided big-game hunting trips in the Rockies, and luxurious resort hotels wherever railroads pushed their way into sublime landscapes. Wilderness suddenly emerged as the landscape of choice for elite tourists, who brought with them strikingly urban ideas of the countryside through which they traveled. For them, wild land was not a site for productive labor and not a permanent home; rather, it was a place of recreation. One went to the wilderness not as a producer but as a consumer, hiring guides and other backcountry residents who could serve as romantic surrogates for the rough riders and hunters of the frontier if one was willing to overlook their new status as employees and servants of the rich.

22   In just this way, wilderness came to embody the national frontier myth, standing for the wild freedom of America's past and seeming to represent a highly attractive natural alternative to the ugly artificiality of modern civilization. The irony, of course, was that in the process wilderness came to reflect the very civilization its devotees sought to escape. Ever since the nineteenth century, celebrating wilderness has been an activity mainly for well-to-do city folks. Country people generally know far too much about working the land to regard unworked land as their ideal. In contrast, elite urban tourists and wealthy sportsmen projected their leisure-time frontier fantasies onto the American landscape and so created wilderness in their own image.

There were other ironies as well. The movement to set aside national parks and wilderness areas followed hard on the heels of the final Indian wars, in which the prior human inhabitants of these areas were rounded up and moved onto reservations. The myth of the wilderness as "virgin," uninhabited land had always been especially cruel when seen from the perspective of the Indians who had once called that land home. Now they were forced to move elsewhere, with the result that tourists could safely enjoy the illusion that they were seeing their nation in its pristine, original state, in the new morning of God's own creation. Among the things that most marked the new national parks as reflecting a post-frontier consciousness was the relative absence of human violence within their boundaries. The actual frontier had often been a place of conflict, in which invaders and invaded fought for control of land and resources. Once set aside within the fixed and carefully policed boundaries of the modern bureaucratic state, the wilderness lost its savage image and became safe: a place more of reverie than of revulsion or fear. Meanwhile, its original inhabitants were kept out by dint of force, their earlier uses of the land redefined as inappropriate or even illegal. To this day, for instance, the Blackfeet continue to be accused of "poaching" on the lands of Glacier National Park that originally belonged to them and that were ceded by treaty only with the proviso that they be permitted to hunt there.

24   The removal of Indians to create an "uninhabited wilderness"—uninhabited as never before in the human history of the place—reminds us just how invented, just how constructed, the American wilderness really is. To return to my opening argument: there is nothing natural about the concept of wilderness. It is entirely a creation of the culture that holds it dear, a product of the very history it seeks to deny. Indeed, one of the most striking proofs of the cultural invention of wilderness is its thoroughgoing erasure of the history from which it sprang. In virtually all of its manifestations, wilderness represents a flight from history. Seen as the original garden, it is a place outside of time, from which human beings had to be ejected before the fallen world of history could properly begin. Seen as the frontier, it is a savage world at the dawn of civilization, whose transformation represents the very beginning of the national historical epic. Seen as the bold landscape of frontier heroism, it is the place of youth and childhood, into which men escape by abandoning their pasts and entering a world of freedom where the constraints of civilization fade into memory. Seen as the sacred sublime, it is the home of a God who transcends history by standing as the One who remains untouched and unchanged by time's arrow. No matter what the angle from which we regard it, wilderness offers us the illusion that we can escape the cares and troubles of the world in which our past has ensnared us.

This escape from history is one reason why the language we use to talk about wilderness is often permeated with spiritual and religious values that reflect human ideals far more than the material world of physical nature. Wilderness fulfills the old romantic project of secularizing Judeo-Christian values so as to make a new cathedral not in some petty human building but in God's own creation, Nature itself. Many environmentalists who reject traditional notions of the Godhead and who regard themselves as agnostics or even atheists nonetheless express feelings tantamount to religious awe when in the presence of wilderness—a fact that testifies to the success of the romantic project. Those who have no difficulty seeing God as the expression of our human dreams and desires nonetheless have trouble recognizing that in a secular age Nature can offer precisely the same sort of mirror.

26 Thus it is that wilderness serves as the unexamined foundation on which so many of the quasi-religious values of modern environmentalism rest. The critique of modernity that is one of environmentalism's most important contributions to the moral and political discourse of our time more often than not appeals, explicitly or implicitly, to wilderness as the standard against which to measure the failings of our human world. Wilderness is the natural, unfallen antithesis of an unnatural civilization that has lost its soul. It is a place of freedom in which we can recover the true selves we have lost to the corrupting influences of our artificial lives. Most of all, it is the ultimate landscape of authenticity. Combining the sacred grandeur of the sublime with the primitive simplicity of the frontier, it is the place where we can see the world as it really is, and so know ourselves as we really are—or ought to be.

But the trouble with wilderness is that it quietly expresses and reproduces the very values its devotees seek to reject. The flight from history that is very nearly the core of wilderness represents the false hope of an escape from responsibility, the illusion that we can somehow wipe clean the slate of our past and return to the tabula rasa that supposedly existed before we began to leave our marks on the world. The dream of an unworked natural landscape is very much the fantasy of people who have never themselves had to work the land to make a living—urban folk for whom food comes from a supermarket or a restaurant instead of a field, and for whom the wooden houses in which they live and work apparently have no meaningful connection to the forests in which trees grow and die. Only people whose relation to the land was already alienated could hold up wilderness as a model for human life in nature, for the romantic ideology of wilderness leaves precisely nowhere for human beings actually to make their living from the land.

28 This, then, is the central paradox: wilderness embodies a dualistic vision in which the human is entirely outside the natural. If we allow ourselves to believe that nature, to be true, must also be wild, then our very presence in nature represents its fall. The place where we are is the place where nature is not. If this is so—if by definition wilderness leaves no place for human beings, save perhaps as contemplative sojourners enjoying their leisurely reverie in God's natural cathedral—then also by definition it can offer no solution to the environmental and other problems that confront us. To the extent that we celebrate wilderness as the measure with which we judge civilization, we reproduce the dualism that sets humanity and nature at opposite poles. We thereby leave ourselves little hope of discovering what an ethical, sustainable, *honorable* human place in nature might actually look like.

Worse: to the extent that we live in an urban-industrial civilization but at the same time pretend to ourselves that our *real* home is in the wilderness, to just that extent we give ourselves permission to evade responsibility for the lives we actually lead. We inhabit civilization while holding some part of ourselves—what we imagine to be the most precious part—aloof from its entanglements. We work our nine-to-five jobs in its institutions, we eat its food, we drive its cars (not least to reach the wilderness), we benefit from the intricate and all too invisible networks with which it shelters us, all the while pretending that these things are not an essential part of who we are. By imagining that our true home is in the wilderness, we forgive ourselves the homes we actually inhabit. In its flight from history, in its siren song of escape, in its reproduction of the dangerous dualism that sets human beings outside of nature—in all of these ways, wilderness poses a serious threat to responsible environmentalism at the end of the twentieth century.

30   By now I hope it is clear that my criticism in this essay is not directed at wild nature per se, or even at efforts to set aside large tracts of wild land, but rather at the specific habits of thinking that flow from this complex cultural construction called wilderness. It is not the things we label as wilderness that are the problem—for nonhuman nature and large tracts of the natural world *do* deserve protection—but rather what we ourselves mean when we use that label. Lest one doubt how pervasive these habits of thought actually are in contemporary environmentalism, let me list some of the places where wilderness serves as the ideological underpinning for environmental concerns that might otherwise seem quite remote from it. Defenders of biological diversity, for instance, although sometimes appealing to more utilitarian concerns, often point to "untouched" ecosystems as the best and richest repositories of the undiscovered species we must certainly try to protect. Although at first blush an apparently more "scientific" concept than wilderness, biological diversity in fact invokes many of the same sacred values, which is why organizations like the Nature Conservancy have been so quick to employ it as an alternative to the seemingly fuzzier and more problematic concept of wilderness. There is a paradox here, of course. To the extent that biological diversity (indeed, even wilderness itself) is likely to survive in the future only by the most vigilant and self-conscious management of the ecosystems that sustain it, the ideology of wilderness is potentially in direct conflict with the very thing it encourages us to protect.

The most striking instances of this have revolved around "endangered species," which serve as vulnerable symbols of biological diversity while at the same time standing as surrogates for wilderness itself. The terms of the Endangered Species Act in the United States have often meant that those hoping to defend pristine wilderness have had to rely on a single endangered species like the spotted owl to gain legal standing for their case—thereby making the full power of sacred land inhere in a single numinous organism whose habitat then becomes the object of intense debate about appropriate management and use. The ease with which anti-environmental forces like the wise-use movement have attacked such single-species preservation efforts suggests the vulnerability of strategies like these.

32   Perhaps partly because our own conflicts over such places and organisms have become so messy, the convergence of wilderness values with concerns about biological diversity and endangered species has helped produce a deep fascination for remote ecosystems, where it is easier to imagine that nature might somehow be "left alone" to flourish by its own pristine devices. The classic example is the tropical rain forest, which since the 1970s has become the most powerful modern icon of unfallen, sacred land—a veritable Garden of Eden—for many Americans and Europeans. And yet protecting the rain forest in the eyes of First World environmentalists all too often means protecting it from the people who live there. Those who seek to preserve such "wilderness" from the activities of native peoples run the risk of reproducing the same tragedy—being forcibly removed from an ancient home—that befell American Indians. Third World countries face massive environmental problems and deep social conflicts, but these are not likely to be solved by a cultural myth that encourages us to "preserve" peopleless landscapes that have not existed in such places for millennia. At its worst, as environmentalists are beginning to realize, exporting American notions of wilderness in this way can become an unthinking and self-defeating form of cultural imperialism.

Perhaps the most suggestive example of the way that wilderness thinking can underpin other environmental concerns has emerged in the recent debate about "global change." In 1989 the journalist Bill McKibben published a book entitled *The End of Nature,* in which he argued that the prospect of global climate change as a result of unintentional human manipulation of the atmosphere means that nature as we once knew it no longer exists. Whereas earlier generations inhabited a natural world that remained more or less unaffected by their actions, our own generation is uniquely different. We and our children will henceforth live in a biosphere completely altered by our own activity, a planet in which the human and the natural can no longer be distinguished, because the one has overwhelmed the other. In McKibben's view, nature has died, and we are responsible for killing it. "The planet," he declares, "is utterly different now."

34   But such a perspective is possible only if we accept the wilderness premise that nature, to be natural, must also be pristine—remote from humanity and untouched by our common past. In fact, everything we know about environmental history suggests that people have been manipulating the natural world on various scales for as long as we have a record of their passing. Moreover, we have unassailable evidence that many of the environmental changes we now face also occurred quite apart from human intervention at one time or another in the earth's past. The point is not that our current problems are trivial, or that our devastating effects on the earth's ecosystems should be accepted as inevitable or "natural." It is rather that we

seem unlikely to make much progress in solving these problems if we hold
up to ourselves as the mirror of nature a wilderness we ourselves cannot
inhabit.

To do so is merely to take to a logical extreme the paradox that was
built into wilderness from the beginning: if nature dies because we enter it,
then the only way to save nature is to kill ourselves. The absurdity of this
proposition flows from the underlying dualism it expresses. Not only does it
ascribe greater power to humanity than we in fact possess—physical and biological nature will surely survive in some form or another long after we
ourselves have gone the way of all flesh—but in the end it offers us little
more than a self-defeating counsel of despair. The tautology gives us no way
out: if wild nature is the only thing worth saving, and if our mere presence
destroys it, then the sole solution to our own unnaturalness, the only way
to protect sacred wilderness from profane humanity, would seem to be suicide. It is not a proposition that seems likely to produce very positive or
practical results.

36   And yet radical environmentalists and deep ecologists all too frequently come close to accepting this premise as a first principle. When they
express, for instance, the popular notion that our environmental problems
began with the invention of agriculture, they push the human fall from natural grace so far back into the past that all of civilized history becomes a tale
of ecological declension. Earth First! founder Dave Foreman captures the
familiar parable succinctly when he writes,

> Before agriculture was midwifed in the Middle East, humans were in
> the wilderness. We had no concept of "wilderness" because everything was
> wilderness and *we were a part of it.* But with irrigation ditches, crop surpluses,
> and permanent villages, we became *apart from* the natural world. . . . Between
> the wilderness that created us and the civilization created by us grew an ever-
> widening rift.

In this view the farm becomes the first and most important battlefield in the
long war against wild nature, and all else follows in its wake. From such a
starting place, it is hard not to reach the conclusion that the only way human
beings can hope to live naturally on earth is to follow the hunter-gatherers
back into a wilderness Eden and abandon virtually everything that civilization has given us. It may indeed turn out that civilization will end in ecological collapse or nuclear disaster, whereupon one might expect to find
any human survivors returning to a way of life closer to that celebrated by
Foreman and his followers. For most of us, though, such a debacle would be
cause for regret, a sign that humanity had failed to fulfill its own promise
and failed to honor its own highest values—including those of the deep
ecologists.

In offering wilderness as the ultimate hunter-gatherer alternative to
civilization, Foreman reproduces an extreme but still easily recognizable

version of the myth of frontier primitivism.* When he writes of his fellow Earth Firsters that "we believe we must return to being animal, to glorying in our sweat, hormones, tears, and blood" and that "we struggle against the modern compulsion to become dull, passionless androids," he is following in the footsteps of Owen Wister. Although his arguments give primacy to defending biodiversity and the autonomy of wild nature, his prose becomes most passionate when he speaks of preserving "the wilderness experience." His own ideal "Big Outside" bears an uncanny resemblance to that of the frontier myth: wide open spaces and virgin land with no trails, no signs, no facilities, no maps, no guides, no rescues, no modern equipment. Tellingly, it is a land where hardy travelers can support themselves by hunting with "primitive weapons (bow and arrow, atlatl, knife, sharp rock)." Foreman claims that "the primary value of wilderness is not as a proving ground for young Huck Finns and Annie Oakleys," but his heart is with Huck and Annie all the same. He admits that "preserving a quality wilderness experience for the human visitor, letting her or him flex Paleolithic muscles or seek visions, remains a tremendously important secondary purpose." Just so does Teddy Roosevelt's rough rider live on in the greener garb of a new age.

38   However much one may be attracted to such a vision, it entails problematic consequences. For one, it makes wilderness the locus for an epic struggle between malign civilization and benign nature, compared with which all other social, political, and moral concerns seem trivial. Foreman writes, "The preservation of wildness and native diversity is *the* most important issue. Issues directly affecting only humans pale in comparison." Presumably so do any environmental problems whose victims are mainly people, for such problems usually surface in landscapes that have already "fallen" and are no longer wild. This would seem to exclude from the radical environmentalist agenda problems of occupational health and safety in industrial settings, problems of toxic waste exposure on "unnatural" urban and agricultural sites, problems of poor children poisoned by lead exposure in the inner city, problems of famine and poverty and human suffering in the "overpopulated" places of the earth—problems, in short, of environmental justice. If we set too high a stock on wilderness, too many other corners of the earth become less than natural and too many other people become less than human, thereby giving us permission not to care much about their suffering or their fate.

It is no accident that these supposedly inconsequential environmental problems affect mainly poor people, for the long affiliation between wilderness and wealth means that the only poor people who count when wilderness is *the* issue are hunter-gatherers, who presumably do not consider themselves to be poor in the first place. The dualism at the heart of wilderness encourages its advocates to conceive of its protection as a crude conflict between the "human" and the "nonhuman"—or, more often, between those

---

* For an argument by Dave Foreman, see pp. 258–266.

who value the nonhuman and those who do not. This in turn tempts one to ignore crucial differences *among* humans and the complex cultural and historical reasons why different peoples may feel very differently about the meaning of wilderness.

40   Why, for instance, is the "wilderness experience" so often conceived as a form of recreation best enjoyed by those whose class privileges give them the time and resources to leave their jobs behind and "get away from it all"? Why does the protection of wilderness so often seem to pit urban recreationists against rural people who actually earn their living from the land (excepting those who sell goods and services to the tourists themselves)? Why in the debates about pristine natural areas are "primitive" peoples idealized, even sentimentalized, until the moment they do something unprimitive, modern, and unnatural, and thereby fall from environmental grace? What are the consequences of a wilderness ideology that devalues productive labor and the very concrete knowledge that comes from working the land with one's own hands? All of these questions imply conflicts among different groups of people, conflicts that are obscured behind the deceptive clarity of "human" vs. "nonhuman." If in answering these knotty questions we resort to so simplistic an opposition, we are almost certain to ignore the very subtleties and complexities we need to understand.

But the most troubling cultural baggage that accompanies the celebration of wilderness has less to do with remote rain forests and peoples than with the ways we think about ourselves—we American environmentalists who quite rightly worry about the future of the earth and the threats we pose to the natural world. Idealizing a distant wilderness too often means not idealizing the environment in which we actually live, the landscape that for better or worse we call home. Most of our most serious environmental problems start right here, at home, and if we are to solve those problems, we need an environmental ethic that will tell us as much about *using* nature as about *not* using it. The wilderness dualism tends to cast any use as *abuse*, and thereby denies us a middle ground in which responsible use and non-use might attain some kind of balanced, sustainable relationship. My own belief is that only by exploring this middle ground will we learn ways of imagining a better world for all of us: humans and nonhumans, rich people and poor, women and men, First Worlders and Third Worlders, white folks and people of color, consumers and producers—a world better for humanity in all of its diversity and for all the rest of nature too. The middle ground is where we actually live. It is where we—all of us, in our different places and ways—make our homes.

42   That is why when I think of the times I myself have come closest to experiencing what I might call the sacred in nature, I often find myself remembering wild places much closer to home. I think, for instance, of a small pond near my house where water bubbles up from limestone springs to feed a series of pools that rarely freeze in winter and so play home to waterfowl that stay here for the protective warmth even on the coldest of winter

days, gliding silently through steaming mists as the snow falls from gray February skies. I think of a November evening long ago when I found myself on a Wisconsin hilltop in rain and dense fog, only to have the setting sun break through the clouds to cast an otherwordly golden light on the misty farms and woodlands below, a scene so unexpected and joyous that I lingered past dusk so as not to miss any part of the gift that had come my way. And I think perhaps most especially of the blown-out, bankrupt farm in the sand country of central Wisconsin where Aldo Leopold and his family tried one of the first American experiments in ecological restoration, turning ravaged and infertile soil into carefully tended ground where the human and the non-human could exist side by side in relative harmony. What I celebrate about such places is not *just* their wildness, though that certainly is among their most important qualities; what I celebrate even more is that they remind us of the wildness in our own backyards, of the nature that is all around us if only we have eyes to see it.

Indeed, my principal objection to wilderness is that it may teach us to be dismissive or even contemptuous of such humble places and experiences. Without our quite realizing it, wilderness tends to privilege some parts of nature at the expense of others. Most of us, I suspect, still follow the conventions of the romantic sublime in finding the mountaintop more glorious than the plains, the ancient forest nobler than the grasslands, the mighty canyon more inspiring than the humble marsh. Even John Muir, in arguing against those who sought to dam his beloved Hetch Hetchy valley in the Sierra Nevada, argued for alternative dam sites in the gentler valleys of the foothills—a preference that had nothing to do with nature and everything with the cultural traditions of the sublime. Just as problematically, our frontier traditions have encouraged Americans to define "true" wilderness as requiring very large tracts of roadless land—what Dave Foreman calls "The Big Outside." Leaving aside the legitimate empirical question in conservation biology of how large a tract of land must be before a given species can reproduce on it, the emphasis on big wilderness reflects a romantic frontier belief that one hasn't really gotten away from civilization unless one can go for days at a time without encountering another human being. By teaching us to fetishize sublime places and wide open country, these peculiarly American ways of thinking about wilderness encourage us to adopt too high a standard for what counts as "natural." If it isn't hundreds of square miles big, if it doesn't give us God's-eye views or grand vistas, if it doesn't permit us the illusion that we are alone on the planet, then it really isn't natural. It's too small, too plain, or too crowded to be *authentically* wild.

44   In critiquing wilderness as I have done in this essay, I'm forced to confront my own deep ambivalence about its meaning for modern environmentalism. On the one hand, one of my own most important environmental ethics is that people should always to be conscious that they are part of the natural world, inextricably tied to the ecological systems that sustain their

lives. Any way of looking at nature that encourages us to believe we are separate from nature—as wilderness tends to do—is likely to reinforce envi-
ronmentally irresponsible behavior. On the other hand, I also think it no
less crucial for us to recognize and honor nonhuman nature as a world we
did not create, a world with its own independent, nonhuman reasons for
being as it is. The autonomy of nonhuman nature seems to me an indis-
pensable corrective to human arrogance. Any way of looking at nature that
helps us remember—as wilderness also tends to do—that the interests of
people are not necessarily identical to those of every other creature or of the
earth itself is likely to foster *responsible* behavior. To the extent that wilderness has served as an important vehicle for articulating deep moral values
regarding our obligations and responsibilities to the nonhuman world, I
would not want to jettison the contributions it has made to our culture's
way of thinking about nature.

If the core problem of wilderness is that it distances us too much from
the very things it teaches us to value, then the question we must ask is what it
can tell us about *home*, the place where we actually live. How can we take the
positive values we associate with wilderness and bring them closer to home?
I think the answer to this question will come by broadening our sense of the
otherness that wilderness seeks to define and protect. In reminding us of the
world we did not make, wilderness can teach profound feelings of humility
and respect as we confront our fellow beings and the earth itself. Feelings like
these argue for the importance of self-awareness and self-criticism as we exercise our own ability to transform the world around us, helping us set responsible limits to human mastery—which without such limits too easily
becomes human hubris. Wilderness is the place where, symbolically at least,
we try to withhold our power to dominate.

46   Wallace Stegner once wrote of

> the special human mark, the special record of human passage, that distin-
> guishes man from all other species. It is rare enough among men, impossible
> to any other form of life. *It is simply the deliberate and chosen refusal to make
> any marks at all. . . .* We are the most dangerous species of life on the planet,
> and every other species, even the earth itself, has cause to fear our power to
> exterminate. But we are also the only species which, when it chooses to do
> so, will go to great effort to save what it might destroy.

The myth of wilderness, which Stegner knowingly reproduces in these remarks, is that we can somehow leave nature untouched by our passage. By
now it should be clear that this for the most part is an illusion. But Stegner's
deeper message then becomes all the more compelling. If living in history
means that we cannot help leaving marks on a fallen world, then the
dilemma we face is to decide what kinds of marks we wish to leave. It is just
here that our cultural traditions of wilderness remain so important. In the
broadest sense, wilderness teaches us to ask whether the Other must always
bend to our will, and, if not, under what circumstances it should be allowed

to flourish without our intervention. This is surely a question worth asking about everything we do, and not just about the natural world.

When we visit a wilderness area, we find ourselves surrounded by plants and animals and physical landscapes whose otherness compels our attention. In forcing us to acknowledge that they are not of our making, that they have little or no need of our continued existence, they recall for us a creation far greater than our own. In the wilderness, we need no reminder that a tree has its own reasons for being, quite apart from us. The same is less true in the gardens we plant and tend ourselves: there it is far easier to forget the otherness of the tree. Indeed, one could almost measure wilderness by the extent to which our recognition of its otherness requires a conscious, willed act on our part. The romantic legacy means that wilderness is more a state of mind than a fact of nature, and the state of mind that today most defines wilderness is *wonder*. The striking power of the wild is that wonder in the face of it requires no act of will, but forces itself upon us—as an expression of the nonhuman world experienced through the lens of our cultural history—as proof that ours is not the only presence in the universe.

48   Wilderness gets us into trouble only if we imagine that this experience of wonder and otherness is limited to the remote corners of the planet, or that it somehow depends on pristine landscapes we ourselves do not inhabit. Nothing could be more misleading. The tree in the garden is in reality no less other, no less worthy of our wonder and respect, than the tree in an ancient forest that has never known an ax or a saw—even though the tree in the forest reflects a more intricate web of ecological relationships. The tree in the garden could easily have sprung from the same seed as the tree in the forest, and we can claim only its location and perhaps its form as our own. Both trees stand apart from us; both share our common world. The special power of the tree in the wilderness is to remind us of this fact. It can teach us to recognize the wildness we did not see in the tree we planted in our own backyard. By seeing the otherness in that which is most unfamiliar, we can learn to see it too in that which at first seemed merely ordinary. If wilderness can do this—if it can help us perceive and respect a nature we had forgotten to recognize as natural—then it will become part of the solution to our environmental dilemmas rather than part of the problem.

This will only happen, however, if we abandon the dualism that sees the tree in the garden as artificial—completely fallen and unnatural—and the tree in the wilderness as natural—completely pristine and wild. Both trees in some ultimate sense are wild; both in a practical sense now depend on our management and care. We are responsible for both, even though we can claim credit for neither. Our challenge is to stop thinking of such things according to a set of bipolar moral scales in which the human and the nonhuman, the unnatural and the natural, the fallen and the unfallen, serve as our conceptual map for understanding and valuing the world. Instead, we need to embrace the full continuum of a natural landscape that is also cultural, in which the city, the suburb, the pastoral, and the wild each has its proper place, which we permit ourselves to celebrate without needlessly denigrating the others. We need to honor the Other within and the Other next door as much as we do the exotic Other that lives far away—a lesson that applies as much to people as it does to (other) natural things. In particular, we need to discover a common middle ground in which all of these things, from the city to the wilderness, can somehow be encompassed in the word "home." Home, after all, is the place where finally we make our living. It is the place for which we take responsibility, the place we try to sustain so we can pass on what is best in it (and in ourselves) to our children.

50   The task of making a home in nature is what Wendell Berry has called "the forever unfinished lifework of our species." "The only thing we have to preserve nature with," he writes, "is culture; the only thing we have to preserve wildness with is domesticity." Calling a place home inevitably means that we will *use* the nature we find in it, for there can be no escape from manipulating and working and even killing some parts of nature to make our home. But if we acknowledge the autonomy and otherness of the things and creatures around us—an autonomy our culture has taught us to label with the word "wild"—then we will at least think carefully about the uses to which we put them, and even ask if we should use them at all. Just so can we still join Thoreau in declaring that "in Wildness is the preservation of the World," for *wild*ness (as opposed to wilderness) can be found anywhere: in the seemingly tame fields and woodlots of Massachusetts, in the cracks of a Manhattan sidewalk, even in the cells of our own bodies. As Gary Snyder has wisely said, "A person with a clear heart and open mind can experience the wilderness anywhere on earth. It is a quality of one's own consciousness. The planet is a wild place and always will be." To think ourselves capable of causing "the end of nature" is an act of great hubris, for it means forgetting the wildness that dwells everywhere within and around us.

Learning to honor the wild—learning to remember and acknowledge the autonomy of the other—means striving for critical self-consciousness in all of our actions. It means that deep reflection and respect must accompany each act of use, and means too that we must always consider the possibility of non-use. It means looking at the part of nature we intend to turn toward our own ends and asking whether we can use it again and again and again—sustainably—without its being diminished in the process. It means never imagining that we can flee into a mythical wilderness to escape history and the obligation to take responsibility for our own actions that history inescapably entails. Most of all, it means practicing remembrance and gratitude, for thanksgiving is the simplest and most basic of ways for us to recollect the nature, the culture, and the history that have come together to make the world as we know it. If wildness can stop being (just) out there and start being (also) in here, if it can start being as humane as it is natural, then perhaps we can get on with the unending task of struggling to live rightly in the world—not just in the garden, not just in the wilderness, but in the home that encompasses them both. ❖

Questions for Meaning

1. Why does Cronon believe that "wilderness" is "a product of civilization"? How has the perception of "wilderness" changed in recent centuries?
2. What is the doctrine of the sublime, and how did it influence the thinking that led to the creation of our first national parks?
3. What kind of values are implicit in our myth of the American frontier?
4. How have race and social class been factors in the creation of national park and wilderness areas?
5. What does Cronon mean in paragraphs 23–29 when he claims that wilderness represents "a flight from history"?
6. How does Cronon think we should respond to nature?
7. Vocabulary: pristine (3), transcendent (3), sojourn (10), icon (13), surrogates (21), tantamount (25), tabula rasa (27), tautology (35), fetishize (43).

Questions about Strategy

1. Consider the memories Cronon tries to invoke in paragraph 4. Who is most likely to have such memories? Is he wise to direct his argument to an audience of this sort?
2. Why does Cronon devote so much space to discussing cultural values that prevailed in the eighteenth and nineteenth centuries?
3. In paragraphs 13–15, Cronon contrasts the experiences of Henry David Thoreau and John Muir. What is the purpose of this contrast?
4. How does Cronon establish that he values wilderness even though he is challenging conventional thinking about it?
5. In his conclusion, Cronon calls for discovering "a common middle ground." Does he give readers any help envisioning what that common ground could be?

ONE STUDENT'S ASSIGNMENT

Drawing on the material in *The Informed Argument,* Brief Edition, and at least two sources that you have discovered on your own, evaluate the current condition of our national parks and recommend how they should be managed in the future. Use the numbered system for documentation recommended by the Council of Biology Editors. (Arrange your reference list in alphabetical order; then number your sources according to this order. When you refer to a source within your paper, cite the corresponding number from the reference list.)

Preserving Our Parks
Amy Karlen

As a girl, I remember traveling many miles cramped between my two brothers in the backseat of our parents' powder-blue Crown Victoria wagon. This trusty old Ford, stocked with enough crackers, chips, pop, and Mad-Libs to last for months, carried our family to a number of national parks around the country. Once, while driving through Yellowstone, my dad had to stop the car to avoid colliding with a half-dozen buffalo making their way across the road. When we started driving again, I turned to watch the buffalo through the back window. It amazed me how fearlessly these animals stepped out in front of us as if to say, "Hey! Get out of the way! This is *our* area. We were here first!"

2   Years later, I came to realize how many of our national parks, which Americans assume to reflect the finest and best in our country's values, often reflect the worst. To most Americans, myself included, the definition of a "park" seems obvious. However, the *concept* of a park has changed over the years. While the early meaning of "park" meant "an enclosed preserve for beasts of the chase," it was later extended to include "a large, 'ornamental' piece of ground, used for recreation"[5]. Today, it seems the mission of many national parks no longer emphasizes a preservation of animals and conservation of natural resources, so much as it focuses on pleasing the public.

I am all for promoting community interaction at the national park level, for without such establishments, many suburban and metropolitan visitors may otherwise not have an opportunity to experience nature. Yet, I still find it disturbing that the mission of species and resource conservation has taken a backseat to keeping Americans self-satisfied. If truly concerned about the environment, Americans should recognize that the preservation of natural habitats is more important than whether their recreational needs are met.

4   To encourage easy access by vacationers, many parks were designed with easy access for motorized vehicles, enabling the Forest Service to lump its wilderness program under the division of recreation. As a result, not only is traffic congestion commonplace during some seasons, but campgrounds fill up early in the morning and muddy trails erode from heavy use. Today, park visitors find that more than "one-third of all roads in the parks need repair"[4]. A 1980 proposal by the Department of Interior, calling for the reduction of accommodations at Yosemite National Park, the elimination of its parking lots, the relocation of some campsites, and a new limit on the number of visitors, collapsed from lack of funding. As a result, by the late 1990s, "the park has made scant headway on the most

challenging problem, the flood of cars, trucks and recreational vehicles that make a mile-long trip through Yosemite Village seem like a Manhattan Rush Hour"[3]. What this demonstrates is that the original function of a park becomes blurred when it tries to equally satisfy the preservation of nature and the recreational needs of the public.

Overuse and underfunding have caused park wildlife to suffer. In fact, the current rate of extinction is as much as "10,000 times the normal background rate documented in the fossil record"[2]. Biologists warn that one-third of our species could die out within 40 years. According to Dave Foreman, director of the Sierra Club, American national park and wilderness areas make up the world's finest nature-reserve service. Why then are we losing so many species? The answer is poor management. As of last year, "officials at many large national parks knew little about the condition of their natural resources"[1]. At Yosemite, for example, the bird, fish, and mammal condition was unknown, and as of 1995, the Park Service had no systematic way to collect data in order to inventory natural resources or monitor their changes over time. As a result, "It is unknown whether the overall condition of many key natural resources is improving, deteriorating, or remaining constant"[1].

6   Although overcrowding threatens our habitats, and although it seems unlikely that Congress could substantially increase the amount of financial resources going to our parks, it is not too late to restore what should be their main mission—"a preserve for beasts of the chase."

Park officials must restrict more tightly which areas are open to the general public—and, in particular, which are open for motorized recreation. Scheduling particular recreations on particular days in particular places would allow visitors to exercise their preferred activity without the interference of other recreational users, and more importantly, without wearing down the same areas of land day after day. While some forms of recreation, such as hiking and mountain climbing, do little harm to the natural resources of the park, motorized recreation threatens to disrupt natural habitats. I do not intend to judge any form of recreation as better than another, but we need to realize that certain activities are more likely to harm our parks than others—and at a much quicker rate. Reserving specific days for specific users will ensure that all visitors have an opportunity to fully experience all the park has to offer—yet not necessarily whenever they choose.

8   Although a proposal of this sort seems unlikely to be implemented soon, Congress has at least taken a step forward, when, in 1996, it approved and President Clinton signed into law a measure to raise entrance fees to our nation's most popular national parks, or in some cases, begin charging for the first time. 1997

introduced the most significant increases under this program when the cost of an annual pass per carload at Yellowstone, Yosemite, Grand Canyon and Grand Tetons parks rose from $15 to $40. The seven-day pass rose from $10–$20 per car. "These new fees will be a down payment on the resource protection, restoration and general maintenance that the parks desperately need," said Paul Pritchard, president of the National Parks and Conservation Association[6].

Whether by recreation or exploration, parks allow visitors to escape the constraints of everyday life. However, while guests may pack up and leave as they wish, our animals *live* in these parks. Isolating animals within a single habitat terminates recolonization by nearby specie members. As a result, species often inbreed, causing severe genetic defects. According to Foreman, America needs to treat the national forests around the parks as integral to the park itself. Connecting habitats by corridors would allow animals to move more freely between the two regions, ceasing inbreeding and recolonizing habitats. As truly concerned Americans, we must allow our animals, as we do ourselves, the freedom to escape from constraint.

10   We need to remember that while national parks may offer sport and recreation for visitors, their primary purpose should be to preserve America's natural resources. I, too, admit falling prey to national park misconception. However, we all need to remember that nature is not a toy. We cannot just play with it one day and ignore it the next. And while we must take care not to play with it any way we choose, this does not mean we cannot play with it at all. By working together and appropriating divisions for both recreation and habitat, all species can share the land.

I only wish that someday, I, too, will buckle my children in our backseat, cramped between bags of low-fat tortilla chips, no-fat cookies, and 100 percent fresh-squeezed, organic orange juice, and show them the beauty, wonder—yet more importantly, the *life*—preserved in our national parks. This time, however, *I'll* be driving with my husband in something more rugged than a powder-blue Crown Victoria wagon.

References

1. Duffus, J. A report from the General Accounting Office. In: Miller R. The informed argument. Brief ed. Fort Worth: Harcourt; 1999. 248–252.
2. Foreman, D. Missing links. In: Miller R. The informed argument. Brief ed. Fort Worth: Harcourt; 1999. 258–266.
3. Golden, T. In Yosemite, nature may have its way yet. The New York Times 1997 Feb 2; Sect 1: 1+ (column 1).
4. Lowry, W. 1994. Promises, promises. Brookings Review. 12: 38–41.

5. Olwig, K. Reinventing nature. In: Cronon W. Uncommon ground: Toward reinventing nature. New York: Norton; 1995. 379–408.
6. Sonner, S. Entrance fees to national parks will rise to fund improvements. St. Paul Pioneer Press 1996 Nov 27; Sect 1: 1+ (column 1).

SUGGESTIONS FOR WRITING

1. Drawing on the argument by Terry Anderson and on additional research, write a plan for making national parks profitable.
2. Synthesize the articles by James Duffus, Terry Anderson, and Dave Foreman in an essay focused on reporting problems in our national park system.
3. Write an essay defining "park," "wilderness," or "nature."
4. Drawing on the work of William Cronon, write an essay explaining the values that led to the creation of our first national parks.
5. Write an argument on behalf of preserving natural resources.
6. If you have ever been to a national park or wilderness area, write an essay describing where you went and evaluating what you experienced there.
7. Write an essay about how to enjoy nature in a city or suburb.
8. Study the painting reproduced on page 271. Locate a color reproduction of this work or another painting by Thomas Cole.
9. Research how publicly held lands are managed in another country and write a report comparing that system with our own.

COLLABORATIVE PROJECT

Looking at photographs or videos of someone else's vacation can sometimes feel like an endurance test, but material of this sort can also be considered historical documents. Ask friends, colleagues, and family members for any pictures they have showing what they consider "nature." Gather a large sample, keeping track of who owns what material so that you can return the contributions at the end of your project. Look for patterns in what people choose to photograph and how they present themselves and others when being photographed in a natural setting. If you have any questions about the material you have gathered, interview the people who contributed it. Then write an essay in which you analyze what this sample group seems to value about nature.

PART 5

SOME CLASSIC ARGUMENTS

Jonathan Swift

A MODEST PROPOSAL

For preventing the Children of Poor People in Ireland from Being a Burden to Their Parents or Country, and for Making Them Beneficial to the Public

Jonathan Swift (1667–1745) was a clergyman, poet, wit, and satirist. Born in Ireland as a member of the Protestant ruling class, Swift attended Trinity College in Dublin before settling in England in 1689. For the next ten years, he was a member of the household of Sir William Temple at Moor Park, Surrey. It was there that Swift met Esther Johnson, the "Stella" to whom he later wrote a famous series of letters known as *Journal to Stella* (1710–1713). Although he was ordained a priest in the Church of Ireland in 1695, and made frequent trips to Ireland, Swift's ambition always brought him back to England. His reputation as a writer grew rapidly after the publication of his first major work, *A Tale of a Tub*, in 1704. He became a writer on behalf of the ruling Tory party, and was appointed Dean of St. Patrick's Cathedral in Dublin as a reward for his services. When the Tories fell from power in 1714, Swift retired to Ireland, where he remained for the rest of his life, except for brief visits to England in 1726 and 1727. It was in Ireland that he wrote *Gulliver's Travels* (1726), which is widely recognized as one of the masterpieces of English literature, and "A Modest Proposal" (1729), one of the most memorable of all essays.

Ruled as an English colony and subject to numerous repressive laws, Ireland in Swift's time was a desperately poor country. Swift wrote "A Modest Proposal" in order to expose the plight of Ireland and the unfair policies under which it suffered. As you read it, you will find that Swift's proposal for solving the problem of poverty is anything but "modest." Even when we know that we are reading satire, this brilliant and bitter essay retains the power to shock all but the most careless of readers.

It is a melancholy object to those who walk through this great town or travel in the country, when they see the streets, the roads, and cabin doors, crowded with beggars of the female sex, followed by three, four, or six children, all in rags and importuning every passenger for an alms. These mothers, instead of being able to work for their honest livelihood, are forced to employ all their time in strolling to beg sustenance for their helpless infants, who, as they grow up, either turn thieves for want of work, or leave their dear native country to fight for the Pretender in Spain, or sell themselves to the Barbados.*

2   I think it is agreed by all parties that this prodigious number of children in the arms, or on the backs, or at the heels of their mothers, and frequently of their fathers, is in the present deplorable state of the kingdom a very great additional grievance; and therefore whoever could find out a fair, cheap, and easy method of making these children sound, useful members of the commonwealth would deserve so well of the public as to have his statue set up for a preserver of the nation.

But my intention is very far from being confined to provide only for the children of professed beggars; it is of a much greater extent, and shall take in the whole number of infants at a certain age who are born of parents in effect as little able to support them as those who demand our charity in the streets.

4   As to my own part, having turned my thoughts for many years upon this important subject, and maturely weighed the several schemes of other projectors, I have always found them grossly mistaken in their computation. It is true, a child just dropped from its dam may be supported by her milk for a solar year, with little other nourishment; at most not above the value of two shillings, which the mother may certainly get, or the value in scraps, by her lawful occupation of begging; and it is exactly at one year that I propose to provide for them in such a manner as instead of being a charge upon their parents or the parish, or wanting food and raiment for the rest of their lives, they shall on the contrary contribute to the feeding, and partly to the clothing, of many thousands.

There is likewise another great advantage in my scheme, that it will prevent those voluntary abortions, and that horrid practice of women murdering their bastard children, alas, too frequent among us, sacrificing the poor innocent babes, I doubt, more to avoid the expense than the shame, which would move tears and pity in the most savage and inhuman breast.

---

* The Pretender was James Stuart, the Catholic son of James II. Exiled in Spain, he sought to gain the throne his father had lost to the Protestant rulers William and Mary in 1688. Attempting to escape from destitution, many Irish people went to Barbados and other colonies as indentured servants.

6   The number of souls in this kingdom being usually reckoned one million and a half, of these I calculate there may be about two hundred thousand couples whose wives are breeders; from which number I subtract thirty thousand couples who are able to maintain their own children, although I apprehend there cannot be so many under the present distress of the kingdom; but this being granted, there will remain an hundred and seventy thousand breeders. I again subtract fifty thousand for those women who miscarry, or whose children die by accident or disease within the year. There only remain an hundred and twenty thousand children of poor parents annually born. The question therefore is, how this number shall be reared and provided for, which, as I have already said, under the present situation of affairs, is utterly impossible by all the methods hitherto proposed. For we can neither employ them in handicraft or agriculture; we neither build houses (I mean in the country) nor cultivate land. They can very seldom pick up a livelihood by stealing till they arrive at six years old, except where they are of towardly parts; although I confess they learn the rudiments much earlier, during which time they can however be looked upon only as probationers, as I have been informed by a principal gentleman in the county of Cavan, who protested to me that he never knew above one or two instances under the age of six, even in a part of the kingdom so renowned for the quickest proficiency in that art.

     I am assured by our merchants that a boy or a girl before twelve years old is no salable commodity; and even when they come to this age they will not yield above three pounds, or three pounds and half a crown at most on the Exchange; which cannot turn to account either to the parents or the kingdom, the charge of nutriment and rags having been at least four times that value.

8   I shall now therefore humbly propose my own thoughts, which I hope will not be liable to the least objection.

     I have been assured by a very knowing American of my acquaintance in London, that a young healthy child well nursed is at a year old a most delicious, nourishing, and wholesome food, whether stewed, roasted, baked, or boiled; and I make no doubt that it will equally serve in a fricassee or a ragout.

10   I do therefore humbly offer it to public consideration that of the hundred and twenty thousand children, already computed, twenty thousand may be reserved for breed, whereof only one fourth part to be males, which is more than we allow to sheep, black cattle, or swine; and my reason is that these children are seldom the fruits of marriage, a circumstance not much regarded by our savages, therefore one male will be sufficient to serve four females. That the remaining hundred thousand may at a year old be offered in sale to the persons of quality and fortune through the kingdom, always advising the mother to let them suck plentifully in the last month, so as to render them plump and fat for a good table. A child will make two dishes at an entertainment for friends; and when the family dines alone, the fore or

hind quarter will make a reasonable dish, and seasoned with a little pepper or salt will be very good boiled on the fourth day, especially in winter.

I have reckoned upon a medium that a child just born will weigh twelve pounds, and in a solar year if tolerably nursed increaseth to twenty-eight pounds. *Expansn*

12   I grant this food will be somewhat dear, and therefore very proper for landlords, who, as they have already devoured most of the parents, seem to have the best title to the children. *Closit to zyrcusm*

Infant's flesh will be in season throughout the year, but more plentiful in March, and a little before and after. For we are told by a grave author, an eminent French physician,* that fish being a prolific diet, there are more children born in Roman Catholic countries about nine months after Lent than at any other season; therefore, reckoning a year after Lent, the markets will be more glutted than usual, because the number of popish infants is at least three to one in this kingdom; and therefore it will have one other collateral advantage, by lessening the number of Papists among us.

14   I have already computed the charge of nursing a beggar's child (in which list I reckon all cottagers, laborers, and four-fifths of the farmers) to be about two shillings per annum, rags included; and I believe no gentleman would repine to give ten shillings for the carcass of a good fat child, which, as I have said, will make four dishes of excellent nutritive meat, when he hath only some particular friend or his own family to dine with him. Thus the squire will learn to be a good landlord, and grow popular among the tenants; the mother will have eight shillings net profit, and be fit for work till she produces another child.

Those who are more thrifty (as I must confess the times require) may flay the carcass; the skin of which artificially dressed will make admirable gloves for ladies, and summer boots for fine gentlemen.

16   As to our city of Dublin, shambles may be appointed for this purpose in the most convenient parts of it, and butchers we may be assured will not be wanting; although I rather recommend buying the children alive, and dressing them hot from the knife as we do roasting pigs.

A very worthy person, a true lover of his country, and whose virtues I highly esteem, was lately pleased in discoursing on this matter to offer a refinement upon my scheme. He said that many gentlemen of his kingdom, having of late destroyed their deer, he conceived that the want of venison might be well supplied by the bodies of young lads and maidens, not exceeding fourteen years of age nor under twelve, so great a number of both sexes in every country being now ready to starve for want of work and service; and these to be disposed of by their parents, if alive, or otherwise by their nearest relations. But with due deference to so excellent a friend and so deserving a patriot, I cannot be altogether in his sentiments; for as to the males, my American acquaintance assured me from frequent experience

---

* François Rabelais (1494?–1533) was the author of *Gargantua and Pantagruel*, a five-volume satire much admired by Swift.

that their flesh was generally tough and lean, like that of our schoolboys, by continual exercise, and their taste disagreeable; and to fatten them would not answer the charge. Then as to the females, it would, I think with humble submission, be a loss to the public, because they soon would become breeders themselves; and besides, it is not improbable that some scrupulous people might be apt to censure such a practice (although indeed very unjustly) as a little bordering upon cruelty; which, I confess, hath always been with me the strongest objection against any project, how well soever intended.

18   But in order to justify my friend, he confessed that this expedient was put into his head by the famous Psalmanazar,* a native of the island of Formosa, who came from thence to London about twenty years ago, and in conversation told my friend that in his country when any young person happened to be put to death, the executioner sold the carcass to persons of quality as a prime dainty; and that in his time the body of a plump girl of fifteen, who was crucified for an attempt to poison the emperor, was sold to his Imperial Majesty's prime minister of state, and other great mandarins of the court, in joints from the gibbet, at four hundred crowns. Neither indeed can I deny that if the same use were made of several plump young girls in this town, who without one single groat to their fortunes cannot stir abroad without a chair, and appear at the playhouse and assemblies in foreign fineries which they never will pay for, the kingdom would not be the worse.

    Some persons of a desponding spirit are in great concern about that vast number of poor people who are aged, diseased, or maimed, and I have been desired to employ my thoughts what course may be taken to ease the nation of so grievous an encumbrance. But I am not in the least pain upon that matter, because it is very well known that they are every day dying and rotting by cold and famine, and filth and vermin, as fast as can be reasonably expected. And as to the younger laborers, they are now in almost as hopeful a condition. They cannot get work, and consequently pine away for want of nourishment to a degree that if any time they are accidentally hired to common labor, they have not strength to perform it; and thus the country and themselves are happily delivered from the evils to come.

20   I have too long digressed, and therefore shall return to my subject. I think the advantages by the proposal which I have made are obvious and many, as well as of the highest importance.

    For first, as I have already observed, it would greatly lessen the number of Papists, with whom we are yearly overrun, being the principal breeders of the nation as well as our most dangerous enemies; and who stay at home on purpose to deliver the kingdom to the Pretender, hoping to take their advantage by the absence of so many good Protestants, who have chosen rather to leave their country than to stay at home and pay tithes against their conscience to an Episcopal curate.

---

* George Psalmanazar (1679?–1763) published an imaginary description of Formosa (Taiwan) and became well known in English society.

22   Secondly, the poorer tenants will have something valuable of their own, which by law may be made liable to distress, and help to pay their landlord's rent, their corn and cattle being already seized and money a thing unknown.

Thirdly, whereas the maintenance of an hundred thousand children, from two years old and upwards, cannot be computed at less than ten shillings a piece per annum, the nation's stock will be thereby increased fifty thousand pounds per annum, besides the profit of a new dish introduced to the tables of all gentlemen of fortune in the kingdom who have any refinement in taste. And the money will circulate among ourselves, the goods being entirely of our own growth and manufacture.

24   Fourthly, the constant breeders, besides the gain of eight shillings sterling per annum by the sale of their children, will be rid of the charge of maintaining them after the first year.

Fifthly, this food would likewise bring great custom to taverns, where the vintners will certainly be so prudent as to procure the best receipts for dressing it to perfection, and consequently have their houses frequented by all the fine gentlemen, who justly value themselves upon their knowledge in good eating; and a skillful cook, who understands how to oblige his guests, will contrive to make it as expensive as they please.

26   Sixthly, this would be a great inducement to marriage, which all wise nations have either encouraged by rewards or enforced by laws and penalties. It would increase the care and tenderness of mothers toward their children, when they were sure of a settlement for life to the poor babes, provided in some sort by the public, to their annual profit instead of expense. We should see an honest emulation among the married women, which of them could bring the fattest child to the market. Men would become as fond of their wives during the time of their pregnancy as they are now of their mares in foal, their cows in calf, or sows when they are ready to farrow; nor offer to beat or kick them (as is too frequent a practice) for fear of a miscarriage.

Many other advantages might be enumerated. For instance, the addition of some thousand carcasses in our exportation of barreled beef, the propagation of swine's flesh, and improvements in the art of making good bacon, so much wanted among us by the great destruction of pigs, too frequent at our tables, which are no way comparable in taste or magnificence to a well-grown, fat, yearling child, which roasted whole will make a considerable figure at a lord mayor's feast or any other public entertainment. But this and many others I omit, being studious of brevity.

28   Supposing that one thousand families in this city would be constant customers for infants' flesh, besides others who might have it at merry meetings, particularly weddings and christenings, I compute that Dublin would take off annually about twenty thousand carcasses, and the rest of the kingdom (where probably they will be sold somewhat cheaper) the remaining eighty thousand.

I can think of no one objection that will possibly be raised against this proposal, unless it should be urged that the number of people will be thereby much lessened in the kingdom. This I freely own, and it was indeed one principal design in offering it to the world. I desire the reader will observe, that I calculate my remedy for this one individual kingdom of Ireland and for no other that ever was, is, or I think ever can be upon earth. Therefore let no man talk to me of other expedients: of taxing our absentees at five shillings a pound: of using neither clothes nor household furniture except what is of our own growth and manufacture: of utterly rejecting the materials and instruments that promote foreign luxury: of curing the expensiveness of pride, vanity, idleness, and gaming in our women: of introducing a vein of parsimony, prudence, and temperance: of learning to love our country, in the want of which we differ even from Laplanders and the inhabitants of Topinamboo: of quitting our animosities and factions, nor acting any longer like the Jews, who were murdering one another at the very moment their city was taken: of being a little cautious not to sell our country and conscience for nothing: of teaching landlords to have at least one degree of mercy toward their tenants: lastly, of putting a spirit of honesty, industry, and skill into our shopkeepers; who, if a resolution could now be taken to buy only our native goods, would immediately unite to cheat and exact upon us in the price, the measure, and the goodness, nor could ever yet be brought to make one fair proposal of just dealing, though often and earnestly invited to it.

30   Therefore I repeat, let no man talk to me of these and the like expedients, till he hath at least some glimpse of hope that there will ever be some hearty and sincere attempt to put them in practice.

But as to myself, having been wearied out for many years with offering vain, idle, visionary thoughts, and at length utterly despairing of success, I fortunately fell upon this proposal, which, as it is wholly new, so it hath something solid and real, of no expense and little trouble, full in our own power, and whereby we can incur no danger in disobliging England. For this kind of commodity will not bear exportation, the flesh being of too tender a consistence to admit a long continuance in salt, although perhaps I could name a country which would be glad to eat up our whole nation without it.

32   After all, I am not so violently bent upon my own opinion as to reject any offer proposed by wise men, which shall be found equally innocent, cheap, easy, and effectual. But before something of that kind shall be advanced in contradiction to my scheme, and offering a better, I desire the author or authors will be pleased maturely to consider two points. First, as things now stand, how they will be able to find food and raiment for an hundred thousand useless mouths and backs. And secondly, there being a round million of creatures in human figure throughout this kingdom, whose sole subsistence put into a common stock would leave them in debt two millions of pounds sterling, adding those who are beggars by profession to the bulk of farmers, cottagers, and laborers, with their wives and children who are beggars in effect; I desire those politicians who dislike my overture,

and may perhaps be so bold to attempt an answer, that they will first ask the parents of these mortals whether they would not at this day think it a great happiness to have been sold for food at a year old in this manner I prescribe, and thereby have avoided such a perpetual scene of misfortunes as they have since gone through by the oppression of landlords, the impossibility of paying rent without money or trade, the want of common sustenance, with neither house nor clothes to cover them from the inclemencies of the weather, and the most inevitable prospect of entailing the like or greater miseries upon their breed forever.

I profess, in the sincerity of my heart, that I have not the least personal interest in endeavoring to promote this necessary work, having no other motive than the public good of my country, by advancing our trade, providing for infants, relieving the poor, and giving some pleasure to the rich. I have no children by which I can propose to get a single penny; the youngest being nine years old, and my wife past childbearing. ❖

Questions for Meaning

1. What do we learn in this essay about the condition of Ireland in Swift's time, and how Ireland was viewed by England? Does Swift provide any clues about what has caused the poverty he describes?
2. What specific "advantages" does Swift cite on behalf of his proposal?
3. Why does Swift limit his proposal to infants? On what grounds does he exclude older children from consideration as marketable commodities? Why does he claim that we need not worry about the elderly?
4. What does this essay reveal about the relations between Catholics and Protestants in the eighteenth century?
5. Where in the essay does Swift tell us what he really wants? What serious reforms does he propose to improve conditions in Ireland?
6. Vocabulary: importuning (1), sustenance (1), prodigious (2), rudiments (6), ragout (9), collateral (13), desponding (19), inducement (26), emulation (26), propagation (27), parsimony (29), incur (31).

Questions about Strategy

1. How does Swift present himself in this essay? Many readers have taken this essay seriously and come away convinced that Swift was heartless and cruel. Why is it possible for some readers to be deceived in this way? What devices does Swift employ to create the illusion that he is serious? How does this strategy benefit the essay?
2. Does the language of the first few paragraphs contain any hint of irony? At what point in the essay did it first become clear to you that Swift is writing tongue-in-cheek?
3. Where in the essay does Swift pretend to anticipate objections that might be raised against his proposal? How does he dispose of these objections?

4. How does the style of this essay contrast with its subject matter? How does this contrast contribute to the force of the essay as a whole?
5. What is the function of the concluding paragraph?
6. What is the premise of this essay if we take its argument at face value? When we realize that Swift is writing ironically, what underlying premise begins to emerge?
7. What advantage is there in writing ironically? Why do you think Swift chose to treat his subject in this manner?

THOMAS JEFFERSON

 # THE DECLARATION OF INDEPENDENCE

Thomas Jefferson (1743–1826) was the third president of the United States and one of the most talented men ever to hold that office. A farmer, architect, writer, and scientist, Jefferson entered politics in 1769 as a member of the Virginia House of Burgesses. In 1775, he was a member of Virginia's delegation to the Second Continental Congress. He was governor of Virginia from 1779 to 1781, represented the United States in Europe from 1784 to 1789, and was elected to the first of two terms as president in 1801. Of all his many accomplishments, Jefferson himself was most proud of having founded the University of Virginia in 1819.

Although the Continental Congress had delegated the responsibility for writing a declaration of independence to a committee that included Benjamin Franklin and John Adams as well as Jefferson, it was Jefferson who undertook the actual composition. His colleagues respected him as the best writer among them. Jefferson wrote at least two, and possibly three, drafts during the seventeen days allowed for the assignment. His work was reviewed by the other members of the committee, but they made only minor revisions—mainly in the first two paragraphs. When it came to adopting the declaration, Congress was harder to please. After lengthy and spirited debate, Congress made twenty-four changes and deleted over three hundred words. Nevertheless, "The Declaration of Independence," as approved by Congress on July 4, 1776, is almost entirely the work of Jefferson. In addition to being an eloquent example of eighteenth-century prose, it is a clear example of deductive reasoning.

When in the Course of human events, it becomes necessary for one people to dissolve the political bands which have connected them with another, and to assume among the powers of the earth, the separate and equal station to which the Laws of Nature and of Nature's God entitle them, a decent respect to the opinions of mankind requires that they should declare the causes which impel them to the separation.

2   We hold these truths to be self-evident, that all men are created equal, that they are endowed by their Creator with certain unalienable Rights, that among these are Life, Liberty and the pursuit of Happiness. That to secure these rights, Governments are instituted among Men, deriving their just powers from the consent of the governed. That whenever any Form of Government becomes destructive of these ends it is the Right of the People to alter or to abolish it, and to institute new Government, laying its foundation on such principles and organizing its powers in such form, as to them shall seem most likely to effect their Safety and Happiness. Prudence, indeed, will dictate that Governments long established should not be changed for light and transient causes; and accordingly all experience has shewn, that mankind are more disposed to suffer, while evils are sufferable, than to right themselves by abolishing the forms to which they are accustomed. But when a long train of abuses and usurpations, pursuing invariably the same Object evinces a design to reduce them under absolute Despotism, it is their right, it is their duty, to throw off such Government, and to provide new Guards for their future security. Such has been the patient sufferance of these Colonies; and such is now the necessity which constrains them to alter their former Systems of Government. The history of the present King of Great Britain is a history of repeated injuries and usurpations, all having in direct object the establishment of an absolute Tyranny over these States. To prove this, let Facts be submitted to a candid world.

   He has refused his Assent to Laws, the most wholesome and necessary for the public good.

4   He has forbidden his Governors to pass Laws of immediate and pressing importance, unless suspended in their operation till his Assent should be obtained; and when so suspended, he has utterly neglected to attend to them. He has refused to pass other Laws for the accommodation of large districts of people, unless those people would relinquish the right of Representation in the Legislature, a right inestimable to them and formidable to tyrants only.

   He has called together legislative bodies at places unusual, uncomfortable, and distant from the depository of their public Records, for the sole purpose of fatiguing them into compliance with his measures.

6   He has dissolved Representative Houses repeatedly, for opposing with manly firmness his invasions on the rights of the people.

   He has refused for a long time, after such dissolutions, to cause others to be elected; whereby the Legislative powers, incapable of Annihilation, have returned to the People at large for their exercise; the State remaining in the mean time exposed to all the dangers of invasion from without, and convulsions within.

8   He has endeavoured to prevent the population of these States; for that purpose obstructing the Laws for Naturalization of Foreigners; refusing to pass others to encourage their migrations hither, and raising the conditions of new Appropriations of Lands.

He has obstructed the Administration of Justice, by refusing his assent to Laws for establishing Judiciary powers.

10 He has made Judges dependent on his Will alone, for the tenure of their offices, and the amount and payment of their salaries.

He has erected a multitude of New Offices, and sent hither swarms of Officers to harass our People, and eat out their substance.

12 He has kept among us, in times of peace, standing Armies without the Consent of our legislatures.

He has affected to render the Military independent of and superior to the Civil power.

14 He has combined with others to subject us to a jurisdiction foreign to our constitution, and unacknowledged by our laws; giving his Assent to their Acts of pretended Legislation:

For Quartering large bodies of armed troops among us:

16 For protecting them, by a mock Trial, from punishment for any Murders which they should commit on the Inhabitants of these States:

For cutting off our Trade with all parts of the world:

18 For imposing Taxes on us without our Consent:

For depriving us in many cases of the benefits of Trial by Jury:

20 For transporting us beyond Seas to be tried for pretended offences:

For abolishing the free System of English Laws in a neighbouring Province, establishing therein an Arbitrary government, and enlarging its Boundaries so as to render it at once an example and fit instrument for introducing the same absolute rule into these Colonies:

22 For taking away our Charters, abolishing our most valuable Laws, and altering fundamentally the Forms of our Governments:

For suspending our own Legislatures, and declaring themselves invested with power to legislate for us in all cases whatsoever.

24 He has abdicated Government here, by declaring us out of his Protection and waging War against us.

He has plundered our seas, ravaged our Coasts, burnt our towns, and destroyed the Lives of our people.

26 He is at this time transporting large Armies of foreign Mercenaries to compleat the works of death, desolation and tyranny, already begun with circumstances of Cruelty & perfidy scarcely paralleled in the most barbarous ages, and totally unworthy the Head of a civilized nation.

He has constrained our fellow Citizens taken Captive on the high Seas to bear Arms against their Country, to become the executioners of their friends and Brethren, or to fall themselves by their Hands.

28 He has excited domestic insurrections amongst us, and has endeavoured to bring on the inhabitants of our frontiers, the merciless Indian Savages, whose known rule of warfare, is an undistinguished destruction of all ages, sexes and conditions.

In every stage of these Oppressions We have Petitioned for Redress in the most humble terms: Our repeated Petitions have been answered only by repeated injury. A Prince, whose character is thus marked by every act which may define a Tyrant, is unfit to be the ruler of a free people.

30   Nor have We been wanting in attentions to our British brethren. We have warned them from time to time of attempts by their legislature to extend an unwarrantable jurisdiction over us. We have reminded them of the circumstances of our emigration and settlement here. We have appealed to their native justice and magnanimity, and we have conjured them by the ties of our common kindred to disavow these usurpations, which, would inevitably interrupt our connections and correspondence. They too have been deaf to the voice of Justice and of consanguinity. We must, therefore, acquiesce in the necessity, which denounces our Separation, and hold them, as we hold the rest of mankind, Enemies in War, in Peace Friends.

    We, therefore, the Representatives of the United States of America, in General Congress, Assembled, appealing to the Supreme Judge of the world for the rectitude of our intentions, do, in the Name, and by Authority of the good People of these Colonies, solemnly publish and declare, That these United Colonies are, and of Right ought to be Free and Independent States; that they are Absolved from all Allegiance to the British Crown, and that all political connection between them and the State of Great Britain, is and ought to be totally dissolved; and that as Free and Independent States, they have full Power to levy War, conclude Peace, contract Alliances, establish Commerce, and to do all other Acts and Things which Independent States may of right do. And for the support of this Declaration, with a firm reliance on the protection of divine Providence, we mutually pledge to each other our Lives, our Fortunes and our sacred Honor.

John Hancock	Thomas Lynch Junr.	Thos. Jefferson
Button Gwinnett	Arthur Middleton	Benja. Harrison
Lyman Hall	Samuel Chase	Thos. Nelson jr.
Geo. Walton	Wm. Paca	Francis Lightfoot Lee
Wm. Hooper	Thos. Stone	Carter Braxton
Joseph Hewes	Charles Carroll	Robt. Morris
John Penn	of Carrollton	Benjamin Rush
Edward Rutledge	George Wythe	Benja. Franklin
Thos. Heyward Junr.	Richard Henry Lee	John Morton
Geo. Clymer	Frans. Lewis	John Adams
Jas. Smith	Lewis Morris	Robt. Treat Paine
Geo. Taylor	Richd. Stockton	Elbridge Gerry
James Wilson	Jno. Witherspoon	Step. Hopkins
Geo. Ross	Fras. Hopkinson	William Ellery
Caesar Rodney	John Hart	Roger Sherman
Geo. Read	Abra. Clark	Saml. Huntington
Thos. McKean	Josiah Bartlett	Wm. Williams
Wm. Floyd	Wm. Whipple	Oliver Wolcott
Phil. Livingston	Saml. Adams	Matthew Thornton ❖

Questions for Meaning

1. What was the purpose of "The Declaration of Independence"? What reason does Jefferson himself give for writing it?
2. In paragraph 1, what does Jefferson mean by "the Laws of Nature and of Nature's God"?
3. Paragraphs 3 through 28 are devoted to enumerating a list of grievances against King George III. Which of these are the most important? Are any of them relatively trivial? Taken together do they justify Jefferson's description of George III as "A Prince, whose character is thus marked by every act which may define a Tyrant"?
4. How would you summarize Jefferson's conception of the relationship between people and government?
5. How does Jefferson characterize his fellow Americans? At what points does he put the colonists in a favorable light?
6. What does Jefferson mean by "the Supreme Judge of the world"? Why does he express "a firm reliance on the protection of a divine Providence"?
7. Vocabulary: transient (2), evinces (2), usurpations (2), candid (2), annihilation (7), render (13), perfidy (26), unwarrantable (30), consanguinity (30), acquiesce (30), rectitude (31).

Questions about Strategy

1. In paragraph 2, why does Jefferson declare certain truths to be "self-evident"? Paraphrase this paragraph and explain the purpose it serves in Jefferson's argument.
2. In evaluating "The Declaration of Independence" as an argument, what do you think is more important: the general "truths" outlined in the second paragraph, or the specific accusations listed in the paragraphs that follow? If you were to write a counterargument to "The Declaration of Independence," on what points would you concentrate? Where is it most vulnerable?
3. Jefferson is often cited as a man of great culture and liberal values. Are there any points of "The Declaration of Independence" that now seem illiberal?
4. Does Jefferson use any loaded terms? He was forced to delete exaggerated language from his first two drafts of "The Declaration." Do you see any exaggerations that Congress failed to catch?
5. For what sort of audience did Jefferson write "The Declaration of Independence"? Is it directed primarily to the American people, the British government, or the world in general?

Mary Wollstonecraft

⌐ THE PLAYTHINGS OF TYRANTS

An English writer of Irish extraction, Mary Wollstonecraft (1759–1797) was an early advocate of women's rights. After working as a governess and a publisher's assistant, she went to France in 1792 in order to witness the French Revolution. She lived there with an American, Captain Gilbert Imlay, and had a child by him in 1794. Her relationship with Imlay broke down soon afterward, and, in 1795, Wollstonecraft tried to commit suicide by drowning herself. She was rescued, however, and returned to London, where she became a member of a group of radical writers that included Thomas Paine, William Blake, and William Godwin. Wollstonecraft became pregnant by Godwin in 1796, and they were married the following year. Their child, Mary (1797–1851), would eventually win fame as the author of *Frankenstein*. Wollstonecraft died only eleven days after Mary's birth.

Wollstonecraft's fame rests on one work, *A Vindication of the Rights of Women* (1792). Although she had written about the need for educated women several years earlier in *Thoughts on the Education of Daughters* (1787), she makes a stronger and better-reasoned argument in her *Vindication*. "The Playthings of Tyrants" is an editor's title for an excerpt from the second chapter, "The Prevailing Opinion of a Sexual Character Discussed." As the excerpt suggests, Wollstonecraft was not especially interested in securing political rights for women. Her object was to emancipate women from the roles imposed upon them by men and to urge women to think for themselves.

To account for, and excuse the tyranny of man, many ingenious arguments have been brought forward to prove, that the two sexes, in the acquirement of virtue, ought to aim at attaining a very different character: or, to speak explicitly, women are not allowed to have sufficient strength of mind to acquire what really deserves the name of virtue. Yet it should seem, allowing them to have souls, that there is but one way appointed by Providence to lead *mankind* to either virtue or happiness.

2 If then women are not a swarm of ephemeron triflers, why should they be kept in ignorance under the specious name of innocence? Men complain, and with reason, of the follies and caprices of our sex, when they do not keenly satirize our headstrong passions and groveling vices.—Behold, I should answer, the natural effect of ignorance! The mind will ever be unstable that has only prejudices to rest on, and the current will run with destructive fury when there are no barriers to break its force. Women are told from their infancy, and taught by the example of their mothers, that a little knowledge of human weakness, justly termed cunning, softness of temper, *outward* obedience, and a scrupulous attention to a puerile kind

of propriety, will obtain for them the protection of man; and should they be beautiful, every thing else is needless, for, at least, twenty years of their lives.

Thus Milton* describes our first frail mother; though when he tells us that women are formed for softness and sweet attractive grace, I cannot comprehend his meaning, unless, in the true Mahometan strain, he meant to deprive us of souls, and insinuate that we were beings only designed by sweet attractive grace, and docile blind obedience, to gratify the senses of man when he can no longer soar on the wing of contemplation.

4   How grossly do they insult us who thus advise us only to render ourselves gentle, domestic brutes! For instance, the winning softness so warmly, and frequently, recommended, that governs by obeying. What childish expressions, and how insignificant is the being—can it be an immortal one? who will condescend to govern by such sinister methods! 'Certainly,' says Lord Bacon,[†] 'man is of kin to the beasts by his body; and if he be not of kin to God by his spirit, he is a base and ignoble creature!' Men, indeed, appear to me to act in a very unphilosophical manner when they try to secure the good conduct of women by attempting to keep them always in a state of childhood. Rousseau[‡] was more consistent when he wished to stop the progress of reason in both sexes, for if men eat of the tree of knowledge, women will come in for a taste; but, from the imperfect cultivation which their understandings now receive, they only attain a knowledge of evil.

Children, I grant, should be innocent; but when the epithet is applied to men, or women, it is but a civil term for weakness. For if it be allowed that women were destined by Providence to acquire human virtues, and by the exercise of their understandings, that stability of character which is the firmest ground to rest our future hopes upon, they must be permitted to turn to the fountain of light, and not forced to shape their course by the twinkling of a mere satellite. Milton, I grant, was of a very different opinion; for he only bends to the indefeasible right of beauty, though it would be difficult to render two passages which I now mean to contrast, consistent. But into similar inconsistencies are great men often led by their senses.

> 'To whom thus Eve with *perfect beauty* adorn'd.
> 'My Author and Disposer, what thou bidst
> '*Unargued* I obey; So God ordains;
> 'God is *thy law; thou mine:* to know no more
> 'Is Woman's *happiest* knowledge and her *praise.*'

---

* John Milton (1608–1674) was an important English poet best known for *Paradise Lost.*

[†] Francis Bacon (1561–1626) was an English statesman, philosopher, and essayist.

[‡] Jean Jacques Rousseau (1712–1778) was an influential philosopher and political theorist best known for *Discourse on the Inequalities of Men* (1754) and *The Social Contract* (1762).

6   These are exactly the arguments that I have used to children; but I have added, your reason is now gaining strength, and, till it arrives at some degree of maturity, you must look up to me for advice—then you ought to *think,* and only rely on God.

Yet in the following lines Milton seems to coincide with me; when he makes Adam thus expostulate with his Maker.

> 'Hast thou not made me here thy substitute,
> 'And these inferior far beneath me set?
> 'Among *unequals* what society
> 'Can sort, what harmony or true delight?
> 'Which must be mutual, in proportion due
> 'Giv'n and receiv'd; but in *disparity*
> 'The one intense, the other still remiss
> 'Cannot well suit with either, but soon prove
> 'Tedious alike: of *fellowship* I speak
> 'Such as I seek, fit to participate
> 'All rational delight—'

8   In treating, therefore, of the manners of women, let us, disregarding sensual arguments, trace what we should endeavour to make them in order to cooperate, if the expression be not too bold, with the supreme Being.

By individual education, I mean, for the sense of the word is not precisely defined, such an attention to a child as will slowly sharpen the senses, form the temper, regulate the passions as they begin to ferment, and set the understanding to work before the body arrives at maturity; so that the man may only have to proceed, not to begin, the important task of learning to think and reason.

10   To prevent any misconstruction, I must add, that I do not believe that a private education can work the wonders which some sanguine writers have attributed to it. Men and women must be educated, in a great degree, by the opinions and manners of the society they live in. In every age there has been a stream of popular opinion that has carried all before it, and given a family character, as it were, to the century. It may then fairly be inferred, that, till society be differently constituted, much cannot be expected from education. It is, however, sufficient for my present purpose to assert, that, whatever effect circumstances have on the abilities, every being may become virtuous by the exercise of its own reason; for if but one being was created with vicious inclinations, that is positively bad, what can save us from atheism? or if we worship a God, is not that God a devil?

Consequently, the most perfect education, in my opinion, is such an exercise of the understanding as is best calculated to strengthen the body and form the heart. Or, in other words, to enable the individual to attain such habits of virtue as will render it independent. In fact, it is a farce to call any being virtuous whose virtues do not result from the exercise of its own reason. This was Rousseau's opinion respecting men: I extend it to women, and confidently assert that they have been drawn out of their sphere by false refinement, and not by an endeavour to acquire masculine qualities. Still the regal homage which they receive is so intoxicating, that till the manners of the times are changed, and formed on more reasonable principles, it may be impossible to convince them that the illegitimate power, which they obtain, by degrading themselves, is a curse, and that they must return to nature and equality, if they wish to secure the placid satisfaction that unsophisticated affections impart. But for this epoch we must wait—wait, perhaps, till kings and nobles, enlightened by reason, and, preferring the real dignity of man to childish state, throw off their gaudy hereditary trappings: and if then women do not resign the arbitrary power of beauty—they will prove that they have *less* mind than man. . . .

12   Many are the causes that, in the present corrupt state of society, contribute to enslave women by cramping their understandings and sharpening their senses. One, perhaps, that silently does more mischief than all the rest, is their disregard of order.

To do every thing in an orderly manner, is a most important precept, which women, who, generally speaking, receive only a disorderly kind of education, seldom attend to with that degree of exactness that men, who from their infancy are broken into method, observe. This negligent kind of guess-work, for what other epithet can be used to point out the random exertions of a sort of instinctive common sense, never brought to the test of reason? prevents their generalizing matters of fact—so they do to-day, what they did yesterday, merely because they did it yesterday.

14   This contempt of the understanding in early life has more baneful consequences than is commonly supposed; for the little knowledge which women of strong minds attain, is, from various circumstances, of a more desultory kind than the knowledge of men, and it is acquired more by sheer observations on real life, than from comparing what has been individually observed with the results of experience generalized by speculation. Led by their dependent situation and domestic employments more into society, what they learn is rather by snatches; and as learning is with them, in general, only a secondary thing, they do not pursue any one branch with that persevering ardour necessary to give vigour to the faculties, and clearness of the judgment. In the present state of society, a little learning is required to support the character of a gentleman; and boys are obliged to submit to a few years of discipline. But in the education of women, the cultivation of the understanding is always subordinate to the acquirement of some corporeal accomplishment; even while enervated by confinement and false notions of modesty, the body is prevented from attaining that grace and beauty which relaxed half-formed limbs never exhibit. Besides, in youth their faculties are not brought forward by emulation; and having no serious scientific study, if they have natural sagacity it is turned too soon on life and manners. They dwell on effects, and modifications, without tracing them back to causes; and complicated rules to adjust behaviour are a weak substitute for simple principles.

As a proof that education gives this appearance of weakness to females, we may instance the example of military men, who are, like them, sent into the world before their minds have been stored with knowledge or fortified by principles. The consequences are similar; soldiers acquire a little superficial knowledge, snatched from the muddy current of conversation, and, from continually mixing with society, they gain, what is termed a knowledge of the world; and this acquaintance with manners and customs has frequently been confounded with a knowledge of the human heart. But can the crude fruit of casual observation, never brought to the test of judgment, formed by comparing speculation and experience, deserve such a distinction? Soldiers, as well as women, practice the minor virtues with punctilious politeness. Where is then the sexual difference, when the education has been the same? All the difference that I can discern, arises from the superior advantage of liberty, which enables the former to see more of life.

16   It is wandering from my present subject, perhaps, to make a political remark; but, as it was produced naturally by the train of my reflections, I shall not pass it silently over.

Standing armies can never consist of resolute, robust men; they may be well disciplined machines, but they will seldom contain men under the influence of strong passions, or with very vigorous faculties. And as for any depth of understanding, I will venture to affirm, that it is as rarely to be found in the army as amongst women; and the cause, I maintain, is the same. It may be further observed, that officers are also particularly attentive to their persons, fond of dancing, crowded rooms, adventures, and ridicule. Like the *fair* sex, the business of their lives is gallantry.—They were taught to please, and they only live to please. Yet they do not lose their rank in the distinction of sexes, for they are still reckoned superior to women, though in what their superiority consists, beyond what I have just mentioned, it is difficult to discover.

18   The great misfortune is this, that they both acquire manners before morals, and a knowledge of life before they have, from reflections, any acquaintance with the grand ideal outline of human nature. The consequence is natural; satisfied with common nature, they become a prey to prejudices, and taking all their opinions on credit, they blindly submit to authority. So that, if they have any sense, it is a kind of instinctive glance, that catches proportions, and decides with respect to manners; but fails when arguments are to be pursued below the surface, or opinions analyzed.

May not the same remark be applied to women? Nay, the argument may be carried still further, for they are both thrown out of a useful station by the unnatural distinctions established in civilized life. Riches and hereditary honours have made cyphers of women to give consequence to the numerical figures; and idleness has produced a mixture of gallantry and despotism into society, which leads the very men who are the slaves of their mistresses to tyrannize over their sisters, wives, and daughters. This is only keeping them in rank and file, it is true. Strengthen the female mind by enlarging it, and there will be an end to blind obedience; but, as blind obedience is ever sought for by power, tyrants and sensualists are in the right when they endeavor to keep women in the dark, because the former only wants slaves, and the latter a play-thing. The sensualist, indeed, has been the most dangerous of tyrants, and women have been duped by their lovers, as princes by their ministers, whilst dreaming that they reigned over them. ❖

Questions for Meaning

1. What is wrong with treating women as children and expecting "blind obedience"?
2. What causes does Wollstonecraft cite for the degradation of women? On what grounds does she defend their "follies" and "vices"?
3. What does Wollstonecraft mean by "false refinement" in paragraph 11? Explain why she believes it is dangerous to acquire "manners before morals."
4. Where in her essay does Wollstonecraft define the sort of education she believes women should receive? Why does she object to educating women privately in their homes?
5. Wollstonecraft was perceived as a radical by her contemporaries, and relatively few people took her ideas seriously. Looking back on her work after two hundred years, can you find any traditional values that Wollstonecraft accepted without question? Could you argue that she was conservative in some ways?
6. Explain why "the sensualist" has been "the most dangerous of tyrants."
7. Vocabulary: ephemeron (2), specious (2), caprices (2), puerile (2), propriety (2), insinuate (3), docile (3), sanguine (10), desultory (14), corporeal (14), enervated (14), sagacity (14), punctilious (15), cyphers (19).

Questions about Strategy

1. What is the premise of this argument? Where does Wollstonecraft first state it, and where is it restated?
2. What is the function of the last sentence in the second paragraph?
3. Why does Wollstonecraft quote Francis Bacon and John Milton? What do these quotations contribute to her argument?
4. Comment on the analogy Wollstonecraft makes between women and soldiers. What type of soldiers did she have in mind? Is her analogy valid?
5. Do you think Wollstonecraft wrote this argument primarily for men or for women? What kind of an audience could she have expected in the eighteenth century?

MARGARET SANGER

THE CAUSE OF WAR

A pioneering advocate of birth control, Margaret Sanger (1883–1966) was one of eleven children. She studied nursing and worked as an obstetrical nurse in the tenements of Manhattan's Lower East Side. She became convinced of the importance of birth control in 1912 when a young woman died in her arms after a self-induced abortion. Sanger went to Europe in 1913 to study contraception, and she is credited with having coined the phrase "birth control." Upon her return to the United States, she founded a magazine, *The Woman Rebel,* in which she could publish her views. In 1916, she was jailed for opening a birth control clinic in New York, the first of many times she would be imprisoned for her work. She founded the National Birth Control League in 1917, an organization that eventually became the Planned Parenthood Federation of America. By the time Sanger was elected the first president of the International Planned Parenthood Federation in 1952, her views had come to be widely accepted.

A lecturer and a writer, Sanger published several books. The following essay is drawn from *Woman and the New Race* (1920). Writing at a time when Europe had not yet recovered from the horrors of World War I, Sanger argued that the underlying cause of the war was excessive population growth. Although most historians would argue that the war had multiple causes, you should consider whether Sanger makes a persuasive case.

In every nation of militaristic tendencies we find the reactionaries demanding a higher and still higher birth rate. Their plea is, first, that great armies are needed to *defend* the country from its possible enemies; second, that a huge population is required to assure the country its proper place among the powers of the world. At bottom the two pleas are the same.

2   As soon as the country becomes overpopulated, these reactionaries proclaim loudly its moral right to expand. They point to the huge population, which is the name of patriotism they have previously demanded should be brought into being. Again pleading patriotism, they declare that it is the moral right of the nation to take by force such room as it needs. Then comes war—usually against some nation supposed to be less well prepared than the aggressor.

Diplomats make it their business to conceal the facts, and politicians violently denounce the politicians of other countries. There is a long beating of tom-toms by the press and all other agencies for influencing public opinion. Facts are distorted and lies invented until the common people cannot get at the truth. Yet, when the war is over, if not before, we always find that "a place in the sun," "a path to the sea," "a route to India" or something of the sort is at the bottom of the trouble. These are merely other names for expansion.

4   The "need of expansion" is only another name for overpopulation. One supreme example is sufficient to drive home this truth. That the Great War, from the horror of which we are just beginning to emerge, had its source in overpopulation is too evident to be denied by any serious student of current history.

For the past one hundred years most of the nations of Europe have been piling up terrific debts to humanity by the encouragement of unlimited numbers. The rulers of these nations and their militarists have constantly called upon the people to breed, breed, breed! Large populations meant more people to produce wealth, more people to pay taxes, more trade for the merchants, more soldiers to protect the wealth. But more people also meant need of greater food supplies, an urgent and natural need for expansion.

6   As shown by C. V. Drysdale's famous "War Map of Europe," the great conflict began among the high birth rate countries—Germany, with its rate of 31.7, Austria-Hungary with 33.7 and 36.7, respectively, Russia with 45.4, Serbia with 38.6. Italy with her 38.7 came in, as the world is now well informed through the publication of secret treaties by the Soviet government of Russia, upon the promise of territory held by Austria. England, owing to her small home area, is cramped with her comparatively low birth rate of 26.3. France, among the belligerents, is conspicuous for her low birth rate of 19.9, but stood in the way of expansion of high birth rate Germany. Nearly all of the persistently neutral countries—Holland, Denmark, Norway, Sweden and Switzerland have low birth rates, the average being a little over 26.

Owing to the part Germany played in the war, a survey of her birth statistics is decidedly illuminating. The increase in the German birth rate up to 1876 was great. Though it began to decline then, the decline was not sufficient to offset the tremendous increase of the previous years. There were more millions to produce children, so while the average number of births per thousand was somewhat smaller, the net increase in population was still huge. From 41,000,000 in 1871, the year the Empire was founded, the German population grew to approximately 67,000,000 in 1918. Meanwhile her food supply increased only a very small percent. In 1910, Russia had a birth rate even higher than Germany's had ever been—a little less than 48 per thousand. When czarist Russia wanted an outlet to the Mediterranean by way of Constantinople, she was thinking of her increasing population. Germany was thinking of her increasing population when she spoke as with one voice of a "place in the sun." . . .

8   The militaristic claim for Germany's right to new territory was simply a claim to the right of life and food for the German babies—the same right that a chick claims to burst its shell. If there had not been other millions of people claiming the same right, there would have been no war. But there *were* other millions.

The German rulers and leaders pointed out the fact that expansion meant more business for German merchants, more work for German workmen at better wages, and more opportunities for Germans abroad. They also pointed out that lack of expansion meant crowding and crushing at home, hard times, heavy burdens, lack of opportunity for Germans, and what not. In this way, they gave the people of the Empire a startling and true picture of what would happen from overcrowding. Once they realized the facts, the majority of Germans naturally welcomed the so-called war of defense.

10   The argument was sound. Once the German mothers had submitted to the plea for overbreeding, it was inevitable that imperialistic Germany should make war. Once the battalions of unwanted babies came into existence—babies whom the mothers did not want but which they bore as a "patriotic duty"—it was too late to avoid international conflict. The great crime of imperialistic Germany was its high birth rate.

It has always been so. Behind all war has been the pressure of population. "Historians," says Huxley,* "point to the greed and ambition of rulers, the reckless turbulence of the ruled, to the debasing effects of wealth and luxury, and to the devastating wars which have formed a great part of the occupation of mankind, as the causes of the decay of states and the foundering of old civilizations, and thereby point their story with a moral. But beneath all this superficial turmoil lay the deep-seated impulse given by unlimited multiplication."

12   Robert Thomas Malthus,† formulator of the doctrine which bears his name, pointed out, in the closing years of the eighteenth century, the relation of overpopulation to war. He showed that mankind tends to increase faster than the food supply. He demonstrated that were it not for the more common diseases, for plague, famine, floods and wars, human beings would crowd each other to such an extent that the misery would be even greater than it now is. These he described as "natural checks," pointing out that as long as no other checks are employed, such disasters are unavoidable. If we do not exercise sufficient judgment to regulate the birth rate, we encounter disease, starvation and war.

Both Darwin and John Stuart Mill recognized, by inference at least, the fact that so-called "natural checks"—and among them war—will operate if some sort of limitation is not employed. In his *Origin of Species,* Darwin says: "There is no exception to the rule that every organic being naturally increases at so high a rate, if not destroyed, that the earth would soon be covered by the progeny of a single pair." Elsewhere he observes that we do not permit helpless human beings to die off, but we create philanthropies and charities, build asylums and hospitals and keep the medical profession busy preserving those who could not otherwise survive. John Stuart Mill, supporting the views of Malthus, speaks to exactly the same effect in regard to the multiplying power of organic beings, among them humanity. In other

---

* Thomas Huxley (1825–1895) was an influential English biologist who supported Darwin's theory of evolution but argued that progress could be achieved through scientific control of evolution.

† Best known for *An Essay on the Principles of Population* (1798).

words, let countries become overpopulated and war is inevitable. It follows as daylight follows the sunrise.

14   When Charles Bradlaugh and Mrs. Annie Besant were on trial in England in 1877 for publishing information concerning contraceptives, Mrs. Besant put the case bluntly to the court and the jury:

"I have no doubt that if natural checks were allowed to operate right through the human as they do in the animal world, a better result would follow. Among the brutes, the weaker are driven to the wall, the diseased fall out in the race of life. The old brutes, when feeble or sickly, are killed. If men insisted that those who were sickly should be allowed to die without help of medicine or science, if those who are weak were put upon one side and crushed, if those who were old and useless were killed, if those who were not capable of providing food for themselves were allowed to starve, if all this were done, the struggle for existence among men would be as real as it is among brutes and would doubtless result in the production of a higher race of men.

16   "But are you willing to do that or to allow it to be done?"

We are not willing to let it be done. Mother hearts cling to children, no matter how diseased, misshapen and miserable. Sons and daughters hold fast to parents, no matter how helpless. We do not allow the weak to depart; neither do we cease to bring more weak and helpless beings into the world. Among the dire results is war, which kills off, not the weak and the helpless, but the strong and the fit.

18   What shall be done? We have our choice of one of three policies. We may abandon our science and leave the weak and diseased to die, or kill them, as the brutes do. Or we may go on overpopulating the earth and have our famines and our wars while the earth exists. Or we can accept the third, sane, sensible, moral and practicable plan of birth control. We can refuse to bring the weak, the helpless and the unwanted children into the world. We can refuse to overcrowd families, nations and the earth. There are these ways to meet the situation, and only these three ways.

The world will never abandon its preventive and curative science; it may be expected to elevate and extend it beyond our present imagination. The efforts to do away with famine and the opposition to war are growing by leaps and bounds. Upon these efforts are largely based our modern social revolutions.

20   There remains only the third expedient—birth control, the real cure for war. This fact was called to the attention of the Peace Conference in Paris, in 1919, by the Malthusian League, which adopted the following resolution at its annual general meeting in London in June of that year:

"The Malthusian League desires to point out that the proposed scheme for the League of Nations has neglected to take account of the important questions of *the pressure of population,* which *causes the great international economic competition* and rivalry, and of the *increase of population,* which is put forward as a justification for *claiming increase of territory.* It, therefore, wishes to put on record its belief that the League of Nations will only be able to fulfill its aim *when it adds a clause* to the following effect:

22   "'That each Nation desiring to enter into the League of Nations shall pledge itself *so to restrict its birth rate* that its people shall be able to live in comfort *in their own dominions without need* for territorial expansion, and that it shall recognize that *increase of population shall not justify* a demand either for increase of territory or for the compulsion of other Nations to admit its emigrants; so that when all Nations in the League have shown their ability to live on their own resources without international rivalry, they will be in a position to fuse into an international federation, and territorial boundaries will then have little significance.' "

As a matter of course, the Peace Conference paid no attention to the resolution, for, as pointed out by Frank A. Vanderlip, the American financier, that conference not only ignored the economic factors of the world situation, but seemed unaware that Europe had produced more people than its fields could feed. So the resolution amounted to so much propaganda and nothing more.

24   This remedy can be applied only by woman and she will apply it. She must and will see past the call of pretended patriotism and of glory of empire and perceive what is true and what is false in these things. She will discover what base uses the militarist and the exploiter made of the idealism of peoples. Under the clamor of the press, permeating the ravings of the jingoes, she will hear the voice of Napoleon, the archetype of the militarists of all nations, calling for "fodder for cannon."

"Woman is given to us that she may bear children," said he. "Woman is our property, we are not hers, because she produced children for us—we do not yield any to her. She is, therefore, our possession as the fruit tree is that of the gardener."

26   That is what the imperialist is *thinking* when he speaks of the glory of the empire and the prestige of the nation. Every country has its appeal—its shibboleth—ready for the lips of the imperialist. German rulers pointed to the comfort of the workers, to old-age pensions, maternal benefits and minimum wage regulations, and other material benefits, when they wished to inspire soldiers for the Fatherland. England's strongest argument, perhaps, was a certain phase of liberty which she guarantees her subjects, and the protection afforded them wherever they may go. France and the United States, too, have their appeals to the idealism of democracy—appeals which the politicians of both countries know well how to use, though the peoples of both lands are beginning to awake to the fact that their countries have been living on the glories of their revolutions and traditions, rather than the substance of freedom. Behind the boast of old-age pensions, material benefits and wage regulations, behind the bombast concerning liberty in this country and tyranny in that, behind all the slogans and shibboleths coined out of the ideals of the peoples for the uses of imperialism, woman must

and will see the iron hand of that same imperialism, condemning women to breed and men to die for the will of the rulers.

Upon woman the burden and the horrors of war are heaviest. Her heart is the hardest wrung when the husband or the son comes home to be buried or to live a shattered wreck. Upon her devolve the extra tasks of filling out the ranks of workers in the war industries, in addition to caring for the children and replenishing the war-diminished population. Hers is the crushing weight and the sickening of soul. And it is out of her womb that those things proceed. When she sees what lies behind the glory and the horror, the boasting and the burden, and gets the vision, the human perspective, she will end war. She will kill war by the simple process of starving it to death. For she will refuse longer to produce the human food upon which the monster feeds.   ❖

Questions for Meaning

1. According to Sanger, what motives have led governments to encourage population growth?
2. From an evolutionary point of view, why is war unacceptable as a "natural check" on population growth?
3. What are the three policies that Sanger believes nations must inevitably choose among? Are there any alternatives that she overlooks?
4. World War II began less than twenty years after the publication of this essay. Do you know anything about the conditions under which that war began that could be used as evidence to support Sanger's thesis that "militarists" and "reactionaries" favor high birth rates?
5. Vocabulary: belligerents (6), conspicuous (6), turbulence (11), debasing (11), foundering (11), inference (13), base (24), jingoes (24), bombast (26), shibboleth (26).

Questions about Strategy

1. Is Sanger ever guilty of oversimplification? Can you think of any causes of war that have nothing to do with population?
2. How useful are the statistics cited in paragraphs 6 and 7?
3. Of the various quotations that Sanger includes in her essay, which is the most effective?
4. How would you describe the tone of this essay? Is it suitable for the subject?
5. Do you detect any bias in this essay? Does Sanger ever seem to suggest that World War I was caused by one country in particular? Is such an implication historically valid?

Adolf Hitler

THE PURPOSE OF PROPAGANDA

A frustrated artist, Adolf Hitler (1889–1945) served in the German Army during World War I, and became the leader of the National Socialist Party (Nazi) in 1920, during the turbulent period that followed the German defeat. In 1923, Hitler led a revolt in Munich, for which he subsequently served nine months in prison, using this time to write *Mein Kampf (My Struggle)*. Under his direction, the Nazis gained political influence throughout the 1920s, and, in 1933, Hitler became Chancellor of Germany. Upon the death of President Paul von Hindenburg in 1934, Hitler assumed dictatorial powers and ruled Germany as Der Führer (The Leader). More than any other individual, he is responsible for World War II and the deliberate murder of millions of people during that war.

Many factors contributed to Hitler's rise to power; one of them was the skill with which the Nazis used propaganda. The 1925 publication of *Mein Kampf*, from which the following excerpt is taken, outlined Hitler's views. But at the time, many people did not take them seriously.

Ever since I have been scrutinizing political events, I have taken a tremendous interest in propagandist activity. I saw that the Socialist-Marxist organizations mastered and applied this instrument with astounding skill. And I soon realized that the correct use of propaganda is a true art which has remained practically unknown to the bourgeois parties. Only the Christian-Social movement, especially in Lueger's time, achieved a certain virtuosity on this instrument, to which it owed many of its successes.

2   But it was not until the War that it became evident what immense results could be obtained by a correct application of propaganda. Here again, unfortunately, all our studying had to be done on the enemy side, for the activity on our side was modest, to say the least. The total miscarriage of the German "enlightenment" service stared every soldier in the face, and this spurred me to take up the question of propaganda even more deeply than before.

There was often more than enough time for thinking, and the enemy offered practical instruction which, to our sorrow, was only too good.

4   For what we failed to do, the enemy did, with amazing skill and really brilliant calculation. [See illustration on page 353.] I, myself, learned enormously from this enemy war propaganda. But time passed and left no trace in the minds of all those who should have benefited; partly because they considered themselves too clever to learn from the enemy, partly owing to lack of good will.

Did we have anything you could call propaganda?

6   I regret that I must answer in the negative. Everything that actually was done in this field was so inadequate and wrong from the very start that it certainly did no good and sometimes did actual harm.

Pollarized / Correct + wrong

The form was inadequate, the substance was psychologically wrong: a careful examination of German war propaganda can lead to no other diagnosis.

8   There seems to have been no clarity on the very first question: Is propaganda a means or an end?

Backround   It is a means and must therefore be judged with regard to its end. It must consequently take a form calculated to support the aim which it serves. It is also obvious that its aim can vary in importance from the standpoint of general need, and that the inner value of the propaganda will vary accordingly. The aim for which we were fighting the War was the loftiest, the most overpowering, that man can conceive; it was the freedom and independence of our nation, the security of our future food supply, and—our national honor; a thing which, despite all contrary opinions prevailing today, nevertheless exists, or rather should exist, since peoples without honor have sooner or later lost their freedom and independence, which in turn is only the result of a higher justice, since generations of rabble without honor deserve no freedom. Any man who wants to be a cowardly slave can have no honor, or honor itself would soon fall into general contempt.

National + Personal Honor

10   The German nation was engaged in a struggle for a human existence, and the purpose of war propaganda should have been to support this struggle; its aim to help bring about victory.   *→ Must renew both for propoganda*   *is important than*

Addrsing critics of Propoganda   When the nations on this planet fight for existence—when the question of destiny, "to be or not to be," cries out for a solution—then all considerations of humanitarianism or aesthetics crumble into nothingness; for all these concepts do not float about in the ether, they arise from man's imagination and are bound up with man. When he departs from this world, these concepts are again dissolved into nothingness, for Nature does not know them. And even among mankind, they belong only to a few nations or rather races, and this in proportion as they emanate from the feeling of the nation or race in question. Humanitarianism and aesthetics would vanish even from a world inhabited by man if this world were to lose the races that have created and upheld these concepts.   *→ realitive*

12   But all such concepts become secondary when a nation is fighting for its existence; in fact, they become totally irrelevant to the forms of the struggle as soon as a situation arises where they might paralyze a struggling nation's power of self-preservation. And that has always been their only visible result. (*In war these values are not relevant to war = morality does not apply; if it does, we loss*)

As for humanitarianism, Moltke* said years ago that in war it lies in the brevity of the operation, and that means that the most aggressive fighting technique is the most humane. (*Eliminate its in 12, then brings it back ?*)

14   But when people try to approach these questions with <u>drivel</u> about <u>aesthetics</u>, etc., really only one answer is possible: where the destiny and existence of a people are at stake, all obligation toward beauty ceases. The

---

* Count Helmuth von Moltke (1848–1916) was a German general who served as chief of staff during World War I.   .

most unbeautiful thing there can be in human life is and remains the yoke of slavery. Or do these Schwabing* decadents view the present lot of the German people as "aesthetic"? Certainly we don't have to discuss these matters with the Jews, the most modern inventors of this cultural perfume. Their whole existence is an embodied protest against the aesthetics of the Lord's image.

And since these criteria of humanitarianism and beauty must be eliminated from the struggle, they are also inapplicable to propaganda.

16   Propaganda in the War was a means to an end, and the end was the struggle for the existence of the German people; consequently, propaganda could only be considered in accordance with the principles that were valid for this struggle. In this case the most cruel weapons were humane if they brought about a quicker victory; and only those methods were beautiful which helped the nation to safeguard the dignity of its freedom.

This was the only possible attitude toward war propaganda in a life-and-death struggle like ours.

18   If the so-called responsible authorities had been clear on this point, they would never have fallen into such uncertainty over the form and application of this weapon: for even propaganda is no more than a weapon, though a frightful one in the hand of an expert.

The second really decisive question was this: To whom should propaganda be addressed? To the scientifically trained intelligentsia or to the less educated masses?

20   It must be addressed always and exclusively to the masses.

What the intelligentsia—or those who today unfortunately often go by that name—what they need is not propaganda but scientific instruction. The content of propaganda is not science any more than the object represented in a poster is art. The art of the poster lies in the designer's ability to attract the attention of the crowd by form and color. A poster advertising an art exhibit must direct the attention of the public to the art being exhibited; the better it succeeds in this, the greater is the art of the poster itself. The poster should give the masses an idea of the significance of the exhibition, it should not be a substitute for the art on display. Anyone who wants to concern himself with the art itself must do more than study the poster; and it will not be enough for him just to saunter through the exhibition. We may expect him to examine and immerse himself in the individual works, and thus little by little form a fair opinion.

22   A similar situation prevails with what we today call propaganda.

The function of propaganda does not lie in the scientific training of the individual, but in calling the masses' attention to certain facts, processes, necessities, etc., whose significance is thus for the first time placed within their field of vision.

24   The whole art consists in doing this so skillfully that everyone will be convinced that the fact is real, the process necessary, the necessity correct,

* A district in Munich favored by students, writers, and artists.

Propaganda = independant of truth of falsity ; political aim ; polarized ; aimd at masses
appeal to emotions

etc. But since propaganda is not and cannot be the necessity in itself, since its function, like the poster, consists in attracting the attention of the crowd, and not in educating those who are already educated or who are striving after education and knowledge, its effect for the most part must be aimed at the emotions and only to a very limited degree at the so-called intellect.　　　WEAK　(An argument for not using argument)

All propaganda must be popular and its intellectual level must be adjusted to the most limited intelligence among those it is addressed to. Consequently, the greater the mass it is intended to reach, the lower its purely intellectual level will have to be. But if, as in propaganda for sticking out a war, the aim is to influence a whole people, we must avoid excessive intellectual demands on our public, and too much caution cannot be exerted in this direction.

26　　　The more modest its intellectual ballast, the more exclusively it takes into consideration the emotions of the masses, the more effective it will be. And this is the best proof of the soundness or unsoundness of a propaganda campaign, and not success in pleasing a few scholars or young aesthetes.

The art of propaganda lies in understanding the emotional ideas of the great masses and finding, through a psychologically correct form, the way to the attention and thence to the heart of the broad masses. The fact that our bright boys do not understand this merely shows how mentally lazy and conceited they are.

28　　　Once we understand how necessary it is for propaganda to be adjusted to the broad mass, the following rule results:

It is a mistake to make propaganda many-sided, like scientific instruction, for instance.

30　　　The receptivity of the great masses is very limited, their intelligence is small, but their power of forgetting is enormous. In consequence of these facts, all effective propaganda must be limited to a very few points and must harp on these in slogans until the last member of the public understands what you want him to understand by your slogan. As soon as you sacrifice this slogan and try to be many-sided, the effect will piddle away, for the crowd can neither digest nor retain the material offered. In this way the result is weakened and in the end entirely cancelled out.

Thus we see that propaganda must follow a simple line and correspondingly the basic tactics must be psychologically sound.

32　　　For instance, it was absolutely wrong to make the enemy ridiculous, as the Austrian and German comic papers did. It was absolutely wrong because actual contact with an enemy soldier was bound to arouse an entirely different conviction, and the results were devastating; for now the German soldier, under the direct impression of the enemy's resistance, felt himself swindled by his propaganda service. His desire to fight, or even to stand firm, was not strengthened, but the opposite occurred. His courage flagged.

Big problem : need dumbies to other people = it will persist + give sinews = but he calls this homoagh nation of dumbies to less statehood = existence

By contrast, the war propaganda of the English and Americans was psychologically sound. By representing the Germans to their own people as barbarians and Huns, they prepared the individual soldier for the terrors of war, and thus helped to preserve him from disappointments. After this, the most terrible weapon that was used against him seemed only to confirm what his propagandists had told him; it likewise reinforced his faith in the truth of his government's assertions, while on the other hand it increased his rage and hatred against the vile enemy. For the cruel effects of the weapon, whose use by the enemy he now came to know, gradually came to confirm for him the "Hunnish" brutality of the barbarous enemy, which he had heard all about; and it never dawned on him for a moment that his own weapons possibly, if not probably, might be even more terrible in their effects.

34   And so the English soldier could never feel that he had been misinformed by his own countrymen, as unhappily was so much the case with the German soldier that in the end he rejected everything coming from this source as "swindles" and "bunk." All this resulted from the idea that any old simpleton (or even somebody who was intelligent "in other things") could be assigned to propaganda work, and the failure to realize that the most brilliant psychologists would have been none too good.

And so the German war propaganda offered an unparalleled example of an "enlightenment" service working in reverse, since any correct psychology was totally lacking.

36   There was no end to what could be learned from the enemy by a man who kept his eyes open, refused to let his perceptions be classified, and for four and a half years privately turned the storm-flood of enemy propaganda over in his brain.

What our authorities least of all understood was the very first axiom of all propagandist activity: to wit, the basically subjective and one-sided attitude it must take toward every question it deals with. In this connection, from the very beginning of the War and from top to bottom, such sins were committed that we were entitled to doubt whether so much absurdity could really be attributed to pure stupidity alone.

38   What, for example, would we say about a poster that was supposed to advertise a new soap and that described other soaps as "good"?

We would only shake our heads.

40   Exactly the same applies to political advertising.

The function of propaganda is, for example, not to weigh and ponder the rights of different people, but exclusively to emphasize the one right which it has set out to argue for. Its task is not to make an objective study of the truth, in so far as it favors the enemy, and then set it before the masses with academic fairness; its task is to serve our own right, always and unflinchingly.

42   It was absolutely wrong to discuss war-guilt from the standpoint that Germany alone could not be held responsible for the outbreak of the catastrophe; it would have been correct to load every bit of the blame on the shoulders of the enemy, even if this had not really corresponded to the true facts, as it actually did.

And what was the consequence of this half-heartedness?

44   The broad mass of a nation does not consist of diplomats, or even professors of political law, or even individuals capable of forming a rational opinion; it consists of plain mortals, wavering and inclined to doubt and uncertainty. As soon as our own propaganda admits so much as a glimmer of right on the other side, the foundation for doubt in our own right has been laid. The masses are then in no position to distinguish where foreign injustice ends and our own begins. In such a case they become uncertain and suspicious, especially if the enemy refrains from going in for the same nonsense, but unloads every bit of blame on his adversary. Isn't it perfectly understandable that the whole country ends up by lending more credence to enemy propaganda, which is more unified and coherent, than to its own? And particularly a people that suffers from the mania of objectivity as much as the Germans. For, after all this, everyone will take the greatest pains to avoid doing the enemy any injustice, even at the peril of seriously besmirching and even destroying his own people and country.

Of course, this was not the intent of the responsible authorities, but the people never realize that.

46   The people in their overwhelming majority are so feminine by nature and attitude that sober reasoning determines their thoughts and actions far less than emotion and feeling.

And this sentiment is not complicated, but very simple and all of a piece. It does not have multiple shadings; it has a positive and a negative; love or hate, right or wrong, truth or lie, never half this way and half that way, never partially, or that kind of thing.

48   English propagandists understood all this most brilliantly—and acted accordingly. They made no half statements that might have given rise to doubts.   (You can't portray) must build up certain aspects of enemy.

Their brilliant knowledge of the primitive sentiments of the broad masses is shown by their atrocity propaganda, which was adapted to this condition. As ruthless as it was brilliant, it created the preconditions for moral steadfastness at the front, even in the face of the greatest actual defeats, and just as strikingly it pilloried the German enemy as the sole guilty party for the outbreak of the War: the rabid, impudent bias and persistence with which this lie was expressed took into account the emotional, always extreme, attitude of the great masses and for this reason was believed.

50   How effective this type of propaganda was is most strikingly shown by the fact that after four years of war it not only enabled the enemy to stick to its guns, but even began to nibble at our own people.

It need not surprise us that our propaganda did not enjoy this success. In its inner ambiguity alone, it bore the germ of ineffectualness. And finally its content was such that it was very unlikely to make the necessary impression on the masses. Only our feather-brained "statesmen" could have dared to hope that this insipid pacifistic bilge could fire men's spirits till they were willing to die.

52   As a result, their miserable stuff was useless, even harmful in fact.

But the most brilliant propagandist technique will yield no success unless one fundamental principle is borne in mind constantly and with unflagging attention. It must confine itself to a few points and repeat them over and over. Here, as so often in this world, persistence is the first and most important requirement for success.

54   Particularly in the field of propaganda, we must never let ourselves be led by aesthetes or people who have grown blasé: not by the former, because the form and expression of our propaganda would soon, instead of being suitable for the masses, have drawing power only for literary teas; and of the second we must beware, because, lacking in any fresh emotion of their own, they are always on the lookout for new stimulation. These people are quick to weary of everything; they want variety, and they are never able to feel or understand the needs of their fellow men who are not yet so callous. They are always the first to criticize a propaganda campaign, or rather its content, which seems to them too old-fashioned, too hackneyed, too out-of-date, etc. They are always after novelty, in search of a change, and this makes them mortal enemies of any effective political propaganda. For as soon as the organization and the content of propaganda begin to suit their tastes, it loses all cohesion and evaporates completely.

The purpose of propaganda is not to provide interesting distraction for blasé young gentlemen, but to convince, and what I mean is to convince the masses. But the masses are slow-moving, and they always require a certain time before they are ready even to notice a thing, and only after the simplest ideas are repeated thousands of times will the masses finally remember them.

56   When there is a change, it must not alter the content of what the propaganda is driving at, but in the end must always say the same thing. For instance, a slogan must be presented from different angles, but the end of all remarks must always and immutably be the slogan itself. Only in this way can the propaganda have a unified and complete effect.

This broadness of outline from which we must never depart, in combination with steady, consistent emphasis, allows our final success to mature. And then, to our amazement, we shall see what tremendous results such perseverance leads to—to results that are almost beyond our understanding.

58   All advertising, whether in the field of business or politics, achieves success through the continuity and sustained uniformity of its application.

Here, too, the example of enemy war propaganda was typical; limited to a few points, devised exclusively for the masses, carried on with indefatigable persistence. Once the basic ideas and methods of execution were recognized as correct, they were applied throughout the whole War without the slightest change. At first the claims of the propaganda were so impudent that people thought it insane; later, it got on people's nerves; and in the end, it was believed. After four and a half years, a revolution broke out in Germany; and its slogans originated in the enemy's war propaganda.

60   And in England they understood one more thing: that this spiritual weapon can succeed only if it is applied on a tremendous scale, but that success amply covers all costs.

There, propaganda was regarded as a weapon of the first order, while in our country it was the last resort of unemployed politicians and a comfortable haven for slackers.

62   And, as was to be expected, its results all in all were zero.   ❖

Questions for Meaning

1. Why did Hitler's interest in propaganda increase after World War I? How important is propaganda in his view?
2. According to Hitler, how did English and American propaganda differ from German propaganda in World War I?
3. Why did Hitler believe that some people do not deserve freedom?
4. How important are truth and aesthetics in propaganda?
5. According to Hitler, what is the key to success in propaganda?
6. How does Hitler characterize the average person?

Questions about Strategy

1. Throughout this argument, Hitler emphasizes that Germany's opponents in World War I used propaganda "with amazing skill and really brilliant calculation." What advantage does he gain from making this point?
2. This argument was first published twenty years before the Allied liberation of Nazi concentration camps. Can you detect any signs of racism within it? Judging from this excerpt, how honest was Hitler in revealing his values before he came to power?
3. In paragraphs 38–40 and 58, Hitler compares propaganda to advertising. Is this a fair comparison? Why is it worth making?
4. Would this argument appeal to the average person? Would it appeal to intellectuals? What sort of audience was most likely to respond favorably to Hitler?

Carl Rogers

DEALING WITH BREAKDOWNS IN COMMUNICATION

Carl Rogers (1902–1987) was a psychotherapist who developed an innovative approach that emphasized the importance of positive reinforcement during therapy. He delivered the following argument at Northwestern University in 1951, when the United States and what was then the Soviet Union were at the height of the Cold War and Senator Joseph McCarthy was questioning the loyalty of many Americans. As you read, note how Rogers refers to these events in order to illustrate his point that understanding begins with careful listening. In recent years, Rogers's views have become influential in rhetoric as scholars have reexamined long-standing ideas about the nature of persuasion. (If you are interested in Rogerian argument, see pages 19–21 and 215–218 of this book.)

It may seem curious that a person whose whole professional effort is devoted to psychotherapy should be interested in problems of communication. What relationship is there between providing therapeutic help to individuals with emotional maladjustments and the concern of this conference with obstacles to communication? Actually the relationship is very close indeed. The whole task of psychotherapy is the task of dealing with a failure in communication. The emotionally maladjusted person, the "neurotic," is in difficulty first because communication within himself has broken down, and second because as a result of this his communication with others has been damaged. If this sounds somewhat strange, then let me put it in other terms. In the "neurotic" individual, parts of himself which have been termed unconscious, or repressed, or denied to awareness, become blocked off so that they no longer communicate themselves to the conscious or managing part of himself. As long as this is true, there are distortions in the way he communicates himself to others, and so he suffers both within himself, and in his interpersonal relations. The task of psychotherapy is to help the person achieve, through a special relationship with a therapist, good communication within himself. Once this is achieved he can communicate more freely and more effectively with others. We may say then that psychotherapy is good communication, within and between men. We may also turn that statement around and it will still be true. Good communication, free communication, within or between men, is always therapeutic.

2   It is, then, from a background of experience with communication in counseling and psychotherapy that I want to present here two ideas. I wish to state what I believe is one of the major factors in blocking or impeding communication, and then I wish to present what in our experience has proven to be a very important way of improving or facilitating communication.

I would like to propose, as an hypothesis for consideration, that the major barrier to mutual interpersonal communication is our very natural tendency to judge, to evaluate, to approve or disapprove, the statement of the other person, or the other group. Let me illustrate my meaning with some very simple examples. As you leave the meeting tonight, one of the statements you are likely to hear is, "I didn't like that man's talk." Now what do you respond? Almost invariably your reply will be either approval or disapproval of the attitude expressed. Either you respond, "I didn't either. I thought it was terrible," or else you tend to reply, "Oh, I thought it was really good." In other words, your primary reaction is to evaluate what has just been said to you, to evaluate it from *your* point of view, your own frame of reference.

4   Or take another example. Suppose I say with some feeling, "I think the Republicans are behaving in ways that show a lot of good sound sense these

days," what is the response that arises in your mind as you listen? The overwhelming likelihood is that it will be evaluative. You will find yourself agreeing, or disagreeing, or making some judgment about me such as "He must be a conservative," or "He seems solid in his thinking." Or let us take an illustration from the international scene. Russia says vehemently, "The treaty with Japan is a war plot on the part of the United States." We rise as one person to say "That's a lie!"

This last illustration brings in another element connected with my hypothesis. Although the tendency to make evaluations is common in almost all interchange of language, it is very much heightened in those situations where feelings and emotions are deeply involved. So the stronger our feelings, the more likely it is that there will be no mutual element in the communication. There will be just two ideas, two feelings, two judgments, missing each other in psychological space. I'm sure you recognize this from your own experience. When you have not been emotionally involved yourself, and have listened to a heated discussion, you often go away thinking, "Well, they actually weren't talking about the same thing." And they were not. Each was making a judgment, an evaluation, from his own frame of reference. There was really nothing which could be called communication in any genuine sense. This tendency to react to any emotionally meaningful statement by forming an evaluation of it from our own point of view, is, I repeat, the major barrier to interpersonal communication.

6   But is there any way of solving this problem, of avoiding this barrier? I feel that we are making exciting progress toward this goal and I would like to present it as simply as I can. Real communication occurs, and this evaluative tendency is avoided, when we listen with understanding. What does that mean? It means *to see the expressed idea and attitude from the other person's point of view, to sense how it feels to him, to achieve his frame of reference in regard to the thing he is talking about.*

Stated so briefly, this may sound absurdly simple, but it is not. It is an approach which we have found extremely potent in the field of psychotherapy. It is the most effective agent we know for altering the basic personality structure of an individual, and improving his relationships and his communications with others. If I can listen to what he can tell me, if I can understand how it seems to him, if I can see its personal meaning for him, if I can sense the emotional flavor which it has for him, then I will be releasing potent forces of change in him. If I can really understand how he hates his father, or hates the university, or hates communists—if I can catch the flavor of his fear of insanity, or his fear of atom bombs, or of Russia—it will be of the greatest help to him in altering those very hatreds and fears, and in establishing realistic and harmonious relationships with the very people and situations toward which he has felt hatred and fear. We know from our research that such empathic understanding—understanding *with* a person, not *about* him—is such an effective approach that it can bring about major changes in personality.

8   Some of you may be feeling that you listen well to people, and that you have never seen such results. The chances are very great indeed that your

listening has not been of the type I have described. Fortunately I can suggest a little laboratory experiment which you can try to test the quality of your understanding. The next time you get into an argument with your wife, or your friend, or with a small group of friends, just stop the discussion for a moment and for an experiment, institute this rule. "Each person can speak up for himself only *after* he has first restated the ideas and feelings of the previous speaker accurately, and to that speaker's satisfaction." You see what this would mean. It would simply mean that before presenting your own point of view, it would be necessary for you to really achieve the other speaker's frame of reference—to understand his thoughts and feelings so well that you could summarize them for him. Sounds simple doesn't it? But if you try it you will discover it one of the most difficult things you have ever tried to do. However, once you have been able to see the other's point of view, your own comments will have to be drastically revised. You will also find the emotion going out of the discussion, the differences being reduced, and those differences which remain being of a rational and understandable sort.

Can you imagine what this kind of an approach would mean if it were projected into larger areas? What would happen to a labor-management dispute if it was conducted in such a way that labor, without necessarily agreeing, could accurately state management's point of view in a way that management could accept; and management, without approving labor's stand, could state labor's case in a way that labor agreed was accurate? It would mean that real communication was established, and one could practically guarantee that some reasonable solution would be reached.

10   If then this way of approach is an effective avenue to good communication and good relationships, as I am quite sure you will agree if you try the experiment I have mentioned, why is it not more widely tried and used? I will try to list the difficulties which keep it from being utilized.

In the first place it takes courage, a quality which is not too widespread. I am indebted to Dr. S. I. Hayakawa, the semanticist, for pointing out that to carry on psychotherapy in this fashion is to take a very real risk, and that courage is required. If you really understand another person in this way, if you are willing to enter his private world and see the way life appears to him, without any attempt to make evaluative judgments, you run the risk of being changed yourself. You might see it his way, you might find yourself influenced in your attitudes of your personality. The risk of being changed is one of the most frightening prospects most of us can face. If I enter, as fully as I am able, into the private world of a neurotic or psychotic individual, isn't there a risk that I might become lost in that world? Most of us are afraid to take that risk. Or if we had a Russian communist speaker here tonight, or Senator Joe McCarthy, how many of us would dare to try to see the world from each of these points of view? The great majority of us could not *listen:* we would find ourselves compelled to *evaluate,* because listening would seem too dangerous. So the first requirement is courage, and we do not always have it.

12   But there is a second obstacle. It is just when emotions are strongest that it is most difficult to achieve the frame of reference of the other person or group. Yet it is the time the attitude is most needed, if communication is to be established. We have not found this to be an insuperable obstacle in our experience in psychotherapy. A third party, who is able to lay aside his own feelings and evaluations, can assist greatly by listening with understanding to each person or group and clarifying the views and attitudes each holds. We have found this very effective in small groups in which contradictory or antagonistic attitudes exist. When the parties to a dispute realize that they are being understood, that someone sees how the situation seems to them, the statements grow less exaggerated and less defensive, and it is no longer necessary to maintain the attitude, "I am 100% right and you are 100% wrong." The influence of such an understanding catalyst in the group permits the members to come closer and closer to the objective truth involved in the relationship. In this way mutual communication is established and some type of agreement becomes much more possible. So we may say that though heightened emotions make it much more difficult to understand *with* an opponent, our experience makes it clear that a neutral, understanding, catalyst type of leader or therapist can overcome this obstacle in a small group.

      This last phrase, however, suggests another obstacle to utilizing the approach I have described. Thus far all our experience has been with small face-to-face groups—groups exhibiting industrial tensions, religious tensions, racial tensions, and therapy groups in which many personal tensions are present. In these small groups our experience, confirmed by a limited amount of research, shows that this basic approach leads to improved communication, to greater acceptance of others and by others, and to attitudes which are more positive and more problem-solving in nature. There is a decrease in defensiveness, in exaggerated statements, in evaluative and critical behavior. But these findings are from small groups. What about trying to achieve understanding between larger groups that are geographically remote? Or between face-to-face groups who are not speaking for themselves, but simply as representatives of others, like the delegates at Kaesong*? Frankly we do not know the answers to these questions. I believe the situation might be put this way. As social scientists we have a tentative test-tube solution of the problem of breakdown in communication. But to confirm the validity of this test-tube solution, and to adapt it to the enormous problems of communication-breakdown between classes, groups, and nations, would involve additional funds, much more research, and creative thinking of a high order.

14   Even with our present limited knowledge we can see some steps which might be taken, even in large groups, to increase the amount of listening *with,* and to decrease the amount of evaluation *about.* To be imaginative for a moment, let us suppose that a therapeutically oriented international group went to the Russian leaders and said, "We want to achieve a genuine

---

* Kaesong is a city near the border between North and South Korea; the Korean War (1950–1953) was being fought at the time Rogers presented this argument.

understanding of your views and even more important, of your attitudes and feelings, toward the United States. We will summarize and resummarize these views and feelings if necessary, until you agree that our description represents the situation as it seems to you." Then suppose they did the same thing with the leaders in our own country. If they then gave the widest possible distribution to these two views, with feelings clearly described but not expressed in name-calling, might not the effect be very great? It would not guarantee the type of understanding I have been describing, but it would make it much more possible. We can understand the feelings of a person who hates us much more readily when his attitudes are accurately described to us by a neutral third party, than we can when he is shaking his fist at us.

But even to describe such a first step is to suggest another obstacle to this approach of understanding. Our civilization does not yet have enough faith in the social sciences to utilize their findings. The opposite is true of the physical sciences. During the war when a test-tube solution was found to the problem of synthetic rubber, millions of dollars and an army of talent was turned loose on the problem of using that finding. If synthetic rubber could be made in milligrams, it could and would be made in the thousands of tons. And it was. But in the social science realm, if a way is found of facilitating communication and mutual understanding in small groups, there is no guarantee that the finding will be utilized. It may be a generation or more before the money and the brains will be turned loose to exploit that finding.

16   In closing, I would like to summarize this small-scale solution to the problem of barriers in communication, and to point out certain of its characteristics.

I have said that our research and experience to date would make it appear that breakdowns in communication, and the evaluative tendency which is the major barrier to communication, can be avoided. The solution is provided by creating a situation in which each of the different parties comes to understand the other from the *other's* point of view. This has been achieved, in practice, even when feelings run high, by the influence of a person who is willing to understand each point of view empathically, and who thus acts as a catalyst to precipitate further understanding.

18   This procedure has important characteristics. It can be initiated by one party, without waiting for the other to be ready. It can even be initiated by a neutral third person, providing he can gain a minimum of cooperation from one of the parties.

This procedure can deal with the insincerities, the defensive exaggerations, the lies, the "false fronts" which characterize almost every failure in communication. These defensive distortions drop away with astonishing speed as people find that the only intent is to understand, not judge.

20   This approach leads steadily and rapidly toward the discovery of the truth, toward a realistic appraisal of the objective barriers to communication. The dropping of some defensiveness by one party leads to further dropping of defensiveness by the other party, and truth is thus approached.

This procedure gradually achieves mutual communication. Mutual communication tends to be pointed toward solving a problem rather than toward attacking a person or group. It leads to a situation in which I see how the problem appears to you, as well as to me, and you see how it appears to me, as well as to you. Thus accurately and realistically defined, the problem is almost certain to yield to intelligent attack, or if it is in part insoluble, it will be comfortably accepted as such.

22   This then appears to be a test-tube solution to the breakdown of communication as it occurs in small groups. Can we take this small scale answer, investigate it further, refine it, develop it and apply it to the tragic and well-nigh fatal failures of communication which threaten the very existence of our modern world? It seems to me that this is a possibility and a challenge which we should explore. ❖

Questions for Meaning

1. According to Rogers, why do people become "neurotic"?
2. What is the purpose of psychotherapy?
3. What keeps people from communicating effectively with one another?
4. What does it mean to "listen with understanding"? Why does this take courage?
5. Does Rogers offer any practical advice for learning how to listen with understanding?
6. How could listening with understanding lead to conflict resolution?

Questions about Strategy

1. How does Rogers establish his authority to speak on the subject of communication?
2. What is the effect of presenting this argument in the second person?
3. What steps does Rogers take to help his audience grasp the key points of this argument?
4. Rogers made this argument in 1951. What assumptions does he make about gender? Could a writer today safely make the same assumptions?

MARTIN LUTHER KING, JR.

LETTER FROM BIRMINGHAM JAIL

Martin Luther King, Jr. (1929–1968) was the most important leader of the movement to secure civil rights for black Americans during the mid-twentieth century. Ordained a Baptist minister in his father's church in Atlanta, King went on to receive a PhD from Boston University in 1955.

Two years later, he became the founder and director of the Southern Christian Leadership Conference, an organization he continued to lead until his assassination in 1968. He first came to national attention by organizing a boycott of the buses in Montgomery, Alabama (1955–1956)—a campaign that he recounts in *Stride Toward Freedom: The Montgomery Story* (1958). His other books include *The Measure of a Man* (1959), *Why We Can't Wait* (1963), and *Where Do We Go from Here: Chaos or Community?* (1967). An advocate of nonviolence, King was jailed fourteen times in the course of his work for civil rights. His efforts helped secure the passage of the Civil Rights Bill in 1963, and, during the last years of his life, he was the recipient of many awards, most notably the Nobel Peace Prize in 1964.

"Letter from Birmingham Jail" was written in 1963, when King was jailed for eight days as the result of his campaign against segregation in Birmingham, Alabama. In the letter, King responds to white clergymen who had criticized his work and blamed him for breaking the law. But "Letter from Birmingham Jail" is much more than a rebuttal of criticism. It is a well-reasoned and carefully argued defense of civil disobedience as a means of securing civil liberties.

April 16, 1963

My Dear Fellow Clergymen:

While confined here in the Birmingham city jail, I came across your recent statement calling my present activities "unwise and untimely." Seldom do I pause to answer criticism of my work and ideas. If I sought to answer all the criticisms that cross my desk, my secretaries would have little time for anything other than such correspondence in the course of the day, and I would have no time for constructive work. But since I feel that you are men of genuine good will and that your criticisms are sincerely put forth, I want to try to answer your statement in what I hope will be patient and reasonable terms.

2   I think I should indicate why I am here in Birmingham, since you have been influenced by the view which argues against "outsiders coming in." I have the honor of serving as president of the Southern Christian Leadership Conference, an organization operating in every southern state, with headquarters in Atlanta, Georgia. We have some eighty-five affiliated organizations across the South, and one of them is the Alabama Christian Movement for Human Rights. Frequently we share staff, educational, and financial resources with our affiliates. Several months ago the affiliate here in Birmingham asked us to be on call to engage in a nonviolent direct-action program if such were deemed necessary. We readily consented, and when the hour came we lived up to our promise. So I, along with several members of my staff, am here because I was invited here. I am here because I have organizational ties here.

But more basically, I am in Birmingham because injustice is here. Just as the prophets of the eighth century B.C. left their villages and carried their "thus saith the Lord" far beyond the boundaries of their home towns, and just as the Apostle Paul left his village of Tarsus and carried the gospel of Jesus Christ to the far corners of the Greco-Roman world, so am I compelled to carry the gospel of freedom beyond my own home town. Like Paul, I must constantly respond to the Macedonian call for aid.

4   Moreover, I am cognizant of the interrelatedness of all communities and states. I cannot sit idly by in Atlanta and not be concerned about what happens in Birmingham. Injustice anywhere is a threat to justice everywhere. We are caught in an inescapable network of mutuality, tied in a single garment of destiny. Whatever affects one directly, affects all indirectly. Never again can we afford to live with the narrow, provincial, "outside agitator" idea. Anyone who lives inside the United States can never be considered an outsider anywhere within its bounds.

You deplore the demonstrations taking place in Birmingham. But your statement, I am sorry to say, fails to express a similar concern for the conditions that brought about the demonstrations. I am sure that none of you would want to rest content with the superficial kind of social analysis that deals merely with effects and does not grapple with underlying causes. It is unfortunate that demonstrations are taking place in Birmingham, but it is even more unfortunate that the city's white power structure left the Negro community with no alternative.

6   In any nonviolent campaign there are four basic steps: collection of the facts to determine whether injustices exist; negotiation; self-purification; and direct action. We have gone through all these steps in Birmingham. There can be no gainsaying the fact that racial injustice engulfs this community. Birmingham is probably the most thoroughly segregated city in the United States. Its ugly record of brutality is widely known. Negroes have experienced grossly unjust treatment in courts. There have been more unsolved bombings of Negro homes and churches in Birmingham than in any other city in the nation. These are the hard, brutal facts of the case. On the basis of these conditions, Negro leaders sought to negotiate with the city fathers. But the latter consistently refused to engage in good-faith negotiation.

Then, last September, came the opportunity to talk with leaders of Birmingham's economic community. In the course of the negotiations, certain promises were made by the merchants—for example, to remove the stores' humiliating racial signs. On the basis of these promises, the Reverend Fred Shuttlesworth and the leaders of the Alabama Christian Movement for Human Rights agreed to a moratorium on all demonstrations. As the weeks and months went by, we realized that we were the victims of a broken promise. A few signs, briefly removed, returned; the others remained.

8   As in so many past experiences, our hopes had been blasted, and the shadow of deep disappointment settled upon us. We had no alternative except to prepare for direct action, whereby we would present our very bodies as means of laying our case before the conscience of the local and the national community. Mindful of the difficulties involved, we decided to undertake a process of self-purification. We began a series of workshops on

nonviolence, and we repeatedly asked ourselves: "Are you able to accept blows without retaliating?" "Are you able to endure the ordeal of jail?" We decided to schedule our direct-action program for the Easter season, realizing that except for Christmas, this is the main shopping period of the year. Knowing that a strong economic-withdrawal program would be the by-product of direct action, we felt that this would be the best time to bring pressure to bear on the merchants for the needed change.

Then it occurred to us that Birmingham's mayoral election was coming up in March, and we speedily decided to postpone action until after election day. When we discovered that the Commissioner of Public Safety, Eugene "Bull" Connor,* had piled up enough votes to be in the run-off, we decided again to postpone action until the day after the run-off so that the demonstrations could not be used to cloud the issues. Like many others, we waited to see Mr. Connor defeated, and to this end we endured postponement after postponement. Having aided in this community need, we felt that our direct-action program could be delayed no longer.

10   You may well ask, "Why direct action? Why sit-ins, marches, and so forth? Isn't negotiation a better path?" You are quite right in calling for negotiation. Indeed, this is the very purpose of direct action. Nonviolent direct action seeks to create such a crisis and foster such a tension that a community which has constantly refused to negotiate is forced to confront the issue. It seeks so to dramatize the issue that it can no longer be ignored. My citing the creation of tension as part of the work of the nonviolent-resister may sound rather shocking. But I must confess that I am not afraid of the word "tension." I have earnestly opposed violent tension, but there is a type of constructive, nonviolent tension which is necessary for growth. Just as Socrates felt that it was necessary to create a tension in the mind so that individuals could rise from the bondage of myths and half-truths to the unfettered realm of creative analysis and objective appraisal, so must we see the need for nonviolent gadflies to create the kind of tension in society that will help men rise from the dark depths of prejudice and racism to the majestic heights of understanding and brotherhood.

The purpose of our direct-action program is to create a situation so crisis-packed that it will inevitably open the door to negotiation. I therefore concur with you in your call for negotiation. Too long has our beloved Southland been bogged down in a tragic effort to live in monologue rather than dialogue.

12   One of the basic points in your statement is that the action that I and my associates have taken in Birmingham is untimely. Some have asked: "Why didn't you give the new city administration time to act?" The only answer that I can give to this query is that the new Birmingham administration must be prodded about as much as the outgoing one, before it will act. We are sadly mistaken if we feel that the election of Albert

---

* A powerful opponent of integration, Connor (1897–1973) used police force against civil rights demonstrators.

Boutwell as mayor will bring the millennium to Birmingham. While Mr. Boutwell is a much more gentle person than Mr. Connor, they are both segregationists, dedicated to maintenance of the status quo. I have hoped that Mr. Boutwell will be reasonable enough to see the futility of massive resistance to desegregation. But he will not see this without pressure from devotees of civil rights. My friends, I must say to you that we have not made a single gain in civil rights without determined legal and nonviolent pressure. Lamentably, it is an historical fact that privileged groups seldom give up their privileges voluntarily. Individuals may see the moral light and voluntarily give up their unjust posture; but, as Reinhold Niebuhr has reminded us, groups tend to be more immoral than individuals.

We know through painful experience that freedom is never voluntarily given by the oppressor; it must be demanded by the oppressed. Frankly, I have yet to engage in a direct-action campaign that was "well timed" in the view of those who have not suffered unduly from the disease of segregation. For years now I have heard the word "Wait!" It rings in the ear of every Negro with piercing familiarity. This "Wait" has almost always meant "Never." We must come to see, with one of our distinguished jurists, that "justice too long delayed is justice denied."

14   We have waited for more than 340 years for our constitutional and God-given rights. The nations of Asia and Africa are moving with jetlike speed toward gaining political independence, but we still creep at horse-and-buggy pace toward gaining a cup of coffee at a lunch counter. Perhaps it is easy for those who have never felt the stinging darts of segregation to say, "Wait." But when you have seen vicious mobs lynch your mothers and fathers at will and drown your sisters and brothers at whim; when you have seen hate-filled policemen curse, kick, and even kill your black brothers and sisters; when you see the vast majority of your twenty million Negro brothers smothering in an airtight cage of poverty in the midst of an affluent society; when you suddenly find your tongue twisted and your speech stammering as you seek to explain to your six-year-old daughter why she can't go to the public amusement park that has just been advertised on television, and see tears welling up in her eyes when she is told that Funtown is closed to colored children, and see ominous clouds of inferiority beginning to form in her little mental sky, and see her beginning to distort her personality by developing an unconscious bitterness toward white people; when you have to concoct an answer for a five-year-old son who is asking, "Daddy, why do white people treat colored people so mean?"; when you take a cross-country drive and find it necessary to sleep night after night in the uncomfortable corners of your automobile because no motel will accept you; when you are humiliated day in and day out by nagging signs reading "white" and "colored"; when your first name becomes "nigger," your middle name becomes "boy" (however old you are) and your last name becomes "John," and your wife and mother are never given the respected title "Mrs."; when you are harried by day and haunted by night by the fact that you are a

Negro, living constantly at tiptoe stance, never quite knowing what to expect next, and are plagued with inner fears and outer resentments; when you are forever fighting a degenerating sense of "nobodiness"—then you will understand why we find it difficult to wait. There comes a time when the cup of endurance runs over, and men are no longer willing to be plunged into the abyss of despair. I hope, sirs, you can understand our legitimate and unavoidable impatience.

You express a great deal of anxiety over our willingness to break laws. This is certainly a legitimate concern. Since we so diligently urge people to obey the Supreme Court's decision of 1954 outlawing segregation in the public schools, at first glance it may seem rather paradoxical for us consciously to break laws. One may well ask: "How can you advocate breaking some laws and obeying others?" The answer lies in the fact that there are two types of laws; just and unjust. I would be the first to advocate obeying just laws. One has not only a legal but a moral responsibility to obey just laws. Conversely, one has a moral responsibility to disobey unjust laws. I would agree with St. Augustine that "an unjust law is no law at all."

16   Now, what is the difference between the two? How does one determine whether a law is just or unjust? A just law is a man-made code that squares with the moral law or the law of God. An unjust law is a code that is out of harmony with the moral law. To put it in the terms of St. Thomas Aquinas: An unjust law is a human law that is not rooted in eternal law and natural law. Any law that uplifts human personality is just. Any law that degrades human personality is unjust. All segregation statutes are unjust because segregation distorts the soul and damages the personality. It gives the segregator a false sense of superiority and the segregated a false sense of inferiority. Segregation, to use the terminology of the Jewish philosopher Martin Buber, substitutes an "I–it" relationship for an "I–thou" relationship and ends up relegating persons to the status of things. Hence segregation is not only politically, economically, and sociologically unsound, it is morally wrong and sinful. Paul Tillich has said that sin is separation. Is not segregation an existential expression of man's tragic separation, his awful estrangement, his terrible sinfulness? Thus it is that I can urge men to obey the 1954 decision of the Supreme Court, for it is morally right; and I can urge them to disobey segregation ordinances, for they are morally wrong.

Let us consider a more concrete example of just and unjust laws. An unjust law is a code that a numerical or power majority group compels a minority group to obey but does not make binding on itself. This is *difference* made legal. By the same token, a just law is a code that a majority compels a minority to follow and that it is willing to follow itself. This is *sameness* made legal.

18   Let me give another explanation. A law is unjust if it is inflicted on a minority that, as a result of being denied the right to vote, had no part in enacting or devising the law. Who can say that the legislature of Alabama which set up that state's segregation laws was democratically elected? Throughout Alabama all sorts of devious methods are used to prevent Ne-

groes from becoming registered voters, and there are some counties in which, even though Negroes constitute a majority of the population, not a single Negro is registered. Can any law enacted under such circumstances be considered democratically structured?

Sometimes a law is just on its face and unjust in its application. For instance, I have been arrested on a charge of parading without a permit. Now, there is nothing wrong in having an ordinance which requires a permit for a parade. But such an ordinance becomes unjust when it is used to maintain segregation and to deny citizens the First-Amendment privilege of peaceful assembly and protest.

20   I hope you are able to see the distinction I am trying to point out. In no sense do I advocate evading or defying the law, as would the rabid segregationist. That would lead to anarchy. One who breaks an unjust law must do so openly, lovingly, and with a willingness to accept the penalty. I submit that an individual who breaks a law that conscience tells him is unjust, and who willingly accepts the penalty of imprisonment in order to arouse the conscience of the community over its injustice, is in reality expressing the highest respect for law.

Of course, there is nothing new about this kind of civil disobedience. It was evidenced sublimely in the refusal of Shadrach, Meshach, and Abednego to obey the laws of Nebuchadnezzar,* on the ground that a higher moral law was at stake. It was practiced superbly by the early Christians, who were willing to face hungry lions and the excruciating pain of chopping blocks rather than submit to certain unjust laws of the Roman Empire. To a degree, academic freedom is a reality today because Socrates practiced civil disobedience. In our own nation, the Boston Tea Party represented a massive act of civil disobedience.

22   We should never forget that everything Adolf Hitler did in Germany was "legal" and everything the Hungarian freedom fighters did in Hungary was "illegal."† It was "illegal" to aid and comfort a Jew in Hitler's Germany. Even so, I am sure that, had I lived in Germany at the time, I would have aided and comforted my Jewish brothers. If today I lived in a Communist country where certain principles dear to the Christian faith are suppressed, I would openly advocate disobeying that country's anti-religious laws.

I must make two honest confessions to you, my Christian and Jewish brothers. First, I must confess that over the past few years I have been gravely disappointed with the white moderate. I have almost reached the regrettable conclusion that the Negro's great stumbling block in his stride toward freedom is not the White Citizen's Counciler or the Ku Klux Klanner,

---

* Nebuchadnezzar, King of Babylon, destroyed the temple at Jerusalem and brought the Jewish people into captivity. He set up a huge image in gold and commanded all to worship it. Shadrach, Meshach, and Abednego refused and were thrown into a fiery furnace from which they emerged unscathed. (See Daniel: 3.)

† In 1956, Hungarian citizens temporarily overthrew the communist dictatorship in their country. Unwilling to confront the Soviet Union, western democracies stood by when the Red Army suppressed the revolt.

but the white moderate, who is more devoted to "order" than to justice; who prefers a negative peace which is the absence of tension to a positive peace which is the presence of justice; who constantly says, "I agree with you in the goal you seek, but I cannot agree with your methods of direct action"; who paternalistically believes he can set the timetable for another man's freedom; who lives by a mythical concept of time and who constantly advises the Negro to wait for a "more convenient season." Shallow understanding from people of good will is more frustrating than absolute misunderstanding from people of ill will. Lukewarm acceptance is much more bewildering than outright rejection.

24   I had hoped that the white moderate would understand that law and order exist for the purpose of establishing justice and that when they fail in this purpose they become the dangerously structured dams that block the flow of social progress. I had hoped that the white moderate would understand that the present tension in the South is a necessary phase of the transition from an obnoxious negative peace, in which the Negro passively accepted his unjust plight, to a substantive and positive peace, in which all men will respect the dignity and worth of human personality. Actually, we who engage in nonviolent direct action are not the creators of tension. We merely bring to the surface the hidden tension that is already alive. We bring it out in the open, where it can be seen and dealt with. Like a boil that can never be cured so long as it is covered up but must be opened with all its ugliness to the natural medicines of air and light, injustice must be exposed, with all the tension its exposure creates, to the light of human conscience and the air of national opinion, before it can be cured.

In your statement you assert that our actions, even though peaceful, must be condemned because they precipitate violence. But is this a logical assertion? Isn't this like condemning a robbed man because his possession of money precipitated the evil act of robbery? Isn't this like condemning Socrates because his unswerving commitment to truth and his philosophical inquiries precipitated the act by the misguided populace in which they made him drink hemlock? Isn't this like condemning Jesus because his unique God-consciousness and never-ceasing devotion to God's will precipitated the evil act of crucifixion? We must come to see that, as the federal courts have consistently affirmed, it is wrong to urge an individual to cease his efforts to gain his basic constitutional rights because the quest may precipitate violence. Society must protect the robbed and punish the robber.

26   I had also hoped that the white moderate would reject the myth concerning time in relation to the struggle for freedom. I have just received a letter from a white brother in Texas. He writes: "All Christians know that the colored people will receive equal rights eventually, but it is possible that you are in too great a religious hurry. It has taken Christianity almost two thousand years to accomplish what it has. The teachings of Christ take time to come to earth." Such an attitude stems from a tragic misconception of time, from the strangely irrational notion that there is something in the very flow of time that will inevitably cure all ills. Actually, time itself is neutral; it can

be used either destructively or constructively. More and more I feel that the people of ill will have used time much more effectively than have the people of good will. We will have to repent in this generation not merely for the hateful words and actions of the bad people, but for the appalling silence of the good people. Human progress never rolls in on wheels of inevitability; it comes through the tireless efforts of men willing to be coworkers with God, and without this hard work, time itself becomes an ally of the forces of social stagnation. We must use time creatively, in the knowledge that the time is always ripe to do right. Now is the time to make real the promise of democracy and transform our pending national elegy into a creative psalm of brotherhood. Now is the time to lift our national policy from the quicksand of racial injustice to the solid rock of human dignity.

You speak of our activity in Birmingham as extreme. At first I was rather disappointed that fellow clergymen would see my nonviolent efforts as those of an extremist. I began thinking about the fact that I stand in the middle of two opposing forces in the Negro community. One is a force of complacency, made up in part of Negroes who, as a result of long years of oppression, are so drained of self-respect and a sense of "somebodiness" that they have adjusted to segregation; and in part of a few middle-class Negroes who, because of a degree of academic and economic security and because in some ways they profit by segregation, have become insensitive to the problems of the masses. The other force is one of bitterness and hatred, and it comes perilously close to advocating violence. It is expressed in the various black nationalist groups that are springing up across the nation, the largest and best-known being Elijah Muhammad's Muslim movement. Nourished by the Negro's frustration over the continued existence of racial discrimination, this movement is made up of people who have lost faith in America, who have absolutely repudiated Christianity, and who have concluded that the white man is an incorrigible "devil."

28   I have tried to stand between these two forces, saying that we need emulate neither the "do-nothingism" of the complacent nor the hatred and despair of the black nationalist. For there is the more excellent way of love and nonviolent protest. I am grateful to God that, through the influence of the Negro church, the way of nonviolence became an integral part of our struggle.

If this philosophy had not emerged, by now many streets of the South would, I am convinced, be flowing with blood. And I am further convinced that if our white brothers dismiss as "rabble-rousers" and "outside agitators" those of us who employ nonviolent direct action, and if they refuse to support our nonviolent efforts, millions of Negroes will, out of frustration and despair, seek solace and security in black-nationalist ideologies—a development that would inevitably lead to a frightening racial nightmare.

30   Oppressed people cannot remain oppressed forever. The yearning for freedom eventually manifests itself, and that is what has happened to the American Negro. Something within has reminded him of his birthright of freedom, and something without has reminded him that it can be gained.

Consciously or unconsciously, he has been caught up by the *Zeitgeist*,* and with his black brothers of Africa and his brown and yellow brothers of Asia, South America, and the Caribbean, the United States Negro is moving with a sense of great urgency toward the promised land of racial justice. If one recognizes this vital urge that has engulfed the Negro community, one should readily understand why public demonstrations are taking place. The Negro has many pent-up resentments and latent frustrations, and he must release them. So let him march; let him make prayer pilgrimages to the city hall; let him go on freedom rides—and try to understand why he must do so. If his repressed emotions are not released in nonviolent ways, they will seek expression through violence; this is not a threat but a fact of history. So I have not said to my people, "Get rid of your discontent." Rather, I have tried to say that this normal and healthy discontent can be channeled into the creative outlet of nonviolent direct action. And now this approach is being termed extremist.

But though I was initially disappointed at being categorized as an extremist, as I continued to think about the matter I gradually gained a measure of satisfaction from the label. Was not Jesus an extremist for love: "Love your enemies, bless them that curse you, do good to them that hate you, and pray for them which despitefully use you, and persecute you." Was not Amos an extremist for justice: "Let justice roll down like waters and righteousness like an everflowing stream." Was not Paul an extremist for the Christian gospel: "I bear in my body the marks of the Lord Jesus." Was not Martin Luther an extremist: "Here I stand; I cannot do otherwise, so help me God." And John Bunyan:[†] "I will stay in jail to the end of my days before I make a butchery of my conscience." And Abraham Lincoln: "This nation cannot survive half slave and half free." And Thomas Jefferson: "We hold these truths to be self-evident, that all men are created equal. . . ." So the question is not whether we will be extremists, but what kind of extremists we will be. Will we be extremists for hate or for love? Will we be extremists for the preservation of injustice or for the extension of justice? In that dramatic scene on Calvary's hill three men were crucified. We must never forget that all three were crucified for the same crime—the crime of extremism. Two were extremists for immorality, and thus fell below their environment. The other, Jesus Christ, was an extremist for love, truth, and goodness, and thereby rose above his environment. Perhaps the South, the nation, and the world are in dire need of creative extremists.

32   I had hoped that the white moderate would see this need. Perhaps I was too optimistic; perhaps I expected too much. I suppose I should have realized that few members of the oppressor race can understand the deep groans and passionate yearnings of the oppressed race, and still fewer have the vision to see that injustice must be rooted out by strong, persistent, and

---

* German for "the spirit of the times."

[†] An important English writer of the seventeenth century, John Bunyan (1628–1688) is best known for his Christian allegory *Pilgrim's Progress from This World to That Which Is to Come.*

determined action. I am thankful, however, that some of our white brothers in the South have grasped the meaning of this social revolution and committed themselves to it. They are still all too few in quantity, but they are big in quality. Some—such as Ralph McGill, Lillian Smith, Harry Golden, James McBride Dabbs, Ann Braden, and Sarah Patton Boyle—have written about our struggle in eloquent and prophetic terms. Others have marched with us down nameless streets of the South. They have languished in filthy, roach-infested jails, suffering the abuse and brutality of policemen who view them as "dirty nigger-lovers." Unlike so many of their moderate brothers and sisters, they have recognized the urgency of the moment and sensed the need for powerful "action" antidotes to combat the disease of segregation.

Let me take note of my other major disappointment. I have been so greatly disappointed with the white church and its leadership. Of course, there are some notable exceptions. I am not unmindful of the fact that each of you has taken some significant stands on this issue. I commend you, Reverend Stallings, for your Christian stand on this past Sunday, in welcoming Negroes to your worship service on a nonsegregated basis. I commend the Catholic leaders of this state for integrating Spring Hill College several years ago.

34   But despite these notable exceptions, I must honestly reiterate that I have been disappointed with the church. I do not say this as one of those negative critics who can always find something wrong with the church. I say this as a minister of the gospel, who loves the church; who was nurtured in its bosom; who has been sustained by its spiritual blessings and who will remain true to it as long as the cord of life shall lengthen.

When I was suddenly catapulted into the leadership of the bus protest in Montgomery, Alabama, a few years ago, I felt we would be supported by the white church. I felt that the white ministers, priests, and rabbis of the South would be among our strongest allies. Instead, some have been outright opponents, refusing to understand the freedom movement and misrepresenting its leaders; all too many others have been more cautious than courageous and have remained silent behind the anesthetizing security of stained-glass windows.

36   In spite of my shattered dreams, I came to Birmingham with the hope that the white religious leadership of this community would see the justice of our cause and, with deep moral concern, would serve as the channel through which our just grievances could reach the power structure. I had hoped that each of you would understand. But again I have been disappointed.

There was a time when the church was very powerful—in the time when the early Christians rejoiced at being deemed worthy to suffer for what they believed. In those days the church was not merely a thermometer that recorded the ideas and principles of popular opinion; it was a thermostat that transformed the mores of society. Whenever the early Christians entered a town, the people in power became disturbed and immediately sought to convict the Christians for being "disturbers of the peace" and "outside agitators." But the Christians pressed on, in the conviction that they were "a colony of heaven," called to obey God rather than man. Small in number, they were big in commitment. They were too God-intoxicated to be "astronomically intimidated." By their effort and example they brought an end to such ancient evils as infanticide and gladiatorial contests.

38   Things are different now. So often the contemporary church is a weak, ineffectual voice with an uncertain sound. So often it is an archdefender of the status quo. Far from being disturbed by the presence of the church, the power structure of the average community is consoled by the church's silent—and often even vocal—sanction of things as they are.

But the judgment of God is upon the church as never before. If today's church does not recapture the sacrificial spirit of the early church, it will lose its authenticity, forfeit the loyalty of millions, and be dismissed as an irrelevant social club with no meaning for the twentieth century. Every day I meet young people whose disappointment with the church has turned into outright disgust.

40   Perhaps I have once again been too optimistic. Is organized religion too inextricably bound to the status quo to save our nation and the world? Perhaps I must turn my faith to the inner spiritual church, the church within the church, as the true *ekklesia* and the hope of the world. But again I am thankful to God that some noble souls from the ranks of organized religion have broken loose from the paralyzing chains of conformity and joined us as active partners in the struggle for freedom. They have left their secure congregations and walked the streets of Albany, Georgia, with us. They have gone down the highways of the South on torturous rides for freedom. Yes, they have gone to jail with us. Some have been dismissed from their churches, have lost the support of their bishops and fellow ministers. But they have acted in the faith that right defeated is stronger than evil triumphant. Their witness has been the spiritual salt that has preserved the true meaning of the gospel in these troubled times. They have carved a tunnel of hope through the dark mountain of disappointment.

I hope the church as a whole will meet the challenge of this decisive hour. But even if the church does not come to the aid of justice, I have no despair about the future. I have no fear about the outcome of our struggle in Birmingham, even if our motives are at present misunderstood. We will reach the goal of freedom in Birmingham and all over the nation, because the goal of America is freedom. Abused and scorned though we may be, our destiny is tied up with America's destiny. Before the pilgrims landed at Plymouth, we were here. Before the pen of Jefferson etched the majestic words of the Declaration of Independence across the pages of history, we were here. For more than two centuries our forebears labored in this country without wages; they made cotton king; they built the homes of their masters while suffering gross injustice and shameful humiliation—and yet out of a bottomless vitality they continued to thrive and develop. If the inexpressible cruelties of slavery could not stop us, the opposition we now face will surely fail. We will win our freedom because the sacred heritage of our nation and the eternal will of God are embodied in our echoing demands.

42   Before closing I feel impelled to mention one other point in your statement that has troubled me profoundly. You warmly commended the Birmingham police force for keeping "order" and "preventing violence." I doubt that you would have so warmly commended the police force if you had seen its dogs sinking their teeth into unarmed, nonviolent Negroes. I doubt that you would so quickly commend the policemen if you were to observe their ugly and inhumane treatment of Negroes here in the city jail; if you were to watch them push and curse old Negro women and young Negro girls; if you were to see them slap and kick old Negro men and young boys; if you were to observe them, as they did on two occasions, refuse to give us food because we wanted to sing our grace together. I cannot join you in your praise of the Birmingham police department.

It is true that the police have exercised a degree of discipline in handling the demonstrators. In this sense they have conducted themselves rather "nonviolently" in public. But for what purpose? To preserve the evil system of segregation. Over the past few years I have consistently preached that nonviolence demands that the means we use must be as pure as the ends we seek. I have tried to make clear that it is wrong to use immoral means to attain moral ends. But now I must affirm that it is just as wrong, or perhaps even more so, to use moral means to preserve immoral ends. Perhaps Mr. Connor and his policemen have been rather nonviolent in public, as was Chief Pritchett in Albany, Georgia, but they have used the moral means of nonviolence to maintain the immoral end of racial injustice. As T. S. Eliot has said, "The last temptation is the greatest treason: To do the right deed for the wrong reason."

44   I wish you had commended the Negro sit-inners and demonstrators of Birmingham for their sublime courage, their willingness to suffer, and their amazing discipline in the midst of great provocation. One day the South will recognize its real heroes. They will be the James Merediths, with the noble sense of purpose that enables them to face jeering and hostile mobs, and with the agonizing loneliness that characterizes the life of the pioneer. They will be old, oppressed, battered Negro women, symbolized in a seventy-two-year-old woman in Montgomery, Alabama, who rose up with a sense of dignity and with her people decided not to ride segregated buses, and who responded with ungrammatical profundity to one who inquired about her weariness: "My feets is tired, but my soul is at rest." They will be the young high school and college students, the young ministers of the gospel and a host of their elders, courageously and nonviolently sitting in at lunch counters and willingly going to jail for conscience's sake. One day the South will know that when these disinherited children of God sat down at lunch counters, they were in reality standing up for what is best in the American dream and for the most sacred values in our Judeo-Christian heritage, thereby bringing our nation back to those great wells of

democracy which were dug deep by the founding fathers in their formulation of the Constitution and the Declaration of Independence.

Never before have I written so long a letter. I'm afraid it is much too long to take your precious time. I can assure you that it would have been much shorter if I had been writing from a comfortable desk, but what else can one do when he is alone in a narrow jail cell, other than write long letters, think long thoughts, and pray long prayers?

46   If I have said anything in this letter that overstates the truth and indicates an unreasonable impatience, I beg you to forgive me. If I have said anything that understates the truth and indicates my having a patience that allows me to settle for anything less than brotherhood, I beg God to forgive me.

I hope this letter finds you strong in the faith. I also hope that circumstances will soon make it possible for me to meet each of you, not as an integrationist or a civil-rights leader but as a fellow clergyman and a Christian brother. Let us all hope that the dark clouds of racial prejudice will soon pass away and the deep fog of misunderstanding will be lifted from our fear-drenched communities, and in some not too distant tomorrow the radiant stars of love and brotherhood will shine over our great nation with all their scintillating beauty.

Yours for the cause of Peace and Brotherhood,
Martin Luther King, Jr.   ❖

Questions for Meaning

1. What reason does King give for writing this letter? What justification does he provide for its length? How do these explanations work to his advantage?
2. One of the many charges brought against King at the time of his arrest was that he was an "outsider" who had no business in Birmingham. How does King defend himself? What three reasons does he cite to justify his presence in Birmingham?
3. King also responds to the criticism that his campaign for civil rights was "untimely." What is his defense against this charge?
4. What does King mean by nonviolent "direct action"? What sort of activities did he lead people to pursue? Identify the four basic steps to a direct-action campaign and explain what such campaigns were meant to accomplish.
5. Why did King believe that a direct-action campaign was necessary in Birmingham? Why did the black community in Birmingham turn to King? What problems were they facing, and what methods had they already tried before deciding on direct action?
6. What was the 1954 Supreme Court decision that King refers to in paragraph 16? Why was King able to charge that the "rabid segregationist" breaks the law?

7. King's critics charged that he obeyed the law selectively. He answers by arguing there is a difference between just and unjust laws, and that moral law requires men and women to break unjust laws that are imposed on them. How can you tell the difference between laws that you should honor and laws that you should break? What is King's definition of an unjust law, and what historical examples does he give to illustrate situations in which unjust laws have to be broken?
8. What does King mean, in paragraph 35, when he complains of the "anesthetizing security of stained-glass windows"? How can churches make men and women feel falsely secure?

Questions about Strategy

1. Why did King address his letter to fellow clergymen? Why was he disappointed in them, and what did he expect his letter to accomplish?
2. Is there anything in the substance of this letter that reveals it was written for an audience familiar with the Bible and modern theology? Do you think King intended this letter to be read only by clergy? Can you point to anything that suggests King may have really written for a larger audience?
3. How does King characterize himself in this letter? What sort of a man does he seem to be, and what role does his presentation of himself play in his argument? How does he establish that he is someone worth listening to—and that it is important to listen to what he has to say?
4. *Ekklesia* is Greek for assembly, congregation, or church. Why does King use this word in paragraph 40 instead of simply saying "the church"?
5. King had much experience as a preacher when he wrote this famous letter. Is there anything about its style that reminds you of oratory? How effective would this letter be if delivered as a speech?

BETTY FRIEDAN

THE IMPORTANCE OF WORK

Betty Friedan was one of the founders of the National Organization for Women, serving as NOW's first president between 1966 and 1970. Born in Peoria, Illinois, and educated at Smith College, the University of California, and the University of Iowa, Friedan has lectured at more than fifty universities and institutes. Her essays have appeared in numerous periodicals, including the *Saturday Review, Harper's, McCall's, Redbook,* and the *Ladies' Home Journal.* Her books include *It Changed My Life* (1976), *The Second Stage* (1981), and *The Fountain of Age* (1993).

"The Importance of Work" is drawn from the book that made her famous, *The Feminine Mystique* (1963). More than a quarter of a century has now passed since Friedan published this book, and the leadership of the women's movement has passed to a younger generation. But if the development of that movement could be traced back to the publication of a single work, it would have to be *The Feminine Mystique*. Friedan believed that women needed to escape from the roles they had assumed as wives and mothers, and if her ideas no longer seem as bold as they once were, it is because she anticipated many of the concerns that would dominate the analysis of male/female relations during the 1970s and 1980s. "The Importance of Work" is an editor's title for the concluding pages of Friedan's book, an excerpt that reveals Friedan's conviction that women need to enter the mainstream of the American workforce—not simply as typists and file clerks, but as the full equals of men.

Appeal to who you are

The question of how a person can most fully realize his own capacities and thus achieve identity has become an important concern of the philosophers and the social and psychological thinkers of our time—and for good reason. Thinkers of other times put forth the idea that people were, to a great extent, defined by the work they did. The work that a man had to do to eat, to stay alive, to meet the physical necessities of his environment, dictated his identity. And in this sense, when work was seen merely as a means of survival, human identity was dictated by biology.

2   But today the problem of human identity has changed. For the work that defined man's place in society and his sense of himself has also changed man's world. Work, and the advance of knowledge, has lessened man's dependence on his environment; his biology and the work he must do for biological survival are no longer sufficient to define his identity. This can be *Defining yourself* most clearly seen in our own abundant society; men no longer need to work all day to eat. They have an unprecedented freedom to choose the kind of work they will do; they also have an unprecedented amount of time apart from the hours and days that must actually be spent in making a living. And ⟶ suddenly one realizes the significance of today's identity crisis—for women, and increasingly, for men. One sees the human significance of work—not merely as the means of biological survival, but as the giver of self and the transcender of self, as the creator of human identity and human evolution.

Problem throughout History

For "self-realization" or "self-fulfillment" or "identity" does not come from looking into a mirror in rapt contemplation of one's own image. Those who have most fully realized themselves, in a sense that can be recog- *Today we do it for us ME* nized by the human mind even though it cannot be clearly defined, have done so in the service of a human purpose larger than themselves. Men from varying disciplines have used different words for this mysterious process from which comes the sense of self. The religious mystics, the philosophers, Marx, Freud—all had different names for it: man finds himself by *Biblical* — losing himself; man is defined by his relation to the means of production; the ego, the self, grows through understanding and mastering reality— through work and love.

4   The identity crisis, which has been noted by Erik Erikson* and others in recent years in the American man, seems to occur for lack of, and be cured by finding, the work, or cause, or purpose that evokes his own creativity. Some never find it, for it does not come from busy-work or punching a time clock. It does not come from just making a living, working by formula, finding a secure spot as an organization man. The very argument, by Riesman and others, that man no longer finds identity in the work defined as a paycheck job, assumes that identity for man comes through creative work of his own that contributes to the human community: the core of the self becomes aware, becomes real, and grows through work that carries forward human society.

Work, the shopworn staple of the economists, has become the new frontier of psychology. Psychiatrists have long used "occupational therapy" with patients in mental hospitals; they have recently discovered that to be of real psychological value, it must be not just "therapy," but real work, serving a real purpose in the community. And work can now be seen as the key to the problem that has no name. The identity crisis of American women began a century ago, as more and more of the work important to the world, more and more of the work that used their human abilities and through which they were able to find self-realization, was taken from them.

6   Until, and even into, the last century, strong, capable women were needed to pioneer our new land; with their husbands, they ran the farms and plantations and Western homesteads. These women were respected and self-respecting members of a society whose pioneering purpose centered in the home. Strength and independence, responsibility and self-confidence, self-discipline and courage, freedom and equality were part of the American character for both men and women, in all the first generations. The women who came by steerage from Ireland, Italy, Russia, and Poland worked beside their husbands in the sweatshops and the laundries, learned the new language, and saved to send their sons and daughters to college. Women were never quite as "feminine," or held in as much contempt, in America as they were in Europe. American women seemed to European travelers, long before our time, less passive, childlike, and feminine than their own wives in France or Germany or England. By an accident of history, American women shared in the work of society longer, and grew with the men. Grade- and high-school education for boys and girls alike was almost always the rule; and in the West, where women shared the pioneering work the longest, even the universities were coeducational from the beginning.

The identity crisis for women did not begin in America until the fire and strength and ability of the pioneer women were no longer needed, no longer used, in the middle-class homes of the Eastern and Midwestern cities, when the pioneering was done and men began to build the new society in industries and professions outside the home. But the daughters of the

---

* Trained by Sigmund and Anna Freud, Erik Erikson (1902–1994) was an influencial American psychoanalyst and writer best known for *Childhood and Society* (1950).

pioneer women had grown too used to freedom and work to be content with leisure and passive femininity.

8   It was not an American, but a South African woman, Mrs. Olive Schreiner, who warned at the turn of the century that the quality and quantity of women's functions in the social universe were decreasing as fast as civilization was advancing; that if women did not win back their right to a full share of honored and useful work, woman's mind and muscle would weaken in a parasitic state; her offspring, male and female, would weaken progressively, and civilization itself would deteriorate.

The feminists saw clearly that education and the right to participate in the more advanced work of society were women's greatest needs. They fought for and won the rights to new, fully human identity for women. But how very few of their daughters and granddaughters have chosen to use their education and their abilities for any large creative purpose, for responsible work in society? How many of them have been deceived, or have deceived themselves, into clinging to the outgrown, childlike femininity of "Occupation: housewife"?

10   It was not a minor matter, their mistaken choice. We now know that the same range of potential ability exists for women as for men. Women, as well as men, can only find their identity in work that uses their full capacities. A woman cannot find her identity through others—her husband, her children. She cannot find it in the dull routine of housework. As thinkers of every age have said, it is only when a human being faces squarely the fact that he can forfeit his own life, that he becomes truly aware of himself, and begins to take his existence seriously. Sometimes this awareness comes only at the moment of death. Sometimes it comes from a more subtle facing of death: the death of self in passive conformity, in meaningless work. The feminine mystique prescribes just such a living death for women. Faced with the slow death of self, the American woman must begin to take her life seriously.

"We measure ourselves by many standards," said the great American psychologist William James, nearly a century ago. "Our strength and our intelligence, our wealth and even our good luck, are things which warm our heart and make us feel ourselves a match for life. But deeper than all such things, and able to suffice unto itself without them, is the sense of the amount of effort which we can put forth."

12   If women do not put forth, finally, that effort to become all that they have it in them to become, they will forfeit their own humanity. A woman today who has no goal, no purpose, no ambition patterning her days into the future, making her stretch and grow beyond that small score of years in which her body can fill its biological function, is committing a kind of suicide. For that future half a century after the child-bearing years are over is a fact that an American woman cannot deny. Nor can she deny that as a housewife, the world is indeed rushing past her door while she just sits and watches. The terror she feels is real, if she has no place in that world.

The feminine mystique has succeeded in burying millions of American women alive. There is no way for these women to break out of their comfortable concentration camps except by finally putting forth an effort— that human effort which reaches beyond biology, beyond the narrow walls of home, to help shape the future. Only by such a personal commitment to the future can American women break out of the housewife trap and truly find fulfillment as wives and mothers—by fulfilling their own unique possibilities as separate human beings. ❖

Questions for Meaning

1. In her opening paragraph, Friedan writes, "when work was seen merely as a means of survival, human identity was dictated by biology." What does this mean?
2. Does Friedan believe that all types of work are equally satisfying? Where does she define the type of work that has "human significance"?
3. According to Friedan, what is the historical explanation for the identity crisis many American women suffered during the twentieth century?
4. What's wrong with "Occupation: housewife"? Why does Friedan believe that women cannot find fulfillment simply by being wives and mothers?
5. Explain Friedan's allusion to "feminists" in paragraph 9. Who were the early feminists, and what did they accomplish?
6. Although you have been given only the last few pages of Friedan's book, can you construct a definition for what she means by "the feminine mystique"?
7. Vocabulary: transcender (2), rapt (3), mystics (3), parasitic (8), deteriorate (8), forfeit (10).

Questions about Strategy

1. What is the premise that underlies Friedan's argument on behalf of meaningful careers for women?
2. Why does Friedan discuss women within the context of psychological "identity"? Why is it important for her to link the needs of women with the needs of men?
3. Comment on Friedan's use of quotation. She refers, for support, to four men (Marx, Freud, Erik Erikson, and William James) and to only one woman, Olive Schreiner. Does her reliance on male authorities help or hurt her argument?
4. When Friedan declares that housewives are "committing a kind of suicide" trapped within homes that are "comfortable concentration camps," is she drawing her work together with a forceful conclusion or weakening it through exaggeration?

SUGGESTIONS FOR WRITING

1. Using "A Modest Proposal" as your model, write a satirical essay proposing a "solution" to a contemporary social problem other than poverty.
2. As a counterargument to Thomas Jefferson, write "A Declaration of Continued Dependence" from the point of view of George III.
3. Drawing on the work of Mary Wollstonecraft, Margaret Sanger, and Betty Friedan, write a "Declaration of Independence for Women."
4. Compare the propaganda posters reprinted on pages 353 and 354. How do they reflect the principles outlined by Adolf Hitler in "The Purpose of Propaganda"? Explain the strategy behind each of these posters and determine their relative effectiveness.
5. Research and report on the conditions in Germany that helped Hitler rise to power.
6. Drawing on the work of Carl Rogers, and other research if necessary, write an essay defining what it takes to be a good listener.
7. Research the influence of Carl Rogers on the teaching of argument, and write a synthesis of what you discover.
8. Write a dialogue between Adolf Hitler and Carl Rogers focused on the importance of respecting the views of people with whom one disagrees.
9. Write a summary of "Letter from Birmingham Jail."
10. Drawing on "Letter from Birmingham Jail," defend an illegal act that you would be willing to commit in order to advance a cause in which you believe.
11. Respond to Betty Friedan by making the case for adults who choose to be "housewives" or "househusbands".

COLLABORATIVE PROJECT

Form a writing group and decide what roles members want to play in creating a dialogue among Thomas Jefferson, Adolf Hitler, Martin Luther King, Jr., and Betty Friedan. Focus the dialogue on what it means to be free and how freedom can be achieved.

FIGURE 1

Figure 1 is an example of an English poster from the First World War (1914–1919). Figure 2 is a Nazi election poster from the early 1930s. It reads, "Work and Bread through List One." (List One refers to the position of Nazi candidates on the ballot before Hitler seized power.) Figure 3 is a Nazi propaganda poster used in Poland after the German invasion of that country in 1939. The caption, in Polish, reads: "England! This is your work!" The picture shows a wounded Polish soldier pointing to the ruins of Warsaw and addressing Neville Chamberlain, the British Prime Minister at the beginning of the war.

FIGURE 2

FIGURE 3

GLOSSARY OF USEFUL TERMS

ad hominem argument   An argument that makes a personal attack on an opponent instead of addressing the issue that is under dispute.

allusion   An unexplained reference that members of an audience are expected to understand because of their education or the culture in which they live.

analogy   A comparison that works on more than one level, usually between something familiar and something abstract.

anticipating the opposition   The process through which a writer or speaker imagines the most likely counterarguments that might be raised against his or her position.

audience   Whoever will read what you write. Your audience may consist of a single individual (such as your history teacher), a particular group of people (such as English majors), or a larger and more general group (such as "the American people"). Good writers have a clear sense of audience, which means that they never lose sight of the readers they are writing for.

authority   A reliable source that helps support an argument. It is important to cite authorities who will be recognized as legitimate by your audience. This means turning to people with good credentials in whatever area is under consideration. If you are arguing about the economy, cite a prominent economist as an authority.

begging the question   An argument that assumes, as already agreed on, whatever it should be devoted to proving.

bibliography   A list of works on a particular subject. One type of bibliography is the list of works cited that appears at the end of a paper, article, or book. Another type of bibliography is a work in itself—a compilation of all known sources on a subject. An annotated bibliography is a bibliography that includes a brief description of each of the sources cited.

bogus claim   An unreliable or false statement that is unsupported by reliable evidence or legitimate authority.

claim   Any assertion that can or should be supported with evidence. In the model for argument devised by Stephen Toulmin, the "claim" is the conclusion that the arguer must try to prove.

cliché   A worn-out expression; any group of words that are frequently and automatically used together. In "the real world" of "today's society," writers should avoid clichés because they are a type of instant language that makes writing seem "as dead as a doornail."

concession   Any point in an argument that recognizes merit in the views of people with whom the arguer disagrees. In argumentation, concessions demonstrate fair-mindedness and help draw different sides together.

connotation   The associations inspired by a word, in contrast to *denotation* (see below).

data   The evidence that an arguer uses to support a claim. It may take the form of personal experience, expert opinion, statistics, or any other information that is verifiable.

deduction   The type of reasoning through which a generally accepted belief leads to a specific conclusion.

denotation   The literal dictionary definition of a word.

diction   Word choice. Having good diction means more than having a good vocabulary; it means using language appropriately by using the right word in the right place.

documentation   The references that writers supply to reveal the sources of the information they have reported.

equivocation   The deliberate use of vague, ambiguous language to mislead others. In writing, equivocation often takes the form of using abstract words to obscure meaning.

evidence   The experience, examples, or facts that support an argument. Good writers are careful to offer evidence for whatever they are claiming (see *claim*).

focus   The particular aspect of a subject on which a writer decides to concentrate. Many things can be said about most subjects. Having a clear focus means narrowing a subject down so that it can be discussed without loss of direction. If you digress from your subject and begin to ramble, you have probably lost your focus.

generalization   Forming a conclusion that seems generally acceptable because it could be supported by evidence. A generalization becomes a problem only when it is easily disputable. You have overgeneralized if someone can think of exceptions to what you have claimed. Be wary of words such as "all" and "every"; they increase the likelihood of overgeneralization.

hyperbole   A deliberate exaggeration for dramatic effect.

hypothesis   A theory that guides your research; a conditional thesis that is subject to change as evidence accumulates.

induction   The type of reasoning through which specific observations lead to a generally acceptable conclusion.

irony   A manner of speech or writing in which one's meaning is the opposite of what one has said.

jargon   A specialized vocabulary that is usually abstract and limited to a particular field; when used in an argument, it should be defined for the benefit of those outside the field.

loaded term   A word or phrase that is considered an unfair type of persuasion because it is either slanted or gratuitous within its context.

metaphor   A comparison in which two unlike things are declared to be the same; for example, "The Lord is my shepherd."

meter   The rhythm of poetry, in which stressed syllables occur in a pattern with regular intervals. In the analysis of poetry, meter is measured by a unit called a "foot," which usually consists of two or three syllables of which at least one is stressed.

non sequitur   Latin for "it does not follow"; a logical fallacy in which a writer bases a claim on an unrelated point.

paradox   A statement or situation that appears to be contradictory but is nevertheless true; for example, "conspicuous by his absence."

paraphrase   Restating someone's words to demonstrate that you have understood them correctly or to make them more easily understandable.

personification   Giving human qualities to nonhuman objects; for example, "The sofa smiled at me, inviting me to sit down."

persuasion   A rhetorical strategy designed to achieve consent. Although there are many different types of persuasion, most involve an appeal to values, desires, and emotions. A persuasive argument would also demonstrate the ability to think critically and support claims with evidence.

plagiarism   Taking someone's words or ideas without giving adequate acknowledgment.

point of view   The attitude with which a writer approaches a subject. Good writers maintain a consistent point of view within each individual work.

post hoc, ergo propter hoc   Latin for "after this, therefore because of this"; a logical fallacy in which precedence is confused with causation.

premise   The underlying value or belief that one assumes as a given truth at the beginning of an argument.

rhetorical question   A question that is asked for dramatic effect, with the understanding that readers will silently answer the way the writer wants them to answer.

rime scheme (or "rhyme")   A fixed pattern of rimes that occurs throughout a poem.

Rogerian argument   A rhetorical approach to conflict resolution that emphasizes treating others with respect and listening carefully and emphatically to what they have to say.

simile   A direct comparison between two unlike things that includes such words as "like" or "as" —for example, "My love is like a red, red rose."

stereotype   An unthinking generalization, especially of a group of people in which all the members of the group are assumed to share the same traits; for example, the "dumb jock" is a stereotype of high school and college athletes.

style   The combination of diction and sentence structure that characterizes the manner in which a writer writes. Good writers have a distinctive style, which is to say their work can be readily identified as their own.

summary   A brief and unbiased recapitulation of previously stated ideas.

syllogism   A three-stage form of deductive reasoning through which a general truth yields a specific conclusion.

thesis   The central idea of an argument; the point that an argument seeks to prove. In a unified essay, every paragraph helps to advance the thesis.

tone   The way a writer sounds when discussing a particular subject. Whereas point of view establishes a writer's attitude toward his or her subject, tone refers to the voice that is adopted in conveying this point of view to an audience. For example, one can write with an angry, sarcastic, humorous, or dispassionate tone when discussing a subject about which one has a negative point of view.

topic sentence   The sentence that defines the function of a paragraph; the single most important sentence in each paragraph.

transition   A link or bridge between topics that enables a writer to move smoothly from one subtopic to another so that every paragraph is clearly related to the paragraphs that surround it.

warrant   A term used by Stephen Toulmin for an implicit or explicit general statement that underlies an argument and establishes a relationship between the data and the claim.

COPYRIGHTS AND
ACKNOWLEDGMENTS

AMERICAN PSYCHOLOGICAL ASSOCIATION Sample screen of PsycLit Database Journal Articles 1/90–12/96. Copyright © 1967–1997 by the American Psychological Association, publisher of *Psychological Abstracts* and the PsycINFO Database. Reprinted by permission of the American Psychological Association.

ANDERSON, JANELLE AND LOVRIEN, CHRISTOPHER "Another Look at the Economics of Immigration." Reprinted by permission.

ANDERSON, TERRY L. "Our National Parks System: It's Time to Privatize." This article appeared in the May 1996 issue of *The World and I,* a publication of The Washington Times Corp. copyright © 1996. Reprinted by permission of The World & I.

BENNETT, WILLIAM J. "An Honorable Estate" (originally titled "Leave Marriage Alone") from *Newsweek,* June 3, 1996. Copyright © 1996 by Newsweek, Inc. All rights reserved. Reprinted by permission.

BORJAS, GEORGE J. "The New Economics of Immigration." First published in *The Atlantic Monthly,* November 1996. Copyright © 1996 by George J. Borjas. Reprinted by permission of the author.

BRIMELOW, PETER "A Nation of Immigrants" (originally titled "Time to Rethink Immigration?"). First published in *National Review,* June 22, 1992. Copyright © 1991 by Peter Brimelow. Reprinted by permission of the Wylie Agency, Inc.

BROWNE, KINGSLEY R. Adapted from "Title VII as Censorship: Hostile-Environment Harassment and the First Amendment" from *Ohio State Law Journal* 1991. Copyright © 1991 by Kingsley R. Browne. Reprinted by permission of the Ohio State Law Journal and the author.

COZZENS, JESSICA "What Managers Need to Know: A Synthesis of Arguments Concerning Sexual Harassment in the Workplace." Reprinted by permission.

CRONON, WILLIAM "The Trouble with Wilderness; or, Getting Back to the Wrong Nature" from *Uncommon Ground: Toward Reinventing Nature* by William Cronon, editor. Copyright © 1995 by William Cronon. Reprinted by permission of W. W. Norton & Company, Inc.

ELSHTAIN, JEAN BETHKE "Accepting Limits" from *Commonweal,* November 22, 1991. Copyright © 1991 by Commonweal Foundation. Reprinted by permission.

FISHER, ANNE B. "Sexual Harassment: What to Do?" from *Fortune,* August 23, 1993. Copyright © 1993 by Time, Inc. All rights reserved. Reprinted by permission.

Foreman, Dave "Missing Links" from *Sierra Magazine,* September/October 1995. Copyright © 1995 by Dave Foreman. Reprinted by permission.

Friedan, Betty "The Importance of Work" from *The Feminine Mystique.* Copyright © 1983, 1974, 1973, 1963 by Betty Friedan. Reprinted by permission of W. W. Norton & Company, Inc.

Hitler, Adolf "The Purpose of Propaganda" from *Mein Kampf,* translated by Ralph Manheim. Copyright © 1943, renewed 1971 by Houghton Mifflin Company. Reprinted by permission of Houghton Mifflin Company. All rights reserved.

Johnson, Fenton "Wedded to an Illusion" from *Harper's Magazine,* November 1996. Copyright © 1996 by Harper's Magazine. All rights reserved. Reprinted by special permission.

Kadi, May "Welcome to Cyberia" by May Kadi, a computer consultant. Originally appeared in the *Utne Reader* under the title of "The Internet . . . As Presented." Reprinted by permission of Jill Stauffer, editor of *h2so4,* San Francisco.

Karlen, Amy L. "Preserving Our Parks." Reprinted by permission.

Katz, Jon "The Rights of Kids in the Digital Age" from *Wired,* July 1996. Copyright © 1996 by Wired Magazine Group, Inc. All rights reserved. Reprinted by permission.

King, Martin Luther, Jr. "Letter from Birmingham Jail" from *Why We Can't Wait.* Copyright © 1963 by Martin Luther King, Jr., copyright renewed 1991 by Coretta Scott King. Reprinted by arrangement with the Heirs to the Estate of Martin Luther King, Jr. c/o Writers House, Inc. as agent for the proprietor.

LaPorte, Kerstin "Preparation for Real Life." Reprinted by permission.

Lexix ®-Nexis ® Sample screens from LEXIS-NEXIS. Reprinted with the permission of LEXIS and NEXIS, a division of Reed Elsevier Inc. LEXIS and NEXIS are registered trademarks of Reed Elsevier Properties, Inc.

Luthar, Harsh and Townsend, Anthony "Man Handling" from *National Review,* February 6, 1995. Copyright © 1995 by National Review, Inc., 150 East 35th St., New York, NY 10016. Reprinted by permission.

Ness, Erik "BigBrother@cyberspace" from *The Progressive,* December 1994. Reprinted by permission of The Progressive, 409 East Main Street, Madison, WI 53703.

Nodzon, B. J. "Regulation of the Internet." Reprinted by permission.

OCLC Online Computer Library Center Introductory screen from OCLC FirstSearch ®, a registered trademark of OCLC Online Computer Library Center, Incorporated. Copyright 1992–1997 by OCLC. Reprinted by permission.

Paul, Ellen Frankel "Bared Buttocks and Federal Cases" from *Society,* May/June 1991. Copyright © 1991 by Transaction Publishers. Reprinted by permission of the publisher.

Rivedal, Karen "To Skip or Not to Skip" and "Absent at What Price?" Reprinted by permission.

Rogers, Carl R. "Dealing With Breakdowns in Communication" from *On Becoming a Person.* Copyright © 1961 by Carl R. Rogers. Reprinted by permission of Houghton Mifflin Company. All rights reserved.

Rulland, Geoff "Homicide." Reprinted by permission.

SilverPlatter Sample screen from *PsycLit* Database, © 1986–1996 American Psychological Association, © 1986–1996 SilverPlatter International, N. V. Reprinted by permission of SilverPlatter Information, Inc.

Simonson, Dana "Speak Now or Forever Hold the Past." Reprinted by permission.

Sullivan, Andrew "Simple Equality." Copyright © 1996 by Andrew Sullivan. First published in *The New York Times.* Reprinted by permission of The Wylie Agency, Inc.

Tackett, Ron "History Is for People Who Think." Reprinted by permission.

Topolnicki, Denise M. "The Real Immigrant Story: Making It Big in America." Copyright © 1995 by Time, Inc. Reprinted from the January 1995 issue of *Money* by special permission.

Willard, Nancy "Pornography on the Internet: The Real Issue Is Values" by Nancy Willard, author of *The Cyberethics Reader,* published by McGraw-Hill. Reprinted by permission of the author.

Wilson, H. W. Sample screens from *Readers' Guide Abstracts* and from *Social Science Abstracts,* an online service, covering 1983–1996. Reprinted by permission of H. W. Wilson.

Yahoo! Sample introductory screen for searching the World Wide Web. Text and artwork copyright © 1996 by Yahoo!, Inc. All rights reserved. Yahoo! and the Yahoo! logo are trademarks of Yahoo!, Inc. Reprinted by permission.

INDEX